The Politics of Interpretation

The Politics of Interpretation

Alterity and Ideology in Old Yiddish Studies

JEROLD C. FRAKES

STATE UNIVERSITY OF NEW YORK PRESS

Published by
State University of New York Press, Albany

Printed in the United States of America

For information, address State University of New York Press, State University Plaza, Albany, N.Y., 12246

Library of Congress Cataloging-in-Publication Data

Frakes, Jerold C.
The politics of interpretation: alterity and ideology in Old Yiddish studies / Jerold C. Frakes.
p. cm.
Bibliography: p.
Includes index.
ISBN 0-88706-845-6. ISBN 0-88706-846-4 (pbk.)
1. Yiddish philology – Historiography. I. Title
PJ5111.F7 1988 *87–37479*
437'.947 – dc19 *CIP*

10 9 8 7 6 5 4 3 2 1

Contents

For roughly five hundred years, Yiddish has attracted far more than sober scholarly interest and popular study. It has persistently drawn an almost obsessive angle-oriented and ax-grinding scrutiny from highly diverse groups of investigators, each of which was driven by its own peculiar ulterior motive. Indeed, an account of the history of literature *on* Yiddish will have to delve deeply into the sociolinguistic phenomena of love and hate of the language, both of which have been (and continue to be) rather intense.

Dovid Katz

Preface

This study has developed over the course of the past four years out of an interest in things Yiddish stimulated initially by the frustration and irritation provoked by recurring, conflicting, and enigmatic references to the Old Yiddish *Dukus Hurnt* in the scholarly literature of medieval German studies. As I became more deeply involved in learning the modern Yiddish language and reading medieval Yiddish texts, the plan for and structure of the present study took shape. It was not to be a "survey" of the history of Old Yiddish studies, nor in itself an analysis – literary, linguistic, or otherwise – of Old Yiddish *per se*. And it has not, I think, become either the one or the other. Rather, it is a study of the critical ideologies that have shaped the perception, reception, and projection of Old Yiddish during the course of the past century. Most likely as a direct result of the path leading to my involvement in this research, my perspective is somewhat skewed, but no more so than those of others who have trod similar paths before me. But be that as it may, it seems to me that this particular sub-field of literary/linguistic studies reveals more clearly the determinant role of ideology in scholarly research than many if not most other literary/linguistic disciplines: even to the point that the form and content of Old Yiddish as a discipline *per se* of scholarly endeavor is itself strictly defined, and its limits marked off by ideological determinants.

The reasons for this determinism are many and complex, most arising out of the very core of the sociological problematic of Jewish existence within (but also, necessarily, always without) European culture. Such cultural prejudices, which are not *simply* manifestations of anti-Semitism (although that is ultimately at the root of the major part of the problem), have so ingrained and integrated themselves into the institutions and thereby the education and thus the mentality of scholars who deal with or might come into contact with this literature/language, that the initially quite obviously ideological claims have in the course of time been reified, taken on the appearance of fact, datum, and information. They are taken for granted, unquestioned and unquestioning. It is these ideologies, petrified into "fact," that are the objects of study here.

This state of affairs in Old Yiddish studies seems to be gradually changing. But that is not to say that ideology is thus left behind; it seems rather that the emerging ideology of contemporary studies of Old Yiddish simply provides a necessary antithesis to that which has come before: a new paradigm of Old Yiddish in its historical context has made possible the relocation and reevaluation of Old Yiddish studies and its place in the present scholarly world. The present study seeks to organize the mass of research devoted to the subject over the past century, extrapolate the ideological constraints on various movements and individual scholars and provide some articulation of the sociological contexts that gave rise to such interpretive ideologies. In the end, I also attempt to contextualize the recent shift in the critical ideology that is now moving to prominence in Old Yiddish studies against the backdrop of what has come before and what has developed in other literary/linguistic fields.

The inherent ideological pre-conceptions concerning the subject of (Old) Yiddish may perhaps best be initially broached anecdotally: after my initial pass through Uriel Weinreich's *College Yiddish*, I began to seek a native speaker of Yiddish among the large Yiddish-speaking community of Los Angeles, with whom I could simply converse in Yiddish to gain some facility in speaking the language and to rid myself of my strong German accent in the language. My efforts were so very frustrating for such an extended period of time that I finally gave up the initial plan. The primary problem did not stem from a dearth of Yiddish-speakers, a lack of interest or enthusiasm on my part, or any unwillingness to compensate the tutor; rather, the stumbling block was one of a pervasive and complete lack of comprehension on the part of my potential tutors of any possible reason for me, a non-Jew, to have any interest whatsoever in (as they said) a dying or already dead, bastardized, pseudo-language, unfit for human usage and incapable of expressing even the most basic human concepts. Thus there were in fact two objections: first, there was simply something suspicious about my not being a Jew, who nevertheless had an interest in Yiddish (if it was in fact suspicion, then, in view of the history of Jewry in the present century, that suspicion of outsiders attempting to insinuate themselves into the inside is fully justified); second, there was a deep-seated, often vehemently-expressed vilification of the "target language" — in every case the native language of my interlocutors. A third objection appeared, if (as happened on rare occasions), I managed to persuade the potential tutor momentarily to disregard the first two objections: there could be no hope of my ever learning to speak Yiddish, since it was too radically different from anything that I, as an adult non-Jew could possibly know. Again, there are two aspects to this objection: that as an adult I could not learn such a complicated language, and that Yiddish is somehow inextricably connected to and defined by Jewishness.

These objections surfaced time and again, until I became rather adept in at least offering quick and relatively coherent responses to them. Since my potential tutors still conversed on a daily basis in Yiddish (with family members and friends), but so rarely came across anyone "interested" in Yiddish (rather only others who *spoke* the language), it was in fact not so very difficult to get them to carry on our conversations in Yiddish almost from the beginning of our tête-à-têtes. Thus I gradually even became rather adept at responding in Yiddish to their objections, and resigned myself to the possibility that, since in fact my only objective was conversational practice in Yiddish, I might be forced to pursue that objective via friendly argumentation (in Yiddish) about the impossibility of achieving any such objective. The culmination of my experiment was an hour-long exchange with a retired professor of Judaic studies, who meticulously and at great length detailed his argument that my very proposition was preposterous, since it would only be after years of study that I could attempt even the simplest conversation in Yiddish. He suggested that I mail him a postcard listing ten English words of my choice per week, which he would then mail back to me with the Yiddish equivalents. The entire conversation, discussion, and argument took place in Yiddish.

Thereafter, I became distracted by other duties from seeking out other opportunities to learn spoken Yiddish.[1] At any rate for the moment I gave up my goal of semi-fluency in spoken Yiddish and resigned myself to being an "outsider" and merely a reasonably fluent reader of the language. My work on the ideological constraints on the study of Old Yiddish language and literature had been proceeding for some time and it became my major research interest. It also became a stimulus for the expression of ideology from unexpected quarters, for when (both Jewish and non-Jewish) friends, acquaintances and, surprisingly even professional academic colleagues (and even my dean) learned of my research, the initial, immediate, invariable reaction was an explosive, almost reprimanding: "But you're not Jewish.

. . . [pause, defensively] . . . Are you?" Nor am I British or German or Roman or Icelandic, but that does not prevent me from having a great interest (even a professional, scholarly interest) in the literary/linguistic traditions of those cultures. Nor, on the other hand, would such an ethnic background predispose me to the study of any of those subjects. But such a response from me was always taken as somehow inappropriate, almost offensive, for in fact no one has ever objected to my research on Greek studies in medieval Switzerland with a protestation that I am neither Greek nor Swiss. Thus it seems that the study of, say, the Anglo-Saxon reception of late antique Neoplatonism via Roman philosophy, or of the thematic significance of the structure of dream sequences in the *Nibelungenlied* is, while not immediately to be expected of any given Tennessean, still perfectly reasonable in certain contexts. On the other hand, the study of Old Yiddish by that same person is in no contexts reasonable and in few justifiable. The point seems to be that Yiddish is conceived of as a cultural phenomenon specifically and exclusively pertaining to, of relevance for, and to be attended to by Jews. It is thought too radically other to be of interest to or even be accessible to the non-Jew, implying also that it is of no importance to the culture of the non-Jew, i.e., the culture of the "Western Tradition." There is a kind of double marginalization at work here: the non-Jewish student of Yiddish is (not altogether effectively) excluded from the language by its native speakers – and thus marginalized from the Yiddish which s/he has centered. On the other hand, the entire project of learning Yiddish or researching some aspect of its history is implied to be inappropriate or even irrelevant by non-Yiddish speakers – thus that project is marginalized by the center. The prospective learner/researcher of Yiddish is lost to the maws of what was in the beginning a perfectly innocent curiosity.

Obviously the researcher suffers no more than slight inconvenience from such ideological games, which at least in my experience with the present project have as often as not been amusing. They do, however, point up the more significant, and not so playful, ideological moves characteristic of the conflicts in the scholarly arena of Old Yiddish studies. And as such, they may provide a bit more "human interest" than does the sometimes merely textual conflicts dealt with in the ensuing analysis.

As an example of the problem inherent in this kind of study, let us again take my own interest in and study of Old Yiddish, for the code of my own ideological determiners is a confusing, inconsistent morass: I am from the Deep South in the United States, a non-Jew, trained initially in philosophy and English literature, then medieval Latin and German*ic* studies. I came to Old Yiddish, as did many other contemporary "Yiddishists," via the decades-long debate concerning the linguistic and cultural identity of *Dukus Hurnt:* Yiddish or Middle High German? My "expertise" is thus that of an amateur, looking over the disciplinary border into the territory of another field. As should already be apparent from the title chosen for the study, and as will become clearer still in the course of the argument, I attempt analysis of the reception of Old Yiddish, without any false pose of objectivity, without any goal of determining Truth, but rather from a consciously polemic perspective – that of the "pro-Yiddish" ideological construct, as opposed to the ideological constructs of the representatives of the anti-Yiddish position, Jewish and non-Jewish, German and non-German, Germanist and non-Germanist. Especially in the critical mode of reception history, it would be easy to *claim* some kind of abstract objectivity, since I have no stake in either the pro- or anti-Yiddish projects, since I am culturally divorced from the whole object of study, since the discipline into which I am herewith intruding is not strictly speaking my own, either by institutional training or present disciplinary employment. But, of course, such notions of objectivity would, like all notions of objectivity, be illusions: they would themselves be no more than a critical move within the larger field of yet another ideological structure.

There may well be a certain amount of presumption and impertinence involved in my attempt to analyze the complex of problems arising in the history of medieval Yiddish studies, since I am not a scholar of Judaic studies, nor even a Yiddishist *per se*. For not infrequently have researchers in the field of Yiddish claimed that in order to perform any valuable work in this field, the scholar must necessarily demonstrate expertise in a myriad of linguistic and literary traditions: Hebrew, Middle High German, Polish (and perhaps another Slavic language).[2] One might add as well: linguistics, medieval economic and social history, paleography, medieval Judaic studies, critical theory, etc. But then, as will become apparent in the course of the study, such a proposal of prerequisites to any scholarly work on Yiddish is in fact simply another example of critical marginalization and definition of the alterity of Yiddish: of rendering it *in*accessible. It is interesting in this regard, and indicative of ideological assumptions, that those who posit such prerequisites oddly never mention a knowledge of Yiddish language, Yiddish literature, nor Ashkenazic culture in general, as necessary prerequisites to a study of Yiddish, and not because these subjects are assumed without mention. Other scholars who have written on Old Yiddish have expressed doubts about the possibility that any single scholar could command the numerous specialized areas of knowledge necessary to deal with Yiddish, especially Old Yiddish, thus attempting to justify the claim that anything less than an interdisciplinary team is inadequate to the task. I, on the other hand, doubt whether their doubts are as much functions of any inherent inability on the part of a single scholar to command sufficiently the necessary areas of expertise, as they are expressions of yet another aspect of that ubiquitous notion of (Old) Yiddish as a sign of the impenetrability of the "hidden code" of Judaism, of Old Yiddish as inapproachably other. And as my discussion of such team projects will illustrate, none has thus far appeared to surpass (or even equal) the work by individual scholars.

I do not point out problems in such prescriptive descriptions of the ideal Yiddishist in order to defend my own lack of expertise in some of the requisite disciplines (although these deficiencies are legion). Despite the fact that the topics dealt with by many, if not most, of the studies examined in this book have to do with linguistic analysis as defined by some school of the past century or with cultural history of medieval European Jewry, I do not here attempt any sort of detailed linguistic analysis, nor an historico-cultural investigation of medieval Jewish culture, as a basis on which to evaluate the modern reception of Old Yiddish. Rather, it is precisely the modern scholarly "attitudes," the schools, the ideologies that concern me: attitudes toward Old Yiddish, which I attempt to explicate in their relevant cultural contexts. Thus some measure of expertise in various of the prerequisite disciplines is indeed of great aid, but I make no pretense to more than a nodding acquaintance with some of them. Deficiencies, and I hope perhaps also sufficiencies, in these areas will be immediately apparent to informed readers. I leave the evaluation of *my* efforts to them.[3]

This is a book about interpretive politics or interpretive strategies or critical ideologies, insofar as they determine the critical evaluation of cultural documents, in this case, specifically Old Yiddish texts. At the same time, however, there is no claim made that this study – as opposed to those books, articles, editions, and reviews examined in its pages – is free of ideological constraints. Just as those (and all) studies arise from ideological assumptions and construct their objects of study on the basis of those same assumptions, so too does this book. In this regard, then, perhaps the present book differs from the majority of those it examines only in that it seeks at every point to be *aware* of its ideological constraints (but not to have the illusion of ever overcoming them), in Gadamer's sense of – "die eigene Geschichtlichkeit mitdenken." The particular object of analysis in these pages and in the studies examined here is, however, perhaps somewhat more peculiar than that normally found in theoretical analyses of cultural history, due, if for no other reason, simply to its necessarily inter- and intra-cultural, inter- and a-national articulation of delayed romantic, nationalistic modes of critical inquiry. The identification of the dominant ideological codes at work in each case is thus always difficult, often all but impossible, and rarely conclusive.

Few studies have dealt directly with the history of scholarship on Yiddish language and literature, but three excellent studies need to be mentioned at the outset: Hans-Peter Althaus gives a brief and general, but insightful overview in his "Die Erforschung der jiddischen Sprachen;"[4] Dovid Katz fills in informational details and adds delightful and interesting anecdotes on some of the nineteeth- and twentieth-century champions of Yiddish and briefly comments on their significance in contexts of cultural history;[5] but it is Maks Weinreich's dissertation, completed while he was a student in Marburg in 1923, "Studien zur Geschichte und dialektischen Gliederung der jiddischen Sprache," that presents the only full-scale history of the field. It is an analytical history of Yiddish studies from the sixteenth century to 1923.[6] In dealing with recent scholarship and his own contemporaries, Weinreich claimed (III, 3) that he did not have the distance from them necessary to judge their work on the basis of personality and also the determinative tendencies of the period (*Zeitströmungen*), so he organizes this section of his study according to topic instead of individuals. The present study is also organized topically, not for Weinreich's reasons, but rather because it seems from the general perspective taken here that individuals are in principle far less important than the determinative *Zeitströmungen*, which can be discerned and traced historically even down to contemporary scholarly schools. Thus here, as in Weinreich's study, numerous scholars appear and are discussed in various chapters, albeit with a different purpose each time.

Most but not all major scholars of the late nineteenth and the twentieth centuries are treated in the following chapters. The attempt is made rather to account for the major critical movements, large and small, in (Old) Yiddish studies, via the comprehensive analysis of the work of scholars representative of those movements and as they relate to larger cultural contexts. The work of Erik, Birnbaum, the Weinreichs and Shmeruk, for instance, is present. Sainéanu is, on the other hand, mentioned more than once but never treated in detail, while the analysis of the work of an insignificant scholar such as Marchand takes up several pages, since it is perfectly characteristic and illustrative of a certain school of thought.

The core subjects of chapters two and three were treated in provisional, preliminary form in conference papers for the Modern Language Association (1984) and the Medieval Association of the Pacific (1985), which then appeared in revised form as "Critical Ideology in Old Yiddish Studies: The Names of Old Yiddish, *Yiddish* 6 (1985), 5-14 and "Audience, Accessibility and Ideology: On Editing Old Yiddish Texts," *The German Quarterly* 59 (1985), 187-202. My thanks to the editors of those journals for permission to make use of that material in this revision and elaboration. For aid in procuring microfilm of manuscripts, I am again pleased to thank Dr. Julian Plante of the Hill Monastic Manuscript Library, St. John's University. The University of Southern California Faculty Research Fund provided partial financial support for a research trip in 1984. My thanks are also due numerous colleagues and scholarly acquaintances who offered much needed and sometimes heeded criticism, advice, and encouragement. Franz Bäuml and Thomas Gustafson offered all this and friendship too.

Note on the Roman Transposition of Hebrew

Since one of the core topics of discussion in the study is the method of transposition of Hebrew-alphabet Old Yiddish into Roman, the treatment of Hebrew-alphabet texts employed here needs to be clarified. I cite Old Yiddish texts only in the Hebrew alphabet. The transpositions of Old Yiddish texts by other scholars are, however, cited in Roman, when those transpositions are at issue. Citations of the titles of Hebrew-alphabet texts (modern Yiddish and Hebrew) and citations from modern Yiddish research literature appear in Roman transposition. The names of scholars appear in the first citation of their works in the various orthographic forms necessary to identify them: e.g., Solomon Birnbaum (Salomo Birnbaum/Shloyme Birnboym). Hebrew and Yiddish terms that have a familiar English form are so cited (e.g., *Haskalah*, not the Ashkenazic *haskole*; otherwise they are spelled according to their Ashkenazic phonemic form (e.g., *yeshivas*, not *yeshivot*).

The orthographic forms of titles of Old Yiddish texts used here do not conform to any one principle, but there is a rationale for the inconsistency. I sometimes use anglicized forms (e.g., *Beria and Simra*), if there is such a common title for a more widespread intercultural legend, or I often use the (modern) Yiddish form (e.g., *Shmuel-bukh*), in each case if there seems to be no compelling ideological issue involved. In at least two cases, however, I choose openly polemical forms, for reasons that will become apparent as the argument of the book progresses: *Vidvilt* and *Dukus Hurnt*, instead of the titles usually assigned to the works, *Wildwilt* (or *Widuwilt* or even *Wigalois*) and *Dukus Horant*. In neither case do I contend that the title I use is more accurate linguistically – especially in the latter case, where *Hurnt* is with near certainty phonetically inaccurate (but probably no more so than *Horant*) – but in both cases I would ague that the blatantly non-German spelling I use is more accurate and appropriate culturally, if for no other reason than that it serves as a constant reminder that the commonly used Germanized or Germanicized titles are equally or even more ideological when assigned to Yiddish texts.

ONE

Alterity, Ideologies, and Old Yiddish

PERHAPS AT THE outset it will be helpful to attempt a definition, or at least delimitation, of my use of the term "ideology," for it is certainly one of the most used and abused terms in the various theoretical and critical vocabularies of the present century, whether in strictly cultural analysis or more recently in literary and linguistic studies. Joseph Roucek's summary discussion of the term, published toward the end of World War II, is a helpful overview of various of the major uses of the term up to that point, but it is interesting for another reason as well, for in itself it illustrates a kind of critical ideology, which, for lack of a more precise term, we could call the hybrid romantic-positivistic perspective, which deals in first principles that of necessity must be capitalized: he assumes an absolute external authority that functions as a guarantor of Truth and of the absolute distinction between Fact and interpretation, between Science and ideology.[1] He thus castigates those who had studied and used the term "ideology" before him (especially Marxians) for their lack of objectivity, their inevitable failure to transcend ideology in their own studies, and ultimately for their inability to deal simply with the Facts, eshewing interpretations. Perhaps most illustrative is his attempted differentiation of science from ideology:

> Scientific method tries to eliminate or minimize all errors or illusions; but ideology, assuming itself to be "scientific," consciously or unconsciously makes use of illusions and even errors. Science questions everything. Ideology takes its illusions (and particularly its premises) for granted; it declines to question them, not even seeking possible contradictions between one factual assumption and another, and refusing to correct the distorting influence of its selected facts. Hence, it often sees what does not exist. In other words, science bases its beliefs on the best available evidence; ideology bases its beliefs on selected facts, frequently on imaginary evidence which will support its philosophico-social assumptions. Ideology employs only that evidence which ratifies the conclusions of its ideological principles. (p. 480.)

It thus seems that Roucek posits an ideal in which "scientists" are not also mothers and fathers, daughters and sons, citizens of various states, Catholics, Jews, Hindus, liberals, monarchists, etc., in which their lives outside the laboratory, their upbringing, their social and political environments do not, have not and can not "influence" their work, their "desired results" even their constitution and definitiion of what a "scientific" problem is, and how it can be solved, nor ultimately even the very selection of problems worthy of "scientific" attention. Only in such an ideal world can he view the "best available evidence," employed by the scientist, as something other than the "selected facts" of the ideologue. In each case, obviously, the "evidence" is isolated, identified, *selected* as being relevant; i.e., this "factual evidence" is factual and evidential only insofar as it is a direct result of the scientist's or ideologue's having decided that it is such. It is not relevant, not factual, not evidential, not scientific, until the researcher uses it as such in constructing her/his view of the world or whatever part of the world the particular experiment or project seeks to "explain."

The whole problem as conceived by Roucek is probably a false one but an important one, nonetheless, since it is an old one that has fueled ideological debates for the length and breadth of the "scientific age."[2] For as James Watson's fascinating reflections on the radically anti-scientific route that led him to the discovery of the structure of the DNA molecule demonstrates on a pragmatic, personal level, and as Thomas Kuhn has shown on a more systematic, theoretical level,[3] the very essence of scientific research, investigatory model development, and experimental design is necessarily a matter of Weltanschauung in the broadest sense. It is a function of the myriad external circumstances that present the scientist with possible ways of seeing, schemata of possible valuations of evidence, definitions of what constitutes evidence, the feasibility of obtaining certain types of financial support for certain types of research projects, etc. Especially these latter aspects of the scientific project are ideological in the broad sense.

"Ideology" in my usage is in fact conceived in a very broad sense, including many of its "common language" connotations. But it is not a pejorative term, as it is, for instance, in Roucek's usage, or in both the traditional Marxist and traditional anti-Marxist code (of which Roucek is in some ways a representative). In a certain sense, my usage of the term is akin to Barthes' notion of *mythologie*, for as he explicates in great detail, "myth is a *parole*. . .myth is a system of communication, it is a form with historical delimitations."[4] It is thus historically bound, not eternal, not "natural", and since it is a necessarily human, social system of language, it is a semiological structure, consisting in its simplest state of the standard structuralist triad of *signifiant/signifié = signe*. This latter, the sign of the *langage* has a conceivably infinite power to generate new *signifiants* on the mythic level.[5] The example given by Barthes – a photograph of a black soldier in French military uniform saluting the tricolor, as first a sign of just that act, then as a mythic sign of the legitimacy and glory of the French empire regardless of race, history, etc. (pp. 221-224) – is clear and well-chosen, but for our present purposes, an equally pertinent example can be taken from the subject at hand, specifically, the representation of Old Yiddish texts by editors, which one would assume would be no more than merely that act – printing the manuscript text, with more or less standard editorial manipulation of the text. But the printed, edited text as sign becomes a signifier of a mythic system as well, for the editor mosts often prints the text in Roman transcription/transliteration of the Hebrew-alphabet original, often in the constructed form of Middle High German, and in so doing subsumes an entire mythological system concerning the origin, cultural identity, and literary value of the text. Thus the mere *appearance* of the text is a mythic signifier. In this case, however, there is a multiplicity of possible mythic systems, for the editor may transform the text into a variety of "dialects," depending on his/her ideology: not just Middle High German, but also modern standard or modern southeastern Yiddish, or a pseudo-neutral linguistic transliteration.

This second sign, which signifies on the mythic level, contains, according to Barthes, the "appropriate" sense of the sign, for it in fact appropriates the entirety of the sign of the *langage* for itself and its mythological system. And unlike linguistic signifiers, mythic signifiers in and of themselves can signify an entire system (Barthes, p. 227), for the myth as a *parole* is defined not by its letter, as is the linguistic sign, but rather by its *intention*, which both presupposes and constructs an entire system. Yet, by virtue of the fact that this system is presupposed, subsumed in a single sign of the system, and that system is divorced and extracted from its previous social and historical context, it becomes depoliticized, dehistoricized, simply natural, universal and eternal.

> Myth is depoliticized *parole*. Here "politics" must of course be understood in the profound sense, as the whole of human relations in their concrete, social structure, in their power to create the world; above all it is necessary to understand the suffix *de-* in an active sense; here it represents an operative movement, continuously actualizing a defection.[6]

And yet, not despite this depoliticization, but precisely because of it, and because it is carried out tacitly, surreptitiously, the mythic system is imbued with political significance, for in actively absenting the political, the key to the entire code becomes politicized.

Mythic constructs and systems are necessarily always functions of specific needs within the dominant social structures. As those needs change, so does the ideology that legitimizes its basic values. Ideo-mythology is thus a set of determinant principles that function as the grid through which experience is perceived, on which it is organized and by which it is imbued with significance. It is the determiner of meaning, of interpretive categories, of the possible set of topics of inquiry and of the possible solutions to the problems that those topics bring to light. The mythological system as a code is more or less permanent: while its component elements may change, the categories, the structural slots in its mythological grid, remain the same; its protean nature adapts to new situations, to new definitions of its component elements. The structure can accommodate virtually any ideological system.

Terry Eagleton's recent comments on the concept of ideology are also pertinent here, despite the fact that he conceives of ideology largely still in terms of the traditionally more narrowly political sense of Marxian thought:

> The largely concealed structure of values which informs and underlies our factual statements is part of what is meant by "ideology". By "ideology" I mean, roughly, the ways in which what we say and believe connects with the power-structure and power-relations of the society we live in. It follows from such a rough definition of ideology that not all of our underlying judgements and categories can usefully be said to be ideological. It is deeply ingrained in us to imagine ourselves moving forwards into the future (at least one other society sees itself as moving backwards into it), but though this way of seeing *may* connect significantly with the power-structure of our society, it need not always and everywhere do so. I do not mean by "ideology" simply the deeply entrenched, often unconscious beliefs which people hold; I mean more particularly those modes of feeling, valuing, perceiving, and believing which have some kind of relation to the maintenance and reproduction of social power.[7]

While one could extrapolate from his "maintenance and reproduction of social power" many of the relations of cultural significance that are essential to my definition of ideology, they are not necessarily implicit therein. But at the same time, it is not clear just how he distinguishes between ideological modes with socio-political significance, and "deeply entrenched beliefs," which, not despite, but rather precisely because of their *personal*, ostensibly non-public, apolitical nature are quite often of paramount importance in determining public, political action.

Peter von Moos' succinct comments and précis of previous definitions derive from a slightly differing perspective than do Eagleton's:

> The definition, which in the present study is in general only negatively suggested, derives from the difficulty of comprehensively defining the indispensable counter-concept of "Truth" developmentally and in its historical context, i.e., without dogmatic fixation – which in itself is an essentially ideological perspective. Nevertheless, in order to avoid the stigma of an assumed objectivity and universal skepticism, I will attempt to point out here in abstract and summary fashion several of the main components of ideology: 1) the legitimation of society in the interest of the dominant groups as a consolation to those who are dominated; 2) the doubt-free, affirmative petrification of historically developed, transmitted and extant relations to self-evident, eternal natural entities; also as a consequence: a paralyzing, anach-

> ronistic insistence on dis-simultaneity, on the "sediments of epochs overcome" (Brecht); 3) "socially inevitable false consciousness" (Marx) or a "rationalization" of entangled volitional goals, a surrogate for the scientific "indicative" in the "unconscious optative" (Freud) which has been collectivized into an obsession; thus also in both cases an accurate image of false reality, symptomatically expressing the truth of the need; 4) the dissolution of the indissoluble connection of theoretical and practical action and the separation of the "pure *Geist*" from the social conditions of its existence; 5) argumentation of compromise for the purposes of consolatory camouflaging of miserable but correctable social contradictions."[8]

This synthesis points to a broader conception of the term and one that seems much more relevant, especially to the present study.

In Karl Mannheim's view, "ideology" includes as relevant indicators not just that which is present, discussed and analyzed, but also, in its absence, "the phenomenon of the counter-concept, the absence of certain concepts, the structure of the categorical apparatus, dominant models of thought, level of abstraction, and the ontology that is presupposed."[9] This notion is related to the problem of the inextricability of centrality and marginality, to be discussed in more detail below.

My use of the term "ideology" will thus not be restricted to the myopic political conceptions and vilifying labeling of the other, whether "communist" or "capitalist", although representatives of these two ideologies, as they are manifested in critical modes are also present among the corpus of studies to be dealt with here: that is, politics certainly has to do with the critical code and mode dominant in any particular scholar's work, since one's political views are also bound up with one's ideology. Nor do I restrict the term to use as a polemical term of castigation, reserved for an evaluative designation of various schools of criticism in the more narrowly defined literary field, such as New Criticism, Structuralism, or Deconstructionism.[10] Rather I use "ideology" in quite a broad sense to denote the social, political, cultural, and intellectual *mentalité*, that shapes the perception, i.e., the construction of reality, to the extent that the reality exists only as an effect of that mentality.

Of central relevance to the present topic of critical ideologies in the study of Old Yiddish is the – in the present century, all too obviously – ideological problem of the "Jewish Question": however, by whomever, where, and whenever that topic is treated in terms of its significance for Yiddish. And in dealing with this central topic, we come to a necessary concern for the concepts of marginality and alterity as they relate to cultural studies in general. For work on Yiddish, especially Old Yiddish has rarely transcended the perspective, the mythology, the ideology that defines Old Yiddish as belonging to the necessarily marginal, as being inalterably other.

One of the most cogent explications of the theory and process of marginality as a culturally significant critical move is Gayatri Spivak's brief, reflective essay on her participation in a scholarly conference on "Explanation and Culture," an examination of the possibilities of interdisciplinary and intercultural exchange of theoretical models, at which she, for a number of reasons, perhaps most importantly because she was the only female on an otherwise all-male panel, was by virtue of the code of the institution of scholarly conferences, radically marginalized.[11] Spivak problematizes the conference and its structure as much as she does the ostensibly given topic of that conference, since they are in fact simply different aspects of the same problem. As such, her essay is pertinent to the present discussion in the same way as was Roucek's, for each of them deals with his/her subject both argumentatively and as a participatory example of the argument.[12]

As the concept is analyzed by Spivak, the opposition of center and margin becomes less an opposition than a set of interchangeable, though rarely interchanged, metonymically substitutable categories, for neither can exist without the other: the margin exists only as other than the center, but the center (self/identity) too, is possible and can exist as such, only by means of the other, to which the self is other (in Saussurean terms of differential definition) by means of its actively determined demarcation from the margin. Alterity thus necessarily precedes identity and makes it possible.[13] But here there is a necessary double-bind as well, for it is only by denying not just the *relevance* of the margin, but rather its very existence, that there can be any production of cultural explanations by the center, for its explanations must necessasrily be uniformly "central", i.e., conform to the code of the center, and thus support, propagate and propagandize its ideology in order to be effective. In so doing, the center must make use of the margin to the extent necessary to define itself, to determine that which is included in the self and excluded from/to the margin. Thus, as Spivak points out, the identification of the inhabitant of "the margin of any particular explanation specifies its particular politics" (p. 204): in seeing what/who is on the outside, the inhabitants of the inside are revealed.

Especially pertinent to Spivak's immediate topic at hand – the marginalization of women in a male-dominated and thus male-defined culture – is her discussion of a typical move in the dynamics of the opposition/symbiosis of center-margin.[14] Spivak quotes Freud and Adrienne Rich as examples of the two conflicting positions in the opposition: Freud replies to female colleagues, who protest the prejudice of male psychologists' stereotyping of the "female psychology," that such labels certainly need not be taken as applicable to women scholar/scientists.[15] The opposition is thus not directly established as consisting of the male/female dichotomy, but rather of science vs. emotion, logic/rationality vs. illogic/irrationality. But these are simply metonymic replacements supplied by the code for the opposition male vs. female, because the realm of science/logic/rationality is for Freud *a priori* the domain of the male. His female colleague has entered that realm (one wonders how bona fide Freud would consider her credentials as a "colleague", since her critique of his position is by (his) definition "typically irrational") and is thus not besmirched by the condition of the female. But this putative transcendence is itself a mere ideological move by the center, which functions to further define it in opposition to the margin. Spivak notes: "The putative center welcomes selective inhabitants of the margin in order better to exclude the margin. And it is the center that offers the official explanation, or, the center is defined and reproduced by the explanation that it can express" (p. 206). Freud's colleague is a member of the club on restricted status, without full privileges: and it is her own fault. No male colleague would have proposed the objection she voices, nor could a male colleague have been placated by Freud's attempted annexation of that colleague into the realm of the center. Her citizenship of the margin has been officially revoked, but has not been replaced by full voting rights in the realm of the center. Rather, the center (Freud) has simply created another district of marginality for her and other "rational" female poseurs like her. In other words, in his seemingly innocuous and conciliatory response, Freud has extracted one subject from the margin on the pretense of accepting her into the center, only simply to create a new category of the no-less-marginal, which is, however, now also marginal to her original home: for she is no longer "simply" female.

Adrienne Rich comments on this same problem of women who are marginalized not just from the male center, but from their original margin: this applies to women who "think like men."[16] As a result of the partial annexation of the female margin, "that power withheld from the vast majority of women is offered to a few, so that it may appear that any truly qualified woman can gain access to leadership, recognition, and reward." Thus this woman is "different," and is instructed by the center *and* the margin to see herself as such, for she has overcome her disadvantaged status through talent, drive, and education. But she is still merely a "woman masquerading as a man in the profession."[17]

The central problem is that the inhabitant of the margin who is granted conditional, partial access to the center still has at her/his disposal no more than the instruments and media of the center, the forms that not only express but also shape and propagate the center's ideology, and – perhaps most devastatingly – the language of the center. It is then in this language, and by means of the center's institutions (the university, the press, academic publishing, scholarly conferences, traditional modes of criticism, etc), that the margin must make do and make a mark on the center. There can rarely be an *attack* as such on the center, but instead more often merely self-deconstruction, self-criticism, and self-hatred.

Spivak also deals with the problem of ideology,[18] in her comments on the false distinction between the epistemic-phenomenological and the cultural (p. 211). In somewhat different terms, this is the same distinction that Roucek posits in his opposition of Fact and interpretation. Since, however, all explanation (Roucek's Fact/Evidence/Science) is no more than the center's defense and redefinition of itself as institution, by means of its delimitation from the margin(s), then in the very act of its explanation and definition, it decentralizes and marginalizes itself by privileging (even if only momentarily and obliquely) the margin as guarantor of its own (the center's) position. Thus there can be no absolute center, no ultimate guarantor, no Fact. All is interpretation and interplay between interpretations, and all explanation is ideological.

Perhaps the most accessible approach to this entire topic of center/margin, identity/alterity with respect to the study of Yiddish is through the brilliantly developed thesis of Sander Gilman's *Jewish Self-Hatred.* He takes language and discourse as the primarily relevant objects of inquiry in his analysis of this complex topic, for he posits language as the hallmark of culture, and perhaps the most visible and accessible measure of culture, however traditionally "culture" is defined.[19] Thus in the use of language, as that usage conforms or does not conform to the norms of the dominant group in society, the cultural identity and thus the value of the self is determined:

> It is in language, then, that the tensions of Otherness and thus eventually of self-hatred can best be examined. The role of a "civilized" language in defining the Other is central to the articulation of the identity of the Jew in the West. The Other cannot ever truly possess "true" language and is so treated. The Other's language is hidden, dark, magical, dangerous, private. So, too, is the language of the Jews.

While Gilman treats the problem of the language and discourse of European Jewish culture in a general sense through the course of a longer period of history than concerns our present subject, many of the theoretical tenets that he proposes are of especial relevance for a discussion of the modern reception of Old Yiddish (a topic not within the purview of his study). For, as he establishes by means of detailed analysis, the history of the Jews in Europe has in one sense been an elaborate working out of the play and interplay of various, ever-changing, almost protean mythological and ideological codes, which invariably *in*clude Jewish culture only insofar as it is excluded: it is ever and always (one of) the inhabitant(s) of the margin, reducible to a mere sign of absolute alterity. This is, as noted above, especially the case with respect to "Jewish language," in earlier periods conceived of most often as Hebrew, an idiom that was utterly alien to the Indo-European languages of Europe and even more demonstratively alien through its use of the Hebrew alphabet, which *de facto* rendered the already incomprehensible language inaccessible as well. Yet at the same time, this secret language of the Jews was one of the *tres linguae sacrae* of early Christianity, the language of the Old Testament, an essential element in the textual structure of Christianity; and this "sacred instrument" was in the hands of the "infidel" Jews. Thus in their linguistic acquisition of Hebrew the Humanists managed to realize a centuries-old desire and complete the process of appropriating and usurping the Hebrew language from the Jews, incorporating it into the Christian code and even denying the Jews access to this code. For while the Jews might command the *language* (Hebrew), they were unable to comprehend its *discourse*.

Thus non-Jewish Humanism admitted Hebrew to the center, but held the culture of the Jews on the margin, for it was only in contrast to their putatively depraved and perverse distortion of Hebrew and its significance through the denial of its function in the redemptive code, that the presence of Hebrew in this Christian, redemptive code could be defined, distinguished, and centered.

With the rise of European Enlightenment ideology in the eighteenth century came a parallel movement in European Jewish culture, the Haskalah, which, while certainly more complex in both origins and goals than any brief summary can demonstrate, strove for the emancipation, education, secularization, and "enfranchisement" of Jewry into European culture. The specific application of these general principles was manifested primarily in terms of an assimilationist ideology: traditional Jewish culture was necessarily, by definition, radically other, due to its "mistaken" identification of religion with a way of life. The Haskalah propagandized more radically and pervasively than perhaps any intellectual movement in Jewish history in order to re-educate European Jewry to the Western model of culture: in public one is a citizen, at home one may be a Jew (or Catholic or Protestant). The movement had its roots in the German Enlightenment and spread from its center in Berlin. The Haskalah was thus initially a movement primarily among (at least partially) assimilated German Jews.

In this context, the concepts of marginalization and alterity must again occupy us, for the parenthetical qualification of the last sentence is perhaps the most explosively pregnant sign in the entire code of European Jewish/Non-Jewish relations: what is *partial* assimilation? Can it exist and if so, how? The tenets of European Rationalism which posited universal brotherhood, citizenship, and the natural rights of man, i.e., the principles that underlay at least the rhetoric (i.e., the ideology) of those marginal and revolutionary societal elements in the British colonies in North America[20] toward the end of the eighteenth century that attempted to establish "democratic" institutions, were ostensibly also extended by the European Enlightenment to European Jewry. But this intellectualized offer of citizenship in the enlightened state(s) was at best an offer of *quid pro quo* – assimilate (external conversion), convert to Christianity and be baptized (internal conversion), and you will be accepted as an equal. The center offered citizenship to the margin in return for renunciation of marginal identity. But as Gilman points out, this offer was itself merely a fraud, for the only means of renouncing marginality (Jewishness) was not assimilation in dress, diet, religion, and speech, but rather ultimately never to have been a citizen of the margin (i.e., not to have been born Jewish). And since such an alteration of cultural citizenship was obviously not possible, from the perspective of the (non-Jewish) center, the assimilated, baptized, Westernized, more-German-than-the-German Jew, could never be more than a Jew masquerading as something other than a Jew: the more assimilated the Jew, the more his assimilation functioned merely as a sign of essential alterity. The situation inevitably leld to the double-bind inherent in all such attempts to move from the margin to the center: a subdivision of the margin and a reprojection of marginality by those attempting to move to the center onto those who do not. In this case, the "assimilated" German Jew defined himself and his strictly European culture via differentiation from the image of the unassimilated, traditional Ashkenazic Jew of the long-standing code of anti-semitism: i.e., the reprojection of alterity by means of self-affirmation through self-denial. As Gilman terms it: self-hatred. The assimilated Jew not only admits the Gentile vilification of Jews as "dirty," "rude," "uncouth," "despicable," "bearded," "profane," "lascivious," "incomprehensible," "diseased," etc. (the "short list" of typical modifiers is of course much longer still), but even extends and expands the portrait of the Jews and their cultural sins: all for the sole purpose of demonstrating one's own non-identity with that type. This object of self-hatred, these most despised, most "typical," most caricatured of Jews, were the Eastern European Ashkenazim, in whose cultural code the most significant signs were not necessarily their alien modes of dress, diet, or general way of life, but rather their language – Yiddish. The most vehement of vilifiers of the Ashkenazim and their language were, obviously, in the context of Jewish self-hatred, non-Yiddish-speaking Jews. The contrast is thus between the (partially) assimilated German Jew and the (wholly unassimilated) Eastern European Jew. The former, having been (partially) accepted into non-Jewish society, was, in appropriately romantic terms, the "noble savage," while the Eastern European Jew was the "ignoble savage."

The most significant manifestation of this relationship between the two groups was in the assimilationist attitude toward Yiddish, which was expressed primarily in terms of the power structure of center vs. margin, i.e., via the means and media of the center, with which the assimilationists *wished* to be identified, that is, through logical analysis (vs. the pilpulistic dialogue characteristic of the Ashkenazim) in published discussions of Yiddish in prestigious, academic journals and presses (i.e., in the organs of the center's power structure), all carried out by means of the language of the center, as well, i.e., in one of the "languages of culture" – English, German, French, or Russian. This use of the language of the center is necessary, since the marginal language is by definition not a "true language". It is "corrupt," "diseased," etc. The use of the center's language in publications on Yiddish is thus in itself a concrete denial of the alterity of the author of the publication. The language of the Other is eliminated quite graphically. It is absent and absented from the discussion, and thus is denied not just all relevance, but even its existence as language. It is not articulate, not printed, and not printable.[21] Thus Gilman's evaluation of the emotional impact of language takes on a dual significance: "The Other's language is hidden, dark, magical, dangerous, private. So, too, is the language of the Jews" (p. 16). The language of the margin is thus often referred to as a pidgin, the language of an inferior class, and the perfect expression of that necessarily *im*perfect class. Yiddish is in fact often characterized as a pidgin or bastard mixture of corrupted German and some "scraps" of Hebrew (and, in later periods, Slavic).

The notion of a "corrupted" German is an interesting one, for it implies the existence of both a non-corrupted, "pure" German, and a single, extant, identifiable, and isolatable form of the "authentic" German language. Both of these implications are tied to the romantic concept of "national language" which arose in the eighteenth and nineteenth centuries, especially in France and Germany. This concept too has mythic significance, for it is projected onto the extant language/dialects as an ideal toward which one strives and is accepted as an accomplished fact and prescribed as a norm. Even so, the radically differing, sometimes mutually unintelligible, spoken dialects of German continued to exist, even as the standard language was constructed and propagated. Yet, the mythology of this notion of "national language" is nourished precisely from this rather unexpected source, for each of the various dialects was perceived as merely a variation on the accepted, normative, "national" language" not as deviant, but as a variant; not as other, but as merely an individual manifestation of self; as an organic, human, "natural" outgrowth of language.

Yiddish, on the other hand, was not a member of this "nuclear family" of languages,[22] since it was not an expression of the culture of any culturally *German* sub-group. Yet there are two possible explanations for the fact that Yiddish was ignored: 1) it was simply subsumed under the linguistic rubric "German," but remained consciously and deliberately undefined, since definition would have required an explanation of its nature; and, 2) its existence as a basically Germanic language was simply denied. On the basis of other kinds of evidence (since both these arguments are silent about the status of Yiddish), it becomes clear that Yiddish is most often simply denied any relationship to German, in terms of Yiddish as *a language*. It must necessarily be not-German, for it is spoken by Jews, who are by definition non-German. It is written in the Hebrew alphabet,[23] which is, to the German "nation," illegible, magical, a very graphic sign of radical alterity. Thus, despite the fact that the morphology, vocabulary, and syntax of modern spoken Yiddish dialects in general differ from modern standard German little more than do, say, some Swiss dialects (even taking into account the Yiddish lexemes of Hebrew/Aramaic and Slavic derivation), it is denied familial relations to German as a whole. And as Gilman notes, this forced distinction between Yiddish and German is a *sine qua non* of the reprojection of alterity onto the Ashkenazim: "This myth of the hidden language of the Jews can exist only if there is an antithesis between the idea of the nature of the national language and that of the language of the Jews. Such a polarity is itself mythic" (p. 20).

The ultimate goal of the anti-Yiddish program of the Enlightenment and its Jewish counterpart, the Haskalah, was obviously the conversion of the Jews to rationalism, to "culture" (i.e., Western cultural norms, assumed without saying). And since the most visible sign of the alterity of Ashkenazic culture was Yiddish, and language is in general held (especially in romantic, national ideological contexts) to be the ultimate sign of one's culture or lack thereof, then the program was first and foremost a concerted effort to eradicate Yiddish. For in bringing about the abandonment of their corrupt language, their discourse and their social use of language, they would be purified, refined, and prepared to participate in society, and would, thus by the adoption of German (or another "language of culture"), be miraculously transformed into citizens of the world, i.e., of the center: always with the proviso, however, that such citizenship would still be no more than a redefinition of, and relocation of the margin. The equation of these various cultural entities is, however, in itself of some interest: speech = discourse = culture. Change one to change them all.[24]

The most common attribute of Yiddish singled out for attack as a sign of the language's deformity and corruption is its essential admixture of Hebrew lexemes, morphemes, and some few syntactic elements into its Germanic linguistic component, usually designated a bastard corruption, neither German nor Hebrew, nor anything else. This case is easily made and easily illustrated with very pertinent and – to a sympathetic audience – even humorously ridiculous examples, such that the image of Yiddish becomes that of a pidgin, consisting of hilariously ungrammatical, mispronounced, and misspelled (in Roman transliteration) German, mixed with equally hilariously ungrammatical, mispronounced Hebrew (i.e., Ashkenazic pronunciation, in contrast to the accepted – among Western scholars of Hebrew – Sephardic pronunciation).

The case is in fact easy to make: not because Yiddish *is* a corrupt, bastardized language, but rather because such cases are by definition easy to make: it is simply the stuff of comparative historical linguistics, especially as conceived in the late nineteenth and early twentieth centuries with its notion of organic growth and decay of languages and pre-sociological approach to such linguistic problems as the analysis of linguistic substrates, influence of bilingualism, and linguistic borrowing from dominant cultures by subordinate subcultures. Such studies abound for the "bastardization" of Anglo-Saxon in the centuries after the Norman Conquest, for the "bastardization" of Norwegian in the period of Danish domination (which, among other effects, launched a debate on the nature of the Norwegian language, or actually language*s*, in the press, the universities, the parlor, the street, the schoolyard, the pubs, which even now shows little sign of resolution), or the "bastardization" of Maltese, etc. But rarely, if ever, is the hybridization of these languages actually termed "bastardization". That is obviously a term of valuation, and whereas those hybrid languages and the processes of hybridization are viewed "objectively" as examples of scientifically quantifiable (and thus legitimate) linguistic processes, the case of Yiddish is and has traditionally always been burdened with value-laden terminology, and not without reason, for the terminology expresses the ideologies of the discussion's participants, to whom the status, the definition, and even the existence of Yiddish is of vital importance in an ideological sense.

The identity of the perpetrators of this mythic definition of Yiddish as other is ideologically quite complex. Unquestionably at the root of it is the non-Jewish center's rejection of Jewish culture as marginal (i.e., a basic, general anti-Semitism). All further treatment of the topic is based on this cultural foundation of ideological definition. The marginalization of Yiddish as the language of the other, which in this role replaced Hebrew as the language of the Jewish other after the appropriation of Hebrew by European Humanism, had a long tradition in non-Jewish European letters before the period in question here, i.e., before the period of "modern" literary and linguistic analysis.[25]

But the most significant, vehement and verbally violent opponents of Yiddish arose in the German Jewish scholarly community of the Enlightenment, in their reprojection of alterity onto the radically other Eastern European Jew, the speaker of Yiddish, especially in the later developments of the Haskalah toward the end of the nineteenth century as "national" movements arose among the Ashkenazim of Eastern Europe with the Bundist goals of self-determination, or those of Poalei Zion or of Zionism proper, or of YIVO or the Wissenschaft des Judentums.[26] One thus sees a casebook manifestation of Gilman's notion of Jewish self-hatred, but one that also transcends his categories to reveal a more far-reaching problematic within the context of linguistic and literary studies and indeed cultural studies in general.

For the virulently anti-Yiddish Maskilim, Hebrew was to be their "Latin," German/Russian/etc., their vernacular, and Yiddish was banished to use by the uncultured and barbaric, who are always located on the margin. For the center, in this case, those in Germany, that margin was both culturally and geographically located in the East, which was already imbued by a long-standing German tradition with the image of (Slavic) barbarism. The harangues against Yiddish took a rather cliché-ridden standard form, containing many elements in common. One of the clichés of this debasement of Yiddish is the recurrent labeling of it as a "woman's language": Hebrew is the learned language of Jewish education and thus that of the Jewish male, while Yiddish is the unlearned pidgin of the uneducated (even in the generally vilified, Ashkenazic context) men and all women. It is thus characterized as a "kitchen language." This is a typical ideological move in attempts to debase a language of whatever kind: by relegating it to inferior status within the culture by assigning it to use by members of a group which is by definition also held to be inferior – in this, as in so many cases, women. With respect to Old Yiddish, this ideological move is also represented in the ubiquitous characterization of the Old Yiddish romance epics as "women's literature" that was shunned by men, who were absorbed with their "legitimate" studies of the Talmud and Torah, but who nonetheless in most cases translated and/or wrote the books, copied, typeset, bound, distributed, sold, and not seldomly read these women's books as well.

Another move in this ideological game was one of self-defense and self-justification. Despite or perhaps ultimately as a result of the fact that Yiddish was defined as linguistically, morally, and culturally corrupt and corrupting, as the means and manifestation of the Jews' antipathy to Christian culture (demonstrated by their debasement of the German language), in short as *the* sign of Jewish anti-culture, it was necessary somehow to render the language harmless and reduce anxiety concerning its subversive nature. This move was carried out by means of still a further characterization of the language as simply the jargon[27] of fools: the language was no more than an attempt by the illiterate, ignorant outcast to speak the language of culture, and as a result, it was comic. The stereotyped Yiddish-speaking or

Yiddish-intoning stage character became a stock figure in comedies of the Enlightenment period and thereafter. In this category of the ideological argument, the speaker of Yiddish is not primarily a corrupter, not sinister, but merely a fool, no more than linguistically inept, just as he is inept in all other social spheres.[28] Still another standard element was the development of a moralistic discourse concerning Yiddish using medical and pseudo-medical terminology, such that the language was described as "diseased," "corrupt," "impure," "degenerate," and needful of "healing."

In the decades around the turn of the century, with the institutionalization of the conflict between pro- and anti-Yiddish ideologies through political parties and research institutes came the attempt to redefine both center and margin. While the Westernized assimilated Wissenschaft des Judentums treated Yiddish as marginal at best, the Yidisher-Visnshaftlekher Institut (YIVO) attempted in part to reverse the polarity by establishing Yiddish literature, language, and culture in general as an inherently valuable cultural entity and thus a legitimate object of study in itself: that is, it was an attempt to center Yiddish. (On this notion of *on* and *in* Yiddish, see Dovid Katz, "On Yiddish, in Yiddish and for Yiddish," pp. 23-36, where, without using the term, Katz discusses the cultural centering of Yiddish, as it arises in the work of YIVO and its allies.) Such a move is, needless to say, by definition threatening to the center. The only legitimate response by the center is therefore to ignore all such moves from the margin. In general such was in fact the reaction of the center to YIVO. In essence, it paralleled the Humanistic usurpation of Hebrew: the center (Humanism, Haskalah) was duty-bound to take over the administration of this cultural entity since the Jew "possessed" Hebrew/Yiddish only in a partial, illegitimate way, and could do no more than corrupt it and distort its nature. One could thus (over)simplify the cultural locus of the entire field of (Old) Yiddish studies by characterizing it as defined by marginality: it exists both within and without the academy only in terms of its relation to the center/margin. In the absence of such definition, the field collapses into a void. This scenario is unfortunately not all that far removed from reality, for most of the ink used in treatments of Old Yiddish has been spilled in addressing one or another aspect of this problem, to the almost complete exclusion of analysis of the traditionally standard problems of literary and linguistic analysis.

Yiddish is thus at times perceived as a German dialect, at times as a mere pidgin-like corruption of German, and at times as no more than a lexical misnomer. It is thus essentially supplemental in the post-structuralist sense: it is inessential to, and non-participatory in the whole (German), but at the same time can and must stand in some relationship to the whole, or even be annexed into the whole in order, one must assume, to make up for some lack in the whole.[29] Old Yiddish studies as a discipline has thus been one plagued by basic conflicts in its own definition, for even some of its champions have assumed its essential alterity while favoring the reification thereof by annexation – the supplemental is simply annexed into the center, for example, by means of the transliteration of Hebrew-alphabet Yiddish texts into Roman, which simultaneously both usurps *and* confirms the alterity of the texts. In general, however, the problem has been one of broader cultural definition, for old Yiddish studies have and have had no history or scholarly identity in the sense that, for instance, Old French has – as the "origin" and earliest period of the "national" language and literature of France. One might thus generalize that Old French texts are important for French "national" culture and must be rendered accessible to the "French nation," as well as to Old French scholars and other interested parties. On the other hand, the modern audience of Old Yiddish literature is less easy to define. There is no Yiddish "nation" and never has been. Thus there has been no national system of secondary schools with courses that deal with the medieval period of the "national literature" and no undergraduate or graduate degree programs for the study of the language and literature at the "national" universities.[30] Moreover, the present century has witnessed the extermination of more than half the world's Yiddish speakers, the dispersal and (apparently) final impulse toward linguistic assimilation of the majority of Yiddish-speaking survivors of the Holocaust,[31] and the founding of the state of Israel, which was initially (and to a lesser degree still is) fundamentally hostile to Yiddish as the idiom of a part of its citizenry.[32] Ironically, only in the present century has a scholarly interest in (Old) Yiddish developed as a distinct, institutional discipline.[33] This scholarly community that deals with Old Yiddish is necessarily *inter*-national, composed of both Jewish and non-Jewish scholars. Among them are few "medieval Yiddishists": those who work in this field are often amateurs (in the best sense), trained as Romance or Germanic philologists, historians of religion or Judaic studies, but sometimes also as chemical engineers.[34] Here the general question of accessibility becomes obscured even in its very formulation: to whom must what aspect(s) of Old Yiddish language and literature be made accessible for what purpose in what form, in what language?[35]

The means here employed to penetrate and elucidate the ideologies present in the modern reception of Old Yiddish literature derive from two recurring topoi in studies of Old Yiddish: the names used to designate the language, and the notion of "accessibility" through text editions. On the surface neither seems a particularly problematic topic nor an especially significant one. But in fact precisely therein lie the inherent possibilities for mytho-ideological manipulation. In the first case, the name assigned by a scholar to the language is in no case a haphazard matter of mere nomenclature, for it presupposes the entire structure of thought that is brought to bear on whatever research problem the scholar happens to address. While the problems involved are quite complex indeed, a mere list of selected names given to the language over the course of the past century will illustrate the myriad possibilities of not just lexical, but also ideological, nuances expressed by the mere *nomen*, which functions as an indicator of the underlying conception of the *res*: Old Yiddish (*Altjiddisch, altyidish*), Judeo-German (*Jüdisch-Deutsch, Judendeutsch, judéo-allemand, yidish-taytsh*), Hebrew-German (*Hebräisch-Deutsch, hébreu-allemand, ivri-taytsh*), Germano-Judaic, *Jüdisch-Mittelhochdeutsch.*

In the second case, regarding the scholarly concern for rendering Old Yiddish "accessible," the problem becomes more complex still, for the myriad possibilities for ideological manipulation are present here, too: indeed for each stage of the editorial process, for each editorial decision, for each text, each word, in fact, each grapheme. And it is most often on this last level, of the single grapheme, that a particular scholar's understanding of the notion of "accessibility" is most clearly revealed: since most editions have appeared in Roman transliteration/transcription, most often without an accompanying Hebrew-alphabet text (or without editorial recourse to it for the purpose of linguistic analysis), the editor may then exercise almost complete freedom in transforming the manuscript text into the form that s/he deems most "accessible," whatever that form might be – an ostensibly Middle High German, modern Yiddish, early New High German, or modern southeastern Yiddish text – with numerous gradations among these various possibilities, or even with added variants. The underlying assumption is, obviously, that the Old Yiddish text in manuscript is *in*accessible, other, bearing a sign of alterity, which can be removed via the editorial procedure: s/he strips the text of its alterity, annexes it (in appearance/alphabet and cultural identity) into the center, and thus renders it accessible to the inhabitants of the center, denying it in the process its originally conceded, now obliterated, alterity. Even so, it is still not a full-fledged member of the center, for it is still only "Judeo-German," "Jüdisch-

Deutsch," etc., not "German" or "Deutsch" *per se*.

Following the analysis of these two seminal problems in the history of Old Yiddish studies, the contemporary movements in the study of Old Yiddish will be investigated and suggestions made for the future course of Old Yiddish studies.

TWO

The Names of Old Yiddish

IN 1932 SOLOMON BIRNBAUM [Salomo Birnbaum/Shloyme Birnboym] remarked in his article "Jiddisch" in the *Encyclopaedia Judaica* that although many names had formerly been used to designate the Yiddish language, "Yiddish" [*Jiddisch*] had finally prevailed.[1] Forty-one years later, Maks Weinreich, in his monumental study of the history of the Yiddish language, the culmination of a lifetime of research, noted the oft-mentioned multiplicity of names attached to the Yiddish language, and made a similar, but much more specific claim.[2] After having outlined the history of the names and sometimes noting their polemic use, he stated that *yidish* had triumphed as the name of the contemporary Yiddish language and also maintained that, although other names had until recently been used for the *earlier* stages of the language, "Yiddish has become the general name for the *entire* language."[3] The statements by Birnbaum and Weinreich are, however, misleading, since in fact the current research literature on Yiddish abounds in names for the language (in general those same ones that have been used throughout the history of Yiddish philology), only one of which is "Yiddish." It thus becomes clear that although these scholars use descriptive terminology here, their statements are in fact prescriptive. Yet with their refined and precise sense of style (in numerous languages), immense erudition in matters of linguistics, literature, and general cultural history and encyclopedic knowledge of the research literature in this and related fields,

Birnbaum and Weinreich were certainly not unaware of the opposition between the descriptive form and prescriptive content inherent in their formulations: it is not an error in thought or terminology. It is the expression of an ideological position common to Yiddish studies, a position from which Birnbaum launched what can only be termed a campaign in the early decades of the century to establish "Yiddish" as the standard name of the language,[4] for during this period he propagated the name *Jiddisch* as the only legitimate name in at least four publications that had wide exposure: in his *Praktische Grammatik der Jiddischen Sprache* (Vienna 1918), the encyclopedia entries, "Jiddische Sprache," in *Jüdisches Lexikon*, vol. 3 (Berlin 1929), "Jiddisch," in *Encyclopaedia Judaica*, vol. 9 (Berlin 1932), and "Jiddisch," in *Der große Brockhaus*, 15th ed., vol. 6 (Leipzig 1931).

This campaign on Birnbaum's part is only one indicator that the subject of the name of the Yiddish language, seemingly trivial and of concern only to terminological pedants, is and has historically been, perhaps one of the most vexing and tenacious questions to occupy – one might almost say plague – scholars of Yiddish language and literature. The problem is even more acute for early Yiddish studies. In reviewing the extensive research literature on Old Yiddish topics published in the twentieth century,perhaps the most striking feature is the plethora of names – old and newly coined – used to designate the language and literature. Rarely has a book, monograph, edition, article, or review appeared on the subject of Old Yiddish without taking a position on what to call the language: "Hebrew-German," ("yidish-taytsh," "Judeo-German," "Jüdisch-Deutsch," "Judendeutsch," "judéo-allemand") or "Old Yiddish" ("alt-yidish," "Altjiddisch," etc.). Whether there is an attempt to justify the terminological choice or not, the choice of what to call the text(s) under examination reveals more of the scholarly method used, the perspective taken, and the historically scholarly "camp" affiliation, than perhaps any other aspect of the argument. After more than half-a-century of often heated discusssion of this topic, one recent scholar has dismissed it entirely by calling it simply a matter of terminology.[5] Yet another scholar was quick to point out that indeed it is *only* a matter of terminology,[6] and precisely for that reason, it is perhaps the most essential of all questions, since behind the seemingly innocuous name assigned to the language lurks an entire infrastructure of critical assumptions that in fact determines not just the name by which the scholar designates the language, but also the critical foundations of the study, the set of questions posed, the answers possible. We are thus concerned here not just, and not even primarily, with a problem of nomenclature, for the variety of names used illustrates a difference of opinion with respect not just to the *nomen* but also to the *res* that determines it, that is, the preconceptions of what the object of study is and can be. The present chapter will examine these names, their ideological underpinnings, and their place in the context of (Old) Yiddish studies and modern European intellectual history.

Weinreich's brief treatment of the history of the names of Yiddish is not unique,[7] and it offers little that goes beyond the outlines presented by his many predecessors. It seems in fact almost *de rigueur* that any author of a lengthy study of the history of some aspect of Yiddish language or literature devote a section or chapter to the names of Yiddish. This preoccupation with the name, status, and even existence of a language is somewhat out of the ordinary, but in fact understandable in context, especially in terms of the cultural marginality outlined in the previous chapter as it is applicable to Yiddish and its cultural home among the Ashkenazim. The ultimate causes of this phenomenon are complex, multifaceted, and hardly classifiable. One might, however, reduce them to a single cause at least initially, simply for the sake of establishing a basis on which to begin the discussion. This single cause is a two-sided coin: non-Jewish anti-Semitism and, in Gilman's formulation "Jewish self-hatred." The process of uncovering and sorting out this morass of intertwined causes and effects may best begin at a more general level.

Yiddish has never been an institutionalized "national language,"[8] in the sense that, for instance, English, French, and German have been; it was never in its early history the language of state, commerce, education, literature, or family in an extensive community in which this was the only or even the primary language of *all* these cultural phenomena. Rather, Yiddish was the language of the "Other," the outsider, the Jew, and most importantly the outsider even among European Jews – the Ashkenazic *Ostjude*. Thus the language of this people on the margins of European society was in turn viewed from the outside as well. For its speakers, inhabitants of the margin, it was simply "our language" (*biloshenu*), "the mother tongue" (*mame loshn*) or "taytsh." For the "insiders," i.e., inhabitants (or would-be inhabitants) of the center, Yiddish was merely the form or dialect of German spoken by Jews: "Jüdisch-deutsch," "Judendeutsch," "Judéo-allemand," "Judeo-German," "Hebrew-German," or even "yidish-taytsh."[9] Thus the language was not seen simply as German *per se*, but rather as a German that is colored by its Jewish speakers, but still in spite of all qualification, a kind of German.[10] The step from this view to a more negative valorization of Yiddish as a degenerated, deformed German, with many Hebrew-Aramaic, Slavic, and some few Romance "scraps" is not a long one.[11] That step was taken both by German-speaking and Yiddish-speaking scholars. Especially in the early nineteenth century, when Germanistic studies arose and "discovered" the German "national" language, literature, and culture, and sought to recast its history into a standard language, a profound distaste for the "substandard" dialects of the language arose.[12] Yiddish, the so-called deformed form of German spoken by the Jews of (primarily) Eastern Europe was still called "Jüdisch-Deutsch" (or a similar name), which took on a strong pejorative connotation, often also expressed with the term "Jargon" whose connotations are obvious.

The problem of the names of Yiddish is, however, much too complex and complicated to be fully elucidated by assigning individual scholars and the names they used to various ideological camps, and little insight would be gained by such affixing of labels into the complex and revealing relationships among the various aspects of linguistic/literary critical methodology, which are involved in this subtle interplay between the names of the language, the general valorization of literature in that language, of the "national" character and origin of the literature. There is no direct path of analysis, but only an intricately interwoven pattern of paths, with multiple switchbacks, connections, and crossroads. The complete history of the names of Yiddish need not be recounted here (although reference will be made to relevant aspects of it in context), for we are concerned with more recent, primarily twentieth-century names of Old Yiddish, i.e., in the period since the beginning of the scholarly and philological analysis of Old Yiddish.

In the past century there have been three approaches to this problem. Here I would like to deal with the method by which the problem of the identity of the language is posed and the presuppositions – the critical ideologies – by means of which the problem itself is constituted. We can view this problem as a matter of the specific formulation of a single question: What *is* the language? For the treatments of the problem are always exercises in ontological criticism. The answers to this variously formulated question are always problematic, but also always adequate, legitimate, and correct – as answers to the particular question posed in its own ideological context. The major problem of course lies in the question's context. With this perspective, the ongoing conflict between the pro- and anti-Yiddish schools of the three ideological stages becomes less important than it has been, since it thus becomes clear that these two categories of scholars are in opposition only in the specific details of their analyses and not in the ideological underpinnings of their arguments. The problem can best be approached by way of examining the three ideological stages. Since the strands of the problem span the last century and are intertwined through schools, countries, and even the various stages of a single career, no strictly chronological or thematic organization is possible. For the purposes of orientation, however, there are four distinct themes to be treated, in relative chronological order: 1) the conflict between the early assimilationists and Yiddish nationalists; 2) the evolution of that conflict into the scientistic debates concerning the texts of the Cambridge codex (especially *Dukus Hurnt*); 3) the analysis of the early modern adaptations of German chapbooks and legal documents into Yiddish; 4) the recent move, especially characteristic of the "Trier School," toward a redefinition of the field on the basis of a socio-linguistic and literary approach.

The first position is that of the addressees of Birnbaum's campaign of the early 1930s: the two rather ill-defined group of scholars loosely associated with the tenets either of the *Wissenschaft des Judentums* or of YIVO. In the latter part of the nineteenth and early years of the twentieth centuries, two schools, both represented almost exclusively by Jewish scholars, began to take a scholarly interest in Old Yiddish studies. The first, the "Wissenschaft des Judentums," one of the many institutional developments arising out of the Jewish Enlightenment (Haskalah), was, with respect to Yiddish, essentially assimilationist in character, and attempted to deny Yiddish the status of a cultural language by advocating its replacement as the language of written communication by German (or in some contexts, Hebrew), and even wanted to replace Yiddish as the spoken vernacular of the Eastern European Jews with "pure" German, or in some cases with the "national" language of the indigenous, non-Jewish population (Polish, Russian, etc.). The various individual reasons for this attempt at linguistic annihilation were complex in their articulation, but ultimately they reflected no more than a simple cultural value judgment: Yiddish was the language of the uneducated (in the Western European sense), unassimilated, traditional Jew of the Eastern European ghettoes. That is, Yiddish was a language of the margin, and a constant and embarrassing reminder to the (primarily) German-Jewish scholars of the Wissenschaft des Judentums, of Jewishness in its pristine, anti-Semitic, caricatured image, which by the nature of anti-Semitism *and* Jewish self-hatred eternally threatened to besmirch them, the "partially" assimilated, partial members of the center. The language was historically German, but had been "corrupted" and was thus no longer fit for any cultured use; its continued use doomed its speakers to a second-class existence beyond the pale of civilized culture. In looking back on the history of Yiddish, the members of the scholarly Haskalah saw a golden age in the pre-sixteenth-century language and literature of their forbears: before the corruption of the language by Hebrew and Slavic influence and the degeneration of grammar, the language was said to have been "pure" German. This argument was very convenient for the entire ideological program of the Haskalah, which attempted to round off the edges of Ashkenazic culture by eliminating those elements of the culture which were identifiably non-central, "non-European," other in some, not to say specifically Jewish, sense. Here, in legislating the prescriptive identity of Yiddish with German, one clearly sees their revisionist program in operation. Four general elements make up the Haskalah evaluation of Old Yiddish. The implications of their program can best be elucidated through an examination of these elements.

1) Yiddish was originally "pure German."

The names used to designate the language reflect this interpretation: "Judeo-German", "Jüdisch-Deutsch," "Judendeutsch," "Hebrew-German." In every case the final element of the compound is determinative, the initial element a modifier, such that even in the names, the primary identification of the language as "German" is apparent. Some aspect of the language is thus specifically "Jewish," although the scholars differ as to what this characteristically Jewish element might be. Leo Landau calls the earliest stages of the language "Hebrew-German," since it is "pure German" in grammar and vocabulary and Hebrew only in its alphabet.[13] Max Grünbaum maintains that the early language is primarily German in form, but Jewish in content, i.e., the subjects of the texts are predominantly Jewish.[14] The meaning of this rather naive, pseudo-linguistic statement becomes clear only in the course of his argument, where the distinctions among linguistic, literary, and cultural elements become further blurred: the language is primarily Jewish in content, since its literature was for the most part translated or adapted from Hebrew books (p. 533). He further remarks that "jüdisch-deutsche" literature is a microcosm of Jewish literature with its primarily ethico-religious tendency. Thus he vehemently rejects secular works, such as *Vidvilt* ["Artus hof"] which he says are Jewish only in script, and otherwise strictly German (p. 534). It seems, however, that he is not commenting on the linguistic identity of the works, for later he maintains that these works are translations *from* German, i.e. not themselves German, as he had claimed earlier (p. 536). At any rate, these works are no more than:

> mere light reading. . . lacking all ethical value and naturally also all moral influence, they are not even remotely comparable to the products of actual and original-authochthonous Judeo-German literature. They do not in any way belong to Jewish literature, and it is questionable whether they belong to Judeo-German.[15]

His next paragraph, however, notes that these works had a much more numerous audience among Jews than did the ethico-religious books which he is willing to call both "jüdisch" and "jüdisch-deutsch". The distinction between these two terms is also problematic: "jüdisch" seems to signify the traditional culture of the Jews, while "jüdisch-deutsch" provides examples of that culture in the "Judeo-German" language. Whatever is not based on Jewish tradition is not Jewish, even if written by and for a Jewish audience in the "Judeo-German" language, containing many Hebrew words, and employing the Hebrew alphabet, as for example, the Old Yiddish text that he singles out for the most vehement attack, *Vidvilt.*

On the other hand, Gustav Karpeles, who calls the language "Judendeutsch," since it was a "mixture of German and Hebrew,"[16] denies any identifiably Jewish characteristics of the early stages of the language, because, according to his view, not only was the language of the medieval German Jews the same as that of their Christian neighbors, but their literature and even culture in the broad sense was identical: The Jews regarded Germany as their "native land" and were "keenly concerned in the development of its poetry."[17] Leo Wiener is of the same opinion in his *A History of Yiddish Literature.*[18] He calls the language "Judeo-German (Yiddish)" (p. xxix), the reasons for which become clear only in the course of his argument: except for their religion, medieval German Jews had the same culture as did their Christian neighbors, including language, conception of life, and popular customs; this Christian literature was comprehensible and "fully acceptable" (p. 2).[19] If one attempts to dissect Wiener's argument, it becomes clear that the Jewish religion, usually thought to be one of the major determinants of Jewish popular and learned culture, is denied relevance as a conditioning factor of culture. Furthermore, what is meant by "Christian literature"? Does he mean ostensibly secular literature, such as the courtly love lyric (with its ambiguous relationship to the developing cult of the virgin)? Or is it the courtly romance (with its hero who is ultimately, although tacitly, a *miles christi*)? Or does Wiener mean St. Thomas' *Summa*? All are certainly "Christian literature," and none could have been "fully acceptable" in any sense to a medieval Jewish audience still several centuries distant from the Haskalah secularization so dear to Wiener's heart (and blinding to his historical perspective).

The most vociferous defender of the identity of Jewish and Christian culture in the Middle Ages was Leo Landau. In the preface to his edition of *Vidvilt*, the first full-scale modern critical edition of a work of medieval Yiddish literature, he discusses in great detail the cultural context of such literature.[20] He denies outright Grünbaum's definition of "Judeo-German" as a language that is German in form and Jewish in content, since, according to him, there is no Jewish content of any sort in this literature; the language should thus be called "Hebrew-German" (p. xxiii), since it is simply German written in the Hebrew alphabet (p. viii). His editions of *Vidvilt* and *Esther* both reflect this conception, in that both are edited on the basis of a posited underlying language in the form of normalized Middle High German.[21] The purity of this language as "German" is apparently not impaired by what he deprecatingly calls "the addition of a few common Hebrew words strewn in here and there" (p. xxx). He also sees the identity of language as a reflection of a cultural identity: medieval German literary genres (lyric and epic) were identical to those found in medieval Hebrew-German literature, and some Jews even became part of the Christian literary tradition.[22] In fact, as soon as there was a fledgling German literature, Landau contends, Jews rushed to participate in it (p. xxiii).[23] In fact he argues that since few Jews were illiterate, as were most of their Christian neighbors, medieval Jews knew more German literature and knew it better than did their Christian neighbors. (p. xviii).

2) The Yiddish language became to some extent independent of German as a result of the displacement of the Jews to Eastern Europe; and
3) The changes in the language which resulted in this relative independence from German were due to "corruption."

Almost without exception scholars of the anti-Yiddish school link the development of Yiddish as a language distinct from German to the exile of the Ashkenazic Jews to Eastern Europe, especially in the sixteenth century, since the language then developed in isolation from its "origin." Wiener's value-laden terms are characteristic of the Haskalah attitude toward the degeneration of Jewish culture in the Slavic East: "Unfortunately in the beginning of the sixteenth century" a "disturbing element" entered the linguistic picture (p. 3). It is not until this period, in this particular geographical environment, that a specifically Jewish literature develops in Yiddish; this literature was the product of the stagnation of Jewish culture, Wiener claims, which was now isolated from its German "homeland" and which thus became ossified in a kind of persistent medievalism that lasted until the late nineteenth century, when the Jews were "liberated" by the benefits of the secular educational system of Czarist Russia (p. 5).

The primary indicators of the change in the language itself was seen in the adoption into Yiddish of Hebrew and Slavic words. The Haskalah attitude is manifested especially in the interpretation of the use of Hebrew words in Yiddish, since Hebrew was viewed as the language of the intellect, while Yiddish was the language of the ignorant peasants. M. Pines even proposes that Judeo-German was *developed* (i.e., apparently actively and consciously) for the purpose of being an adaptable and easy instrument of commerce and communication for a people of the ghetto, while Hebrew was the language *appropriate* to the Jewish "race."[24] Pines posited the adoption of Hebrew words into Judeo-German by the thirteenth century for the purposes of some technical expressions (p. 1). But these words were clearly foreign to the idiom, he maintains, since they were always enclosed in quotation marks (pp. 3-6).[25] It is also very difficult to determine how Pines could in any particular case distinguish between foreign and borrowed/assimilated terms in a language sample several centuries old, since such distinctions can only be made on the basis of a well-developed sense of style in the language and are often quite difficult even for contemporary native speakers, since a term may be appropriate in one register (say, academic prose), but not in another (casual conversation or poetic style).

Wiener implies that it was only in the absence of another language capable of intellectual expression (i.e., German and excluding Yiddish) that Hebrew, the language of Jewish education, came to exert an influence on Yiddish (p. 16). In this view, the Slavic languages also contributed to the corruption of the mother tongue. Landau argues that it was not until translations were made from Latin, Hebrew, French, and other languages that non-German words appeared in Yiddish – such translations were, he contends, the source of all Hebrew words in the the Jews' German.[26] The Hebrew words used in Yiddish were also only the "most common" of Hebrew words (p. xxx). One might well ask how Landau came to consider these and not other Hebrew words "common," the most likely answer being that they were simply the most *frequent* in Yiddish texts. This is hardly compelling evidence for denying significant influence by Hebrew on Old Yiddish. The "archaisms" (with respect to modern standard *German*) for which Yiddish is well known are explained by Landau as the result of the exclusion of the Jews from education in the medieval period (p. xxx); one wonders then how they managed to know Christian literature better than the Christians did, as Landau maintains only two pages earlier.

Wiener adheres to the romantic notion of the organic nature of language – that for instance languages experience "natural growth and decay" (p. 14); Judeo-German had thus been in a state of decay since the sixteenth century.[27] The fusion character of Yiddish is described in terms of the corruption of the "mother tongue"; perhaps even in the pre-sixteenth-century period some Hebrew words were introduced into Judeo-German, "relating purely to the Mosaic ritual," and in the East, Slavic vocabulary and grammar also exerted an influence on Yiddish (p. 15). With regard to the first kind of influence, Wiener further reduces the importance of the Hebrew language and literature on Diaspora Jewish culture in general to a neat formula and thus misrepresents the nature of the influence: medieval Christians used the sacred language of their culture, Latin, for their "higher literature," and the Jews *modeled* their use of the Jewish sacred language, Hebrew, on the Christian practice (pp. 1-2). The effect of this linguistic fusion was felt not only in the language of the Eastern European Jews, but, through the export to the West of Judeo-German books published in the East, the language of the Western European Jews was also colored and slowly corrupted by what Wiener, the "semi-assimilationist" terms a "Semitic infection" (p. 16).

The notion of linguistic corruption does not stop here, however, but is even applied in the reverse direction: he calls the attempts by members of the Enlightenment to purify Judeo-German by re-Germanizing it an "evil practice" (p. 22).[28] The use of German in Judeo-German, he maintains, is characteristic of "lower writers" and "scribblers" who have corrupted the literature and language of the Jews (p. 22). Wiener's argument thus disintegrates of itself, since he sees the Judeo-German language as originally pure German which was corrupted by the influx of Hebrew and Slavic words,[29] only to be re-corrupted in the attempt to purify the language of the corrupting

Hebrew and Slavic elements through the re-introduction of "pure German."

The most polemic of the proponents of Yiddish as a corruption of German is Karpeles, who calls the language:

> This Judeo-German jargon . . . this German linguistic heritage . . . that has been allowed to degenerate here for such a long time through disuse . . . whose only law seems to have been its lawlessness . . . . When one speaks of inflections, one may not think of definite grammatical forms, which are, on the contrary, carelessly mixed up in this macaronic language.[30]

He first claims that the language consists of four elements, then lists six: 1) Hebrew words; 2) periphrastic phrases containing both Hebrew and German words; 3) combined terms, with Hebrew roots and German inflections; 4) arbitrary abbreviations and combinations; 5) illegitimate and error-ridden German; 6) foreign words (p. 1003). The literature is in no sense original or of any value, he claims (pp. 1005-1009); it is merely a literary weed patch (*literarischer Wildwuchs*), characterized by its tastelessness (*Geschmacklosigkeit*) and poverty (*Armseligkeit*), in which the German language has become no more than babbling (*ein Lallen*).

The last of the elements of the Haskalah treatment of Old Yiddish, which grows out of the previous three elements and provides the ultimate justification of the general argument, has ostensibly little to do with Old Yiddish *per se*:

> 4) *Modern* Yiddish is essentially German, i.e., not a language or even a discrete dialect of German, but merely German in a corrupt form.

This argument justifies the attempt by the Haskalah to "purify" Yiddish and thus return it to its alleged pristine state. Wiener praises the Haskalah unabashedly for forcibly separating the Jews from their medieval culture (in the pejorative sense of the "Dark Ages"). It was only through Mendelssohn and other representatives of the Enlightenment that "the Jews were once more brought back into the fold of the German nation," in that they abandoned Judeo-German for pure German (p. 6). Here he is writing only of the Jews of Germany, however, since the Jews in Eastern Europe persisted in their use of their "homely dialects" instead of their "mother tongue" (i.e., German).

Landau also maintains the same argument regarding Modern

Yiddish, claiming that relations between Jews and Germans were "intimate" for centuries, and even at the time of his writing, the language of the European Jews was "a slightly modified German" (p. xxii). His term for Yiddish is, as noted above, "Hebrew-German"; the term is, however, not merely used for the earlier stages of the language, but also applied to the Yiddish literature of Landau's day in Russia, Poland, England, and the Americas (p. xxx). Thus in his view and according to his definition of "Hebrew-German," Eastern European Jews in the twentieth century were still speaking "a slightly modified German" and writing this language in the Hebrew alphabet. Karpeles' interpretation is similar, insofar as he also views modern Yiddish as Judeo-German that was still surviving in Eastern Europe of the time, and still producing a literature without form, character, or originality, for an audience that was "klein und eng," a suitable audience, he contends for "dieses dürftige und armselige Schrifttum" ("this wretched and miserable literature," p. 1029).

This argument has as one offshoot the notion that modern, just as early Yiddish, can shed light on the phonetics of Middle High German, since the language is written in the Hebrew alphabet and thus sometimes contains more specific phonetic information than that rendered by the Roman alphabet used for Middle High German. In fact, it often seems to be the case that these scholars see little use for Yiddish (medieval or modern) beyond this putative value in reconstructing Middle High German pronunciation.[31]

Perhaps the description of Yiddish that has the most consistently Haskalah bent is to be found in the utterly unpolemical article by the eminent linguist, Edward Sapir. He calls the language "Judeo-German," but in identifying his topic calls it the "Judeo-German or 'Yiddish' dialects":[32] the language did not begin to develop until the early sixteenth century; Eastern European Jews then spoke pure German, and "the basis has remained thoroughly German, the foreign accretions and influences are, at best, of only secondary importance" (p. 233); archaic features have been preserved, while radical simplifications have also occurred (pp. 234-237); and, the phonology of both vowels and consonants of *modern* Yiddish is discussed in detail strictly in terms of Middle High German (pp. 237-266). He concludes: "I trust that I have shown that a thorough investigation of the phonology, morphology, and vocabulary of Judeo-German will prove abundantly fruitful to students of German dialectology" (p. 266). Again, it seems that the only value of Yiddish is for the linguistic analysis of German.

It would be unfair to leave the discussions of the scholarly

Haskalah's attention to Old Yiddish without attempting to put my criticism of their endeavors into context. As Schulman notes (pp. vii-viii) in his introduction to Leo Wiener's *History*, and Wiener himself indicates in his preface (p. xxix), there was little preliminary research (bibliographical, biographical, linguistic, or literary studies) of any significance on nineteenth-century Yiddish literature. Essentially Wiener had to start with a *tabula rasa*. How much more so was this the case with Old Yiddish literature (as Landau's note on the lack of prior interest in and publications on the topic hardly serves to fully document; *Arthurian Legends*, p. vii). There had been some previous attempts at scholarly work,[33] but no real foundation had been laid. These scholars were in essence attempting to lay that foundation themselves. Their failure, if it must be called such, lay therein that, lacking much of the necessary materiel, editions, lexica, grammars, and monographic studies of linguistic and literary phenonomena, they substituted their own critical and cultural ideologies for that materiel and laid them qua foundation of their discipline. Even here, however, a word of caution against unbridled criticism of their methods is in order: by proceeding in this manner, they were following a precedent set by the "discovery" and foundation of medieval European philologies in various countries almost a century beforehand, and it would not be too far-fetched to suppose that they were conscious of that model, especially in Germanic philology, in laying the foundations of their own field, especially since they themselves emphasize their affiliations with the tradition of Germanic philology at every opportunity, for they view their field as merely a subdiscipline of German.

Certainly not all of the scholars dealt with here were devoted to the systematic malignment of Old and modern Yiddish language, literature, and culture, and few of those deserving of that label would have admitted to the accuracy of such a description of their efforts. Pines, one of the most polemic of the group, denies categorically that Judeo-German, *Jüdisch-deutsch* in Hecht's translation,[34] was "Kauderwelsch," since it was, he notes, a rule-governed language, capable of linguistic description (pp. 14-15).

Although Felix Perles calls the language "Jüdisch-deutsch" in the title of one of his articles,[35] in his text he also designates it "jüdisch" (p. 197, n. 1), for the same reasons as had Pines:[36] because, as he claims, that is the name given to the language by its Ashkenazic speakers. But he chooses to use that name here only "der Kürze halber," i.e., for the sake of convenience and without investing the name with any significance in itself. But one must further note that this name, "jüdisch," is a cultural rather than a linguistic designation and is in fact *not* the name given to the language by its speakers, but is rather obviously the *German* translation of that name, which is, of course, *yidish.* The difference is certainly slight, but in the present context, a significant distinction: it is simply inaccurate and furthermore has a sharp chauvinistic edge. How many native speakers of English, for instance, would agree that in that language they designate their native tongue *anglais* or *angliski iazyk*? Both of these are in fact accurate designations of the language, but not (commonly) what speakers of English accept as the English name of the language.

Wiener introduced his analysis of the language with a discussion of the general polemic directed against Yiddish: "There is probably no other language in existence on which so much opprobrium has been heaped as on the Judeo-German" (p. 12). He cites several examples, some of which are blatantly anti-Semitic in their condemnation of Yiddish as a language and as a medium of cultural expression. He further notes that writers on the subject seem compelled to apologize for the nature of the language, its usage, and even its existence (pp. 12-13). This he sees as an example of a prejudice against all things Jewish, which is, ironically, especially apparent in Haskalah examinations of Yiddish: Karpeles, Wiener asserts, is ignorant of the language; Grünbaum "displays an ignorance of the dialect which would put to shame a sophomore newspaper reporter of a scientific lecture" (p. 13). Wiener condemned this attitude, since, as he noted, Yiddish was the language of more than five million people at the time of his writing. Nonetheless, he immediately undermines his own *apologia* and enters the camp of his apparent opponents: "It cannot be maintained that it is desirable to preserve the Judeo-German, and to give it a place of honor among the sisterhood of languages . . . ." (p. 14). His subsequent remarks on the language and the culture (or lack thereof, as he sees it) further illustrate the essential dichotomy inherent in his position – for in claiming that the Yiddish language is uncouth, its literature merely a product of a stagnated medievalism, arising only in the total absence of culture (i.e., German and Russian culture), he hardly distinguishes himself from the detractors of Yiddish whom he so vehemently castigates. Furthermore, one might ask, what is his purpose in writing an entire book about such literature, if it is indeed as poor as he claims? One would hope that Wiener could have answered such questions, although there is doubt, since his general evaluation of Yiddish literature – that it compares favorably with other national literatures such as the Bulgarian – can hardly be read today in any but an ironic sense.[37]

The other "school" of Old Yiddish studies developed especially in the earlier decades of the present century, at least in part in reaction to the *Wissenschaft des Judentums*, but also in conjunction with the rise of Zionism, the freedom of ethnic self-determination, -education, and cultural preservation granted by the Soviet government in the years immediately after the Russian Revolution, and in the general cultural context of the rise of "nationalistic" movements among the Ashkenazim of Eastern Europe. Perhaps we could best call this movement the "Yiddish nationalists" on the basis of the initially insignificant (in practical terms) but soon-to-be influential (at least symbolically) conference at Tshernovits in 1908, at which the delegates from numerous countries overwhelmingly voted Yiddish *a* "nationalist language" of the Ashkenazim .[38] The first paper of the linguistics section was read (in Yiddish) by Matisyohu Mieses; it was revolutionary, in that he described Yiddish as a unique linguistic structure and used this foundation for further linguistic and sociological analysis. Fist fights broke out on the conference floor; confirmed Hebraicists burst into tears. Katz remarks: "On the tumultuous floor of the Tshernovits Conference was born, or almost born, a new science of Yiddish, combining progress in linguistic theory of the West with the Jewish cultural renaissance in Eastern Europe" (p. 32). Scholars under this banner not only viewed the language and content of the surviving early documents in their language as the "dawn" or "birth" of their discrete, separate, national culture, but also enthusiastically used such terms in their evaluations. European Romanticism had thus come even to the Ashkenazim, a century later than it had arrived in Western Europe, to be sure, but its impact and its manifestations among the Ashkenazim resembled those in, for instance, England, France, and Germany, especially with respect to the treatment of medieval language and literature, and in reaction to the Enlightenment in all its forms.

The Enlightenment (Haskalah) had of course also come to the Ashkenazim, also with some delay, as compared with its Western European manifestations. The impact of the Romantic, nationalistic movements in Europe on literary and linguistic scholarship is concisely formulated by Robert Holub in his discussion of Hans-Robert Jauß's critique of that scholarship: "The breakdown of this [earlier] paradigm in the eighteenth and nineteenth centuries is a part of the 'scientific revolution' of historicism, which arose in the wake of the establishment of nation-states and the strivings for national unity throughout Europe. As a result of political changes and ideological necessities, literary history became an idealized moment of national legitimation. Consequently, activity centered on source studies, attempts to reconstruct the prehistory of standard medieval texts, and the editing of critical editions in the national tradition. The generally accepted positivistic approach of this paradigm produced the celebrated national histories of literature associated with Gervinus, Scherer, De Sanctis, and Lanson. Methodologically, this 'historicist-positivist' approach is often identified with a mechanical approach to literary texts and a narrow, almost chauvinist outlook. Remnants of this paradigm exist today . . . . By the First World War, though, it had outlived its usefulness for productive literary research."[39] One of the reasons for the problem with this movement in Old Yiddish was that there was no "national" substrate to which recourse could continually be had in order to provide even basic guidelines for interpretive problems. To give a roundabout example: Geoffrey of Monmouth and Aldhelm regularly appear in literary histories of England, as do *Waltharius* and *Ruodlieb* in literary histories of Germany. But all belong strictly to Latin literature. There is simply a cultural *and* national interpretive substrate operative in most definitions of the bounds of a literature and a language. In Yiddish, not even Old Yiddish texts are necessarily and consistently considered part of Yiddish literature: there is no solid natio-cultural foundation on which interpretation can be based.

In the present context, however, one of the major results of the Romantic and Yiddish nationalistic movement among the Ashkenazim was the realization of one of Ber Borokhov's dreams of a Yiddish-language scientific academy in the foundation of the Yidisher Visnshaftlekher Institut in Vilna (1925) by Nokhem Shtif (1879-1933), Maks Weinreich (1894-1969), and Zalman Reyzen (1887-ca. 1940), since most proponents of this movement were in spirit, if not actually in fact, allied with YIVO.[40] One should not, however, expect of the scholarly publications of the Yiddish nationalists either a contrast in all respects to the tenets of the assimilationists, or a point-by-point refutation of the latters' arguments, for the Yiddish nationalists quite simply had a different perspective from which they viewed the Yiddish language and the history of its literature, and thus they were concerned with different topics. For instance, they accepted the origin of the language in the medieval German cultural environment and its affinities with the language of that environment as a fact of social and linguistic history, but they never spoke of Yiddish as ever having been pure German, nor of Ashkenazic culture as essentially German at any point in its history. They note that the majority of Old Yiddish texts are derivative, in that they are translations or adaptations of literary works in other languages

(French, German, Italian, Hebrew), but do not for this reason deny literary value to Old Yiddish literature, since in fact (as they often note), the adaptation of a given work from, say, Middle High German, into Old Yiddish was no more than a single additional example of the medieval literary reception of a given text from, for instance, Greek via Latin, Old French, Middle High German (and perhaps even Hebrew) to Old Yiddish. There is, however, a more pronounced tendency toward linguistic analysis and comparison to be found here, in order to demonstrate a distinction between Middle High German and Old Yiddish, but even in this regard, no rigorous refutation of the assimilationists' views is presented, primarily due to the paucity of editions of Old Yiddish texts available at the time, but also to a general lack of trained linguists among those working on Old Yiddish.[41]

One of the major illustrations of the difference in perspective found in the two schools is in their proposal of the dates of "beginnings" – the assimilationists seek to establish a time (usually a century) at which Yiddish had become different enough from German to be called a distinct language, or at least a "corrupt" form of German, distinct from German *per se*. The Yiddish nationalists accept the integrity and distinct existence of Yiddish from the very beginning of Ashkenazic culture (i.e., from the initial settlement of Jews in German-speaking territory), usually without any argument for the justification of this premise, since they are primarily interested in proposing a conjecture for the earliest date of Yiddish literary documents. The distinction is subtle, but telling. The latter school's purpose, of determining the date of the origin of Old Yiddish literature presupposes the existence of the Yiddish language, a logical presupposition in context, since they assume Yiddish as the language of the Ashkenazim *ab ortu*. Thus the assimilationists see in the earliest connected texts (i.e., more than mere glosses) evidence that the Yiddish language *per se* did not exist before the texts, while the latter sees the text as evidence of a long tradition of literature in the language which, beginning with isolated glosses in the eleventh century, had developed into a full-scale literature at least by the time of the longer texts, although perhaps even earlier, since as is generally the case with older, especially medieval European literature, relatively few documents have survived the centuries.

One of the earliest pioneers in the philological analysis of early Yiddish literature was Maks Erik (pseudonym of Zalmen Merkin), whose two major studies *Vegn altyidshn roman* and *Geshikhte fun der yidisher literatur* essentially founded the literary and linguistic study of Old Yiddish.[42] Erik never deals specifically with the questions at issue here. He tacitly accepts the term "yidish" and "altyidish" as appropriate and does not defend his choice. At the same time, however, he concurs with Güdemann's assessment of the strong cultural ties between Jews and Christians in medieval Germany.[43] Not until the fifteenth century were the Jews isolated from Christian culture to the degree that cultural exchange, especially with respect to literary influence, was reduced to insignificant levels, although beginning with the first Crusade, Jews were more isolated than before. Due to his subject in *Vegn altyidishn roman*, Erik concerns himself most with the commonality of the so-called German *Spielmann*/Yiddish *shpilman* literature,[44] and in this regard his view of the cultural ties between Germans and Jews resembles Landau's.[45] The similarities proposed by Erik sometimes almost reach assimilationist proportions: he asserts that yeshiva and Christian students were similar if not identical in their attitudes toward study, love, jesting, and the world in general (*Geshikhte*, p. 9).

The language of this early secular literature is, according to Erik, Yiddish, not German or Hebrew-German as Landau calls it, and Erik posits the beginning of Yiddish literature in the thirteenth century, although the earliest works known at Erik's time were fourteenth-century; he argues that the high level of literary technique in the surviving works shows that an older tradition existed in the adaptation of *Spielmann* literature. These adaptations are characterized by Erik as omitting Christian and adding Jewish cultural features; many melodies were appropriated with the texts, while many new ones were also added from the Jewish tradition; thus the works became specifically *Jewish* literature (2nd p. 9). He does not distinguish between secular and religious *shpilman* epics, but considers both as expressions of the same literary impulse and productions for essentially the same audience.[46]

This same type of approach, with a similar ambiguity of contrast with the assimilationist perspective, is also characteristic of many other pro-Yiddish studies. Moses Gaster's brief characterization of the language which he calls "Yiddish," also includes many arguments similar to those found in assimilationist studies: Yiddish is "preponderantly German," especially early Yiddish, where "scarcely a single Hebrew word is to be found."[47] Even so, he does not propose that Yiddish is merely German written in the Hebrew alphabet, nor German with Hebrew admixture, nor corrupt German; it is always Yiddish, and he even briefly defends its legitimacy against assimilationists.[48]

Perhaps the most characteristic spokesman for this school was the chemical engineer, Yisroel Tsinberg (Israel Zinberg), who died in Stalin's purges and whose monumental *Geshikhte fun der literatur bay yidn* includes one volume on pre-Haskalah Yiddish literature.[49] He calls the language "yidish," except once in a reference to the earliest deviations of the language from its German base, where he also uses the term "yidish-daytsch" in quotation marks, as if not quite appropriate, in deference to the use of this term elsewhere in the research literature (p. 22). He supports the position of Isaac Marcus Jost that Yiddish must date at least from the thirteenth-century immigration of Provençal Jews to the upper Rhineland, and thus opposes those scholars who place the origin of Yiddish in the period after the migration to the Slavic East (p. 23). Tsinberg points up one of the most significant arguments against the Haskalah analyses of Old Yiddish, but does not pursue it to its logical end: since the Haskalah sought to prove the origins of Yiddish in a corruption of pure German, they could not but date it to a period after the beginning of the sixteenth century, when the language rapidly distanced itself from German; anything else would have rendered their case illegitimate. In the pre-sixteenth century texts, they rationalized the use of Hebrew as isolated, technical, learned, or religious intrusions which did not reflect actual language usage, and even omitted or replaced these terms with German in their editions of the texts. At a number of points in his study, Tsinberg notes two points which are essential in analyzing any medieval document as evidence of the nature of the spoken language of its author and audience: 1) the oft-cited legal documents are necessarily of an official nature, usually couched in a style specifically characteristic of the chancery, which in its customary archaisms bears little resemblance to the spoken language of the time (pp. 26-27); and 2) religious works naturally draw more heavily on the language of the religion – Hebrew (or analogously, Latin for Christian Europe) – than would be the case in common speech.[50] Thus the use of Hebrew (or Slavic) words in written texts of various kinds is not indicative of the extent of fusion in vernacular speech. Tsinberg notes Zunz's categorization of the kinds of Hebrew words which are used in Yiddish:[51] 1) objects related to Judaism, 2) concepts associated with yeshivas and schools, 3) some expressions of daily life, and 4) conscious avoidance of certain German terms. Tsinberg adds a fifth category: commerce, which established ties among Jews throughout Europe, North Africa, and the Near East. In the end, however, Tsinberg seems to reject the mere counting of Hebrew (and other non-Germanic) words as a criterion of identifying the language of a text as Yiddish *per se*, for Yiddish differed not only in vocabulary, pronunciation, and syntax, but also, and most importantly for Tsinberg, in its expression of a way of life distinct from that expressed and expressible by German (pp. 24-25). On a sociological level, such an argument is compelling, but Tsinberg does not demonstrate his case for the distinction between the Germans and Jewish cultures in medieval Germany (nor is it his purpose to do so in the book), which would have refuted the arguments of the assimilationists that Jews were in some (equally ill-defined) sense integrated into medieval German culture. Nor does (or can) Tsinberg elaborate on his proposition that the authentic Yiddish (i.e., in his sense, the spoken) language differed from German in syntax and phonology, two criteria which, if proven would have stilled the controversy that has continued to rage on this question.

The study of Yiddish by Jechiel Bin-Nun [Fischer] is ultimately a defense of Yiddish, written and accepted as a dissertation at the Universität Heidelberg in 1935 on the eve of the Holocaust, and partially printed in Leipzig in 1936. It was at that time accepted for publication by Hermann Niemeyer in Tübingen. The Nazis disallowed the publication of the book, and it did not appear in print until 1973.[52] Bin-Nun calls the language Yiddish in the title of his study, but adheres to an essentially assimilationist definition of the developmental stages of the language (pp. 39-50): *Juden-Deutsch* (pre-ninth-century), *Jüdischdeutsch* ("jüdisch gefärbtes Deutsch," ninth-thirteenth century), *Urjiddisch* (from thirteenth century), and *Jiddisch* (not until inclusion of the Slavic determinant in the sixteenth century).

Despite his knowledge of the language, in an excurse on the name of the language, Bin-Nun claims that the Yiddish name of the Yiddish language is "Jüdisch." A problem arises when he then attempts to explain the ambiguity of the term, which designates both language and culture as "Jewish." He claims to have derived the solution to this problem of possible ambiguity from the English transcription of the language's name as *Yiddish*, which can then be adopted into German orthography as *Jiddisch* to contrast with *Jüdisch* "Jewish." But it is never made clear why it is necessary to go to English to obtain that distinctive (and apparently mystical) /i/ in *Yiddish/Jiddisch*, when it is oddly enough already present in the Yiddish name of the Yiddish language which is of course not "Jüdisch" (the German translation of the Yiddish name), but rather *yidish*. Even stranger than the fact that he thus takes the *German* term as definitive (despite the parallel lexical ambiguity in both German and

Yiddish in this case),[53] is, however, that at the end of this explication he in fact cites the two usual Hebrew-alphabet orthographic forms of *yidish* (p. 19).

N. Siskind's remarks on the early history of Yiddish differ little from those of assimilationists.[54] He claims the language is independent only when its speakers and non-speakers recognize that it differs in phonetics, grammar, syntax, and vocabulary (p. 99). He calls the earliest period of the language "ivri-taytsh" (p. 98), and initially posits the existence of an independent language, named Old Yiddish, not before 1350, when the language no longer participated in the phonetic changes characteristic of Middle High German (p. 106). This separation was due to the persecution of the Jews and their exile and isolation in ghettoes, which led to the emergence of new mixed dialects ("koylel-shprakh," pp. 105-106) unlike any single German dialect.[55] Later he contradicts his initial dating of the beginning of Yiddish as an independent language, for he claims that it was not until the Middle Yiddish period (1500-1750) that Yiddish speakers became aware that their language was different from German (p. 106). Only in the East did Yiddish become a cultural language (pp. 107-108), since in Germany, Jews used German as their literary language, and they spoke Yiddish "against their will" (p. 107).

Yitskhok Shiper's brief studies, noted above, are interesting if for no other reason, than the impossibility of classifying them ideologically. Shiper castigates Erik and Weinreich for positing a thirteenth or fourteenth-century beginning for Yiddish literature, since the earliest texts known (at the time Shiper wrote) were from a century later ("Problemen," pp. 38-41). On that basis, one would logically expect Shiper to propose that perhaps no earlier texts existed or that the earliest texts were not Yiddish, but German. Instead, however, he conjectures that Yiddish literature began in the twelfth century, on the basis of mention in the early modern period of other works, which, he speculates, must have been written in the twelfth century.[56] He further attacks Erik for proposing that the Yiddish and German culture and languages were similar in the twelfth and thirteenth centuries, because that would render Erik's thesis of a pre-fourteenth-century Yiddish literature impossible: that literature would have to be considered German, not Yiddish (p. 41).

A. A. Roback's somewhat later study, equally difficult to classify, concurs with the basic tenet espoused by the Yiddish nationalists that Old Yiddish literature is written in the Yiddish language and that this literature developed before the sixteenth century.[57] Otherwise he has almost nothing in common with them. He carries the latent tendency toward a Romantic nationalism, inherent in most studies by members of this school, to an extreme, especially in his terminology, while he eschews almost all attempts at literary or philological analysis. He often refers to the "genius of the [Jewish] race," and the "psychology of the race," all in a positive sense, ostensibly unmarked by the unavoidably macabre connotation these terms now evoke, especially when one considers that Roback's study was published in 1940. He rejects the notion that German and Jewish culture were closely aligned in the Middle Ages, and can thus argue that Yiddish had already developed into an independent language by that time, due to its isolation from German (pp. 37-43), beginning perhaps even by the Carolingian period.[58] He counters the argument that Yiddish is merely German in the Hebrew alphabet with the explanation that a literature and language are not just modes of expression, "but an ideational substance which lends it its peculiar value as a creative emanation" (p. 44). The meaning of these words is obscure at best. He does, however, attempt a more concrete analysis in categorizing the differences between Old Yiddish and German romances, which thus might aid in distinguishing the languages (p. 48): 1) lexical, grammatical, and syntactic variations; Yiddish contains biblical and Talmudic allusions even in secular works; 2) the plots are adapted to incorporate Jewish customs; 3) the reflective interludes are examples of a specific Jewish flavor; 4) monstrosities are avoided in Yiddish; and 5) in the Yiddish romances there is a prevalence of reason and justice and a lack of bloodshed. Most of his argument disintegrates under inspection, however, due to his appalling lack of understanding of his *general* subject, but especially with respect to the literature, as one example may suffice to illustrate – his comparison of the German "Lay of Hildebrand" with the Yiddish version. In the former, he contends, the father kills his son in combat, while in the latter, under the same conditions, the two are reconciled (pp. 49-50). The comparison is ill-conceived, since the Old High German *Hildebrandslied* (presumably the German poem to which he refers, since in a later Middle High German version, the father and son are reconciled) is preserved in only one fragmentary manuscript which breaks off during the battle, before either combatant has gained an advantage. Thus there can be no more than speculation on the outcdome.[59] Most likely Roback knew the poem only in a popular translation or "scholarly reconstruction" of a proposed "original," and thus was unaware that his argument had no textual basis. In any case, his interpretation of the poem is hardly solid evidence for a contrast of "national" or "racial" psychology.

At times it almost seems as if Roback turns the weapons of the assimilationists back on them, especially when they deny all cultural value to early Yiddish culture, for he maintains that medieval Jewry had a "cultural tradition" with a "social," as well as "biological heredity," while the Italian, French, Teutonic, and Spanish "tribes" did not (p. 52). It is difficult to refute an argument such as this one, since its meaning is almost impossible to extrapolate – what is one to understand as a *French* "tribe" (in any period, but especially duing the Middle Ages), or what is to be made of the posited absence of a cultural tradition among medieval Italians? His argument – already successfully self-refuted on sociological and historical grounds – disintegrates linguistically as well when he maintains that the developmental relationship between Yiddish and Hebrew, with the former constantly drawing nourishment from the latter, contrasted with the development of the Romance languages, which grew on the "dead debris" of the Latin language (p. 53), as if Latin had simply died at some identifiable point in history, and its former speakers only then set about consciously constructing a vernacular replacement for it; and as if Latin did not continue to be used throughout the length and breadth of the Middle Ages, at times more or less "classical" in style and grammar, but with few exceptions consistently as the language of learning. In this context of biological metaphor, decaying linguistic humus, and the death of languages, it is only appropriate that Roback proposes that Yiddish literature was "born"; he dates the joyous event (without further comment on the determination of the date) to "a little after 1000, or at any rate in the twelfth century" (p. 53).

In his brief and general history of Yiddish literature, Yudl Mark devotes two pages to a discussion of the language.[60] He places the origin of the Yiddish language at the time of the first settlements of Romance-speaking Jews in the Rhineland, 1000 years ago, and intimates that even then their language differed from that of their Christian neighbors. Thus he calls the language "yidish" in all periods. Since his book's intended audience is not linguistic or philological, but popular, he attempts no close analysis of the criteria for distinguishing Yiddish from German.

In 1947-1948, F. J. Beranek, who later attracted a group of students interested in Yiddish to the Universität Gießen and edited a journal devoted to Yiddish studies,[61] published a clearly well-intentioned, but, from a contemporary perspective, rather extraordinary article, which relates obliquely to our present topic.[62] His plea for scholarly research on Yiddish seems to be grounded in a desire to set his post-holocaust house – a (Jewish) German house – in order:

since Yiddish took its origin “aus dem Schoße der deutschen Sprache” (p. 163), it is the duty of German scholars to tend its study. He finds this to be especially pressing, since the field is untilled – “Es ist noch so gut wie alles zu tun” (p. 170). It is unclear how he can make this statement, especially since by this point in his article he had already discussed YIVO (p. 168). But he does claim that it is the duty of *Germanistik* to take advantage of the YIVO collections, as apparently the only scholars qualified to do so (p. 168), but also out of penance and good will, due to the “role fate has forced on the German *Volk*,” apparently herewith referring to the Nazi extermination of Jews and others (p. 170).[63] Thus Germanistik is, in his view, morally bound to preserve Yiddish language and literature as subjects of scholarly study (especially since they may not exist much longer as living cultural phenomena). As he notes in his conclusion, who better to study the culture of the people of the book than “das Volk der Dichter und Denker” (p. 174). The use of these clichés in a scholarly article published in 1947 must have been especially macabre for its initial audience.

Yiddish as an independent language is, according to Beranek, apparently the product of the linguistic influence from Slavic, for he distinguishes between East Yiddish and West Yiddish, the latter of which he would prefer to call “Judendeutsch” since it has remained as he sees it so closely related to German. Old Yiddish then, one must assume, did not exist as such, since it would have to be posited at a time before the development of East Yiddish in the Slavic lands – i.e., in the period when Yiddish was still “Judendeutsch.” On this point, Beranek’s arguments are generally strained and strange: he characterizes the exile of the Jews to Eastern Europe as a “concomitant phenomenon to the medieval German colonial movement to the East” (“Begleiterscheinung der mittelalterlichen deutschen Ostkolonisationsbewegung,” p. 164), thus as an innocuous, apparently voluntary migration which participated in a German national migratory movement; and as a result of this view, he can propose that East Yiddish is related to West Yiddish as the German of the “Neustämme” is to that of the “Altstämme” (p. 165). In the context of such remarks, his general views on the study of Yiddish as a subdiscipline of Germanistik are not surprising.

The brief history of Yiddish literature written by S. Lastik is interesting, and not just for reasons of content, as even a brief characterization of it demonstrates: it is dominated by a Marxist critical perspective, intended as a secondary school textbook, published in Warsaw, in 1950 – in Yiddish![64] Lastik places the origin of the Yiddish language in the period after the resettlement of the Jews in Eastern Europe, where the Slavic language altered its syntax and lexicon to the extent that it became an independent language; also contributing to this process of separation from German was the tradition of the three preceding centuries in which rabbis had translated and explicated (Hebrew) religious texts for children in the vernacular, which caused a great influx of Hebrew and Aramaic words into the language (p. 7). Up to the time of the settlement in the Slavic lands, the language of the Ashkenazic Jews was "yidish-taytsh," which had its origin in a Middle High German dialect and had added some few Hebrew and Romance words. "Yidish-taytsh" persisted in Eastern European cities that had a substantial German-speaking population and also in the territories bordering on German-speaking communities (p. 7). Yiddish did not achieve independent status as a language until the end of the seventeenth century (p. 7); its literary language was conservative – due both to this general tendency in literary styles and to the deliberate attempt on the part of the East Yiddish publishers to retain their West Yiddish market – and remained "yidish-taytsh" until the beginning of the nineteenth century. The literary standard only changed when this archaic language ("taytshmerisher loshn," p. 7) became incomprehensible to the reading public. The literary language then adapted to the spoken language and thus became the authentic language of the proletariat, "folks-yidish" (p. 8). Lastik here touches on a problem of immense importance for the study of the historical development of Yiddish literature, for the means of production and distribution of that literature, through publishers and booksellers, is to a great extent determinant of the kinds of literature to be promoted. His underlying purpose – to ground Yiddish literature in the *folk*, the proletariat, as opposed to the rising bourgeoisie of the industrial revolution – may also be applicable, since Yiddish was certainly more strongly based in the working class than the middle and upper classes among the Ashkenazim, who were more open to assimilationist influences. Perhaps most interesting here, however, is his proposal of two identifiably distinct literary languages, dependent on audience needs. This distinction is not new in Lastik, but is more cogently formulated than it had been before.[65]

Thus far we have dealt only with studies published up through the fifth decade of the present century, and generally found there two names, with variant forms in the languages of modern scholarship (and some few variations within those languages): "Judeo-German" (Hebrew-German," "Jüdisch-Deutsch," "Judendeutsch," judéo-allemand," "yidish-taytsh"/"evri-taytsch") and "Yiddish" ("Jiddisch," "yidish"), which in general reflect the scholars' conception of the nature of the language so designated: the former view the language as German in a determinant sense, i.e., that the language is German in essence, though "corrupt" in some manner; this name and conception of the language are seen as valid for the period up to the sixteenth century (and by many of the scholars even up to the time of their writing). On the other hand, the scholars who call the language "Yiddish" tend to view the language as a separate linguistic entity from its very early stages (some even from its initial adoption as the vernacular of the immigrant Jews in Germany). As has been noted, neither of the schools attempted to present detailed linguistic or sociological justifications for either the name of the language or their conceptions of its nature. There was little argument directly concerning the problems discussed in the present essay; battle lines were hardly drawn, defined, or defended. Often it seems almost as if the two schools were unaware of their opponents' existence, but such poses were most likely no more than that, since the scholars simply differed so radically in their interpretations as to be practically unable to communicate about such issues.[66] Also noted was the relative paucity of published texts, general introductions, or histories of the literature and grammars, which made study of the entire field difficult. The studies by members of each of the two schools, however, formed the basis on which further scholarly work could be and has been founded.

A number of factors worked in combination (though not always in cooperation) to promote Old Yiddish studies: the rise of Modern Yiddish literature to prominence, which stimulated interest in the earlier periods; the impetus given to Yiddish studies in general (not just literary, but historical, sociological, and folkloristic) by YIVO, especially after the Institute transferred to New York and began to train professional Yiddishists for academic careers; the founding of the state of Israel and its eventual foundation of university departments for the study of Yiddish language and literature; and the development of interest (scholarly and to a certain extent also lay) in things Yiddish in reaction to the Nazi extermination of European Jewry. This interest is often purely nostalgic, but it just as often arises from a spirit of preservation – to prevent the total loss of those aspects of Ashkenazic culture that can be preserved for study even after the living culture has perished. Perhaps the most important single factor contributing to the rise of Old Yiddish studies is the rediscovery and publication of a number of Old Yiddish texts, which in effect altogether change the profile of Old Yiddish literature from that known by Pines, Roback, Wiener, and Erik.[67]

In general, the scholars of neither of the two schools of this first ideological stage attempted to establish linguistic or other criteria on the basis of which one could distinguish Old Yiddish from Middle High German texts. Nor did they even express the question of language as a significant one. In the context of the present investigation, their work may be characterized as that of the pre-question stage, in which mere assumption suffices. The implicit question proves to be determinative nevertheless. The object of study, the language, the specific text *was*, without further comment or reflection, either "Hebrew-German," that is, Middle High German as spoken by Jews (and that language was by definition "reines Deutsch"), or simply Yiddish. The various kinds of textual evidence to the contrary were not accepted as evidence in either case, and the editors/critics simply suppressed them and, especially in the case of the anti-Yiddish group, they stripped the text of as many of its inherently "Jewish" features as possible, but not without doing violence to the text and its context. Thus in the editorial process, the editors restored the text to its pristine state of purity, such that in the end, they were in fact correct in their initial assumption: the text was (now) purely German or Yiddish, as the case demanded.

This conflict between the pro- and anti-Yiddish groups is an interesting variation on the theme of center vs. margin. In their attempt to dissociate themselves from the marginal existence of Jewishness in its, for them, inferior manifestation of Ashkenazic culture and language, the anti-Yiddish group, consisting primarily of members of the (partially) assimilated German Jewish community, annexed Yiddish as a language by characterizing it as a corrupt form of German, i.e., as a partial member of the center (with all the ideological implications of partiality). The culture that produced this language was allegedly once purely German, as was the language, but was corrupted over the course of the centuries, distancing itself further and further from the center's culture. In this process, the anti-Yiddish group attempts selectively to marginalize the submarginal group of Ashkenazim by banning their culture to the margin, while depriving that margin of its very language, which is usurped for the center. At the same time, they also annex the intellectual rights to Yiddish, as the Humanists had done with Hebrew centuries earlier: only they are capable of and empowered to carry out the editing and analysis of texts, for the margin itself is by its very nature unable to perform such tasks legitimately, accessibly, or objectively.

The pro-Yiddish group consists primarily of Ashkenazim whose native language is Yiddish.[68] This group displays far less uniformity of purpose and argument, however, as the above analysis demonstrates. Nevertheless a certain common thread runs through their diverse arguments: their view of the problem is also that of the opposition center-margin, which predetermines their treatment of it just as it does for their antagonists. But the pro-Yiddish group attempts a substitution and relocation of the entities within the given structure: they attempt to center Yiddish as a legitimate language, research subject, and cultural phenomenon in itself and banish to the margin its relationship to German and German culture.[69] Rather than viewing Yiddish as a sub-heading in the history of the German language, they locate it within the boundaries of the now-centered category of Ashkenazic culture. Yiddish thus takes its place as the linguistic manifestation and voice of the entirety of Ashkenazic culture. As such, it is central to the work of, for instance,YIVO, which has established four research sections to deal on a scholarly level with all aspects of Ashkenazic culture.[70] The scholarly publications were almost exclusively in Yiddish, thus establishing a body of research in the language on a broad basis, including histories of the language, literature, press, theatre, intellectual history, and even an encyclopedia, so that Yiddish was truly to become of the voice of a modern, fully developed intellectual and popular culture, on a par with the cultures and languages of the traditional center.

The two groups thus operated within the bounds of the same intellectual model – both were concerned with valuations of culture via its language, with establishing this valuation by means of delimiting the centered culture from the margin, and with establishing their arguments via traditional, scholarly, and central means: the scholarly press, conferences, and research institutes. They worked within the same intellectual structures and differed almost only in the respective items assigned to the various structural slots in those systems.

This first stage in this reception of Old Yiddish occurred in the years immediately preceding the turn of the century and continued into the first decades thereafter, with some few later progeny, that is, before Yiddish studies had really been established on a modern scholarly basis (and Landau, et al., one must not forget, helped in this establishment); before the most basic descriptive linguistic studies of the language had been carried out; before the seminal publications by Maks Weinreich and Solomon Birnbaum; before those of Uriel Weinreich, Khone Shmeruk, Josef Weissberg, and Judah Joffe; before YIVO had become the international center of scholarship that it is today; and, before Yiddish (and Old Yiddish) had become a university discipline in the (still restricted) sense that it is now. One could thus expect a remarkable difference between the first and second stages in the reception of Old Yiddish: a different initial question (implicit or otherwise), and method, and on that basis, different conclusions. These expectations are only partially satisfied, however. The primary question of the second stage – of the immediate pre- and post-World War II period – is the same as that *implied* in stage one, but here it is made explicit, perhaps most succinctly – though not for the first time – formulated by Birnbaum in the title of his 1961 article, "Old Yiddish or Middle High German?"[71] This approach is by nature necessarily one of contrastive analysis, in the positivistic, philological sense, and thus it deals closely with texts, textual analysis, textual criticism, and editing. This positivist method of minute philological analysis is found in both pro- and anti-Yiddish arguments. In fact, their arguments differ again (as in stage one) only in detail and rarely in structure.

One text in particular, the *Dukus Hurnt*, is more important in this regard than all others, for its subject derives from the well-known medieval Hilde-saga (among other motifs); it is a full-scale medieval narrative "epic"; and its form resembles in many respects that of the so-called *Spielmann* epic. The work is found in a manuscript which also contains a number of other texts, all of which are more clearly identifiable as "Jewish" in their cultural origins. For the sake of this text, if for no other, the battle lines were finally sharply drawn and the battle joined with all the weapons at the disposal of modern scholarship: descriptive, historical and socio-linguistics, genre and reception theory, comparative folklore, history, sociology, and comparative motif analysis. To illustrate the point: in the decade after the *editio princeps* of the manuscript in 1957, there were two additional editions of the whole manuscript and numerous further editions of various individual poems from the manuscript, comprising an unprecedented amount of editorial attention to a group of texts to which ironically almost all substantial literary value was systematically denied by their editors.

Interestingly enough, the scholarly conflicts, although fought with more precise, more modern weapons (including computer analysis), are generally the same as those fought indirectly by scholars of previous generations, and the names attached to the language of the texts are also essentially the same, often for identical reasons, although the arguments are generally much more detailed, and the justifications more specifically focused on that subject. The difference is that in this scholarly controversy, there is an exchange, a direct conflict of proposition, argument, and rebuttal, by which means the *res* of Old Yiddish literature and language, while still not satisfactorily defined, does at least gain more precision: for here finally the justification of the *nomen* becomes all-important. But here again, the problem is stated in reverse, if one is to take the entire problem as one to be dealt with by scholarship: in terms of traditional, empirical scholarship, should one not in fact determine the nature of the *res* before assigning it a *nomen*, rather than merely attempting to justify *a priori* the name by taking recourse to the object? Ideally and theoretically the answer is yes, and many recent studies of Old Yiddish have made a great noise about their having carried out just this sort of "objective" scientific investigation. Their sound and fury, however, signifies no more than is customary in such cases, for they also make the same *a priori* judgments as do other scholars; they distinguish themselves from the others merely in that they ostensibly avoid the use of names altogether or invent "objective" pseudo-scientific names or acronyms, which they claim do not prejudice their studies. In the analysis of these more recent studies, it is not possible to divide the scholars into separate groups in order to categorize them and analyze their programmatic interpretive purposes. The proposition-rebuttal nature of the scholarly discussion thus determines the form of the remainder of the chapter.

While the manuscript Cambridge, T.-S. 10. K. 22 was not published until 1957 by Lajb Fuks, the controversies surrounding the texts of the manuscript and the methodologies employed to deal with them have provided the focal point of Old Yiddish studies since that publication, and we may thus legitimately begin the investigation of contemporary names of Old Yiddish with these studies and work outwards. The manuscript was brought to Cambridge by Solomon Schechter in 1896 from the Fostat Genizah in Cairo[72] and thereafter "discovered" at least twice, once by Ernest-Henry Lévy, who transcribed the manuscript into normalized Middle High German and planned to publish a critical edition. He died in World War II and the manuscript of his edition was lost. Lévy's plan was in part finally realized in the dissertation of a doctoral candidate studying under Lévy's former student, the eminent Germanist Jean Fourquet.[73] The second discovery was by Fuks, the librarian at the Rosenthaliana in Amsterdam, who was made aware of the manuscript by J. L. Teicher, a lecturer in Hebrew at Cambridge. Fuks published a number of announcements (in both English and Yiddish) of the discovery of the manuscript and its value as the most ancient Yiddish codex in existence; the edition itself was finally published in 1957 in two volumes.[74] The edition consists of an introduction, facsimile, transliteration into Hebrew square script (from the Ashkenazic cursive of the manuscript), transliteration into Roman, and modern German translation. As the numerous reviews immediately demonstrated, this *editio princeps* was inadequate in almost all respects, in each of its five constituent parts. Most likely due in large part to its grave inadequacies (but also to its making available a text which was in some sense related to the medieval German literary tradition), the edition was the spark which ignited an explosion of scholarly interest in Old Yiddish.

Fuks himself denies that his edition is more than a "rendering of the text 'as the reading eye sees it'" (I, xxxvii)[75] and claims that he attempts no interpretation of any kind, since the nature of Old Yiddish texts requires expertise beyond the ken of any one scholar. He thus attempts to offer the raw material to scholars of various disciplines. Despite his disclaimer, however, his brief introduction to the edition is inevitably interpretive in all respects. In general, he follows his predecessors in the field of Old Yiddish studies (both assimilationists and Yiddish nationalists), in that he posits a close cultural bond between medieval Jews and Christians (I, xiv), and he designates the texts "shpilman" literature (I, xvii).

He calls the language of the manuscript "Old Yiddish" and gives a brief explanation of his understanding of the name's legitimacy (I, xxvi-xxviii): the texts are linguistically Middle High German, written in the Hebrew alphabet,[76] Fuks thus implies that linguistic criteria are inadequate to the task of identifying the language. He proposes two legitimate criteria: cultural distinctions and the linguistic perceptions of the language's speakers. Thus since the language represented in the codex was spoken by a culturally, historically, sociologically, and economically distinct group, the language must also be distinct and separate, despite the fact that it allegedly shows no linguistic dissimilarity to cotemporal German.[77] And since the speakers of Yiddish perceived that their language was different from German, it must have been Yiddish.[78] In essence, then, Fuks posits that the language of the manuscript is Yiddish, not on the basis of the evidence which would seem immediately relevant (i.e., linguistic evidence), but rather in spite of that evidence, and he is thus compelled to introduce extra-linguistic arguments to resolve a linguistic problem. His *a priori* argument, coupled with the lack of any detailed evidence for his extra-linguistic criteria have justifiably been attacked by his reviewers. As will be seen, however, Fuks is not alone in proposing the significance of extra-linguistic factors in the history of Yiddish; rather his discussion of the specific nature of their relevance is merely one of the less successful.[79] Fuks' major failing was in not providing detailed evidence. While he claims sociology and history are of the utmost importance, he does little more than cite the assimilationists, Grünbaum and Landau, on the generally close cultural relations of medieval Jews and Christians (I, xv); but even this slight evidence contradicts his later argument for the independence of Yiddish, based directly as it is on Jewish cultural isolation and alterity. His second tenet, that a language is a distinct linguistic entity only if its speakers perceive it to be such, is untenable by any standards.[80]

Fuks' edition was greeted by a storm of reaction. It seems that his brief, repetitious articles announcing the discovery and forthcoming edition of the codex had raised expectations and caused some impatience in the scholarly community.[81] When the edition finally appeared and was generally recognized as an embarrassingly botched job, there was a note of anger and betrayal to be sensed in many of the reviews.

Especially with respect to Fuks' ill-supported arguments concerning the language of the texts, there was vehement response. Even so, there was no concerted, united front opposing all of the interpretive remarks in Fuks' introduction: scholars variously commended his brief treatment of the genre of *shpilman* literature, the suggestion that the manuscript originated in the thirteenth-century Jewish community of Yiddish speakers in Cairo, the discussion of the possible topical sources of the lion fable, or the analysis of metrics; others attacked the same sections. Only the most relevant reviews will be treated here, since many are by nature repetitive, do not address the present issue, or are not well enough informed on the subject to be of value.[82]

H. Beim proposes the question of the language of the texts as the most important (and rejects Fuks' criteria as inadequate), but one which can be answered only after a thorough linguistic analysis of the texts has been carried out.[83] Thus he does not attempt an analysis or designation of the language in his brief review. His corrections of Fuks' misreadings nonetheless betray his own preconceived assumption of the language: e.g., ". . .*shlekht* – the last word is mhg. 'sleht.'"[84] This kind of slip in the "objective" methodological mask of scholars dealing with this problem is surprisingly common and indeed often seems not to be recognized as a methodological error: the text lemma is identified, analyzed and categorized on the basis of its Middle High German cognate, as if it is only when coupled with that term that it can be identified and defined.

In his rather uncritical review, J. Carles assumes the texts were written by a Jewish troubadour;[85] the language is called "judéo-allemand" without an explanation of the precise meaning of the term. But in his concluding evaluation of the edition, Carles indirectly identifies the relevant audience for these texts, as he conceives it – medieval Germanists: the edition presents "an entirely new element of medieval literature and a valuable research document for Germanists" ("un élément entièrement nouveau de littérature médiévale et un instrument de travail précieux pour les germanistes," p. 351).

Solomon Birnbaum, the doyen of Old Yiddish studies, deemed Fuks' remarks (or rather Hellinga's, as Fuks acknowledges I, xxvii, n.1) on the language problem interesting, but irrelevant, since we do not and can not know what the linguistic perceptions of the Jews and Christians of the time were, but "presumably both Jews and Christians assumed the language of the Jews to be simply German" (p. 52). Documentary evidence *per se* for Fuks' criteria do not appear before the fifteenth century. But Birnbaum claims that in general the perception of linguistic independence is not relevant, since, as he had argued elsewhere, the Yiddish language had existed since the ninth century, and thus the Cambridge codex could not in any respect be seen as representative of the initial stages of the linguistic separation of Yiddish and German.[86]

Leonard Forster (who admits what many of us cannot bring ourselves to do – that he is a hobby-Yiddishist) does not ostensibly concern himself with the problem of language. His assumptions are obvious, however: he transcribes text citations into normalized Middle High German, since the unpointed Hebrew alphabet is "singularly unsuited to the rendering of *German* sounds" (my emphasis).[87] His analysis of *Dukus Hurnt* and criticism of its form and content are based on what Forster deems *appropriate* in Middle High German literature.[88] The poem shows no "Jewish coloring" beyond the medieval "Hebrew" word *dukus* of the title, the use of "Hebrew" *tifle* "church" (11. 485 & 584) and the omissions of specifically Christian references in the Crusader song (*Dukus Hurnt* 243 from Gottfried von Straßburg's *Tristan* 11, 538).[89] But despite this tacit rejection of the work as in any sense Yiddish or even Jewish, Forster notes at the end of his review that "this manuscript was presumably compiled, like most early Yiddish literature, for the edification of Jewish women" (p. 284), and thus he subsumes the text under the rubric of Old Yiddish literature in its traditionally defined character as "women's literature."[90]

In her review of Fuks' edition, Ingeborg Schröbler maintains at one moment that the language of the codex is late Middle High German, even though "the guise of the foreign script" ("das Gewand der fremden Schrift") does not allow recognition of it as such in all cases; at the next moment, she notes that until the history of Yiddish is better known, these texts should be provisionally called "Hebrew-German" (she uses the English term in her German text and notes Landau's use of the term), since they show hardly any characteristics of later Yiddish.[91] She does not otherwise address the question of language, except, as customary in Germanistic-oriented treatments, to identify the vowels of the text with their Middle High German "equivalents" (p. 142).

Peter Ganz argues that the linguistic question is much more intricate than Fuks suggests, especially since the poet of *Dukus Hurnt* employs the literary techniques and vocabulary characteristic of Middle High German epic poetry: thus "this purely literary language must have differed considerably from the conventional idiom of the Jewish audience before whom it was recited or sung."[92] It seems then that Ganz identifies the text as Middle High German, although if one were to concede his point here, then one would also at least have to question whether Gottfried's *Tristan* and especially Wolfram's *Parzival* were "Middle High German," since their language is also a very stylized, literary idiom, far removed from that of the common speech of their audience – in fact the same literary language which Ganz proposes for *Dukus Hurnt*. He does not decide for either Middle High German or Yiddish, however, as even his plea for a transcribed edition – which he deems necessary as a prerequisite for any literary analysis – shows: such an edition should transcribe the text into either a "conventional Middle High German"[93] or "some other system such as that employed by Solomon Birnbaum."[94] He thus implies that the linguistic form of the text edition is of little importance in conditioning the literary interpretations based on that edition (p. 248).

Ganz had apparently modified his views by the time of the publication of his article on *Dukus Hurnt* in the *Journal of Jewish Studies* a year later.[95] Not just in the title of the article, but in his argument as well, Ganz identifies the language of the poems of the manuscript as Yiddish: the manuscript "contains the earliest datable Yiddish poems" (p. 48). He argues that the texts may be analyzed as literature only after the issue of their language has been settled, but he sees this issue as especially problematic in the case of Yiddish, since its origins are obscure, and since the Hebrew alphabet does not adequately represent its phonetic system (p. 53). He divides the early stages of the development of Yiddish into three periods (pp. 53-55): 1) pre-Carolingian (no texts extant); Jews spoke Old High German with some Romance and Hebrew loan words and with a "certain characteristic flavour," but the language was not yet a "specifically Jewish language" (p. 54); 2) 900-1200; the language is fundamentally Middle High German and can be called "Jewish-German"; and 3) 1250 – the beginning of a specifically Jewish language, called "early or proto-Yiddish," which develops phonetic features distinct from German and combines features of many German dialects.[96]

While *Dukus Hurnt* was written in the period of "early Yiddish," according to Ganz, its "language appears to be pure Middle High German with Central German characteristics" (p. 55). This "appearance" is, however, not due to the identity of the language with Middle High German but rather "to the literary nature of the evidence" (p. 55); i.e., the texts are written in a conventional literary style distinct from the colloquial Yiddish language of the time[97] and influenced by the cotemporal German literary conventions. Some Yiddish features are present in syntactic constructions, such as the use of the reflexive pronoun with verbs not commonly so used in Middle High German (p. 55, n. 36). Despite this argument for Yiddish as the language of the texts, Ganz uses the Middle High German phonetic system as his "starting point" in the analysis of the phonetic system of *Dukus Hurnt*, as he says, "for the sake of convenience" (p. 55). He argues against Jewish authorship of the poem, since the subject is not specifically Jewish,[98] and cites the use of *tifle* and the adaptation of the Crusader song as exceptions to, rather than arguments for, the non-Jewish character of the work (p. 59, n. 54).

Werner Schwarz, who later participated in the team edition of *Dukus Hurnt* with Norman and Ganz, calls the text "Jiddisch" in the title of his review article,[99] and maintains that the text is evidence of the "beginning" of Yiddish as a language independent of German,[100] but then remarks that "the language of the Yiddish manuscript is essentially German" ("die Sprache des jiddischen MS. [ist] im wesentlichen deutsch," p. 329). What the sentence is intended to mean is unclear, unless Schwarz thinks that the texts can be Yiddish and German simultaneously. His argument proceeds, however, toward an identification of German as the language of the manuscript, since, for example, final *aleph* (as a posited *schwa*) is used consistently in this manuscript but not elsewhere in Yiddish texts:[101] thus the scribe knew German and this text is merely German written in the Hebrew alphabet.[102] Schwarz notes at the end of his review that he, Frederick Norman, and Peter Ganz are preparing an edition of

Dukus Hurnt to supersede Fuks' "courageous effort". He calls the text at this point a "jiddische[n] Text in Mitteldeutsch" ("Yiddish text in Central German"), i.e., again neither Yiddish nor German, but both (p. 332).

Probably the most provocative, and in terms of the present study, most relevant review of Fuks' edition was that by James Marchand,[103] since he stages a full frontal assault on Fuks' identification of the texts' language as Yiddish. Three years after his review appeared, he and F. Tubach published an edition and analysis of one poem from the codex, "Yosef Hatsadik," in which Marchand's position is further elaborated.[104] Marchand calls the texts "Hebrew-German," i.e. "German written in Hebrew characters," thus adopting the name used by Landau a half-century earlier with the same justification.[105] Marchand/Tubach claim that these texts are in "linguistically pure German" ("reindeutscher Sprache"), but then explain the lack of attention to such texts on the part of medieval Germanists by noting not only their difficulty of access (since 'disguised' in the Hebrew alphabet), but also that they are written in a foreign language (p. 30). Do they mean that "pure German" is a foreign language? Certainly such is the case for most of the world, but one would hardly consider that to be true for medieval Germanists, their apparently intended audience, whom they address in German in a journal of Germanistic studies. Or do they mean that Middle High German (the form of "pure German" they have in mind, one must assume) is a foreign language, since it is not *modern* German? Or is this simply another instance of their recurring terminological (conceptual?) confusion? The texts of the codex are said to be written in "aschkenasische[r] (deutsche[r]) Hand"; the scribe was German, and the manuscript is attributable to a German ("Josef," p. 35). It seems that the only possible reason for designating the Ashkenazic variant of the Hebrew script "German" is to further divorce the entire codex from any Jewish association whatsoesver, for "Ashkenazic" means "German" in only a very restricted, qualified, and strictly Jewish – not German – sense. The same caveat is also necessary in speaking of the manuscript's scribe or the person who commissioned the manuscript as "German" – there is no evidence of any kind for the existence of either (Christian) German scribes who could write entire manuscripts in Hebrew script[106] or German patrons of Hebrew-alphabet texts. Or are we again being misled by Marchand/Tubach's imprecise terminology? Do they really only wish to say that the Jewish scribe was "German" in the sense that, from the assimilationists' perspective, all medieval Jews in Germany were German, i.e., that they were fully integrated into German culture in the broadest sense? This is most likely the "correct" interpretation of their argument.

Marchand/Tubach continually chip away at all evidence of the Jewishness of the manuscript. The Hebrew titles of the poems are, for instance, said to be later additions to the manuscript (i.e., not a part of the original German texts), as is evident from their having been written with ink recognizably different from that used for the texts themselves (pp. 35-36). This argument would command attention were it not for the fact that Marchand/Tubach's examination of the text consisted solely of reading the black-and-white facsimile plates in Fuks' edition, which have little value since they were not made under the ultra-violet light essential for deciphering much of the manuscript, and are certainly inadequate to the task of distinguishing various ink compositions. In another context, Marchand/Tubach themselves even go so far as to say that the facsimiles of Fuks' edition – the sole textual basis of their own study – are "zu wissenschaftlichen Zwecken einfach unbrauchbar" ("quite simply useless for scholarly purposes," p. 36). Surely it is then senseless to attempt an analysis of the physical aspects of the manuscript on the basis of these photographs.

Marchand distinguishes himself from Landau and the early assimilationists by attempting to establish verifiable criteria for identifying the language of the text, and he thus attempts to give an empirical, "scientific" basis to his arguments, something Landau had not done. Yet in trying to justify their use of the term "Hebrew-German," Marchand/Tubach show their ideological colors quite clearly when they seemingly call the roll of assimilationist Yiddishists – Steinschneider, Güdemann, Grünbaum, Perles, and Zunz – and appeal to their putatively unassailable authority that these texts were only German in Hebrew characters. They then accuse modern researchers of ignoring the work of these great scholars when they use the illegitimate term "Jiddisch" ("Josef," p. 32, n. 14). In this regard Marchand/Tubach also presume to have better access to the true convictions of Solomon Birnbaum than he himself, since they claim that in one of his publications that dealt with the oldest Yiddish document discovered up to that time (so named by Birnbaum), "[he] realized that his 'oldest dated Yiddish document' was actually German."[107] In making this claim, Marchand/Tubach even manage to ignore the fact that Birnbaum's stated purpose in the cited article (pp. 197-198) was to demonstrate, through the establishment of a transliteration system applicable to the text in question and to Old Yiddish texts in general, that editions of such texts should not be based on the German grapho-phonemic system, since the resulting texts would be more translation than transliteration/transcription and thus altogether useless for scholarly purposes.

Marchand counters Fuks' argument concerning the perceptions of a language's speakers as definitive of the language's identity by pointing out its circularity (p. 385). He maintains that on this ground the Old Yiddish *Shmuel-bukh* would also have to be called German, since its author "thought" he was writing German. As authorities for this argument, Marchand cites Siskind, Erik, and Weinreich.[108] It is not clear to what purpose he does so, for no argument should be countenanced that presumes to identify the thoughts of anonymous authors, dead for half a millenium, whose century, country, and often even continent of residence can rarely be determined. Appeals to the names they attached to their language are notoriously problematic.[109] Marchand also gives a counter-example to Fuks' anecdote on Dutch-German linguistic perceptions: Black English,[110] he claims, is recognized by "everyone" as different from "white English," but that does not mean that it is a different language, he argues, since Black English is simply derived "from Southern areas where [Black] speech was the same as that of the Whites."[111] The anecdote reveals Marchand's lack of linguistic sophistication even more clearly than did Fuks in his case: "everyone" must mean only non-White Southerners, since White Southerners apparently have the same speech as [all?] Blacks and would thus not recognize a difference between their own speech and Black English. One may apparently also group all Blacks together into a single dialect group of southern emigrés. Marchand here fails, among other things, to 1) differentiate among the various "southern" dialects which purportedly gave rise to Black English; 2) to take into account the relative date of Black immigration to the North; 3) to take into account the regional origin of the Blacks in the South; 4) to differentiate among varieties of Black English, and 5) to comment on the ultimate inappropriateness of the term and concept of "Black English."[112]

At times it almost seems as if Marchand were attempting a point-by-point parody of Fuks' arguments by exaggerating them *ad absurdum*: Fuks claims, with little attempt at proof, that Yiddish as a distinct language was as old as the use of *loshn ashkenaz* as its designation. In turn Marchand claims simply that the term means "German," and cites two examples, which do no more than distract attention from the very long and complex history of this term and its various conflicting uses through the centuries.

He dismisses Fuks' claim that the texts are Old Yiddish since, if one concedes the argument by the chief proponents of the pro-

Yiddish position, Weinreich and Birnbaum, that Yiddish was from the beginning a fusion of Romance, Hebrew, and German elements, then the language of the Cambridge manuscript cannot be Yiddish, since it is not such a fusion (rev., p. 386). This argument is clarified in his discussion of the criteria by which a text can be identified as German or Yiddish:[113]

1) If the text contains .01% Hebrew vocabulary = Old Yiddish.[114]
2) If the theme is, *ceteris paribus*, "particularly Jewish" = Old Yiddish.[115]
3) If the text contains any non-Yiddish dialect forms = German.[116]
4) If the text contains evidence of having been copied from a Roman-alphabet source, *ceteris paribus* = German; if on the other hand, a text shows an influence from the Hebrew alphabet and scribal practice, then the text is Yiddish [Three Basic Problems," p. 39].

Two other criteria concern German vs. Jewish cultural identity:

5) If the material departs from the non-Jewish tradition in ways derived from the Jewish tradition = Jewish.
6) If the material shows traces of Jewish cultic usage, the Jewish conceptual realm or the Jewish religious perspective = Jewish.

In applying the first criterion to the codex, he finds only one Hebrew word, *tifle*, and thus the text is said to be German. In determining the Hebrew word count, he excludes as a matter of course all biblical names, the titles of the poems (all of which are Hebrew), and the names of the gems in text 6 (Ms. p. 40).[117] He does not justify his arbitrary omission of these numerous Hebrew words (beyond his indefensible claim, noted above, that the Hebrew titles were later additions). Nor does he explain how he arrived at the figure .01%. One might well ask why he does not rather demand, for instance, .005% or .02%? The answer is in fact not far to seek – if he eliminates all words except *tifle* (which occurs twice, although he counts only one occurrence), the percentage of Hebrew words is just under .01%, and thus the text is by (his) definition not Yiddish. Convenient for his argument, one might say, but hardly of any value with such a small sample: if one were to add a single Hebrew word to his count, or counted each of the occurrences of *tifle*, his count would double; or if one were to count the Hebrew titles, the count would more than double, and suddenly the text would become Yiddish.

The themes of the poems on Moses, Paradise, Abraham, Joseph, the lion fable, and *Dukus Hurnt* are not, according to Marchand, "particularly Jewish," since the themes are also known in Middle High German and later literature. One would expect this very problematic generalization concerning the thorniest of philological questions – thematic sources – to be argued in some detail. It is not, however; Marchand instead promised a forthcoming study on this topic in collaboration with Tubach.[118] Most intriguing here is Marchand's complete omission of text 6 – the list of weekly Pentateuch readings and the list of the gems on the high priest's breastplate; by ignoring it altogether, he frees himself from what would have been a rather difficult task – denying its "particularly Jewish" character.

The dialect is identified as Central German, specifically Hessian, and thus, Marchand argues, it can not be Yiddish. The implication is that Marchand – although his ostensive purpose in the article is to establish criteria for the identification of Yiddish – is already capable of recognizing Yiddish and non-Yiddish. He does not indicate the documentary basis of his knowledge of Yiddish dialect features, but simply assumes that *any* dialect features identifiable as "German" in any form are proof of the non-Yiddish nature of the text.

He interprets the presence of doubled consonants,[119] the use of Germanic as opposed to Hebrew names for Egypt and Spain, and the construction איגעש for Middle High German *ich ez*, as evidence of a Roman-alphabet source manuscript. He thus concludes that he has "demonstrated conclusively that the language of the document is German" and warns that the use of the text in the study of Old Yiddish as Fuks and others propose "would be disastrous" (rev., p. 391). He is then confident enough in his results to reconstruct 11. 205-219 of *Dukus Hurnt* in the putative Middle High German "original," written in the Roman alphabet (rev., p. 391).

Marchand seems to be carried away by his own rhetoric and the grand conclusions he extrapolates from his arguments and thus concludes his tirade by first denying that the *Shmuel-bukh* and *Vidvilt* are Yiddish texts and then proclaiming: "In fact, I know of no example of specifically Yiddish literature before ca. 1500" (rev., p. 392).[120] In his later article, however, Marchand calls *Shmuel-bukh* and *Vidvilt* (among others) "actual works of Yiddish literature" ("Denkmäler der eigentlichen jiddischen Literatur," "Josef," p. 30) as opposed to those texts designated "Hebrew-German." Is this a change in Marchand's interpretation, or simply another instance of his inconsistency?

Two years after the appearance of his review of Fuks, Marchand published an article on *Dukus Hurnt*, the title of which immediately reveals his view of the subject: "Einiges zur sogenannten 'Jiddischen Kudrun.'"[121] Here again he claims the text is "Hebrew-German" (with reference to his previous articles). He posits a Roman-alphabet source manuscript for this manuscript on the basis of the scribal error *lanc* for *lant*, with the *t-c* confusion possible in medieval Roman-alphabet, but not Hebrew-alphabet documents (p. 58). He then denies that the language is Yiddish and gives essentially the same four reasons as in his review of Fuks (pp. 59-62). In denying that the poem has any specific Jewish character, he claims that the Jewish scribe replaced *junger* with *juden* in the Crusader song, "since it was forbidden to write the names of Christian deities in Hebrew script" ("da es verboten war, Namen christlicher Gottheiten in hebräischer Schrift zu schreiben," p. 63, n. 28). This statement prompts several rather embarrassing questions, such as: can one seriously speak of Christian deit*ies*? Or Christ's *disciples* as "deities"? Perhaps one would do better to pass over Marchand's argument altogether here.

In denying that the text is Yiddish, Marchand claims to refute most scholars who had previously written on the text and who, he maintains, had either silently assumed that the text was Yiddish, or ignored the question altogether. While the Wissenschaft des Judentums and the Yiddish nationalists *had* in fact made silent assumptions about language identity, they had *not* done so about this particular text, since it was not yet known, and as the foregoing pages of the present study have demonstrated, there had in fact been anything but silence on this topic and few tacit assumptions that this text was Yiddish.

One might expect that Marchand's review and articles would have elicited a widespread and even more animated and heated response than had Fuks' disappointing edition. For at least two reasons, however, such was not the case: first, each of Marchand's argumentative points was immediately and conclusively (and, one might add, rather graciously) refuted in print; second Marchand's arguments were even more blatantly circular than were Fuks' and he additionally seems to have grossly manipulated evidence to suit his argument. Thus his articles ultimately carried little weight in the scholarly forum, since perhaps the best refutation of his theses is simply a close reading of his publications.

The clearest argumentative demonstration of the failings of

Marchand's arguments was given by Khone Shmeruk in his analysis of the Hebrew acrostic in "Yosef Hatsadik."[122] Marchand's claim that the codex was copied from a Roman-alphabet source was thus not just refuted, but made an embarrassment, since one could scarcely maintain that the supposed Roman-alphabet source manuscript also contained a Hebrew-language acrostic. Shmeruk also notes the paucity of Hebrew words in the codex, but does not for this reason deny that the texts are Yiddish. Rather, they are said to adhere to the principles of a literary style of Yiddish which rejects Hebrew words as inappropriate to the content – the exception being generally in titles and words used to avoid specifically Christian words with troublesome connotations (such as *tifle* in the present text).[123]

In his 1960 article ("Old Yiddish Poetry") Maks Weinreich published a full-scale, point-by-point refutation of Marchand's criteria for distinguishing Old Yiddish from Middle High German as they were presented in his review of Fuks' edition. He praises Marchand for changing the direction of the scholarly discussion of this problem by finally attempting to establish verifiable criteria for the differentiation of the two languages; especially commendable was Marchand's proposal of two linguistic and two extra-linguistic criteria. In moving from the abstract to an evaluation of the specific criteria. however, Weinreich finds nothing more to praise. He notes first that neither Marchand's use of the term "Hebrew-German" nor its specific meaning is innovative; the term dates at least to Schadäus in the sixteenth century[124] and was of course popularized by Landau in 1912. He responds to Marchand's criteria concerning the "particular Jewish theme" by pointing out first of all (as Marchand himself admits) that with respect to the lion fable, there is no extant German parallel; second that the theme is international; and third, that the Jews were well-known as mediators of diverse literary motifs from a variety of cultures during the Middle Ages. Marchand's contention that the theme was necessarily a borrowing from German is therefore baseless. Marchand's notion of the German origin of the biblical themes is even less compelling; such a derivative relationship would have to be shown by minute comparison of the German and Yiddish versions in each particular case. With respect to the proposition of a Roman-alphabet source manuscript, Weinreich notes Marchand's misrepresentation of Siskind and Erik as supporting his position, although neither even remotely posits Roman-alphabet sources for the *Shmuel-bukh* as Marchand claims (p. 103). Marchand's conclusion that Hebrew-German and German versions of "Kalila and Dimna" and "Barlaam and Josaphat" exist is refuted by his own bibliographical references to works supposedly in support of his thesis, but which in fact demonstrate only that the subject has not yet been adequately studied. Weinreich also notes the Hebrew acrostic in "Yosef Hatsadik" (p. 107) and its inherent refutation of Marchand's position.

In this article Weinreich advances perhaps the most important extra-linguistic argument concerning linguistic identity thus far to be found in Old Yiddish research: Landau's splitting Old Yiddish into "Judeo-German" (i.e., Yiddish?) and "Hebrew-German" (i.e., German in the Hebrew alphabet) ignores the fact that both had the same *audience*. Weinreich does not pursue the point, however, and it has been up to more recent researchers to deal with this seminal question of audience.[125] Later in the essay, Weinreich argues that the distinction, for instance, between language and cultural identity (dominant themes, percentage of Hebrew vocabulary, etc.) in texts as ostensibly "Jewish" as the list of Pentateuch readings and as "non-Jewish" as *Dukus Hurnt* might better be seen as distinctions in style and linguistic register, since each language has several registers ranging from the very colloquial to the conventionally literary.[126] Even the same author might write works which exhibit different registers – some quite clearly colloquial Yiddish, and some partaking of the literary conventions characteristic of a language one might almost call a literary *koine*.[127] Weinreich posits two styles in Old Yiddish literature – both literary and both divorced from colloquial speech: the "horizontal style," dominant in "minstrel poetry and patterned after the Middle High German model"; and the "vertical style," dominant in the tradition of Jewish literature and characteristic of translations of biblical literature and prayers which closely follow the Hebrew originals (p. 109). The two styles coexisted in Yiddish into the eighteenth century. The problem in Yiddish is further compounded by the inherent componential nature of the language, which is a fusion[128] of elements of Germanic, Slavic, Hebrew, and Romance. The writer can achieve different stylistic effects not only through the use of intrinsic techniques known and used generally by *literati*, but also by appeal to the diversity of the Yiddish componential lexicon (as is for instance to a degree also possible for English language authors with the language's Germanic *and* Romance vocabulary): e.g., the use of a recherché Hebrew instead of the colloquial Germanic or Slavic term; or, on the other hand, s/he may choose the colloquial Hebrew term instead of a Germanicized (*daytshmerish*) term. Thus the identifiable lexical composition of a Yiddish text of any period is not necessarily only (or even primarily) of linguistic, but also of literary-stylistic significance: the avoidance of Slavic words in Middle Yiddish literature was deliberate in order to retain the Western European readers (and book buyers) whose colloquial language had little if any Slavic component; or with respect specifically to the Cambridge codex, the avoidance of Hebrew words was characteristic of the conventional style of Old Yiddish poetry, since the Hebrew component was, as Weinreich argues, conventionally "unpoetic" vocabulary.[129] The stylistic register of the language must thus be independently determined for each text. The general absence of Hebrew lexemes from texts such as *Dukus Hurnt* need not mean more than an adherence to convention and certainly cannot be used as evidence that the text is not Yiddish but German.

With respect to Fuks' argument that the medieval German Jews perceived their language to be distinct from that of their Christian contemporaries, Weinreich sides with Marchand, that there was probably no perception of linguistic distinction in the modern sense.[130] He also notes that *both* Fuks and Marchand are correct in their conflicting definitions of the use of *loshn ashkenaz*: the term signified the language of the Ashkenazic Jews (i.e., Yiddish), as well as German; those two languages were distinguished by phrases specifying, for instance, the "*loshn Ashkenaz* which is customary among us Ashkenazim," i.e., Yiddish (p. 108, n. 20).

Directly responding to Marchand's two linguistic criteria, Weinreich finds neither "serviceable" (p. 110). Not only is Marchand's figure of .01% arbitrary, but also "once a fusion language has formed, proportional representation of the components in a given text is immaterial" (p. 110): componential percentages can only be descriptive, not prescriptive. But even if one accepts Marchand's procedure in principle, Weinreich points out, it is not enough to seek Hebrew words in the texts, but rather one must also seek non-German words. Here even Marchand's demands would be satisfied: *dukus* < Latin *dux; tolme* < Latin *thalamos* (both from Zarphatic, the Romance component of Yiddish), and thus, including *tifle* (which means "church" only in *Ashkenazic* Hebrew, otherwise "tastelessness"), there are three non-German, "Hebrew" words among the fifteen thousand = .02%, even if one omits the Hebrew names and titles, which in fact can hardly be legitimately omitted. Other ostensibly "German" features not present in any German dialect are also present: e.g., *lernen* "to study the Talmud" (twice).[131]

Marchand's criterion of dialect isolation is also faulty, since he considers any feature present in any German dialect and not in Yiddish (Marchand does not here specify what he means by "Yiddish" in this sense: Old, Middle, modern, or otherwise)[132] to be evidence that the text is not Yiddish. But the presence of German dialect features and the Yiddishness of a text are not mutually exclusive, since Yiddish is in its very essence a fusion not only of various linguistic components, but also of various dialectal elements within the German component. Weinreich also rejects Marchand's argument that the dialect of the texts is Hessian, since there are simply too many clearly non-Hessian features present (listed and analyzed, pp. 114-115). This fact would indeed rather point more to the possibility of the text as Yiddish, due to the fusion of German dialectal features in Yiddish (p. 113). Weinreich even proposes that since many other Old Yiddish texts have been generally labeled "Hessian,"[133] one might better posit the possibility of a super-dialectal literary dialect of horizontal Old Yiddish that was distinct from the Alemannic-Bavarian literary dialect of Middle High German courtly poetry but which paralleled it in that neither was the native dialect of any speaker of Old Yiddish on the one hand, or Middle High German on the other (p. 115). An important point here is the distinction between the Middle High German literary language and the spoken dialects of Middle High German.[134]

Weinreich's argument thus demonstrates that even if the derivation of Yiddish from Middle High German is granted,[135] then this Middle High German source was not the normalized Middle High German constructed by the Benecke-Lachmann school of textual criticism, nor even the actual language of the Middle High German literary manuscripts, but the language of the populace, which rarely penetrates into the literary style.[136] Birnbaum also notes that Yiddish derives from Middle High German dialects, not modern German or the Middle High German literary language ("Two Problems," p. 63). While this point may seem obvious, it was not until the Landau school that the origin of Yiddish was sought in the medieval period (i.e., in some form of Middle High German) and not viewed as a mere corruption of New High German, as the original proponents of the Enlightenment had proposed. Weinreich calls this innovation by Landau and others a "turning point" in Yiddish studies ("Prehistory," p. 73). Thus Old Yiddish derived from the various *spoken* dialects of coterritorial Middle High German and, as a result of the commerce, migration, and exile that were essential aspects of medieval Ashkenazic history, fused them into a supra-dialectal Old Yiddish vernacular. The literary language of Old Yiddish was, however, again not this vernacular, but rather also a literary language with the varying stylistic registers generally characteristic of literary languages. Thus modern German dialects are of as little aid in determining the "origin" of Old Yiddish as is literary Middle High German in analyzing the Old Yiddish literary language ("Prehistory," p. 76). No modern Yiddish dialect can be identified with a German dialect. In general, the development of Yiddish cannot be conceived of as a gradual breakaway of a German-speaking group from its former language: "There was NO period in history before the nineteenth century [i.e., Haskalah assimilationism] when any Jewish GROUP had spoken anything approximating 'pure German'" ("Prehistory," pp. 78-79).[137] Weinreich concludes by 1) calling the practice of editing Old Yiddish texts in normalized Middle High German transcription "outright detrimental"[138] to the study of both Old Yiddish and the history of the German language; and 2) rejecting the term "Hebrew-German" altogether in the study of Old Yiddish language and literature (p. 116).

In addition to his specifically linguistic and sociological arguments for the existence of both the Old Yiddish colloquial language, independent of German, in the period of the Cambridge codex, and an Old Yiddish literary language distinct from both the Old Yiddish vernacular and Middle High German (literary and colloquial), Weinreich elaborates a protracted and detailed argument in his *Geshikhte*, which is difficult to categorize, but which he terms "symbolic." He initially presents the argument with reference to "Judeo-Romance" languages: the distinctions between the names Western Laaz and Judeo-French, Southern Laaz and Judeo-Italian, Chuadit and Judeo-Provençal, and Dzhudezmo and Judeo-Spanish may seem insignificant and even pedantic, but the former names in each pair have symbolic significance, in that they do not treat the Jewish languages as an integral element of each particular Romance language, which nevertheless exhibit some few particularly "Jewish" features, but rather view them as separate linguistic totalities in themselves. By naming the languages such, their Romance affiliations are not endangered. The languages are instead merely viewed from within rather than from without (*Geshikhte*, I, pp. 120-131). These languages not only differ from their coterritorial Romance counterparts in having a Hebrew component, but also in having a Romance component identifiably dissimilar to those counterparts (*Geshikhte*, I, 130). Such is even more the case with respect to Yiddish and its Germanic component.

The basic elements of this argument are already present in 1923 in Weinreich's Marburg dissertation on the history of Yiddish studies, where he grapples with this problem of the names of Yiddish: "Not so very much depends on the name we attach to a thing, as long as we all agree on the meaning of the term."[139] The problem lies of course precisely in achieving this kind of consensus on the definition. He justifies his use of the name *Jiddisch* as "the only appropriate name for its (the Jewish people's) language" by means of a brief analysis of the various names for Yiddish used and in use.[140] The use of *Jüdisch-deutsch* is no more appropriate for Yiddish than "Franco-Latein" would be for French or "Brito-Westgermanisch" for English, he argues, since it falsifies the relationship of Yiddish and German and "wird der Materie nicht gerecht." He maintains that the best German name for the language would probably have been the *translation* of the Yiddish name, *yidish*, into German, i.e., *Jüdisch*,[141] instead of simply borrowing the English term (from Wiener's "Yiddish"), but that would have caused some lack of precision in expressions such as "jüdische Literatur" ("Yiddish" or "Jewish"?).

The argumentation of Weinreich's dissertation in a certain sense denies the marginality of Yiddish and proposes its centering, but does not take an extreme position in this regard, for he still remarks: "German studies . . . legitimately includes Yiddish among its areas of research."[142] This position may have reflected an attempt to arouse some interest in Yiddish among the generally not unsympathetic scholarly audience of the time, but it was certainly not a moderate position. The fact that we now view it as relatively tame obviously derives from our post-Holocaust perspective and the unavoidable contrast to the more radical position of the *Geshikhte*, in which Weinreich denies the marginality of each of the Jewish languages in the context of the center's perspective, and proposes a reorganization of the structure, such that the specifically Jewish language is also centered and in some significant way independent of the traditional center.

In 1960 Hans Neumann published a lengthy article on the texts of the Cambridge codex, which, like Marchand's publications, attempts to provide an empirical basis for the pro- vs. anti-Yiddish conflict. The title of the article already shows his interpretive orientation: "Sprache und Reim in den judendeutschen Gedichten des Cambridger Codex T.S. 10.K.22."[143] Neumann views the language of the texts as the German of the Jews living in the Holy Roman Empire, and the texts as evidence of the Jews' participation in the German literary tradition of the period (p. 145). This "judendeutsche" literature is of minor significance as literature, he contends, but of great importance "for the friend of early German literature."[144]

His definition of the term "judendeutsch" is the same as Landau's "Hebrew-German" – the German spoken (and written) by

Jews. He rejects Fuks' term "Old Yiddish," because the term and the language it putatively designates lack definition. He does not attempt such a definition, since he considers the language German from the outset and the script a "hebräische Transliterierung" ("Hebrew transliteration," p. 149) without any consistent system of orthography (p. 153). He also notes that the fact that *Dukus Hurnt* is written in the Hebrew alphabet is not in itself evidence for Yiddish as its language (p. 164).

His purpose in the article is a legitimate and commendable one (in the context of the then prevailing empirical mode of research): to compare possible rhymes in the texts to determine details of the phonetic system represented by the "defective" graphemic system, which is especially problematic with respect to the representation of vowels. Unfortunately, the results of the study are rendered irrelevant by one of Neumann's methodological principles, which is simply noted but not justified, and whose significance is not acknowledged: "I give the text in Roman characters and add the unwritten vowels and consonants. In the remaining quotations from the Cambridge manuscript, I write the words in normalized Middle High German."[145] Thus it is not surprising that Neumann ends his phonetic analysis of these normalized Middle High German rhyme words by concluding that the phonetic system of *Dukus Hurnt* exhibits no Yiddish characteristics (p. 162). Furthermore, the use of *tifle* in the sense of "church" is, according to Neumann, non-Hebrew and thus its use makes Jewish authorship improbable (p. 162). Yet the Hebrew word, as noted by Weinreich (see above), generally signified "tastelessness" in "whole Hebrew contexts," in medieval Yiddish contexts, however, the word consistently signified "church." Even disregarding this explanation, however, one might well wonder how Neumann conceives the word *tifle* to have been part of the German poetic vocabulary.

The texts other than *Dukus Hurnt* are not as unambiguously characterized by Neumann: he first concedes that these poems are not so very obviously Hebrew transliterations of Roman-alphabet German originals, but then immediately thereafter apparently rejects the possibility of German originals altogether, when he speaks of "dies jüdischer Dichter" and "diese jüdischen Poeten" ("the Jewish poet(s)," pp. 162-163) – but only apparently, for he conceives of the poet as Jewish and German at the same time, such that the language of the Jews is identical to that of *Dukus Hurnt* and thus shows no traces of a Judeo-German language of the fifteenth century.[146] Here one must ask if Neumann proposes a recognizable distinction between "Judendeutsch" of the fourteenth and that of the fifteenth century, and if so, what is that distinction? Or is his use of terms here simply imprecise, such that he calls both the language of the Cambridge codex and the (one must surmise) "Jewish-colored German" vernacular of the following century "Judendeutsch." His attempt at elucidation of the point is unsuccessful, however, because the proposed contrast is made with the rhymes in the "judendeutsche[m] 'Wigalois,'" which he also constructs and cites in normalized Middle High German.[147]

Neumann concludes his study by conceding that a Yiddish language may have existed in the fourteenth century, but that none of the texts analyzed from the Cambridge codex have any relevance to a discussion of that language, since they are written in German and demonstrate on the contrary that even if Yiddish existed at the time, Jewish poets could also compose in the German tradition even when they used Jewish material. It thus seems that Neumann at least acknowledges indirectly the possible existence of various registers of language, but he does not develop the idea, since he sees it only in terms of Middle High German (the putative Jewish literary medium) vs. Yiddish (a conceivable Jewish spoken medium). The audience of such poetry was, according to Neumann, Jewish and German-speaking – i.e., he posits an elite German-speaking Jewish group (essentially a Haskalah perspective). He thus discounts the theory that the Cambridge codex is a *shpilman's* repertoire for recitation before "common" Jewish audiences at fairs and in Jewish ghettoes (p. 165). Rather, except for *Dukus Hurnt*, the poems are learned compositions for a sophisticated audience of German-speaking Jews.

Neumann contends that one may posit an independent Yiddish only when the phonetics, grammar, syntax, and vocabulary (especially Hebrew words) of the texts present "ein spezifisch nicht-Deutsches Gepräge" (a "specifically non-German character," p. 164). He deals with only two of his criteria, phonetics and vocabulary, and treats them, one must admit, in a rather cavalier fashion (rendering his conclusions suspect), since: 1) he does not in fact analyze the phonetic system of the texts in question, but rather only that of his normalized Middle High German transcription; and 2) he does not acknowledge that the Hebrew word, *tifle*, used in *Dukus Hurnt* in a uniquely Yiddish signification, is indicative of a Jewish context, but rather, apparently, wishes to add the word to the lexicon of Middle High German.

In 1963 and 1965, Josef Weissberg published two articles analyzing the phonetic system of the Cambridge codex.[148] In the first he immediately notes that the primary question confronting scholars with respect to the codex is whether the language is Old Yiddish or Middle High German. Initially, it seems that his approach is different from those of his predecessors, since he attempts to define the constraints on strict linguistic analysis in relation to this group of texts (pp. 38-40): 1) it is always difficult to distinguish closely related languages, especially at an earlier period in their history, when their similarities were even more pronounced than at present; 2) this problem is further compounded when an apparently uniform language is used by two "national" groups (he gives U.S. vs. British English and modern German vs. Austrian as examples); 3) it is even more problematic with respect to medieval documents which had no rigid orthographic rules; 4) in its earliest stages, the use of the Hebrew alphabet alone distinguished Yiddish from Middle High German, and only later did the linguistic form of the two languages diverge; 5) with respect to *Dukus Hurnt* the problem also arises of the relation of the language of the text to the rather strict tradition of the conventional literary style associated with courtly poetry, which avoided regionalisms and the vernacular; and, 6) the Middle High German literary language of the manuscripts is an artificial construct, which has been further obscured by the standard, "normalizing" practice of modern editors, thus rendering a comparison of the language of the Cambridge codex to "Middle High German" more problematic still.

Having briefly drawn attention to these intriguing and vital problems in the cultural setting of the texts of this codex, Weissberg then shifts to his analysis, which surprisingly begins by immediately identifying the texts as the Middle High German typical of courtly literature, with certain Central German dialect features,[149] only to add immediately thereafter as a methodological premise that linguistic analysis is prerequisite to any identification of the language.[150]

It seems thus that despite the fact that he has already identified the language of the texts as the Middle High German courtly language, Weissberg still wishes to maintain a distinction between two forms of that language – one in Roman and one in Hebrew script, since the latter are somehow involved in the beginnings of Yiddish.[151] His phonetic analysis thus proceeds on the basis of identifying the possible Middle High German phonemes represented by the Hebrew graphemes of the text.

While ostensibly differing from previous studies, in that he intimates that there is a significant distinction between Middle High German and Old Yiddish, his analysis in fact follows the same procedures used by scholars who call the language of the Cambridge codex German, and one can expect no more from his analysis since he distinguishes the languages only in their graphemic representation (i.e., Roman or Hebrew alphabet). On the one hand, Weissberg denies that the language/dialect can be determined, due to our lack of knowledge of Middle High German and Old Yiddish dialects, to the inadequacy of normalized Middle High German as a basis of comparison, and finally to the defective representation of *German* phonetics by Hebrew graphemes. He nevertheless forges ahead with his plan to identify language/dialect and graphemic/phonemic relationships by comparing the Hebrew graphemes to their normalized Middle High German correspondences.

His method and its shortcomings may be illustrated with a single example ("Vowel System," pp. 43-45): the grapheme ו. He lists and gives examples of this grapheme's use in the codex to represent the following posited normalized Middle High German vowels: a/u/ö/ü/ô/û/æ/e/uo/üe/ou/a. These possible interpretations of the grapheme are ostensibly based on rhyme words, but Weissberg rarely provides the rhyme words to confirm his hypothetical identification of the vowels, and in any case, the vowels of those "confirming" rhyme words are hardly evidential, since they must also be interpreted, a fact that he fails to mention. The arbitrariness of his method becomes clear in his interpretation of יור, which he maintains may be read either *jor* or *jur*, for the reason that both forms occur in modern Yiddish dialects – i.e., he suddenly offers a new basis of comparison, in place of his established Middle High German base. On the other hand he argues that the word cannot be read as *jâr* – the *only* possible normalized Middle High German form – since that form does not occur elsewhere in the manuscript. And of course he is right: it does not, nor does *jor* or *jur*, for only יור occurs, here and everywhere else, and that form must be interpreted in each individual case. Furthermore, since the grapheme ו also (infrequently) apparently can represent /a/, as he had already claimed, there is actually no reason why the word cannot be read as *jor/jur/jar*; or for that matter even *jüer* would be theoretically possible, since /üe/ is also one of his posited interpretations.[152] In order to decide between these possibilities, he must interpret. He does so sometimes on the basis of normalized Middle High German, and sometimes on the basis of modern Yiddish dialects, depending on the needs of his argument. Thus his proposal of a consistent orthographic system, based on both the tradition of Hebrew orthography *and* Middle High German usage, is not convincing.

The premises and conclusions of such exercises in positivism as Marchand's and Weissberg's were examined and confirmed or refuted in great detail in the course of other similarly positivistic studies, and it is not to our purpose to review these refutations here.

Rather, it is the underlying conception of the problem, its manifestation in a single question, and its determinative properties that are of paramount interest. In the mere act of posing the question – Old Yiddish or Middle High German? – there is a determinative presupposition involved: that an answer is possible. In order for this to be the case, however – and this is a further, unstated, *a priori* principle – it is assumed as a given that Old Yiddish and Middle High German *per se* have already been sufficiently defined, such that the distinction between them can also be identified and defined. But this definition, identification, and distinction are, taken together, in fact the *conclusions* sought by these studies. The definition and distinction are thus assumed in order to, in the end, posit the definition and distinction. To take Marchand's arguments as illustrative here, he is misled by his positivistic premises: that he may take *de*scriptive data of, for instance, the percentage of Hebrew versus Germanic lexical components as *pre*scriptive evidence in defining the language; that the *script* in which the proposed source text was written is relevant in identifying the *language* of the given text; that the identity of medieval Ashkenazic culture may be quantified and defined as a subset of German culture on the basis of affinities of certain aspects of the one language and literature to the other.

These detailed philological investigations arose out of a late resurgence of that initial stage of positivism that was more than merely objective and descriptive, for it attempted to be prescriptive as well, and as such it is especially characteristic of the pioneering stages of the study of a newly established scholarly discipline (as was the case at the time in Old Yiddish studies). The limits on the results of such a methodology eventually made themselves apparent and the impulse to such studies was finally exhausted. Thus, whether it was due to the inadequacies of the particular applications of empirical principles, or to the general methodological difficulty of establishing such principles, there have in any case, been few further concrete attempts, after Marchand's publications and the initial reactions to them, to set up verifiable criteria for distinguishing Middle High German from Old Yiddish. This debate did, however, serve as a significant spur to further studies of the general subject, and it even gave rise to a later period of extreme positivism that eschewed even the slightest hint of prescription and interpretation.[153] With this modulation in the methodological tone of Old Yiddish studies after the early 1960s, the raging controversy provoked by the Cambridge codex abated somewhat, as has the controversy surrounding our present topic. It seems indeed that the explicit question itself was suppressed, but that is not to say that it has disappeared. The possible answers to the unexpressed question continued to dominate the discussion, and the question still determined the set of possible answers.

The debates of the previous decade, based almost exclusively on *a priori* interpretive, transcribed evidence finally led to a second edition of the entire Cambridge codex by Eli Katz.[154] He approaches the problem of the name of the language much more from the perspective of cultural history than from strict linguistics, although not from any lack of linguistic expertise on his part. He rejects both the names "Hebrew-German/Judeo-German" (i.e., German written in the Hebrew alphabet)[155] and Birnbaum's arguments for "Yiddish,"[156] and proposes a new name for the language, "Germano-Judaic." The manuscript is "an early representative of the literary tradition which gave rise to Yiddish literature," and the term Germano-Judaic is "a convenient designation for this tradition at a stage where linguistic differentiation cannot yet be determined" (p. 1, abstract); the term designates a "Jewish literature written in a Germanic dialect to which the origin of Yiddish literature must be traced" (p. 73, n. 21). Thus he, like many of his predecessors in the later positivistic stage of Old Yiddish studies, avoids the term "Yiddish" and in so doing attempts to sidestep the Yiddish vs. Middle High German controversy; he differs from most of them in many respects, however, perhaps most obviously in that his "sympathies" lie in the direction of Yiddish rather than Middle High German. His term Germano-Judaic accounts for what Fuks and others had called the Jewish cultural background of the codex and also for the Germanic linguistic affiliation, but without trying to make the text in any way specifically German. The term Germano-Judaic refers thus to a body of literature and not to a language *per se*.[157] The literature is to be defined not just by language, but also by sources and audience. The sources were primarily Jewish, and the audience was quite simply Jewish, for which the author served as a "literary broker," adapting the source material – whether from German or Jewish cultural traditions for his Jewish audience (p. 9). Thus Katz's argument attempts to take the sources and audience into account as important elements in a definition of the literature – at least as important as language identity: the Jewish author chose what to omit, adapt and accept, and therefore everything that is present in these Germano-Judaic texts is by definition now "Jewish," whether its ultimate source was in the Jewish tradition or not. This process of selection and adaptation is clearly significant since not all German literature, for example, was adapted into the Jewish literary tradition. Katz adapts Birnbaum's formulation here, when he asserts that German and Jewish literature do not coincide, but rather seem to "overlap in significant areas of theme and motif" (p. 10) as did most literatures of the Middle Ages, where it was (and is) often difficult to determine which of the two was the source and which the borrower. In the case of the texts of the Cambridge codex, Katz maintains that the sources seem to be clearly Jewish for all poems except *Dukus Hurnt*, and even here Jewish adaptation is obvious and has transformed the material into Jewish literature (pp. 13-17).

Katz further concedes (p. 19) that the texts are not linguistically identifiable as Yiddish,[158] but rather *seem* indeed to be Central German, as Marchand, Ganz, and Neumann (among others) had argued before him,[159] but not so clearly Hessian. In fact, he notes, the dialect features present are not uniform enough to identify the manuscript with any single German dialect. It is not simply Middle High German, but neither does it show "directional deviation" toward modern Yiddish (p. 21). He also follows Birnbaum and Weinreich here in positing a Yiddish literary dialect not identical to either Middle High German or modern spoken Yiddish (p. 21). Thus one must assume that Katz conceives of these texts as "Jewish," in that they were adapted or written by Jews for a Jewish audience and transmitted in the Hebrew alphabet – i.e., in his view they are "Yiddish" in all senses but that of identifiably (modern) Yiddish linguistic features: "The Ms. can be properly assessed only in terms of the Yiddish literary tradition of which it is an early representative."

Katz's position is thus a difficult one to categorize – the texts are Jewish; as literature they belong to the Yiddish literary tradition; but as to their linguistic affiliations, few premises can be advanced, and no conclusions can be drawn: the texts are not standard literary Middle High German; they are not identifiable representatives of a single, uniform German dialect. What are they? Katz answers only – "Germano-Judaic." Many scholars have argued polemically and otherwise for Yiddish or Middle High German on far less evidence than Katz adduces. There is no sense of urgency in his argument concerning the language, no sense of defense or attack, and above all no critique of scholars drawn along identifiable party lines – he rejects, for instance, some views of the extremists Marchand on the one hand, and Birnbaum on the other, but accepts other interpretations of each. His is perhaps the most measured and informative of all treatments of these texts.

In 1964 the editorial team of Frederick Norman, Werner Schwarz, and Peter Ganz published an edition of *Dukus Hurnt* in the estimable Altdeutsche Textbibliothek series that promised to be the critical edition of the poem that was to become the long hoped-for standard, often said to be possible only through the combined efforts of an interdisciplinary team of experts.[160] These three editors are, however, all scholars of medieval German.[161] Perhaps for this reason they also enlisted the aid of the renowned Yiddishist and Hebrew paleographer, Solomon Birnbaum, who wrote a brief analysis of the manuscript's script (pp. 7-14). The edition has indeed become the standard in some respects, but it is in general at least as great a disappointment as was Fuks' edition a decade earlier, albeit for different reasons.

The conceptions of the editors as to what the apparatus of a critical edition of the poem should include and the proportions of the sections of the introduction provide perhaps the most immediate insight into the failings of the edition:[162] 1) a brief introduction to the recent history of the manuscript, a description of the manuscript and contents (Ganz, pp. 1-6); 2) an analysis of the script (Birnbaum, pp. 7-14); 3) the grapho-phonemic systems of the text (Schwarz, pp. 15-74), and 4) the literary-historical affiliations of the text (Norman, pp. 75-131). The subject of the cultural milieu of this text and its place in this codex are not dealt with in more than a perfunctory manner in occasional remarks and footnotes.[163] The question of language is not dealt with as a topic of significance anywhere in the editors' introduction. Yet in Ganz/Norman/Schwarz's collaborative article, "Zu dem Cambridger Joseph," published the year before, where they attempt to correct the errors of the Marchand/Tubach edition of that poem, they call the poem, "a 'German' poem written in Hebrew letters" ("ein in hebräischen Buchstaben geschriebenes 'deutsches' Gedicht").[164] The significance of their inverted commas in "deutsches" is unclear – do they imply that the poem is not unambiguously German, only German in a restricted sense, or German for lack of a better name? They never specify their understanding of the term. Perhaps as a result, the editors come to conflicting conclusions in their edition of *Dukus Hurnt* (if they are conclusions in any sense), and sometimes a single editor's contribution is inconsistent. Norman's essay on saga and literary history is the most disappointing, for methodologically it is a nineteenth-century treatise on *Sagengeschichte*, replete with discussions of posited (i.e., non-extant) stages in the development of this tale and their interrelationships, but not of the literary problems (in the modern sense) of the extant text ostensibly under examination. This is not to say that the editors misrepresent their method: after all, Norman's section is even entitled

"Die sagen- und literaturgeschichtlichen Probleme." Rather, it seems that in 1964 the editors might well have attempted to produce a modern edition of the poem which treated the text as a cultural and literary document, rather than one in which it appears solely as an example of what they oxymoronically term "unterliterarische Unterhaltungsliteratur" ("subliterary light literature," p. 104), i.e., in their view, as a philological artifact useful only for the purposes of reconstruction of posited earlier stages of the (*German*) literary tradition.

Their reasons for patterning their edition on the archaic philological model of nineteenth-century Germanistic textual editing are obvious, however, and have strictly ideological implications. They are thus relieved of any responsibility to address the problems which arise from the ambiguous and peculiar character of this text, both in general as a cultural document and specifically as a part of a codex of texts which, as Norman does obliquely admit (p. 77), clearly derive from a medieval Jewish cultural milieu. This method also – and this is perhaps the most insidious element – clothes their efforts in the traditional, somehow still respectable robes of textual editions for which the ATB series has long been known.[165] And by virtue of the edition's appearance in this particular series, with its specific title – Alt*deutsche* Textbibliothek – and in the traditional form characteristic of medieval German text editions, this text in effect *becomes* a German text without the necessity of argument or presentation of evidence by the editors. This generalized critique of the underlying premises of the edition arise out of the actual practice of the editors, especially with respect to the problem of the *res* and *nomen* of the language.

In his essay on the grapho-phonemic system of the text, Schwarz's procedure is characteristic of the edition in general. His orientation immediately becomes clear when he labels the extant twelfth-century (Germanic) glosses of Hebrew texts "deutsch . . . in hebräischen Buchstaben" ("German . . . in Hebrew letters"), a tradition which was continued in the "Judeo-German [jüdisch-deutschen] Bible translations" of the thirteenth century (p. 15). As a theory this one is, *prima facie*, as legitimate as any other. In this "standard critical edition" of the poem, one would, however, expect such a premise concerning the tradition of Hebrew orthography and the vital question of its use in representing vernacular (i.e., non-Hebrew) texts to be supported by evidence and integrated into Schwarz's larger discussion of the phonetic system. Schwarz does not offer any evidence or attempt any integration; in fact he relieves himself of the responsibility to do so by claiming that it is impossible to compare the relationship of graphemes to phonemes in texts written both before and after *Dukus Hurnt*, since the relevant texts are either not edited or available only in editions with undefined systems of Roman transcription. In making this disclaimer, he undermines his own claim that the language of the aforementioned glosses is "German," since it is thus apparently not possible to determine the phonetic value of the graphemes: i.e., he does not and, by his own admission, can not know what sounds the letters represent. The apparently well-intentioned, innocuous disclaimer reveals yet another problem, however, which is devastating in its implications: one must conclude that the editor did not attempt to analyze the grapho-phonemic relations of other texts similar to and originating in the same general time period as the text under his editorship, since they were available only in manuscript or poor editions. Does this mean that editorial recourse to the manuscripts, a *sine qua non* of any thorough analysis of medieval texts (and one deserves at least thoroughness from the 'standard edition'), was either considered irrelevant or unfeasible?[166] Generally Schwarz's terminology is disconcertingly imprecise: he calls the Roman alphabet "ein europäisches System" ("a European system") or "deutsche Buchstaben" ("German letters"), and manuscripts written in the Roman alphabet "in deutschen geschriebenen Hss." (sic: "in-German written manuscripts," pp. 16-17).[167] The fact that the text is written in Hebrew alphabet is viewed as insignificant, except insofar as it is an obstacle to the determination of the phonetic system of the text: "the difficulty in interpreting the phonetic value of an alphabet system is intensified in our case even more through the use of an alphabet alien to German" ("die Schwierigkeit, die Lautwerte eines Buchstabensystems zu interpretieren, wird in unserem Fall noch durch den Gebrauch eines dem Deutschen fremden Alphabets vergrößert," p. 16). Thus the language is simply assumed to be German, which the scholar must reveal by stripping off the disguising garb of a "foreign" alphabet.[168]

The problem of the cultural source of the poem is treated in contradictory fashion. Since it was impossible for Schwarz to determine the cotemporal system of orthography, for the reasons just noted, he need not deal with the text as a part of that tradition. Even so, he finds examples of the influence of Hebrew orthography in the manuscript (pp. 18-20). He rejects Neumann's theory ("Sprache und Reim," pp. 146-47) that *Dukus Hurnt* was copied (i.e., transliterated/transcribed) from a Roman-alphabet, German-language manuscript. Rather, he proposes that the text was written down from the oral tradition (p. 18). The implications are thus that the analysis of the phonetic system of the text need not deal with problems of a direct transmission in the traditional orthography, since the text is "oral" and therefore apparently outside of the orthographic tradition.

In a nine-line identification of the phonetic system of the text, which *prefaces* his analysis, Schwarz claims that its language is "mitteldeutsch" ("Central German," pp. 20-21); neither here nor elsewhere in his fifty-page essay on the grapho-phonemic system does he attempt any justification of this guiding principle of the investigation.[169] In his article, "Prinzipielle Erwägungen," published two years later, however, Schwarz does address this issue that he had ignored in the edition. Here he calls the texts of the manuscript "deutsche Texte in hebräischen Buchstaben" ("German texts in Hebrew letters," p. 141). One of his "principles" is that since such a text can yield excellent information on the history of German phonetics and the pronunciation of Middle High German, one must proceed with an investigation of the texts without prejudice as to their possible phonetic character: a strange requirement of "objectivity," since it is conditioned by his wish to use this principle to prove the language to be German, and enunciated here immediately after he has claimed the language as German.[170] He nevertheless maintains the pretense of objectivity in establishing the context of the investigation: "wenn die Sprache dieser Hs. deutsch wäre . . ." ("If the language of this manuscript were German," "Prinzipielle Erwägungen," p. 141), as if his conclusion had not already been drawn and preposed to his investigation, *and* as if this "objective" premise could in any way fulfil his requirement of non-prejudicial premises. This is indeed a revealing practice in an article whose stated purpose is one of methodological analysis. Schwarz then lists the questions which he views as seminal, one of which is whether the scribe attempted to accurately render via the Hebrew alphabet the German pronunciation known to him, or rather followed a traditional system of orthography; i.e., in either case, the language is again simply assumed to be German.

In denying that the more recent history of Yiddish can be relevant to an analysis of the texts of the manuscript, Schwarz undermines his methodological principles still further by trying to justify this claim by noting that the early history of Yiddish is not yet known "in allen Einzelheiten." Yet at the same time he nonetheless finds it legitimate to draw on German data in analyzing this manuscript, in order to define the development of medieval German phonetics. But if the study of medieval German phonetics could profit from definition via analysis of these texts, then one must assume that the subject is also not yet known "in all its details." And in fact he admits that the details of early German phonetics are so obscure that we know almost nothing about Middle High German dialects ("Prinzipielle Erwägungen," pp. 142-143). One might then well ask how Middle High German phonetics can aid in the definition of the grapho-phonemic system of this manuscript, only in turn to be defined by that same system.

He expresses the hope that an analysis of the kind he envisions here might result in proving the manuscript to be "Mittelhoch-deutsch" or "Mitteldeutsch" (pp. 142-143), but, he cautions, until the manuscript has been deciphered and detailed philological analysis carried out, nothing can be said (p. 143). His wish is perplexing, for if he seeks unprejudiced investigations, why would he *hope* that the language would be identified as one language rather than another; does this hope expressed here mean that he doubts his already stated conclusion earlier in the article that the language is German, and that it is specifically Central German, as he maintained in his edition of two years before? Are those conclusions also merely expressions of his scholarly hopes? Furthermore, what can his intent be here when he states that the decipherment of the codex is a prerequisite to all philological analysis? At the time of this article there had already been two editions of the entire manuscript and several editions of individual poems, *one of them his own*, published two years earlier! Had they not already at least deciphered the manuscript? Had not each edition, review, article and monograph deciphered the manu-script *and* offered philological analysis, especially the articles by Marchand, Weissberg, and Weinreich? In the abstract then, Schwarz's article seems to have been written without consultation of the rele-vant research literature, although in fact he does cite it (albeit spar-ingly). Perhaps his attempt to offer "first principles" leads him to assume this pose of abstract theoretical objectivity, unsullied by prac-tical analysis and the groundbreaking work that had already been done in the field. Whatever the purpose for this pose, Schwarz's methodological house collapses under the weight of its own ideologi-cal pretense of objectivity.

Norman's essay on *Sagengeschichte* is no more consistent in itself than Schwarz's, and additionally also often contradicts the claims of the other editors.[171] He immediately identifies the language as "mhd."[172] and supports his claim (p. 75) with the reference "(siehe Lautstand)" [that is, one must assume, Schwarz's essay], but there is no page reference here, since there is none to cite, because Schwarz never claims that the language is Middle High German and in fact denies that one can be more specific than Central German, which is, one must assume, different in his view from Middle High German, although he does take Middle High German as his basis of analysis. Norman then notes, "ob sie [sc. die Sprache] schon jüdisch gefärbt ist, läßt sich *auch* mit literarischen Mitteln nicht feststellen" ("whether it [the language] already had a Jewish tinge is indeterminable by literary means *as well*," p. 75; my emphasis). With this statement, Norman assumes: 1) that Schwarz has conclusively proven that the language is a Middle High German that is not susceptible to any identification of "Jewish coloring"[173] and 2) that the text is not to be associated with medieval Jewish culture, despite the fact that it exists in a single manuscript written in the Hebrew alphabet, containing "Jewish" poems, and found in a Jewish Genizah thousands of miles from the home of Middle High German literature.[174] He notes the medieval Jewish interest in and versions of Middle High German Arthurian and heroic literature, but asserts that although those works are not "rein deutsch,"[175] it is irrelevant whether they are "jiddisch" or "Hebrew-German," since "in dem vorliegenden Falle . . .handelt es sich ganz sicher um deutsch" ("in the present case, it is quite certainly a matter of German," p. 75).

Let us attempt to determine what distinction Norman establishes here between "Hebrew-German" and "Deutsch" (as he identifies the language of *Dukus Hurnt*). Landau and Marchand define the term as German written in the Hebrew alphabet.[176] Is that not in fact the language Norman and Schwarz have proposed: "Mitteldeutsch" or "Mittelhochdeutsch," grudgingly conceded to have been written in the Hebrew alphabet? How does this differ from Landau/Marchand's "Hebrew-German"? Ganz/Norman/Schwarz do not explain this distinction, but one can speculate on the basis of their method: if they were to call it "Hebrew-German," the language and literature, even in the name itself, would somehow be linked with medieval Jewish culture. Yet the editors are uncompromisingly consistent in denying such an association (a consistency that is uncharacteristic of their method in general): from their perspective, the text of *Dukus Hurnt* is quite simply German. The transmission of the text in the Hebrew alphabet with some Jewish adaptations is not, as the use of the term "Hebrew-German" would imply, a qualification of the German-ness of the document, but rather an irrelevant, removable bit of debris; the Hebrew alphabet is merely the vehicle by which this German literary tradition, with its variant versions (all other versions – including the posited German ones – except this example are now lost), has been transmitted. It is not a factor of any significance in an interpretation of the text. In their inclusion of Birnbaum's very brief remarks on the script, the editors had already forced their readers to venture far enough away from the familiar Germanistic center toward the margin, into the exotic realm of ultra-Germania; and therewith had also made the required bow to the fact of the use of the Hebrew alphabet in this text. And with that, the matter was, apparently, settled.

Norman maintains that except for the lion fable (which "mag deutsch sein") and *Dukus Hurnt*, the other texts of the manuscript are "certainly of Jewish origin" ("sicher jüdischer Herkunft," p. 75).[177] This claim apparently has no relevance for the language of the texts, however, for Norman cites the final line of "Gan Eden" in "normalem Mittelhochdeutsch" (p. 76).[178] Furthermore, he notes that the Abraham poem is written "in fließendem Mittelhochdeutsch" (p. 76), employing a term, "fluent," generally used in evaluations of the quality of a non-native speaker's competence in a foreign language. Does he thus assume the author's language was not the putative Middle High German of his composition?[179] Or does he simply mean that the poem's language is too "proper" and "correct" to be associated even remotely with a "Jewish-tinged German" (i.e., something resembling the unmentioned and unmentionable, and therefore ever-present, Yiddish)? Due to the presence of the Hebrew acrostic, he concedes that "Yosef" was written by a Jewish poet.[180] Yet even here, where the "Jewish coloring" is most evident, and even conceded by the editors, it is denied that the poems are anything but "deutschsprachige Literatur," although it is briefly and in this context enigmatically noted that they must have been written for a Jewish audience (p. 77).

The question of the original script of the texts is again touched on obliquely when Norman notes that it seems that the authors of the texts knew the principles of post-classical Middle High German metrics very well, although it is difficult to discern their skill, due to the problems caused by the "aschkenasische Umschrift" (p. 77). With "*Um*schrift" it is implied that the poems were transposed from, one must assume, a Roman-alphabet source. But Schwarz has already maintained that the text of *Dukus Hurnt* was the written recording of the oral tradition and not a copy of any manuscript in either Hebrew or Roman script. And Norman himself had just argued that the poet of "Yosef" composed the poem in the Hebrew alphabet – which is of course the only possible explanation for the existence of the acrostic. What then is the significance of Norman's sudden claim, by implication, that the poems are transcriptions?

The inconsistencies continue to accumulate, as Norman later

notes that it is not possible to prove a Hebrew-alphabet source for *Dukus Hurnt*, although certain addenda (*Nachträge*, p. 83) would seem to indicate that to be the case, and thus he again contradicts Schwarz's proposition of an oral source for *Dukus Hurnt*. He then notes "bei Sammelhandschriften ist Abschrift das Gegebene" (p. 83). Does this mean that the manuscript (or certain of its texts) was copied either from Roman or Hebrew-alphabet sources, or a combination thereof? Norman does not address the question with his irrelevant generalization, but again one can extrapolate information from his elliptical remarks: "Yosef Hatsadik" and the other poems signed by Isaac and Abraham were copied from (an) existing manuscript(s) (p. 83), and most likely *Dukus Hurnt* was *also* (*auch*, p. 84) copied from a *Hebrew* alphabet source, thus implying that the other poems were written in the Hebrew alphabet. Here again, however, he uses the term "aschkenasische Umschrift," and therewith implies an ultimate source in (one must assume) the Roman alphabet (p. 84), only in the next sentence to deny that it is possible to determine whether *Dukus Hurnt* was copied from a Roman alphabet source ("deutschschriftliche Quelle") or written down from the oral tradition.

He denies that the poem could have been written by a Jew, since the presence of the Christian "Reisesegen," the Crusader poem and the treatment of the Church and Mass would all have to be explained away (p. 103). He even goes so far as to maintain that the poet's assumption of the aesthetic sensibilities of wild boar (which, the poet says, are soothed by music) would have been impossible for a Jew (p. 118).[181] Would Norman have us seriously consider that this – for modern tastes – at worst ridiculous and at best amusing bit of medieval anthropomorphism was more proper for Christians than Jews, merely due (one must assume, since he gives no reason) to the – in this case certainly irrelevant – Jewish dietary laws? The same patronizing technique is employed to dismiss the entire notion of Jewish authorship when Norman remarks in a footnote, without deigning to provide even a summary of the many complex arguments advanced before him, that "was bisher für eine solche Auffassung [i.e., Jewish authorship] geltend gemacht worden ist, hält kritischer Prüfung nicht stand" ("what has up until now been advanced as evidence for such an interpretation, does not stand up under critical examination," p. 124, n. 87). This "critical examination," which the reader of this standard edition would expect to find here (since not elsewhere) is not forthcoming, however.[182] The flippant method of dismissing one's opposition on a seminal question of the poem's significance as a cultural document is unsettling. After having called the poem "unterliterarisch" (p. 104), he nonetheless grants that it is "eine . . . merkwürdige Erscheinung . . . in der deutschen Literatur" (p. 123). I would certainly agree that no other place than that of "a remarkable phenomenon" could be granted this poem "in *German* literature."

Norman's speculations on the earlier, non-extant stages of the Horant legend are relevant here only insofar as the construction of an entire historical and literary tradition of the tale provides an ideological interpretive framework for the details of the editors' method. The implied conclusions of Norman's rambling essay are that *Dukus Hurnt* is only a late, derivative, and sub-literary version of a long, complex tradition in Middle High German. *Dukus Hurnt* is thus denied intrinsic literary value, and is rather characterized as valuable only insofar as it allows the scholar to delve into the posited earlier stages of the tradition.[183] That the present text is the only version extant from this tradition is only an accident of history and especially textual history, and that it is written in the Hebrew alphabet and thus for a Jewish audience is of no relevance for Norman's purpose, since the source-hunter can easily identify and strip away later accretions (i.e., in the present case, "Jewish coloring") to the legitimate tradition in order to reveal an earlier stage of that tradition.[184]

It has never been denied that the Horant legend derives directly from the Germanic literary tradition, and Norman's practice in constructing a stemma of the posited pre-*Dukus Hurnt* stages of the tradition does not simply participate in the tradition of source studies, but is exemplary as such. Its inappropriateness here lies in part certainly in the fact that such studies have been obsolete, and justifiably so, for decades (although they do still appear from time to time even now), since they have long since been recognized as more a test of the modern scholar's ingenuity in composing (usually non-extant) medieval literary texts than in dealing with texts in their extant form. But the main objection to Norman's essay must be that here, as the major portion of the introductory matter to the standard edition of this particular poem, it does not attempt to deal with the text as: 1) a literary work of intrinsic value (to be determined on some stated criteria); 2) a work of cultural significance which would provide information about precisely that phenomenon that they take such pains to obscure – the nature, practice, and purpose of Christian-Jewish literary relations, as revealed in such a cross-cultural adaptation; and 3) a massive data base for linguistic analysis, possibly yielding conclusions on the state of the Jewish literary language of the time. The editors do not treat these questions directly at any point. One can, as I have attempted to do here, extrapolate much information concerning the editors' *a priori* answers to these questions, but that does not mitigate their failure to address the problems as such.

One might hope that many of the problems in interpreting the conflicting claims presented obliquely by the editors derive from their imprecise terminology, rather than from actual incoherency of argument (although the former is often merely a manifestation of the latter); especially is this the case with Norman's essay. But the result is in any case chaotic, since one is never sure what is meant by any of his (often newly-coined) undefined terms, nor how his opinions are to be viewed in light of the differing conclusions drawn by his co-editor, Schwarz, on the basis of the same material. The most disturbing aspect of the edition is that at few points does it seem relevant to the editors to present evidence for their opinions.[185] This lack of evidence, argument, and scholarly discussion is probably at the root of the editors' inconsistencies: since they have no argumentative system of premise, evidence, or conclusion, they are not obligated to develop a consistent set of terms for expressing their case (at any rate they do not do so). But perhaps one cannot fault them for more than their lack of argument, since in its absence, one cannot expect them to follow any principles of argumentation.

The editors never refer to the text as Yiddish, nor do they even hint that a discussion of the text's language as Yiddish has been of relevance in prior scholarship, and thus they in effect misrepresesnt the scholarly context of the work. They in general do not cite much of the abundant scholarly literature on the subject of Old Yiddish, nor on *Dukus Hurnt* itself,[186] and thus they not only fail in their duty as editors of the standard edition to come to terms with the seminal questions occupying their colleagues working on the same and related texts, but also as a result of their ignoring other studies, they undermine the validity of their own position and render it obsolete even at the moment of its appearance. Finally, in ignoring the majority of the research literature and in presenting an introduction to the edition consisting exclusively of a pseudo-objective description of the grapho-phonemic inventory of the text and its speculative literary prehistory, they present an eminently "German" text: the possibility of its being otherwise is in the rule ignored, and if mentioned, then only to be derisively denied in the relative obscurity of the footnotes. The edition is an insidious failure – not principally through errors of commission (although they also occur), but rather errors of omission, exacerbated by the editors' proclivity for the pronouncement of their opinions as self-evident truths rather than hypotheses requiring argument.

Their pose of objectivity and purely philological analysis is a clear manifestation of the denial of the existence of Yiddish. The editors expend little energy on a refutation of arguments in favor of the identification of the text's language as Yiddish (in fact they hardly mention them at all and never take them seriously); instead they simply annex the (Yiddish? certainly Jewish) text for the German literary and linguistic tradition. They do so especially by institutional means, for they publish the text in traditional Germanistic form in a traditional bastion of Germanistic text editions. They have thus not just denied the alterity of the text and annexed it to the center, but in doing so have "deprived" the margin of one of its major (and newly "discovered") texts. Again the critical move signifies on several levels: the margin is denied a cultural element (a text, a language) which is incorporated into the center, but there it is denigrated to the level of a mere defective corpus of linguistic (but not literary, since "unterliterarisch") information about the center's language. Most significantly of all, this annexation has taken place without confrontation, argument, or refutation of the margin's position – it has rather all taken place merely implicitly, tacitly, and with the customary arrogance of the imperialist center for all things marginal.

Reviews of Ganz/Norman/Schwarz's edition were not as numerous as those of Fuks' edition, nor as important for the continuation of the scholarly discussion. Rauh accepts Norman's claim that the texts are "linguistically Middle High German," but notes that many of the linguistic features that are interpreted as evidence for Central German are also characteristic of Yiddish (review, p. 154). Even so, she notes "es wäre absurd, eine deutsche Sprachform als jiddisch zu characterisieren, nur weil Juden sie übernommen haben" ("it would be absurd to characterize a linguistic form of German as Yiddish simply because Jews had adopted it," p. 154), [187] and then makes an equally absurd claim of her own: that the presence of the Hebrew alphabet does not necessarily make the language written in that alphabet Yiddish, but that the use of the Hebrew alphabet is a precondition for a language's being Yiddish. Thus on the one hand, the Hebrew alphabet is unimportant, and on the other a *sine qua non.* An equally problematic claim is that since ח does not correspond to any Middle High German sound and that Hebrew letter is rare in this text, then the text is "reines Mittelhochdeutsch" ("pure Middle High German," p. 154, n. 1).[188] It thus becomes clear that for Rauh "language" is simply literary language, and the language of this text is significant for the existence and character of spoken languages of the time; Yiddish then does not yet exist. She criticizes Ganz for reducing the necessary discussion of Jewish-Christian cultural exchanges to a footnote reference to Friedrich Heinrich von der Hagen's century-old article (p. 156), since the topic is of seminal importance for a discussion of the text. She argues against Schwarz's proposal of an oral source and for a Hebrew-alphabet source text, since the nuancing of the Hebrew alphabet for non-distinct forms in the Roman alphabet is based on the traditional Hebrew orthographic system (p. 157).[189] In the very existence of *Dukus Hurnt* – as German literature written in the Hebrew alphabet – she sees evidence that Jews were well assimilated to German culture. The editors' bibliography draws criticism for its incompleteness and she thus appends a "Gesamtbibliographie" (pp. 160-164) to supplement it; her bibliography is, if anything, even less satisfactory and more error-ridden, full of incomplete references and enigmatic abbreviations (although she criticizes the editors for this last fault in their bibliography and adds a list of abbreviations herself, in which many of her own are, however, unfortunately not found).[190]

H. Stopp's review addresses the problem of language by noting that further study of the problem is necessary before one can identify it as either Central German or Yiddish; i.e., he implies that the editors have not presented a definitive discussion of the problem.[191] Stopp argues for the importance of the Bavarian-Central German dialect mixture characteristic of Regensburg as evidence for that city as the poem's place of origin (p. 460).[192] He laments Norman's fantasies about the prehistory of the work as "wieder einmal eine Filiation über eine Reihe von Unbekannten" ("yet another filiation via a succession of unknowns," p. 460), which is based on no more than "an impressionistic selection" of motifs from the work and relations between this work and others. Schröbler, on the other hand, praises Norman's "selbstverständliche . . . Sachkenntnis und wohlerwogene Zurückhaltung ("obvious . . . expertise and deliberate restraint," p. 74). Paucker concurs that Norman "lucidly and convincingly" outlines the place of *Dukus Hurnt* in German literature (p. 274). Röll accepts Norman's proposal of a lost *Herbortlied* as the source of *Dukus Hurnt* as "irrefutable" ("unabweisbar," p. 271).[193] Kaplowitt criticizes Norman's lack of explicitness on the dates and content of his supposed older Rother source (p. 540). In general, he finds Norman's discussion of the Hilde-saga too diffuse and irrelevant for all purposes except as support for the editor's own speculations (p. 541). But he accepts Norman's notion of only minor adaptation by a Jewish scribe (i.e., the poem had no Jewish author; p. 541). Stopp, however, notes as if an obvious fact that Norman failed to disprove Jewish authorship (p. 463).

In his review, Rosenfeld objects to Norman's outmoded method and his ignoring more recent research, which leads the editor to many unnecessary errors.[194] He also argues for a Jewish poet, since: 1) the motif of loans plays an important role, due to Jewish involvement in money-lending in this period; 2) the role of women is less honorable than in the Christian courtly literature of the time, in that the princess is forced to come to Hurnt, the courtly suitor; 3) that *even* wild boars are affected by Hurnt's music would argue for, not against Jewish authorship; 4) typically Yiddish reflexive constructions are present in the text; 5) *tifle* "church"; and, 6) the problematic loss of /h/ in the traditional name Hetan is explained as a replacement of that German king with the Jewish king Etan from the Old Testament (p. 128). Except for the last argument, none of Rosenfeld's points are new, nor are they presented in a more convincing manner than they had been before, but the last point is telling. He concludes that the poet was a Jew and adapted the Hilde section of the Middle High German *Kudrun* of 1233 for a Jewish audience, and in doing so set up a monument to the riches and nobility of urban Jewish merchants (p. 128). In the context of his generally pro-Jewish/Yiddish arguments and conclusions, it is surprising that he calls the language of the text "judendeutsch" not Yiddish (p. 129); one can only speculate what specific connotation the term has for him, but it can hardly be an unmarked term that means simply "Yiddish."

In view of the generally accepted duality of nomenclature, it is surprising that Siegfried Colditz added yet another name – *hebräisch-mittelhochdeutsch* – only two years after the publication of Ganz/Norman/Schwarz's edition of *Dukus Hurnt.*[195] He patronizingly notes that some few scholars have "remained faithful" to the name "Jiddisch,"[196] despite a preponderance of evidence against such an identification, but that most have chosen Landau's term, "Hebrew-German," which Colditz identifies as simply a translation of Friedrich C. B. Avé-Lallemant's "Ibri-, Iwriteutsch,"[197] i.e., German in the Hebrew alphabet, a suitable name for *Dukus Hurnt* and many other such texts (p. 303). The name is too daring in his view to be used as a general term for all secular Jewish poetry of the twelfth through the fourteenth centuries, and Landau's use of it in this way is an example of his uncritical acceptance of "the late romantic ideas" ("die spätromantischen Vorstellungen") of von der Hagen and Delitzsch.[198] The specific problem with such late Romantic conceptions is that Jewish poetry was said to be "national-deutsche Singekunst" ("German national vocal art") in pure German. Colditz counters this assumption by pointing out that the majority of secular literature in Yiddish was lost as a result of the persecutions of the time. He proposes a "neutral designation" – "'Hebräisch-Mittelhoch deutsch' (Hebrew-Middle High German)" (p. 304)[199] – for this poetry, since "Hebrew-German" covers too broad a time span. Thus it seems that he differs from the typical Haskalah argument in proposing a distinct Yiddish language for later periods, but he agrees with the assimilationists that the origin of Yiddish was "pure German," despite his claims that "Hebräisch-Mittelhochdeutsch" is somehow neutral. His affiliation with the assimilationists is also apparent in his proposal of *Dukus Hurnt* as evidence of a Jewish-Christian German cultural community (p. 304). In this regard, he inexplicably criticizes Ganz/Norman/Schwarz for their failure to integrate the poem into German literary history.

Despite his designation of the language, Colditz argues vociferously in favor of Jewish authorship of the poem, and rejects the arguments of Ganz/Norman/Schwarz for German authorship as an inappropriate transferral of the literary situation of the sixteenth-seventeenth century (when German works were commonly adapted into Yiddish) to *Dukus Hurnt*, which he finds "irritating." He takes the adaptation of the Crusader song, the use of *tifle*, and the merchant atmosphere of the poem as indications of Jewish authorship (p. 306) and agrees with Rosenfeld that Etene derives from the Old Testament *Etan* and that Regensburg is the likely origin of the poem.[200]

More important than any reviews of Ganz/Norman/Schwarz was the summary of the research on *Dukus Hurnt* included by Michael Curschmann in his study of *Spielmann* literature.[201] Specifically on the present topic, he calls the language of the Cambridge codex "Jüdischdeutsch," notes that the question of Middle High German vs. Yiddish is more urgent for Yiddish than German studies, points out that Weinreich (in "Old Yiddish Poetry") had successfully refuted Marchand's arguments (p. 43), concurs with Colditz's proposal[202] of Jewish authorship of *Dukus Hurnt*, even though the evidence is not vast, and rejects Fuks' theory of the origin of the poem in a Jewish ghetto and Menhardt's that it was written in Regensburg (p. 44). He also notes that the edition by Ganz/Norman/Schwarz comes closer to the needs of scholars than had Fuks', but cautions that this edition also has its glaring inadequacies, especially the bibliography and the lack of critical appraisal of and response to the research literature (pp. 42 & 44).

As noted above, the positivistic method did not disappear from Old Yiddish studies with the refutation of Marchand's theses, but rather simply became more extreme. Eschewing all apparent intent to interpret, it sought only to compile data, primarily linguistic data, which could then be used by scholars as the basis of their interpretive studies. In such studies the dominant questions of language identity and nomenclature were strictly and consciously deferred until after the preliminary data base had been established; that is, they were ostensibly eliminated from the set of possible topics of discussion and analysis. Yet they nevertheless continued to be determinants of the methods involved in the compilation of the data: they still determined the ideological tenor of the discussion, for by the very fact of their consciously enforced absence from the discussion, they were pervasive. Especially characteristic of this movement are the editions by Heikki J. Hakkarainen and Hans-Peter Althaus.[203]

The last editor of the Cambridge codex in its entirety, Heikki J. Hakkarainen, again takes the entire manuscript into account and deals with his editorial task in three volumes.[204] His proposed method is one of pure objectivity, "with no interpretation of any kind on the part of the editor" ("ohne irgendwelche Interpretation seitens des Herausgebers," I, 5). Thus he sees his task as one of "deciphering" (*Entzifferung*, I, 14) the manuscript and linguistic analysis without prejudicing the case of language identification prior to the study: "Ich will hier absichtlich nicht eine Deutung and Etikettierung der Sprache vorwegnehmen" ("I deliberately want to avoid anticipating/prejudicing an interpretation and labeling of the language," I, 16). He seems to promise that such a question can be answered only after and on the basis of his study. Yet even in the first sentence of his introduction, he already calls the manuscript "die jüdisch-deutsche Handschrift," and in the midst of his protestations of objectivity, he says the language of the text is "in ihrer Substanz Deutsch" ("substantially German," I, 16). The context of this last phrase is interesting, for it is here that he provides his revealing definition of "jüdisch-deutsch": "Ich verwende diese Bezeichnung, da wir es ganz offenbar mit einer Handschrift zu tun haben, die (1) von Juden geschrieben wurde und (2) deren Sprache in ihrer Substanz Deutsch ist. Nur in diesem Sinne möge sie verstanden werden" (I, 13, n. 2).[205] In the last sentence of the quotation, the signification of the pronoun "sie" is ambiguous and could refer either to "Bezeichnung" (i.e. *Jüdisch-deutsch*) or "Handschrift." In either case Hakkarainen is simply adhering to the Haskalah notion of "Jüdisch-deutsch" as German written by Jews and derived from a Jewish cultural milieu that is itself strictly German. But he delves no more deeply into the entire problem. He makes the disclaimer that at this point in the study, it is not his purpose to deal with the language and literary content, implying thereby that he will return to this topic after his editorial task and linguistic analysis are complete. He thus claims that it is legitimate for him initially to treat the entire codex as a single corpus of data, without reference to the distinctions among the various texts in topic, style, genre, etc.[206] There is an insidious bit of dissimulation to be discerned here, since Hakkarainen pretends to a kind of objectivity that would allow him to first mechanically transpose the texts into "readable" form (i.e., transliteration into Roman), analyze them linguistically, and only then draw conclusions.[207] This tendency toward an idealization of pure objectivity is further emphasized in his use of computer analysis, which even for the initiated carries some aura of "scientific" objectivity and freedom from interpretation.[208]

Significantly, Hakkarainen never deals with the deferred topics of literary and cultural significance, nor does he even get to the promised conclusions, based on his descriptive analysis, since there are few which one can draw from the mass of raw statistical data, divorced from all context, *and* since his conclusions on such topics are already present in the first sentence of volume one, and as such determine his conception of his research tasks, his definition of evidence, and his entire notion of what data to seek and value.[209] As he proceeds with his analysis, Hakkarainen is compelled to call the language by some name, but he silently passes over his newly defined "jüdischdeutsch" and instead calls the language "deutsch"[210] and even characterizes it briefly when he deals with the presence of Hebrew words in the manuscript:

> Hebräisch tritt im "deutschen" Text in einzelnen Wörtern auf, die den Charakter eines Fremdworts haben und spezifisch jüdische Angelegenheiten bezeichnen, sowie in einigen rein hebräischen Wörtern – losgelöst vom "deutschen" Text – am Ende der einzelnen Abschnitte der Hs. . . . Im ganzen kann festgestellt werden, dass hebräische Wörter und hebräische Sprache in dieser Hs. sehr selten sind. (I, p. 16)[211]

The passage is enlightening on a number of points, especially with regard to Hakkarainen's preconceptions of the character of these texts: there are, apparently, two kinds of "texts" present in the codex – German and Hebrew. Although the Hebrew texts (sections, words, phrases, and titles) form an integral part of the poems which they open, close, or are enclosed by, they are viewed as distinct, since they are in the Hebrew language. The German texts also contain intrusive, foreign Hebrew words. These Hebrew words are, apparently, of a different kind from the "purely Hebrew words" of the distinct Hebrew texts, and they are used for "specifically Jewish affairs," while the latter are apparently not. These contrasts do not seem to be of great import for the details of Hakkarainen's further argument, however, since he says no more about them. Nor could he have carried the point much further, since it seems that the Hebrew words in the German texts are "intruders" for no other reason than that they are simply not of Germanic etymology; when Hakkarainen labels them such, however, he assumes that he is capable of determining the state of lexical integration (or lack thereof) of the vocabulary of a language sample that is more than half a millenium old, in a language that he ostensibly refuses to identify.

Perhaps the most significant ideological notion in Hakkarainen's argument is, however, the minor aside noted above that a given poem that is ostensibly a single text, in fact comprises two texts, one German and one Hebrew. It implicitly refutes the layman's (and erstwhile scholarly) characterization of Yiddish as a "German dialect with some Hebrew admixture," such that a vaguely dialectal "German" text with some Hebrew lexical admixture would, from this perspective, immediately be open to identification as a possibly Yiddish text. But according to Hakkarainen's posited double textuality, there is no such German-Hebrew mixed text here. Rather, there are two texts, one discrete German text and one discrete Hebrew text, or rather two *types* of texts, which are shuffled together, so to speak. And of course neither German texts nor Hebrew texts can be suspected of being Yiddish, and thus one need not even address the problem of Yiddish vs. German. Consequently he in fact does not do so.

The reviews of Hakkarainen's three volumes rarely deal with the problems here at issue (since Hakkarainen does not do so himself), but do occasionally touch on issues of methodological import. Lindgren faults Hakkarainen for allowing his knowledge of the content of the texts to influence his interpretation of graphic problems and thus advocates an even more extreme form of objectivity than that toward which Hakkarainen strives.[212] In passing he invents still another name for the language: "jüdisch-mittelhochdeutsch . . . in hebräischer Schrift" (p. 724) and later notes the "obvious" character of the texts as "Deutsch im weiteren Sinne" (p. 726). Neither of the terms is defined, nor do they need to be in the context of Lindgren's remarks, since for him there is no controversy, and the terms speak for themselves.[213]

In his edition of the lion fable, the briefest of the literary texts from the Cambridge codex, Hans-Peter Althaus attempts to establish a methodological model for editions and analyses of Old Yiddish texts.[214] Like Hakkarainen's, his proposed method is one of objective linguistic analysis, completely uninfluenced by preconceptions of language/dialect identity, since as he notes in his discussion of the three major theories of the texts' language – German, Yiddish, and Hebrew-German – and their proponents' arguments, any decisions concerning the linguistic identity of the texts predetermines all further editorial decisions (pp. 31-32), and by implication thus denies that his study will be so prejudiced. If anything, however, his aspirations toward a purely objective analysis are even stricter than were Hakkarainen's, and as a result the deficiencies and failings of the study are even more glaring. The method leads him to convolutions in terminology and argument which are only partially successful in obscuring the fact that they are more often than not either statements of "common sense" or intricately ideological (that is, if they can be decoded at all),[215] i.e., hardly objective in any sense.

He maintains that previous determinations of dialect have all been based on faulty methodology (p. 32). His own is to be free of such faults, due to its analytical objectivity. Yet even before beginning his analysis of the linguistic forms of the text, he asserts that there is no lexical or grammatical evidence for proposing a distinction between the language of this text and Middle High German (p. 30) and further remarks that due to the isolation of Jewish communities from their Christian neighbors, the mixture of dialects, and the exile of the Jews, it was not until after the mid-fourteenth century that Yiddish existed as a language distinct from Middle High German (p. 39).[216] With this sweeping generalization, he determines the course of the remainder of his study. In the context of his argument, however, the language of the lion fable *could* not exhibit any specifically Yiddish characteristics and could *only* be Middle High German, since he dates the text to 1300, that is, to a period *before* the time at which he posits the emergence of a distinct Yiddish language. Despite the clear implications of these preconceptions, he initially avoids any explicit identification of the language as Middle High German, since that would invalidate his pose of objectivity: such an identification could only legitimately be proposed *after* the completion of the analysis of the data.

Instead of committing himself to a named designation of the language, he devises a set of camouflaging acronyms for designating the graphic and phonemic forms of the language of medieval German Christians and Ashkenazic Jews:

MhdPhoChr = Middle High German spoken by Christians
MhdPhoJud = Middle High German spoken by Jews
MhdGraLat = Middle High German "oriented toward" the Roman alphabet
MhdGraHeb = Middle High German "oriented toward" the Hebrew alphabet.[217]

As the acronyms indicate, however, the language under discussion is in all cases considered Middle High German, whether spoken by Christians or Jews, whether "oriented toward" [presumably written in] the Hebrew or Roman alphabet. Althaus further assumes that the Jewish form of this language, written in the Hebrew alphabet, was a representative of the "mittelalterliche deutsche Phonemsprache,"[218] a unique term that he declines to define, despite the fact that in its vagueness, it could refer to such diverse languages/dialects and historical stages of the "German" language as eighth-century Low German or fifteenth-century Austrian and everything in between. His acronyms demonstrate that even at this point, the language of the document, both graphemic and phonemic, is identified as Middle High German, despite the apparent attempt by means of the acronyms to avoid any and all such identification. The legend to the table accompanying this passage, however, indicates an implied contrast between "mhd./altjidd." (p. 68, tab. 5), but it is never defined.

Althaus attempts to lend an aura of scientific objectivity to his subjective interpretations through the use of a strained hyper-scientifistic terminology, such as the acronyms noted above, and for instance the linguistic term "Nullgraphem" (p. 210), used by Althaus to designate a posited phoneme which, though not represented graphemically in the actual (Hebrew-alphabet) text, he nonetheless analyzes phonemically in great detail as if it were.[219] In the end he can only conclude that the language is Middle High German, and thus his critical edition of the text is presented in a form of Middle High German remarkably similar (if not identical) to the normalized language of Middle High German text editions (pp. 210-218). Thus he offers as the conclusion of his study no more than the basic premise of his investigation that had guided his efforts throughout. Like Landau, Althaus does not express the question of language but devotes his entire study to answering the implicit question of language identity, but Althaus does so by means of a rigorous linguistic investigation, which is to lend a measure of legitimacy to his answer. But in fact the results of his study can only confirm his initial premise, since that premise predetermines the conclusions possible, as he himself notes in the abstract at the beginning of his study!

With Althaus' edition, the period of radical positivism in the study of Old Yiddish drew to a close. In this field it was halted by the same methodological aporia that had led to its demise in other disciplines. Neither the pro- or anti-Yiddishists triumphed in the process; nor had either side been defeated. The game simply at some seemingly random point stopped, and there was no more to say. Positivism flourishes only in an environment of a relatively widespread acceptance of a body of basic "facts," which can then serve as the foundation on which "analysis" can proceed. In Old Yiddish studies, there are fewer facts in this sense than is characteristic of other disciplines and sub-disciplines, and thus positivism necessarily had a relatively short life span in the field, for it soon became apparent that it was impossible to achieve any kind of objectivity beyond that which is legislated by the tenets of one's own ideological construct. Thus the legitimacy of the dominant question of Old Yiddish studies up through this phase of study – Old Yiddish or Middle High German? – so pervasively present in the case of extreme positivism precisely because of its legislated absence from all analysis, has itself been called into question and may in fact have now disappeared as a topic of major import. Perhaps the question was recognized as too volatile and subjective, in the pejorative, positivistic sense, and the minute objective linguistic analysis that is posited as a prerequisite to the determination of language identity (which would then be founded on that preliminary data base) was recognized as an unrealizable ideal in a field where "facts" are so rare.

The problem of the relationship of Yiddish and German has been dealt with in other ways, however, and on the basis of quite a different kind of text: early modern Hebrew-alphabet texts which are demonstrable adaptations of Roman-alphabet, German texts. Most common among such texts are adaptations of chapbooks [*Volksbücher*] and brief legal documents. Here too the evidence is open to the interpretation that the close linguistic relationship of the Hebrew-alphabet adaptation to the German original proves that Yiddish as an identifiably distinct language had not yet emerged. But there have been few attempts to advance this thesis in recent decades.

Florence Guggenheim-Grünberg's work relates indirectly to the present topic, since she deals with fourteenth- and fifteenth-century German legal documents also extant in Hebrew alphabet versions,[220] and because many scholars have viewed some or all of Old Yiddish literature merely as German written in the Hebrew alphabet. Since the documents in question exist in both Roman and Hebrew script, a comparison is possible, and Guggenheim-Grünberg demonstrates that the dialects of the texts differ, but also that the Hebrew alphabet texts still present little evidence of a specifically Yiddish linguistic form. Therefore she concludes with a question: from what period can one legitimately speak of West Yiddish *per se* (p. 246)? She thus implies that such documents argue against the existence of West Yiddish at this period. Argument to that end would be very difficult on the basis of these documents for a number of reasons: legal documents are by nature quite a conservative genre and their phraseology is traditional and has its own specific, legal significance. For this latter reason they are not open to paraphrase if they are to retain their official, legally binding character. The language of the documents – in Roman and Hebrew script – is thus unlikely to reflect the actual speech of either Christians or Jews of the time. In fact legal documents are less likely to yield such information as many other kinds of documents, due simply to their stylized conservative language. Most significantly in this case, the dominant legal tradition in which these bilingual texts participate is of course the non-Jewish tradition of the center; and thus the conservative, normative language is in this case German. The documents are interesting as attempts to render German into Hebrew script, but have little direct relevance for the state of the West Yiddish language of the time.

Arnold Paucker addresses a similar problem in his analysis of Yiddish translations of early German prose novels (*Volksbücher*).[221] The Yiddish works show great adaptation in the omission and addition of material and motifs, but, as is usually the case with strict translations of one language into a closely related one, the Yiddish texts are greatly influenced by the German originals and use few specifically Yiddish turns of phrase and few Hebrew words. As Paucker points out, however, there is no evidence for identifying these texts as Hebrew-alphabet transliteration from the Roman-alphabet German text, nor one might add for denying the existence of Yiddish *per se*, since the *prologues* to these texts are very clearly Yiddish in vocabulary, grammar, and phraseology. The texts themselves simply participate in the tradition of literary style (*Kunstsprache*) and not in the spoken language.[222]

The same ideological position as that proposed by Marchand is found in the work of two other scholars who have dealt with late medieval/early modern Yiddish adaptations of German chapbooks. In his edition of the Yiddish *Hildebrandlied*, W. B. Lockwood makes no pretense of coming to terms with the theoretical problems addressed by Marchand, but simply calls the language of the text *Jüdisch-deutsch* without definition or discussion, and notes that the Hebrew graphs represent German phones. There is no controversy as far as he is concerned.[223]

John A. Howard on the other hand does devote some attention to the theoretical problems in language identification, but only insofar as he reiterates Marchand's principles and in some cases even applies more stringent restrictions to an identification of the language as Yiddish. In the title of his article on the scholarly misuse of the concept of Spielmann literature in Old Yiddish studies,[224] he calls the literature in this language *altjiddisch*, but in his introductory remarks consistently uses the doublet "hebräisch-deutsche und frühjiddische [or "frühe jiddische"] Literatur."[225]

Once he begins discussion of the topic at hand, however, he uses "jiddische Literatur,"[226] albeit sparingly, until he comes to a consideration of the Cambridge codex, when the inverse doublet "altjiddische oder hebräisch-deutsche Literatur" appears (p. 10). *Dukus Hurnt*, however, "ist ganz einfach ein Stück deutscher Literatur" ("quite simply a piece of German literature," p. 11). His justification of this usage is a summary paraphrase of Marchand's previously published criteria.

In his discussion of the persistence of the Spielmann theory in Old Yiddish studies, he denies that a specifically Yiddish shpilman literature could have existed in the Middle Ages, since the language as such did not exist until after 1450 (pp. 12-13).[227] His argument here is again essentially the same as Marchand's, with the addition of Siskind's misrepresentation of Weinreich's theory of proto-Yiddish. He points out that there was no uniform proto-Yiddish from which all modern Yiddish dialects derive, and then apparently wishes to extrapolate from that point the conclusion that there was no Yiddish during the period in question.[228] He attempts to supply further evidence for this contention by pointing to the absence of contemporary satirical diatribes mocking the language of the Jews, adduces as authority the claim made by I. Abrahams a century ago in his layman's historical overview that in the Middle Ages the Jews spoke a German indistinguishable from their Christian neighbors (pp. 13-14),[229] holds fast to Marchand's interpretation of *loshn ashkenaz* as German (p. 15),[230] and concludes that Yiddish did not exist during that period. In the end he outdoes even Marchand's criteria by maintaining: "Es wäre keinesfalls unmöglich, daß . . . jüdischer Inhalt, deutscher Dialekt und hebräische Buchstaben in einem einzigen Dokument zusammenfallen, ohne daß die Sprache Jiddisch wäre" ("It would not at all be impossible for . . . Jewish content, German dialect and Hebrew letters to come together in a single document, without the language's being Yiddish," p. 18). By the end of the article the language and literature have been so stripped of all conceivably non-German traits that they are suddenly designated simply "altjüdisch" (p. 20), which, out of the context of this particular article, one would most likely decode as a reference to ancient Hebrew or Aramaic. Ironically, however, here it simply means German language and/or literature that happens to pass through the mouths or pens of Jews.

The same underlying program is at work in his article on the *Fortunatus* text, although, perhaps due to its appearance in the journal *Yiddish*, it is not so blatantly anti-Yiddish. He first maintains that the Hebrew-alphabet text agrees "virtually verbatim . . . in both language and content" with a German edition of 1680 in the British Museum (p. 16). But from the summary discussion of the types of adaptation undertaken in the Hebrew-alphabet version, it become clear that Howard's sense of "verbatim" with respect to content is as unique as that concept itself, for as he himself notes more than once in the brief article, "the tale has been adapted for a Jewish audience," including consistent adaptation and/or omission of Christian material, phrases, terms, and episodes. Despite the fact that it is a "virtually verbatim" reproduction of the posited extant source text, it is nonetheless by no means "merely a slavish transcription of the German text" (p. 17). But (again) despite even that fact, "the language cannot be designated as any other than the standard German of the day simply rendered in the Hebrew alphabet. The Bodleian text is not a Yiddish *Fortunatus*."[231] Even so, there are numerous linguistic forms in the text that are clearly open to identification as Yiddish, such as *mir/nit/jo* (inconsistently) as opposed to standard German *wir/nicht/ja*. Howard counters with the typically Marchandian notion, however, that since these forms are also characteristic of some German dialects, they are not Yiddish (p. 17). Conveniently for his argument, he does not deem it relevant to indicate whether there is consistency in the German dialect used (in either of the texts), whether these German "dialectal" forms are present in the German text, or if they were substituted for the "standard" forms by the Jewish adapter.

Finally it is necessary at least to mention four additional scholars whose work seems somewhat anachronistic in context, but which also illustrates the methodological pluralism of approaches to Old Yiddish studies at any given period: Siegmund Wolf's *Jiddisches Wörterbuch*, Werner Weinberg's recent article on "Jüdischdeutsch," and the edition of *Akedas Yitskhok* by Percy Matenko and Samuel Sloan. Wolf's dictionary, published in 1962, could, in light of its method and argumentation, have been published a century ago without having been out of place.[232] Although he calls the language "Jiddisch" in the title of the book, Wolf immediately implies that "Jüdisch-deutsch" is the more appropriate name, since even Jews have called the language by that name (p. 7). The language is said to be a *Mischsprache* based primarily on Middle High German and early New High German (p. 8).[233] Older manuscripts and printed works in this language are, according to Wolf, simply German in the Hebrew alphabet; the alphabet is "das einzig Jüdische" in such texts and thus "Jüdisch-deutsch" is a better term for them than Yiddish (p. 8). West Yiddish is said to be a misnomer, since it designates merely a German dialect and not a language (pp. 12-13). Yiddish did not become a separate language until the Jews moved to Eastern Europe, at which time their language was merely a "jüdisch gefärbtes Deutsch" ("Jewish-tinged German"); this German dialect was then influenced by the Slavic languages (p. 15). The inadequacies of his conclusions on such points are made especially clear through an examination of his general method, two examples of which may suffice here: 1) in order to have free reign in interpreting the texts phonetically, he attempts to demonstrate that the Hebrew alphabet is incapable of reflecting German phonetics (primarily vowels), which is especially problematic since early writers "thought" they were writing German (p. 16), and thus wanted to preserve the German *Schriftbild* though not the phonetics of German. His table of consonants, listed to demonstrate this latter point, is indeed problematic for his argument, since in all innocence it refutes his claim: Hebrew ש = *sch* hardly preserves the *Schriftbild*, but on the contrary does represent the posited phonetic form accurately; 2) he prints all Yiddish entries in his dictionary spelled as if they were German: e.g. אויף = auf, ש = *sch*. Thus he makes no attempt to indicate the Yiddish graphemic or phonemic system, but rather presents *modern* Yiddish as if it were (a slightly dialectal variant of) modern German.

Weinberg seems to view the entire problem of linguistic nomenclature as one of the natural development vs. artificial imposition of terms; his goal is to rehabilitate the "natural" term *Jüdischdeutsch* as the name for the German mixed with some Yiddish expressions and idioms spoken in Western Europe after the distinct dialect/language Yiddish was no longer spoken.[234] His argument seems ultimately to have a personal basis, despite the barrage of scholarly apparatus issuing forth from his argument. Along the way, numerous elements of the assimilationist argument appear, for instance, that the name "Yiddish" may legitimately apply only to the language of the Ashkenazim that developed under Slavic influence after their move to Eastern Europe in the sixteenth century; up until that time their language had been German, and those who remained behind in Germany continued to speak German, until their language was corrupted by Yiddish-speaking Eastern European Jews who moved back to the West (pp. 266-267). Nor is this tendency surprising, for Weinberg is ultimately arguing in favor of his native dialect and the perceptions of the speakers of that dialect (including himself): Westphalian Jews of his youth viewed Yiddish as a foreign language – the language of Eastern European Jews; they viewed their own association with Yiddish to be closer than with other foreign languages only on an emotional level (pp. 254-256); but they designated their own speech *Jüdischdeutsch*, while the terms *Ostjiddisch* and *Westjiddisich* were unknown terms to them.

Thus for him the perceptions of the native speaker are determinative, as they also were for previous scholars who claimed that the Ashkenazim spoke German since they called their language *taytsh*, or that they spoke *Jüdisch* since that was allegedly (but not actually) their name for the language, or that any and all of them spoke *yidish* from the instant of 'birth' of Ashkenazic civilization, since that is what (many) modern speakers call the language. This problem is obviously not nearly as simple as Weinberg and the others sometimes pretend, but at the same time, it hardly seems unreasonable that the native speaker's perception of the identity, integrity, and name of his/her native language is somehow relevant. Even so, the linguist need not be ruled by that perception, for among the linguist's tasks are the determination of linguistic relationships beyond the experience or interest of the layman native speaker: the native speaker's designation of the language as *zhargon* or *mame loshn*, in their nineteenth-century usages, clearly identify the language in question as Yiddish, but that need not have any bearing on the linguist's naming of the language, *if* another name is more accurate for his/her purposes.

Weinberg extends the bounds of his argument to take this unmentioned objection into account by including lists of scholars who used the name *Jüdischdeutsch* and its equivalents in other languages throughout the ages as proof of its legitimacy; he notes that its use in Latin (*Hebraeo-Germanica/Teutonica, Judaeo-Germanica/Teutonica*, etc.) since the early sixteenth century also lent the term a certain amount of prestige in its later competition with "Yiddish"; it further appeared in language textbooks and glossaries written in German, and, interestingly, he also finds it relevant to give two separate lists of *Jewish* scholars who have used the term, as if their Jewishness were to lend their judgment more weight.[235] Yet later in the article this view is again modified in his response to Maks Weinreich's rejection of the notion of Zunz, Steinschneider, Perles, and Güdemann that Yiddish and Middle High German are identical. Weinreich so argues because these scholars had neither any scholarly interest in Yiddish nor in fact any knowledge whatever of the actual language. Weinberg objects that neither of these points is relevant, but rather only the fact that they call the language *Jüdischdeutsch* (p. 268).

The artificial imposition of the name "Yiddish" came about, according to Weinberg, as a result of the campaigns waged by Birnbaum and Weinreich: after World War II there was a general attempt to view Yiddish as a unified linguistic unit, and thus the name "Yiddish" came to dominate, so much so that the second postwar generation "ist diesem Namenszwang fast gänzlich erlegen" ("has all but completely succumbed to this terminological tyranny," p. 272). Weinberg indicates that he is aware of the fact that to use *Jüdischdeutsch* fifteen years after World War II is to risk being labeled "altmodisch oder gar dilettantisch." With this artifical revision of the name, he remarks, there was also necessary a revision of attitudes toward the history and development of the language, such that the old notions of early Yiddish/*Jüdischdeutsch* as being merely Middle High German with scattered Hebrew borrowings were no longer accepted as legitimate. He would apparently also like to rehabilitate these notions, for he reverts to Marchandian word counts and to Marchandian interpretations of such word counts. In so doing, he generally ignores or makes light of the studies by Birnbaum, Weinreich, and Dreeßen, especially regarding the two literary standards and thus relative paucity of Hebrew words in older texts as an indication of a particular stylistic register (pp. 268-270), which he calls "die alte 'apologetische' . . . Deutung." He attempts little argument here, but seems content with polemic alone, consisting in large part of lambasting unnecessarily frequent and lengthy quotations taken out of context.

The primary problem for Weinberg is the displacement of *Jüdischdeutsch* by "West Yiddish," the origins of which he traces (p. 273) to Maks Weinreich,[236] N. Prylucki's "mayrefyidish,"[237] M. Mieses' "westj. = westjiddisch, die ehemalige Mundart der ethnographisch deutschen Juden"[238] and Birnbaum's "westjidd."[239] Weinberg nonetheless attempts to make the claim that since none of these uses is emphasized or defined as a new term by these scholars, none is really conscious of creating a new term or changing established terminology, and thus their use of these terms is nothing of note, and the implications may be ignored. This notion does not bear close scrutiny.

The development of the term "West Yiddish" passed through several stages (pp. 274-275): 1) *Jüdischdeutsch* can no longer be used for East Yiddish; 2) "Yiddish" includes *Jüdischdeutsch*; 3) West Yiddish and East Yiddish are both geographical/dialectal and historical/etymological designations; 4) there is an antipathy toward *Jüdischdeutsch*; 5) "West Yiddish" comes to dominate, but *Jüdischdeutsch* continues to be used. In the end Weinberg argues for a restricted use for *Jüdischdeutsch*: when it is a matter of "a self-referential aspect of the earlier language of the German Jews that is not being considered as part of a larger historical, philological, or geographical unity."[240] West Yiddish is to be preferred in cases where distinctions such as geographical, temporal, lexical, phonetic, grammatical, or literary are to be made. Furthermore, he maintains, the remains of the idiom in the West are to be called *Jüdischdeutsch*, since they are not the same language as East Yiddish, and especially becauses speakers of Yiddish will be "angered" by the designation of these "kümmerlichen Reste" with the name of their language, while speakers of *Jüdischdeutsch* would object just as vehemently to the designation of their language as Yiddish. He claims (p. 278) that this problem has become especially acute now that Yiddish as a term has won, for it should not be allowed to usurp further territory and be charged with "Expansionspolitik, Sprachimperialismus, Fanatismus und Arroganz." Perhaps such emotional outbursts should best be seen in the light of his initial anecdote: he simply does not wish his native dialect to be designated with that term of opprobrium *Jiddisch*, no matter what historical or linguistic affinities they may have. It is ultimately a personal, not a scholarly matter.

The edition by Matenko and Sloan of *Akedas Yitskhok* seems as out of touch with modern research as does Wolf.[241] They generally cite out-dated editions and studies, and offer little justification for their editorial method. They call the text Old Yiddish, and although they mention the relevance of Middle High German in the discussion of their method of transliteration (pp. 44-46), they dwell primarily on modern Yiddish, and it becomes clear that in the actual practice of editing the text, they take almost as many liberties in accommodating the text to modern Yiddish as other editors do in transforming their texts into normalized Middle High German.[242] Most importantly, however, they practice this method seemingly without awareness of the ideological struggle that goes on around them: for them the identity of the language and the implications of that identification are of little moment, and thus their edition serves as an ideological counterpart to Weinberg's and Wolf's work, and at least Wolf and Matenko/Sloan seem utterly oblivious to the scholarly context which they innocently enter. Their publications thus seem almost to hark back to the ideological positions of the initial stage of the scholarly reception of Old Yiddish, when *a priori* assumption sufficed.

Thus we see in the history of the names of Old Yiddish up until recent decades an interesting case of variation on a single methodological and ideological theme. The unargued assumption of the assimilationists that the Old Yiddish language and literature was in fact Middle High German language and literature and thus important in the study of the medieval culture of German Christians and Ashkenazic Jews is an exemplary instance of the ideology of the Wissenschaft des Judentums (and its later permutations). That group was opposed by the Yiddish nationalists (among them Erik and Tsinberg), who saw this literature as the origin of the Yiddish national literary tradition. Yet neither school progressed methodologically beyond its individual ideological concerns, and their arguments differed only in detail, but not in the conception of the essential critical problem to be solved. Nor was this conception of the problem radically transformed by the rise of descriptive linguistic studies, with its notions of objective analysis that could produce verifiable conclusions. Here also, there were at least two sides: Marchand was, for instance, opposed at every turn, but again, as in the first stage, by arguments based on the same conception of the problem, the same initial question, and with the same set of possible conclusions.[243] The inadequacies of this method led to an extreme form of assumed objectivity – as in Althaus' edition – in which the question itself was suppressed, although its all-pervasive, determinative significance remained, as did the set of possible answers to the question.

This determinative significance is the subject of the following chapter, for the intial assumption of the identity and character of the language, revealed in the scholar's choice of a name for the language, continues to determine the ideological course of the scholar's work (especially after that ideology has been "legitimized" by having its research topic identified and named). The magnitude of potential ideological power manifested in projects such as the naming of a language becomes especially apparent when that naming takes place as one of the initial tasks in a project to edit an Old Yiddish text, such that it is rendered accessible to a particular audience. A consideration of the ideological implications of editorial principles in Old Yiddish studies is thus the next step and the focus of the following chapter.

THREE

Alterity, Accessibility, Audience, Alphabet: On Editing Old Yiddish Texts

ONE OF THE MOST basic purposes of text editions of all forms is to render the texts accessible to a wider audience than would be possible if the texts were available only in manuscript. The concept of accessibility is, however, in itself problematic, for in order to achieve its goal, it initially demands a conscious identification of audience. Moreover, just as the expectations of the intended audience condition both form and content of other scholarly and literary genres, so too does this apply to the genre of text editions. In making the text accessible to the intended audience, the editor necessarily manipulates the manuscript text to a greater or lesser degree. Depending on the specific scholarly purpose and audience conceived by the editor, the text may be presented in photographic facsimile, diplomatic transcription, or critical edition, with or without introductory essays of varying length on the manuscript, date and authorship of the text, cultural background, language, metrics, literary evaluation, bibliography, glossary, with or without historico-cultural explanatory notes and textual notes, etc. Even within one sub-genre, critical editions of medieval literary works, the gamut runs from the formidable abundance of apparatuses of, for instance, Manly and Rickert's edition of the *Canterbury Tales*, to the relatively unencumbered, student edition of de Boor's *Nibelungenlied.*[1]

The implication of the notion of accessibility is that the text as extant in manuscript(s) is *in*accessible in some way, for some reason, for some conceivably interested group of readers. The key word is, of course, *accessible*: how is accessibility defined by the editor with respect to the text s/he edits? What critical principles are brought to bear in order to render the text accessible? One might generalize on the relative accessibility of various kinds of editions, thus: the further one moves from the manuscript, the more accessible the text becomes – the facsimile edition is in many cases more accessible than the manuscript only by virtue of its wider distribution (each manuscript exists by definition as a unique phenomenon, even if direct copies are extant, since they necessarily differ from the original), since the text is often distorted in some way through the format of the edition (e.g., reduction of the size of the original) or poor photographic reproduction of faded original script. But in any case, the facsimile is the least accessible of the editions (according to the present provisional definition) simply by virtue of its requiring some degree of paleographical expertise on the part of the reader. The diplomatic edition takes the next step toward accessibility by eliminating the paleographical barrier and presenting the reader with a printed text, which is, depending on the rigor of the editor's diplomatic principles, a more or less faithful transliteration of the manuscript text into (for Western European texts and audiences, usually) modern Roman typeface. Such editions still contain barriers to accessibility, however, in that they often do not resolve abbreviations in the text, punctuate (or repunctuate according to modern principles), do not emend passages rendered unintelligible in the process of textual transmission, or standardize spelling and capitalization. The reader may thus still be confronted with a radically "Other" kind of text. The editor of the critical text usually performs the just-listed tasks for the reader and offers in addition explanatory notes on linguistic, cultural and paleographical matters, textual notes on variants in other manuscripts, literary parallels and sources in other works, a glossary, a full introductory essays. A subset of the critical edition is the student edition, with a relatively "laundered" text, usually based on a previously published standard critical edition, but now relatively or completely free of textual notes and purged of textual cruces. One further step can be taken to make the text even more accessible – translation into a modern language with or without a facing-page original text.

Thus in each successive kind of edition (which in practice are not so very clearly distinguished), the text is made more accessible - at least in the sense that it is accessible to a progressively wider potential audience, ending, in the last case, with a possible audience of all readers of the given modern language. But this view of accessibility - the size of the potential audience - is obviously not the only definition possible, nor the most pertinent scholarly definition. Each kind of edition serves a different purpose, even if the makeup of its audience overlaps with that of another type of edition. A Chaucer scholar may, for instance, use Manly/Rickert's eight volumes for some research tasks, Robinson's edition for others and as a class text for university courses in Chaucer, and Lumiansky's modern translation of the *Canterbury Tales* in literary survey courses.[2] The students in this latter course would, on the other hand, have little use for Manly/Rickert. The *Nibelungenlied* scholar might cite de Boor's text in an article on a general literary problem, but would need to consult an edition with fuller textual apparatus for linguistic or textual studies.[3] Thus each type of edition and each particular text within that type is tailored to the *needs* of the audience as conceived by the editor. Yet often the conception of audience is not just based on projected needs, but is also conditioned by the national, disciplinary, or general cultural tradition of textual editing, sometimes even by the editorial tradition of a particular text.

Each successive stage in rendering the text more accessible in the above-described sense requires and thus empowers the editor to manipulate the raw material of the manuscript text to a greater extent, in transcribing, printing, normalizing, standardizing, and repunctuating the text. We generally accept some or all of these procedures simply as the editor's task. But even the ostensibly most innocuous editorial decision and mechanical task is interpretive, an exercise of judgment, and thus also of editorial power. As in the exercise of any form of power, here, too, there can be abuse: depending on their degree of extremity, unity of purpose, and guiding principle, the editor's interpretations can be(come) ideological. The critical editor can, for instance, base the edition not on the manuscript(s), but rather on other (facsimile, diplomatic, or critical) editions; s/he can conflate readings from various manuscripts to produce a text that was never written, read, or heard by anyone in the Middle Ages, s/he can reject attested manuscript readings as "corrupt," "inappropriate," or "late medieval additions/emendations." The resultant text is ostensibly accessible, but can in fact be so far removed from the medieval text as to be a different literary work altogether – a "medieval" text that is in essence composed by a nineteenth or twentieth-century textual editor. Such editorial practices are relatively rare, although the last century has seen several of them. Their practice seems to skew the entire notion of accessibility through editing.

For both textual and cultural reasons, the problem of accessibility with regard to Old Yiddish literary texts is somewhat more complex than usual and than these oversimplified remarks concerning textual editing in general indicate. A simple list of some basic facts of the Old Yiddish textual tradition demonstrates the potential for the abuse of editorial power: Old Yiddish manuscripts are written in the Hebrew alphabet; yet at the time that the traditional Hebrew orthography was adapted for use in representing Old Yiddish texts, it had no established tradition of graphemically representing the vowels of a non-Hebrew language text. Vowel pointing in Old Yiddish texts is very rare; and only five graphemes represent all Old Yiddish vowels (in addition to their consonantal functions). Thus specific identification of vowel phonemes is, except in rare cases, never transparent and is in many, perhaps most, cases all but impossible. Yet the determination of vowel quality plays perhaps the most important role in the identification of medieval, Continental Germanic dialects. As a further complication, the Old Yiddish *literary* language in general resembles its Germanic determinant much more closely than does modern Yiddish. In addition, the literature itself has thematic and formal affinities to both Middle High German and medieval Hebrew literature, as well as to the later tradition of Yiddish literature. Thus the editor's freedom to manipulate the text to conform to his/her own conception of language, dialect, cultural origin, and derivation of literary form is almost without limit. This manipulation already begins at the level of grapho-phonemic interpretation of vowels, for most editors of Old Yiddish texts have chosen to transcribe or transliterate the texts into Roman. This seemingly innocuous procedure of transposition can, for instance, transform the alien (to a general audience) appearance of the Hebrew alphabet, which lacks a complete and consistent system of vowel graphemes, into the (for some audiences) more familiar Roman alphabet, with the grapho-phonemic system of, for instance, Middle High German, early modern German, or some form of modern Yiddish. And second, as sketched in chapter one above, there is also a problem of cultural identity and audience identity in Old Yiddish studies, since there is no pre-defined audience (e.g., no "national" audience) and no "national" tradition of scholarship.

Thus to an even greater degree than in text editions from other medieval literary traditions, the Old Yiddish editor must not just identify his/her audience, but even to some extent *invent* it, as a composite potential *scholarly* audience.[4] This invention of audience is a powerful factor in establishing criteria for editorial principles, and by the same token, the editor's conception of the text conditions his/her view of the possible audience. Both factors thus mutually influence the final result: the text edition.

Due to the extreme situation in Old Yiddish studies and to the range of problems both internal and external to the text, the major task of the editor of Old Yiddish texts has become something quite different from that set by editors of texts in other classical and medieval languages, even as those tasks evolve due to changes in methodological climate. To provide an illustrative contast: traditionally, the Old Yiddish editor has not sought either the archetype (in Lachmann's or Housman's sense) or the best manuscript (in the standard sense of textual criticism) of the text. The editor has not been concerned with constructing a stemma or collating readings – at least not as the *primary duty* in producing a text edition. S/he normally does perform these tasks, but usually only after and as an adjunct to the primary task s/he sets for her/himself, which is to identify, define and justify the identification of the *language* of the text, as explicated above in chapter two. This may be surprising as the editor's primary task, but it is understandable in the historical context of Yiddish studies: it is a response to the culturally orphaned status of the Yiddish language, the existence of which scholars have historically either denied as an independent language, or acknowledged as such only to set it up as an object of vituperation – as the modern bastardized corruption of the "pure" Middle High German idiom adopted by Jews in the Middle Ages. Voices in opposition to (but still defined by) this view have been vehement and just as ideological in proclaiming Yiddish the fountainhead of the modern language and literary culture. And thus one finds in this latter group a belated, twentieth-century attempt to do for Yiddish what early nineteenth-century nationalistic Romanticism had done for the medieval languages and literatures of France, Germany, and England.

Under slightly different banners, these two columns of Yiddish scholars still march and still edit texts, and one may with some qualification categorize their general projects as attempts not so much to provide an answer to a single, specific, and seemingly irrelevant question, i.e., the one dealt with above in chapter two – Old Yiddish or Middle High German? – but rather to justify and support that initial decision by means of presenting a text that confirms it. The answer to the question concerning language identity is ostensibly rather innocuous and certainly insignificant when viewed from the perspective of traditional principles of textual editing, but it in fact has a profound and pervasive influence on all remaining tasks and decisions of the editor. As one editor of Old Yiddish texts has pointed out, the answer to this question quite simply predetermines all further editorial decisions.[5] One need only recall the results of Frings' transformation into a constructed Old Limburg dialect of Heinrich von Veldeke's Middle High German adaptation of the *Aeneid* or Krogmann's transformation into Lombardic of the *Hildebrandslied*,[6] in order to recognize the full implications of such ideological editing, based on the identification of the putatively original language of the text, that is, the editor's forcing a text into a preconceived form in spite of a preponderance of manuscript evidence to the contrary. In these two cases, as in Old Yiddish editions, the editor's decision as to the original language of the text is paramount and determinative, and leads not just to a textual but also a cultural transformation of the document, with a concomitant radical redefinition of the audience.[7]

At this point let us note the ubiquitous litany of Old Yiddish scholars, which rises in a multilingual choral refrain, calling for texts to be *accessible* (French/English), *zugänglich*, or *tsutritlekh*. The attainment of accessibility seems at times indeed to be the ultimate *telos* of Old Yiddish studies, and the editor's procedure in making the text accessible to the intended audience is as extreme as the circumstances demand. There have traditionally been three types of Old Yiddish text editions: 1) Those whose editors consider the text Middle High German that was written in the Hebrew alphabet. They transcribe (or as is often claimed, "retranscribe," since a Middle High German text in Roman is posited as the "original") the text into the Roman alphabet, "reconstructing" its putative original Middle High German linguistic form, i.e., almost invariably "normalized Middle High German," that artificial dialect of Middle High German that was more or less invented in the intellectual climate of romantic idealism by nineteenth-century philological editors and which has since become the standard of Middle High German text editions.[8] The introduction to such an edition deals with the history of Middle High German literature and the derivation of the given text from that tradition. The intended audience (often directly identified) consists of students and scholars of medieval German literature, for whom the Hebrew alphabet would, from this critical perspective, be no more than an artificial obstacle to be removed by the editor, so that they may again have access to "their" literature.[9] 2) Those whose editors consider the text one of the earliest examples of the literary tradition of the Yiddish language and its proper audience as those interested in that tradition. The text is normally printed in the Hebrew alphabet with or without an attempt to modernize the language for the reading convenience of the specialist and non-specialist, Yiddish-reading, intended audience, and with or without conjecture concerning the vowels represented by the Hebrew graphemic system. The introduction to the edition deals with the Jewish cultural and literary context from which the text, according to this editor, derived. The audience is generally conceived of as Yiddishists *and* the educated Jewish lay reader. 3) Those who claim to avoid all such arguments of cultural and linguistic identification and merely present the text "as it is in the manuscript," so that linguistic and literary scholars can themselves analyze the text.[10] Strangely, however, with few exceptions, this kind of diplomatic edition of Old Yiddish has been somewhat less than rigorously diplomatic, since most such editions are in Roman transcription/transliteration. Thus although such editors ostensibly take no position regarding the language or cultural origin of the text (that is, the determinant problems of text types one and two), and often even go to great lengths to document the objectivity of their studies, they must necessarily make assumptions concerning these problems in order to perform even the most basic editorial tasks. These editors call their pose of pure objectivity and the entire notion of objective, mechanical transliteration into question when they, as is almost always the case, reject all previous systems of transcription/transliteration as inappropriate, inaccurate, interpretive, and ideological, and devise an *ad hoc* system for use in the edition – which in turn does no more nor less than support their own ideological arguments. For in the very rejection of the appropriatenes of other systems, the editor has *eo ipso* demonstrated that such systems are by nature interpretive. This practice also has major repercussions for the definition of the editor's audience.

Facsimile editions of Old Yiddish texts are few. Diplomatic editions in the strict sense (i.e., not in transcription/transliteration) are even less common; critical editions are in the majority, but exist in name only, since in fact they consist by and large of translations into twentieth-century constructions of Middle High German, archaic modern Yiddish, or transliterations into arbitrary grapho-phonemic systems based on the Roman alphabet, but which are nonetheless practically illegible even for the trained linguist; this last practice is especially counterproductive, since one must learn a new system for each of the dozens of relevant editions, articles, and reviews.

In the following pages, an attempt will be made to identify the specific nature of the various kinds of editions of Old Yiddish texts, their intended audience, the appropriateness of the conception of that audience, the editor's success in making the text accessible, and the resultant transformations of the text in the process of this editorial manipulation. Thus the three principal types of editions will form the primary organizational schema of the analysis, but that schema must be adapted to take into account the demands of the scholarly dialogue that developed out of the publication by Fuks of the Cambridge codex, which elicited responses representing all three textual types. And since the problem, broadly defined, concerns the conception of the old Yiddish *text*, and not simply particular editions of a given text, the chapter will also take into account conceptions of the text expressed not just by editors *per se* but also by a wide range of scholars who have dealt with that problem.

As was the case with the chosen designation of the language, so too with the conception of the text among adherents of the tenets of assimilationism, whether in the early part of the century when the political battle between the various parties of Zionism, nationalism, and assimilationism was openly waged, or more recently when only the general theoretical principles (though no longer the socio-political goals of these parties) still obtain.[11]

In his study of primarily nineteenth-century Yiddish literature, Leo Wiener notes that since his book is intended for the general public and not for lingusts, "there was no choice left for the transliteration of Judeo-German words but to give it the modified orthography of the German language"; and to render the texts more accessible still, he uses the Lithuanian dialect of Yiddish, since it is "least distinct from literary German" (p. xxxii). His Yiddish texts are thus consciously and admittedly adapted (practically translated) into German. This practice is not exceptional, especially in books with a broadly conceived audience, nor is it even a period-specific occurrence: Waxman still follows the same practice in 1943, even in citing the titles of modern Yiddish-language publications and institutions – "Schriften" for "shriftn"; "Yiddisch" for "yidish" (in the name of YIVO!).[12] While the practice is in principle ideologically unjustifiable, it lacks the insidious misrepresentation inherent in the similar practice in the presentation of *Old* Yiddish texts, where the phonetic system is all but unrecoverable, rendering any transcription a radical interpretation. The transcription of modern Yiddish texts into a generally German orthography is thus, perhaps by the very nature of its conscious, blatant ideology, somewhat less offensive.[13]

The primary early spokesman for the editorial principles of text type one was Landau, in his edition of *Vidvilt* ("Artus Hof"). He certainly views his task as making his subject accessible, for he notes that few scholars have dealt with Hebrew-German literature before, primarily because the subject requires one to know both German and Hebrew literature.[14] The question is, of course, how does Landau make the material accessible, and in answering that question, we can determine his intended audience. In his designation and definition of the language, Hebrew-German (i.e., Middle High German as spoken by Jews), Landau's goal of accessibility already begins to become clear. As noted above in chapter two, he considers Hebrew-German literature merely German literature written in the Hebrew alphabet. Thus when Hebrew-German is printed in the Roman alphabet, it is stripped of its "Hebrew-" qualification and becomes merely German. And he does print the text in Roman, without discussion of the Hebrew-alphabet original.[15] Landau's argument consistently denies the cultural integrity and especially the alterity of Jewish civilization, while at the same time simply reprojecting that alterity onto another aspect of historical Jewish culture. Not only did he view the medieval Ashkenazim as German in culture and language (and claim that medieval German Jews even knew German literature better than did the Germans), but he moreover denied that Hebrew-German literature had any Jewish content or that its themes differed from those of Middle High German literature. For Landau, Yiddish (even modern Yiddish) is relevant only for the light that it can shed on medieval German, due to its many archaisms.[16] He constantly reiterates that the language of the medieval Ashkenazim was "pure German."

Even in the choice of type fonts used to print the various languages cited in his introduction to the edition of *Vidvilt*, his assimilationist tendencies are manifest: quotations in Yiddish are transliterated into Roman and printed just as are those from German - i.e., in Gothic, while cited English is in italics: thus even in typeface, Yiddish has "become" German. He calls the script of the manuscript "Hebrew-German cursive writing" (pp. xxxii-xxxiii) and does not note that this is in fact the Ashkenazic cursive form of the *Hebrew* alphabet. The difference in terminology is slight, but the ultimate difference in meaning is significant. He abbreviates the name of the language – Hebrew-German – to "H.-G.", which bears a striking resemblance to Landau's "target language" and its standard abbreviation "M.H.G.," thus assimilating the language toward German even in his abbreviated designation of the language.

In his discussion of the phonetic characteristics of the text, Landau takes little note of the fact that the text was written in the Hebrew alphabet; in the context of his denial of the alterity of the literature, a discussion of this topic would be at cross-purposes to his goal and would perhaps offend or at least confuse his intended audience.[17] Generally his discussion of phonetics is less than enlightening, even in the context of early twentieth-century linguistics: the author of *Vidvilt* "did not like" diphthongization and umlaut and thus omitted them at every opportunity (p. lii). Since both of these phonemic phenomena are expected in Middle High German documents of this period, their absence from this text would be damaging to Landau's "Hebrew-German" theory, if in fact they were clearly absent. But Landau sidesteps the entire complex issue of graphemic representation of the desired phonemes and avoids mentioning the complexities of a discussion of the potential use of the Hebrew alphabet in representing umlaut by appealing to the linguistic likes and dislikes of the author (more likely – scribe).

He discusses the phonetic system of the text from the perspective of Middle High German and cites the standard Middle High German grammars as authorities (i.e., just as Althaus does two generations later), which in the context of his study is certainly legitimate, since he identifies Hebrew-German as essentially Middle High German. The phonetic system differs slightly from the German standard, but from this perspective, it is nonetheless classifiable, rule-governed (even by Middle High German rules), not foreign, not other. At one point, however, confusion results from Landau's inconsistency, for in explaining the distinction between /man/ and /men/, he incongruously opts for accuracy: he notes that /a/ in "man" is represented in the manuscript, while the /e/ of "men" is not, and one can thus distinguish the two words (p. lix). He does not say how this /a/ is represented, nor does he indicate what this whole discussion can possibly mean without a discussion of the graphemic system of the original and of his transcription system. Furthermore, he notes that "fro sin" governing the accusative case in *Vidvilt* is a grammatical mistake, since according to the standard grammars of Middle High German, the construction must govern the genitive (p. lxiii). He thus manages to turn potential evidence for the characteristically Yiddish loss of genitive into a simple grammatical mistake. This point is not without ideological implications either: as a harbinger of the later putative corruption of the German language by Jews and as a justification for further editorial emendation of the text.[18]

According to Landau, the tale itself is derived in its entirety from sources in German romances (pp. lxvi-lxxxv) and not from Jewish sources nor even from sources in any other language. It is thus purely German in language, content, sources, and underlying grammar. He does not dwell on the task of rendering the text accessible, because he does not propose the text as one that is necessarily inaccessible. In general Landau's introduction is a systematic attempt to deny the alterity of *Vidvilt* and Old Yiddish ("Hebrew-German").

The attention directed to Old Yiddish by Jechiel Bin-Nun was not that of an editor *per se*, but his usage in the presentation of texts in his study is nonetheless interesting as an example of an ostensibly pro-Yiddishist but implicitly assimilationist ideology.[19] When the pronunciation of the language of a given Yiddish text is known, he transcribes it into Roman, according to the phonetic rules of that form of Yiddish. Yet since the pronunciation of Old Yiddish is unknown, he notes, it is necessary to "transcribe" those texts according to the orthographic rules of modern German; thus he essentially translates the texts into modern German, while maintaining that the process is mere transcription.

As was pointed out above in chapter two, Franz J. Beranek's 1947-1948 article seems a belated assimilationist *apologia.*[20] It bears the marks of the immediate post-war period, but at the same time displays a remarkably patronizing Germanistic stance. In order to accomplish the task he sets for the Germanistic study of Yiddish, a task of "good will and penitence" (p. 170), he proposes an Institut zur Erforschung der jiddischen Sprache. The field of study is, according to his view, ripe – "es ist noch so gut wie alles zu tun" ("it is practically an untilled field," p. 170), and he thus displays either ignorance of or reprehensible disregard for the multitude of varied work already done by 1947, or perhaps he is simply carried away by what in tone seems to be an impassioned sermon. One of the tasks of the proposed institute would be the publication of Yiddish books - in German translation, or at least in Roman transliteration (p. 174); no possibility of publishing Yiddish books in the original is mentioned. Such an institute in general would be an attempt to recompense world Jewry, a reconfirmation of the universality of the German scholarly community, and also an intellectual reparation to the Jewish people by the German people. This kind of nationalism in the guise of atonement for the irreparable excesses of another era of nationalism hardly past is nothing less than macabre.

Viewed in terms of its educational project, the program of Siegmund Wolf's *Jiddisches Wörterbuch* is perhaps even more ideological than was Landau's editorial method or Beranek's vision of the institutionalization of Jiddistik under the aegis of a nationalistically conceived, penitential, and purely German scholarship. The book includes fifty-five pages of Yiddish texts, one hundred pages of dictionary entries, plus facsimiles and a bibliography. As a dictionary, a reference book, and a putatively definitive (though brief) treatment of the language, it purports to provide the interested party with the tools necessary to "deal with" the language. Wolf attempts to render Yiddish accessible to an audience that is easily identifiable on the basis of his remarks on the obscurity and inaccessibility of the Hebrew alphabet: "Diese ausschließliche Wiedergabe des Jiddischen in Schrift und Druck durch hebräische Buchstaben dient heute der Germanistik als willkommene Begründung für seine völlige Nichtbeachtung" ("This exclusive representation of Yiddish in script and print with Hebrew letters today serves Germanistic as a welcome justification for ignoring it altogether," p. 7). His intended audience is obviously Germanists, who apparently will no longer be able to ignore Yiddish once the vocabulary and texts have been published by Wolf in Roman transcription.[21]

Needless to say, he was in large part wrong: Germanists have not by and large become Yiddishists of any ilk. And his other assumption is equally erroneous: scholars and pseudo-scholars had been rendering Yiddish texts "accessible" by means of Roman transcription for at least a century before him without interesting the broad spectrum of Germanists, and such was even the case during the nineteenth century, when, according to Wolf (one wonders how accurately), a basic knowledge of Hebrew was an integral part of the elementary training of Germanists. At any rate, he justifies the use of the Roman alphabet with the claim that the basic vocabulary of Yiddish is Middle High German and early New High German (p. 8). Here, too, one of the recurring ironies of the Germanist version of the accessibility topos is touched on by Wolf: his intended audience is composed of students and scholars of German language and literature, who know nothing of Yiddish language and literature because of their simple inability to read texts printed in the Hebrew alphabet (Wolf implies that this inability is justified) and their disinterest in learning, or perhaps inability to learn, the Hebrew alphabet. Wolf thus assumes, as do most scholars who publish on any topic, that his subject is somehow valuable and that his intended audience is intellectually curious and competent and is or can be interested in his topic. He nevertheless accuses this same audience of willful ignorance, incompetence, and irresponsibility; he presents his material to them in laundered form (i.e., in the "German," alphabet), since they will otherwise not have access to it. His stated purpose (p. 9) is to inform Germanists of the Germanic vocabulary of Yiddish, which they had ignored until the present time. He makes the further claim, as had others before him, that the master of Yiddish must be a polyglot, among whose languages Yiddish is nonetheless not mentioned.

Despite his naming the language "Jiddisch" in the title of his dictionary, Wolf quite simply pretends that Yiddish is German and constructs his dictionary accordingly. In order to have free reign in interpreting the texts phonetically, he attempts to demonstrate that the Hebrew alphabet is incapable of reflecting German phonetics (primarily vowels), which is especially problematic since early writers "thought" they were writing German (p. 16), and thus wanted to preserve the German *Schriftbild*, though not the phonetics of German - a bizarre claim since this attempt was made using the Hebrew alphabet, since many of the vowels were simply not represented in the Yiddish texts, and since, the table of consonants he provides as evidence for his claim quite innocently and conclusively refutes his claim: Hebrew ש = Roman /sch/ and Hebrew כ = Roman /ch/ hardly preserve the *Schriftbild*, but on the contrary *do* represent the posited phonetic forms accurately.

In his discussion of the vowels (pp. 20-21), Wolf's confusion about the intelligence and needs of his audience, about his material and subject, and about his own argument become painfully obvious. Yiddish vowels are discussed only in terms of which German vowel they *replace* ("steht für...") or as which German vowel they "may be read." He notes (p. 22) that some readers may object to his transcription, but defends it by noting that: 1) a transcription is not a transliteration, 2) the Hebrew alphabet is phonetically "unzulänglich," and 3) Yiddish phonetics is represented in the transcription as accurately as possible on the basis of the inadequacies of the Hebrew alphabet in representing *German* consonants and vowels. Thus he again allows his conception of Yiddish as merely a (mis)representation of German via the Hebrew alphabet to govern his practice. But if, as he claims, he is concerned to represent Yiddish phonetics with the Roman alphabet, how is the putative inadequacy of the *Hebrew* alphabet in representing *German* phonetics relevant? In any case, Wolf's attempts at justification are inadequate to the task, for his "Yiddish dictionary" has turned all Yiddish words into German. אויס, אויף, ש become "aus/auf/sch-". There is no attempt to represent Yiddish phonetic, phonemic, or graphemic information; the dictionary presents Yiddish as modern standard German, with a few slight dialectal deviations. Is this not a further insult to the ignorant, irresponsible

Germanist, who in the first place could not be bothered to learn the Hebrew alphabet, and who must now discover that Yiddish is actually more closely related to standard German than is perhaps Austrian dialect? But this scenario assumes that Wolf's estimate of his audience is accurate; that is, that Germanists are at least as ignorant as he implies. And such has not proven to be the case, as the response to Wolf's book – or rather lack thereof – has demonstrated. And research on what he calls "indubitably the next and most important task of Yiddish studies in Germany" – the study of the dialects of the prefaces of the early printed books in Yiddish (p. 22) – has continued, but without increased intensity. His audience has proven even more intransigent, or rather probably merely more intelligent than he had anticipated and was thus no audience at all for his book.

In the period before the publication of the Cambridge codex, the proponents of text type two were somewhat less numerous than those of type one. Their *a priori* principles are just as unassumingly determinative as those of type one, and they often involve the same kind of operations on texts, albeit with a different goal and a different audience in mind.

Maks Erik notes in his *Geshikhte* that one of the major goals of the book was to make Old Yiddish literature accessible to a wider reading public, in response to a growing interest among his contemporaries in gaining a historical overview of Yiddish literature. He thus attempts to present a survey for both scholars and lay readers (pp. iv-v). This combined audience was in general quite a different group of people from those addressed by Landau, however, simply by virtue of the fact that Erik's book was written in Yiddish. The procedure of rendering the material accessible was nevertheless not that different in principle from Landau's method, for the language of the text was to be accommodated to the intended audience. Erik notes that in order not to plague the reader, he quotes from older literature in modern orthography/language (i.e., modern Yiddish, p. vi).[22]

The gap between theory and practice is perhaps best illustrated in Chaim Ginninger's article on the work of Lévy and Fourquet on the Cambridge codex, which appears in the same volume of *The Field of Yiddish* as did one of Fuks' announcements of the Cambridge Codex and his forthcoming edition.[23] He includes information on Lévy's system of transcription, which had as its main purpose to devise a system "readable by Germanic scholars, but which would distinguish the reconstructed vowels and the consonant values which were based on his conjectures from those which were really attested."

The goal of this transcription was obviously normalized Middle High German, which was Lévy's standard. Ginninger also prints fifteen lines of Fourquet's transcription into normalized Middle High German, as he says, "for lack of the only proper thing, an unravelled Yiddish original" (p. 277). It thus seems that his ideal is to present the text in (Hebrew-alphabet) Yiddish, but lacking that, he is surprisingly ready to compromise and conform to general Germanistic practice by printing the text as normalized Middle High German.

The most extreme example of text type two, the edition by Matenko and Sloan of *Akedas Yitskhok*,[24] appeared after the initial flurry of scholarly activity in response to the publication of the Cambridge codex, but the editors were seemingly oblivious to the methodological controversies raging around them. In their explanation of the transliteration it becomes clear that the editors have been overwhelmed by the complexity of the problems involved in the task: they transliterate Yiddish words of Germanic etymology according to their own system and Yiddish words of Hebrew etymology according to Gesenius' system,[25] except in references from *The Jewish Encyclopaedia*, whose Hebrew transliteration system is preserved in those references, and except in the case of Hebrew ח (misprinted as ת), which is transliterated as "ḥ". But that is all only relevant for Yiddish and Hebrew words prior to about 1912. All modern Yiddish and Hebrew words since that time are transliterated phonetically according to Uriel Weinreich's system in *College Yiddish*.[26] This practice initially seems far more complex than need be.[27]

The primary problem in the study by Matenko and Sloan is the unnoted interpretation involved in their transliteration. Just as Middle High German was the normative *telos* for Landau's transcription and modern German was for Wolf, so modern Yiddish is for Matenko/Sloan: ו is rendered as /u/ or /o/ "as necessary": זון = "zun," not "zon"; קומן = "kumn," not "komn," but תון = "ton," not "tun." The practice of taking modern Yiddish as the norm goes even beyond such cases of grapho-phonemic interpretation to cases of putative emendation to conform to modern Yiddish: they argue for the transliteration of the nominal suffix ניש as *-niš* (stanza 25, 1. 4), as opposed to the Middle High German form *-nisse*, "because this pronunciation seems to have become universal in Yiddish at an early period" (p. 53, n. 11). The note is confusing for a number of reasons, not the least of which is their positing of "universal" phonetic developments on the basis of evidence that is anything but consistent. Secondly, it seems that they are here attempting to justify an emendation of manuscript evidence for *-nisse*; but in fact the manuscript clearly reads ניש at this point![28]

The most significant contribution to the development of editorial practice in Old Yiddish came as a result of Fuks' publication of the Cambridge codex, for that publication generated more scholarly interest in the topic than has any other in Old Yiddish studies during the present century. Fuks' *editio princeps* of the codex is an excellent example of the problematic of accessibility. Fuks notes the esoteric nature of the field of Old Yiddish, which requires specialists to have expertise in numerous other fields, among them Judaic culture, Jewish history, Jewish language and literature, geography, distribution of dialects, paleography, orthography, and transliteration. Studying such a manuscript is, he suggests, like solving a puzzle, and is indeed so difficult and demanding that no single person can hope to perform competently in the areas necessary for producing an edition (p. ix). This claim was echoed by many other scholars who reviewed Fuks' rather disappointing attempt at a one-man edition, and it has resurfaced more than once in recent years, at least in practice, if not in stated principle, for team editions have become rather common: Ganz/Norman/Schwarz's (with Birnbaum) *Dukus Hurnt*, Marchand/Tubach's *Yosef*, Matenko/Sloan's *Akedas Yitskhok*. This seems to be a variation on the topos of (Old) Yiddish as a hopelessly inaccessible subject, similar to Wiener's and Wolf's demand that scholars know multiple languages (none of them Yiddish) before claiming to be a competent Yiddishist.[29]

Fuks' solution to the problems of the limitations on individual expertise was a fourfold edition in order to render the manuscript accessible to a broad audience: 1) photographic facsimile, 2) Hebrew square script transliteration, 3) Roman transliteration and, 4) modern German translation. Thus exhausting the possibilities of editorial types noted at the beginning of the present essay (excepting the critical edition), his edition could theoretically have satisfied the requirements of all scholars, students, and lay readers, except those who require either the manuscript itself or a critical edition. Unfortunately, for numerous reasons Fuks' edition satisfied few requirements of few members of his audiences: his facsimile is of little value because it was not photographed under ultra-violet light; his readings and transliterations are far too often inaccurate or incomplete; and his German translation is inaccurate and often simply non-idiomatic. This translation is a fascinating phenomenon in general in Fuks' edition: why include a German translation of an Old Yiddish manuscript (as he identifies the language) to which he writes an English introduction to be published in the Netherlands? What is the intended audience of such a polyglot undertaking? And why does

Fuks defend his inclusion of a German translation as necessary "in order to draw attention to the codex C.Y. beyond the circle of specialists" (p. ix)? That is, one must assume the specialists addressed by such an edition will be able to deal with the text in one or more of its three edited forms (and with the apparatus in English), while the non-specialist who *might* be interested in such a text is thought to be a reader of German rather than, say, the English of the introduction. This is certainly an interesting train of thought.[30] The subsequent history of scholarship on this manuscript and Fuks' edition demonstrate, however, that his inclusion of a German translation was appropriate for part of his potential audience.

His edition seeks primarily to be one of type three, merely presenting the text *per se* without interpretation; but with its Hebrew transliteration, it also approximates type two; and with its modern German translation, it at least makes a bow to the putative needs of the audience of type one. His edition fails as edition type three not just because all editing requires interpretation, but also because, as his introduction makes quite clear, it is a strictly pro-Yiddish ideology that governs this project, which in the prevailing anti-Yiddish context of type three editions, could only lead to the rejection of his edition's legitimacy as an objective transliteration. In this intellectual climate, Fuks' omnibus edition (as the *editio princeps*) could only fail, for it did not address or even acknowledge the legitimate existence of the ideological concerns of those text types.[31]

His transliteration into Roman is called a transliteration into "characters derived from the European writing system" (p. xxxvi).[32] His transliteration is justified as a preservation of the "semiologic system" of the original. Yet his claim that "our sole purpose is the rendering of the text 'as the reading eye sees it,' " and thus that he attempts no interpretation of the material, is somewhat naive in its denial of editorial interpretation, especially in an edition with as many versions of the text as Fuks includes.

To a much greater degree than the texts edited by Fuks, his notions of audience and accessibility occupied his reviewers, which is in fact to be expected. Since he attempted to appeal to a wide audience or in fact several distinct audiences at once with his *editio quadrupartita*, he was bound to displease not just a portion of one scholarly audience (as all editions inevitably do), but a portion of at least four different scholarly audiences and various combinations of those four. Thus the reviewers' response to Fuks is initially an interesting chapter in reception, audience, and accessibility. A common section of these reviews and of the genre in general is, of course, lists of errors or types of errors. It is interesting to note the types found here. The reviewers most often castigate Fuks for his sins of omission rather commission, since they apparently do not understand (or in some cases, one would have to say that they have temporarily suspended such understanding of) either the basic types of editions or the editor's responsibilities in preparing them.

Ganz objects to Fuks' notion of presenting the text "as the reading eye sees it," for this is, the reviewer contends, simply an abdication of editorial responsibility to analyze the orthographic system such that a solid basis for reading and conjecture is presented.[33] Yet Fuks had claimed only to lay the foundation for further philological study, and thus Ganz objects to Fuks' stated purpose *not* to present a critical edition. Certainly there are myriad problems with Fuks' edition, but the fact that a diplomatic edition (even a poor one) is not a critical edition is not one of them. Ganz objects in general to the lack of linguistic analysis in Fuks' edition, on which an edition of the manuscript could be based (p. 247). He thus apparently does not consider Fuks' text an edition. This notion becomes clearer when Ganz suggests that for literary analysis, scholars need a transcription into "conventional MHG or some other system such as the one employed by S. Birnbaum" (p. 248).[34] With the suggestion of Middle High German as a possible transcription model, the leitmotif of the "ignorant Germanist" is established, to recur regularly in the years following - the texts are obviously relevant for medieval Germanists, who, however, apparently cannot make use of any of Fuks' texts, but must wait for a transcription into (apparently) normalized Middle High German. In fact, since Ganz does not identify this audience only as Germanists, we must assume that he envisions this frustrated, expectant audience as all literary scholars, who are unable to proceed on the basis of texts in the raw state (i.e., facsimile or transliteration). It seems thus that it is the necessity for some form of transcription that is paramount. The actual form is, however, irrelevant, or it apparently does not matter for the purpose of literary analysis if the text is translated into a scholarly construct of normalized Middle High German or into another form.

In dealing with and editing Old Yiddish texts, the concepts of transliteration, transcription, and translation are of major significance, and Ganz treats these problems in some detail in criticizing Fuks' practice. For Ganz himself, the concepts are very problematic, as is demonstrated in his critique of Fuks' treatment of איטנא (p. 41, 1.4). Ganz claims that Fuks transliterates the word as "Etten" (p. 247). But in fact Fuks transliterates first into Hebrew square script with the same Hebrew letters, and then into Roman as /'itn'/ and *translates* as "Etten" (I & II, 41). Thus Ganz' objections to Fuks' interpretation of phonological evidence in transliterating the word are irrelevant. This technical misunderstanding would be of minor importance in a review, were it not for the fact that Ganz was to become one of the editors of the "standard edition" of *Dukus Hurnt.*

Forster's review in *German Life and Letters* is interesting not just for its comments on Fuks' edition, but also as a revelation of audience: the edition of the Cambridge codex is thought to be relevant enough to be reviewed for this journal's audience of general Germanists.[35] Forster nevertheless feels compelled to define immediately the limits of his expertise in the field: he knows little Hebrew and has a hobby interest in texts such as *Dukus Hurnt* - as if it were a "crossword puzzle" (p. 276). Three of his eight pages are devoted to a plot summary of *Dukus Hurnt* for his non-medievalist, Germanistic audience. He then deals briefly with the history and possible derivation of character and theme in the work. The text is cited in normalized Middle High German, since the unpointed Hebrew alphabet "is singularly unsuited to the rendering of German sounds" (p. 276). He thus implies by example that the text is to be analyzed not in the form of Fuks' edition, but in Middle High German form. One suspects then that this attitude is also responsible for Forster's assuming that it is relevant to note Fuks' "scanty" knowledge of medieval German (p. 276).

Birnbaum notes the restricted relevance of Fuks' second transliteration (into Roman), which is of little service to non-specialists and "very forbidding."[36] He also points out that Fuks' printed Hebrew text is itself a transliteration and as such, a work of interpretation, not one of mechanical substitution. He remarks as well that errors in Fuks' transliteration and translation are legion and unfortunately cannot be checked by recourse to the half-tone facsimile, which is too faint to be read in all cases.

Schramm calls Fuks' transliterations "Druckwiedergaben" and says his four texts make for the best possible scholarly use.[37] He points out that discrepancies between Fuks' transliteration and translation exist which seem to indicate that the translation was made without the use of ultra-violet light to decipher the manuscript and is thus less complete than the transliteration (p. 213). Fuks is said to be too cautious in refusing to offer conjectural readings on the basis of rhyme, and thus Schramm, like Ganz before him, also ignores Fuks' avowed intent of producing a diplomatic edition. Schramm cites the second poem of the collection ("Paradise") in normalized Middle High German and emends it freely, since the scribe Isaac "spoiled" much of the poem (especially in the rhymes). It is then surprising when after five pages of Middle High German reconstruction, Schramm suddenly shifts to a "versuchsweise angesetzter jiddischer Lautung," only immediately to shift yet again in order to reconstruct "die originale Lautung nach dem Text von Fuks" (p. 219). At least initially it seems that Schramm wishes to shift from normalized Middle High German to Yiddish and thence to a posited "original" form, but there is in fact no shift at all - all texts are simply normalized Middle High German: with umlaut vowels, diphthongs, and long vowels marked with macrons. Thus in order to account for Schramm's seeming inconsistency, we must recognize that his shifts are merely terminological, and not alterations of his transliteration/transcription or editorial method - i.e., for him, normalized Middle High German, Old Yiddish *and* the original form of the text are identical.[38] He denies that Fuks produced more than the raw material that could be used for a critical edition, which would have to be presented in the form of the "reconstructed original" (p. 220) and include emendations and conjectures without "false caution." The edition should be done not in reconstructed normalized Middle High German, in which, as he notes, he cites the texts, but rather in "original Old Yiddish form" (p. 220). (Taking his example as an illustration of this distinction, the difference is, well, only academic.) He notes further that the Germanist who wishes to deal with the texts of this codex in manuscript form for the purpose of textual criticism, historical linguistics, and literary history, need only know Middle High German and the Hebrew alphabet, and "does not necessarily need to be well-travelled *in iudaicis*" (pp. 220-221). But then he strangely remarks that in questions of the literary tradition, the "five religious texts" can be dealt with only by Hebrew scholars - that is, for five of the seven texts contained in the manuscript, the Germanist *sine iudaicis* cannot in fact deal with the literature. Momentarily it seems the texts were accessible, only to be withdrawn again immediately beyond the pale of disciplinary alterity, a border apparently not to be crossed by mere Germanists.

Schwarz, who was later to work with Norman and Ganz on the Tübingen edition of *Dukus Hurnt*, twice expresses thanks to Fuks for attempting such a difficult task[39] – in the context of his pointing out the many failings of Fuks' edition, implying that the given task was too difficult for Fuks. He notes Fuks' difficulties with the attempted translation, and imputes that difficulty to the fact that Fuks is not a

Germanist – i.e., his knowledge of (Middle High) German is not sufficient; on the other hand, he is nevertheless praised for his ability to read Yiddish (p. 330). On the form of the edition, he objects to Fuks' not using Birnbaum's transliteration system[40] and notes that "the primary duty *(Hauptaufgabe)* of the editor" is the presentation of the *Hebrew* text.[41] He then accuses Fuks of having used non-ultraviolet photographs under magnification as the basis of his transcription, instead of ultra-violet photographs (such as the ones that Schwarz owns) or the original under ultra-violet light. He attempts to prove this allegation by quoting two sentences from Fuks' introduction in which the editor remarks on his use of ultra-violet light and the microvist (Fuks, ed., I, xxxvi). Schwarz claims the passage is ambiguous (p. 331). It is not: both here and in the discussion of the damage to the manuscript (I, xxi), it is clear that Fuks read the manuscript under ultra-violet light and microfilm of the manuscript with a microvist. Schwarz's purpose here is not quite clear, since, as everyone who has examined the edition realized, Fuks had certainly committed a sufficient number of errors; there is no need to try to invent new ones. When Schwarz says "Fuks hat also geglaubt, dass die Vergrösserung eines normalen Mikrofilms besser sei, als das Original, das mit Hilfe von ultravioletten Strahlen gelesen wird" ("Thus Fuks believed that the magnification of a normal microfilm was better than the original, read with the aid of ultraviolet rays," p. 331), he betrays either a procrustean inability to evaluate Fuks' work on a scholarly level, or an inability to understand relatively straightforward English prose.

Schwarz concludes by again thanking Fuks for making the text accessible, which would not have been published without him, since, Schwarz claims, no one else would have attempted it. This praise is then transformed into a patronizing jibe, when he immediately claims that there must now be a new edition of "these Yiddish texts in Central German" ("dieser jiddischen Texte in Mitteldeutsch," p. 332), i.e., the one he plans with Norman and Ganz.[42] These last sentences of the review are rather bizarre, for after having claimed that with the exception of Fuks, no one would have attempted such an absurdly difficult task, he announces that three other scholars, himself included, are prepared to do it again immediately. They obviously see an audience that is still unreached or dissatisfied. And, in view of the inordinate editorial attention focused on the codex since Fuks' edition, they were obviously not alone in this opinion.

Schröbler's review remarks on Fuks' insufficient knowledge of both Middle High German and modern German and the consequences thereof for his edition and translation.[43] She praises his non-interpretative transposition, but notes that it must be further analyzed to determine the grapho-phonemic system (p. 142). After a lengthy evaluation of the literary motifs as Middle High German literature and detailed correction of Fuks' misreadings and mistranslations, Schröbler remarks: "Whoever undertakes to make such a text accessible to the scholarly world must be aware of the responsibility which is connected with the enterprise and which is all the greater since quite different disciplines are interested in such an edition," and notes that Fuks' edition "doubtless sprang from an intimate/insider's interest in the history and culture of Judaism," but is nonetheless "philologically inadequate."[44] The implications here are disturbing. Apparently since the present edition was produced by a scholar intimately acquainted with Jewish history and culture, allegedly without consideration of an audience beyond that group, it has failed and perhaps even demonstrates the editor's irresponsiblity; there is a contrast implied between Jewish scholarship and "philological competency," between consideration of the demands of all potential audiences (one wonders which one Schröbler envisions, beyond Germanists, of course), and responsible scholarship. A "responsible" edition would have to be in Middle High German, one would assume, since Schröbler identifies the language of the manuscript as such, merely disguised in the "guise of the foreign script" ("Gewand der fremden Schrift," p. 136); and, one must further assume, such an edition would potentially be philologically competent; and it would satisfy the needs of the audience of Germanists. But would that suffice as well for any of the other unnamed audiences envisioned by Schröbler (the Yiddishist, for instance)? What Schröbler suggests is a commonplace in Germanistic criticism of Yiddish, but its implications are myriad and extend to the demand that the edition must *conform* to the critical ideology of one segment of its potential audience and disregard the rest. This particular segment is, however, located at the center, and apparently reserves the right and has the institutional power to define research tasks, relevant audiences, and the means to reach them – all implicitly, without addressing the topics directly.

Carles criticizes many of the same aspects of Fuks' edition as have others, but goes on to add *expressis verbis* that the edition was of prime interest for Germanists.[45] The audienc*es* envisioned by Schröbler are reduced to one by Carles, in fact the only one that had concerned Schröbler in the end as well – medieval Germanists.

In addition to Carles' brief article, Fourquet's review, which appeared in *Études germaniques* in the following year, while not of great moment otherwise, served to inform French Germanists of

Fuks' edition and addresses points of significance for our present argument. He notes that Fuks' work was "un peu hatif" and very graciously points up specific failings, including those of Fuks' lack of expertise in Middle High German and errors in modern German syntax (pp. 53-54). He also hints at the necesssity of a cooperative edition, without suggesting it outright, for as he remarks, an edition of this manuscript would require a paleographer of "judéo-allemande," a medieval German dialectologist, and an expert in the phraseology of the various epic genres. At the beginning of his review, however, he briefly summarized Lévy's occupation with the manuscript and laments the loss of this one-man edition (pp. 50-52 & 56). He then notes further that Lévy's work was in spirit and principle being carried on by S. Roelly, one of Fourquet's students, who was to edit *Dukus Hurnt* in normalized Middle High German, "such as those we use for *Kudrun*."[46] Such an edition, Fourquet suggests without further discussion, would be more arbitrary than *Kudrun*. But he nonetheless views such an edition in normalized Middle High German as "la tache la plus urgente, pour répondre aux besoins de l'histoire littéraire" ("the most urgent task, in order to respond to the needs of literary history," p. 55) and despite all the arbitrariness in the transposition into normalized Middle High German, "ce serait déjà un progrès sérieux" ("that would already be significant progress," p. 55). At any rate, the basic principle of the proposed edition would be to indicate clearly all textual problems and unintelligible or suspect passages, thus leaving judgments to the reader (p. 56). There is an incongruous juxtaposition of editorial objectivity with radical editorial manipulation – the editor proposes to transcribe the text from its Hebrew alphabet original into Roman in the form of normalized Middle High German, entailing a radically interpretive transformation of the linguistic form of the text (whether it is in fact Old Yiddish or Middle High German is immaterial here, since unquestionably the texts are not *normalized* Middle High German); after this massive reconstitution of the texts, then all scribal, metrical, and logical errors in the "text" will be noted so that there is no danger that the reader will be forced to rely on the editor's judgment! C'est vraiment très bizarre!

Marchand's review of Fuks' edition, treated in some detail above in chapter two, addresses the present topic as well. He finds Fuks' system of transliteration acceptable, noting only that indication of finals would be helpful. In his construction of a portion of his posited Roman alphabet *Vorlage*,[47] he demonstrates his notions of editorial practice rather clearly. In determining the dialect of the text he first transcribes the text into its "original" Roman-alphabet form, a process which demands that he determine the target dialect in order to decide on the conjectured vowels to be inserted into the text. He chooses Central German and thus transcribes קוניק as "kunec"; he notes that *v* (i.e. ו) "corresponds to MHG *o, u, â* (occasionally *a*), *o, u*, not to mention *ö, ü, uo*, etc." This lack of distinction is said to be characteristic of Central German, and although one could thus conceivably interpret the text as *kunec, konec, kunic* or *konic*, it must, according to Marchand, be read as *kunec*, the Central German form. He further intimates that the scholar who has "a great deal of experience with MHG, especially central German, manuscripts" (p. 391) will recognize such features and if such a scholar performs the text reconstruction (i.e. of the "original" Roman-alphabet *Vorlage*), then the accuracy of the reconstruction is "fairly certain" although it "can lay no claim to absolute accuracy." Thus Marchand, the Central German expert, posits that experts in Central German are the best editors of such texts, since they are Central German texts, which is proven by transcribing them into Central German and then demonstrating that their grapho-phonemic form is Central German. The case, such as it is, is so solid that Marchand can then conclude: "It is hoped that the above remarks will have demonstrated conclusively that the language of the document is German. To use this manuscript in the study of Old Yiddish as Fuks and others advocate, would be disastrous" (p. 391).

The errors in Fuks' German translation are no more than annoying, says Marchand, since the "German specialist" can easily clear them up for himself; non-German specialists must thus be on guard. The inclusion of a translation is commended by Marchand, although for a strange reason – not to reach a wider audience, but because "a translation will inevitably reveal any weaknesses in the readings adopted" (p. 394). It is unclear to whom this revelation will be made – certainly not the "specialist," who will presumably be able to recognize false or weak readings without a pony; and not to the lay reader who may use the original texts (facsimile or transliterations) little, if at all. Again it seems that another of Fuks' reviewers is dissatisfied with Fuks' attempt at a facsimile/diplomatic edition and projects his desires for an idealized critical edition on the present edition – i.e., for a critical edition so perfectly constituted that its readings could be easily, clearly, lucidly, and transparently translated into a modern language without textual complications, ambiguity, or uncertainty, that is, without interpretation. Unfortunately such medieval texts do not exist nor are such translations conceivable, except from an extreme, positivistic perspective. In any case, it is unreasonable to expect such a purged text from Fuks' facsimile/diplomatic edition.

The audience of the edition is briefly mentioned by Marchand – Yiddish and German specialists, who "owe Fuks a vote of thanks for having called the attention of the scholarly public to this manuscript and to the field of Early Yiddish and Hebrew-German studies in general. We must expect a great deal of renewed interest among the wide audience the book will undoubtedly reach" (p. 394). Even so, he claims that the edition is useless for scholarly purposes and contends that the manuscript must be re-edited before scholars can study the texts. This projected new edition must be prepared by means of the "collaboration of several scholars" (p. 394).

Despite the general problems with Marchand's method, there are many positive aspects of his work, especially in treating the problem of accessibility. In his 1960 article in *Orbis*, he announces his debut as a fledgling Yiddishist who enters the field from medieval German studies and thus brings a fresh perspective – one perhaps occasionally offensive, as he remarks, but at least different and provocative.[48] From this perspective he summarizes the three *practical* problems confronting the field of Old Yiddish studies and hindering progress (p. 34),[49] and in fact all three have to do with the present topic: 1) a lack of good texts and textual studies, including facsimile and critical editions (the latter due to a lack of comprehensive paleographical analyses), and microfilm of manuscripts and rare books (pp. 35-37); 2) the lack of a definitive grapho-phonemic analysis of Old Yiddish (termed "pronunciation," p. 37); and, 3) the lack of training in Middle High German and early New High German among Yiddishists and lack of training in Judaic studies among Germanists. He has two suggestions: first, manuscript texts should be accessible on microfilm so that uninformed polemic is replaced by informed discussion, so that dissertations (as a genre of scholarly studies, rather dependent on relative accessibility) can be written on the subject and thus broaden knowledge and train scholars. Second, there must be more cooperation between Yiddishists and Germanists for the mutual benefit of Old Yiddish and medieval German studies.

The tone is a positive one and the suggestions are certainly pertinent, but here again Marchand is unsure of the direction of his argument, for in addition to these suggestions, he also requires that no one not thoroughly grounded in Middle High German and early New High German and their dialects be allowed to edit Old Yiddish texts (p. 41). This is the only basic requirement noted.[50] In a later article, he also calls for cooperation between Germanists and Yiddishists, but the note again goes a bit flat when he proposes as the goal of this cooperation the wider accessibility of Hebrew-German literature,[51] for the term "Hebrew-German" can only antagonize Yiddishists, who regard this literature as Old Yiddish. If the literature were in fact Hebrew-German, then Yiddishists *per se* would logically be no more drawn to it than would, for instance, medieval Germanists to Old Yiddish. Finally, what is one to understand as Marchand's "wider audience" ("weitere Kreise")? Apparently, according to his program. both Germanists and Yiddishists (who have been trained as *Altgermanisten*).

The scholarly audience of these texts is directly addressed and at least partially defined by Marchand in this article, where he notes the interest that the edition of the Cambridge codex has aroused among Germanists (p. 55) and cites seventeen publications that had dealt with the text (pp. 60-61, n. 1). He then laments the lack of interest in the text by Yiddishists.[52] The cause of this dismay is clear on the one hand, since he ignores six reviews of Fuks' edition and numerous articles by eminent Yiddishists. On the other hand, however, it is also necessary to point out that among the seventeen publications listed as indicators of Germanistic interest, seven are written by Yiddishists and five others by scholars whose research deals in large part with medieval Yiddish studies, a fact that is actually obliquely revealed in his second bibliographical note which lists the "few" exceptions to his claim that Yiddishists had all but ignored the text: the list consists of scholars whose publications make up a great part of those listed in the first note. He then immediately proceeds to the stated purpose at hand, which is to clarify some few philological problems with the text - since it had been ignored by Germanists up to this point. This morass of confusing claims and self-refutation all takes place in the space of a few lines.

In 1962, five years after Fuks' edition and the controversy it provoked, Marchand and Tubach ostensibly "announced" the discovery of the codex and its edition by Fuks.[53] The manuscript is suitable, they claim, "to awaken the interest of German literary scholarship in Hebrew-German literature" *(hebräisch-deutsche Literatur,* p. 34). This literature is one that had been ignored by scholarship up to then, they lament, and one which they cannot even find mentioned in the handbooks of Yiddish literary history, among which they list Erik, Wiener, Pines, Weinreich, and Shiper.[54] Their putative expectation of finding reference to the work is doomed and their disappointment fictive, since those studies were of course all published a generation before the manuscript containing "Yosef" was edited and published.

In fact, however, their implied criticism of these studies is even more of a distortion, since they discuss the topic of Hebrew-German literature as if it were the major discovery of a new (corpus of) literature, while in fact, they are merely announcing their own personal rediscovery of Landau's name for Old Yiddish literature, which was, understandably, not used by the authors of the histories of Old Yiddish literature (who generally designate it "Yiddish") in which they pretend to have searched in vain for mention of this ignored corpus. It is not that the literature has been either discovered or ignored by anyone. Marchand/Tubach have simply decided to join the Old Yiddish vs. Middle High German fray and add a new polemic twist by "inventing" a new literature and seeking a Germanistic audience for it.

As editors of the text, Marchand/Tubach see their task to be "das Gedicht in einer dem Germanisten zugänglichen Gestalt vorzulegen" ("to present the poem in a form accessible to the Germanist," p. 36). No further audience is sought and, as is customary with the "accessible to Germanists" genre of Old Yiddish editing, Marchand/Tubach see their task to be one of presenting the work in its putatively original form: Middle High German purged of its Hebrew-alphabet disguise. This is a particularly difficult task since, according to Marchand/Tubach, it involves, in the case of Hebrew-German documents, the transliteration of the text into the Roman alphabet from the Hebrew transliteration of the Roman-alphabet original. In order to see the Roman-alphabet original behind the Hebrew alphabet, one must know 1) the value of the Hebrew graphs, 2) the scribal tradition, 3) the etymology of the lexemes in each case, and, 4) the German dialect of the original text. Even when all these conditions are fulfilled, arbitrary decisions ("willkürliche Entscheidungen") are unavoidable in many cases (p. 36). But in the case of "Yosef," Marchand/Tubach maintain, there are few such arbitrary decisions necessary, since they *know* that the dialect is Hessian. According to the criteria just established, one wonders how this recognition of dialect frees them from arbitrary decisions. In fact, it seems that this knowledge is itself merely an arbitrary decision, since Marchand/Tubach proceed to an analysis of the language of the text without presenting a table of their transcription system (or even mentioning the possible relevance thereof), and the reader thus never knows what the manuscript might possibly contain. In any case, argument for any particular dialect is prejudiced to say the least when based on a transcription of the text *into that dialect.*

An example can illustrate the practice and its implications (p. 37):

> Für *he* and *eh* (mit offenem *e*) steht immer *x*, ohne Vokalzeichen. Die Herkunft dieser Praxis ist uns unklar.* Beispiele: *xr (her), gzxn (gesehen).*
> * Nach oder vor *x* kann im Hebräischen kein *e* stehen; *he* wäre vielleicht als *ha-ee* gelesen und mißverstanden; *hj* wäre *he*, so hat unser Schreiber einfach *x* geschrieben nach einer Art Akrophonie. Der Gebrauch von *e* als offenem *e* ist wohl spät im Abendlande...

Such passages confuse more than they enlighten. The editors do not distinguish between transcription (*he*) and transliteration (*x*). Without any information concerning the system of transliteration/transcription,[55] many editorial statements are simply meaningless, such as: "...kann im Hebräischen kein *e* stehen." Without a context, one can only agree that the statement is undeniably correct: the Roman letter *e* is never used in Hebrew.[56] But a statement like "*hj* wäre *he*, so hat unser Schreiber einfach *x* geschrieben" admits no interpretation.

The first point to be made here is that all such editions must inform the reader of the system of transposition either via an *ad hoc* table or a reference to a published system of transposition. If we are to take Marchand/Tubach's claim seriously – that they are dealing with a newly discovered literature, for which there logically can not yet be a standard transliteration system established – then a table would be necessary. Second, their intended audience is Germanists who, the editors imply, not only do not know, but also do not need to know Yiddish [since the text in question is (Hebrew-)German], and for whom the editors have dutifully purged the text of its Hebrew-alphabet disguise, so that this audience can have access to the text. But if this is in fact the intended audience, then for whom are the pseudo-textual notes written? Certainly not for the intended reader with no knowledge of the Hebrew alphabet, for s/he can not even begin to guess what they mean; and just as certainly not for the reader who *does* know the Hebrew alphabet, because even if s/he could "reconstruct" the manuscript reading, such a lack of precision would still remain that no analysis *per se* could take place, for the problems of grapho-phonemic relations in Old Yiddish are so complex that even the mere attempt to deal with them by means of an undefined system of transposition is an exercise in futility.

At some point the reader's faith and stamina simply no longer suffice to deal with the tasks required, as for instance in the editors' argument for Hessian dialect features such as *e* for *ae*, *ou* for *iu*, while the manuscript reads only י for both posited /e/ and /ae/, and ו or וו for posited /ou/ and /iu/.[57] They also cite as evidence for Central German dialect the forms *muchte/duchte* as rhyme words (as opposed to normalized Middle High German, *möhte/duhte* which would not rhyme, p. 42). Yet in their edition of the poem, they print *mochte/dochte* (ll. 7-8, p. 39). Unfortunately for their argument, however, *dochte/duhte/duchte* is merely a phantom – no more than their own editorial conjecture, conjured up in order to fill a manuscript lacuna, and thus it can hardly be used as evidence of dialect identity. Here Fuks reads דו⟨כטא⟩ *dv⟨xt'⟩* (ms. p. 34, l. 10), but the manuscript is in poor condition. The readings of other editors resemble each other but not Marchand/Tubach: Hakkarainen: "?n tvxt' " (I, 70); Ganz/Norman/Schwarz: "entochte" (*ZfdPh*, p. 88); Katz: אנטוכטא (p. 113). In other words, Marchand/Tubach's evidence for Hessian is quite simply invented.

Their general ability to use and work with manuscript sources does not inspire confidence,[58] when they deny that /'/ (i.e., א) ever signifies anything but /a/, since /'/ as /o/ is a development post-dating this manuscript – that is except in a few cases, but these are "wohl nur fehlerhafte Lesungen von Fuks" (p. 38, n. 28). That is, it seems that their edition is based on Fuks' "readings," i.e., his Roman transliteration, for otherwise their indecision about the accuracy of Fuks' reading /o/ would be unintelligible.

In general Marchand/Tubach's handling of the editorial task they set for themselves – presenting a text in transcription – is disappointing. They claim that the transliteration/transcription of the document is a rather mechanical task without interpretation. Yet their almost impenetrable (since based on an undefined transliteration system) and polemical arguments about the grapho-phonemic system demonstrate clearly that they are indeed interpreting, for otherwise it would be neither possible nor necessary for them to claim that their interpretation is correct and that of their opponents incorrect. And thus in the attempts to invent a new field of literary endeavor, establish a scientifically verifiable scheme of dialect identification, impose Middle High German as the original of Hebrew-German documents, and thus also the editorial *telos* of transcription, Marchand/Tubach present a full program of pseudo-positivistic, ideological textual editing.

The general tenor of Marchand's editorial practice was continued by John Howard and W. B. Lockwood. The introductory comments in Howard's edition of the "Bärmuttersegen" indicate the ideological program at work, for he assumes without further comment that Hebrew-alphabet (Germanic language) chapbooks are German "cast in Hebrew letters."[59] He notes that since libraries normally catalogue Hebrew-alphabet chapbooks under Hebraica, Germanists rarely discover their existence, a task usually left to Hebrew scholars. Such literature "in time came to be appropriated by persons in the Yiddish field," an unfortunate state of affairs for German studies, since, he contents, the field thereby has remained unaware of a rather large body of documents "which belong part and parcel" to it.[60] This is clearly a reiteration of the Marchandian thesis of "Hebrew-German." Howard further maintains that serious study of these works has begun only recently, despite the fact that Yiddishists have known of them for more than a century (p. 129), thus not merely disparaging, but rather denying the existence of serious scholarship on the texts prior to Marchand/Tubach's ideological entry into the field.

His initial edition of the "Bärmuttersegen" is based on Güdemann's printed version from the *Sefer ha'assufoth*, which he, like Güdemann, simply assumes is Middle High German (p. 214). He prints the Hebrew-alphabet text (from Güdemann's article) and a transposed text according to a rather strict system of transliteration.[61] The following year he again published an edition of the text, after having become aware of the existence of Güdemann's source text in London.[62] The edition consists of a photographic facsimile (facing p. 256), a Hebrew-alphabet text based on ultra-violet photographs, and a transliteration (called *Transkription*, p. 255).

In his edition of the Yiddish adaptations of the younger *Hildebrandlied*, W. B. Lockwood makes a standard claim: that this edition will make the texts accessible (*zugänglich*).[63] He suggests that these early- to mid-sixteenth-century texts were very possibly copied from a printed German text, and without further comment assumes that they are simply German texts in the Hebrew alphabet, since as he remarks, the twenty common Hebrew graphs are used to represent all German sounds (*deutsche Laute*, p. 434). His edition consists of a rather strict transliteration, which is followed – at the request of the editors of the journal – by a transcription "in conventional orthography," that is – German. Lockwood nevertheless notes that this "normalization" of the orthography obscures both graphemic and phonemic problems. We may, however, also note, that the point was apparently not of sufficient import to him that he abandon this tradition of editing and perhaps seek a less prejudicial journal in which to publish.

In quite a different context, in his article analyzing the Hebrew acrostic in "Yosef," which revealed the basic theses of Marchand/Tubach to be rather more of an inept embarrassment than merely an inaccurate edition, Khone Shmeruk brings up two points relevant to the present argument.[64] As Germanists had done before, Shmeruk also calls for scholarly cooperation "between Germanists and Yiddish researchers who are generally competent in Judaic studies" (p. 67). He does not note any specific reasons for the necessity of this cooperation, but the topic of his article can of course be taken as an illustration of the possible problems arising from a lack of such cooperation - Germanists or Germanist-oriented scholars had simply overlooked or ignored the importance of the acrostic in determining the scribal tradition, cultural origin, and perhaps even language of the text. The implications of this Germanistic orientation are briefly outlined by Shmeruk and deserve to be quoted in full:

> The Hebrew acrostic is obscured or totally lost in the Latin-letter transliterations and transcriptions of the published versions of the poem. It is really unimportant whether there is awareness of the acrostic (as in Hakkarainen, [I] p. 24 [n. 40]) or if its existence is passed over in silence (as in Marchand/Tubach). In this connection, it is worth passing a basic comment in criticism of the newly revived older Germanistic practice of publishing Yiddish texts only in transliteration or even transcription into Latin letters – a practice that has recently found a stout defender. No matter how consistently and well the principles of such transliterations and transcriptions are applied – and regardless of other problems that may be involved – it is entirely clear that they are inadequate for poems with Hebrew acrostics. They cannot really reflect the original text. And we cannot imagine that we can agree to a variety of rules for such publications of Yiddish texts - with or without a Hebrew acrostic. (pp. 68-69)[65]

Shmeruk thus takes the misrepresentation (or even lack of recognition) of the Hebrew acrostic not as an exceptional, but rather as a representative example of the effects of Roman transposition. Such editions can only be misrepresentations in some degree. The further problem of whether a transposition standard is possible will be addressed in more detail below.

Shmeruk also printed an edition of the brief poem in this article. Since his purpose was to "explain ... the acrostic and its significance" (p. 67), he arranges the text according to its stanzaic structure. Otherwise there are few editorial changes made (beyond transliteration into Hebrew square script) in this edition. He indicates line and page breaks from the manuscript, brackets posited omissions, illegible text, and (few) conjectures. Since, as he notes, his is the sixth published edition of the poem, he does not include textual notes, but refers generally to Hakkarainen's edition, with whose readings he usually agrees. His edition consists thus of a single, Hebrew-alphabet edition.

As Shmeruk points out, Weinreich spoke out even more strongly in response to Marchand's publications, when he contended that "transposing" Old Yiddish texts into normalized Middle High German "is outright detrimental"[66] since, as he remarks on Landau's edition of *Esther*, such an edition falsifies the text altogether. Weinreich goes even further in opposing Marchand's requirement that no one should edit "Hebrew-German" texts who does not know Middle High German and early New High German by cautioning that the better the editor knows Middle High German, the greater the "danger of his superimposing the Middle High German norms upon the Hebrew-letter text" (p. 116). Thus he claims that an edition of the Cambridge codex by a Germanic scholar would not be as good as Fuks', unless it includes a facsimile and printed (Hebrew-alphabet) Yiddish text (p. 117).[67]

Solomon Birnbaum's essay of 1961 is important specifically with respect to the problem of transposition,[68] for here he contends that through the use of normalized Middle High German "an extraneous pattern is thereby imposed on the material," but then goes on to add an ideologically unexpected consequence of such an imposition – "and this prevents the scholar from uncovering new information which the M.H.G. sources cannot reveal" (p. 21). Thus in the first part of the sentence, Birnbaum declares that transcription into normalized Middle High German is an inadequate representation of the text, but then intimates that the value of an accurate representation of the text would be in its ability to convey phonetic information not present in Middle High German documents. One might counter that Old Yiddish texts naturally convey phonetic information not found in Middle High German texts. But the problem is obviously more complex, as Birnbaum's note 5 (p. 21) shows – for he is not stating a truism here, but rather claiming, as had assimilationists before him, that Old Yiddish texts are of major significance in the study of Middle High German phonology. The point is thus not that the texts might be important for a study of Old Yiddish phonology, nor does Birnbaum discuss the basic problems inherent in the use of Old Yiddish data in this pursuit, which are admittedly relevant to some degree to the study of the history of medieval German, some stage of which also supplied Yiddish with one of its determinant linguistic components.

Birnbaum then proposes a comparison of the Old Yiddish and Middle High German "system of spelling" in order to determine whether Old Yiddish texts are merely Middle High German texts *transliterated* into the Hebrew alphabet. While such claims have been made from time to time, few scholars – even among those opposed to Old Yiddish – take them seriously. Often the problem may simply be the imprecise use of terminology — transliteration vs. transcription. That is, it would be conceivable that such texts are Middle High German transcribed/translated into the Hebrew alphabet/Yiddish. It is, however, nonsense to argue that they are transliterated.

For some reason, Birnbaum nonetheless concerns himself with proving that Old Yiddish is not *transliterated* Middle High German and in so doing involves himself in numerous absurdities. For instance, he gives several examples of Middle High German words as they would be transliterated into the Hebrew alphabet and as the cognate forms actually appear in Yiddish:[69]

in	ינ	אין
ich	יקה/יכה	איך
grüeʒen	גרוֹעצענ/גרוּצֵנ	גרושן
retten	רעתּתּנ/רֵתתֵנ	ריטן

The entire argument is exagerrated and distorted. Transliterating ן as נ is inaccurate and misleading. Yet since a strict transliteration simply reproduces symbol-for-symbol in one graphemic system (alphabet) the sequence in the other system, there is some theoretical legitimacy in the absence of initial א in Birnbaum's transliteration of "in," as there is in the transliteration of "ich" as יקה. But the point here cannot be one of strict transliteration in the modern linguistic sense, and thus these proposed transpositions are *impossible* in Hebrew-alphabet texts. Furthermore, Birnbaum misleads, for instance, when he suggests that Middle High German "retten" would appear as noted above in Hebrew transliteration. The reason for including this example at all is most likely the presence of the double consonant in German, rarely present in Old Yiddish words, but often cited as evidence for a Roman-alphabet source of Old Yiddish texts. Yet Birnbaum not only demonstrates that actual Old Yiddish ט contrasts with Middle

High German /tt/, but he also uses תת for /tt/ in the proposed transliteration, while ט of course appears in the actual Old Yiddish orthography. Thus he makes the artificial *ad hoc* creation of the inaccurate transliteration visibly even "less acceptable" by using letters that strike the eye of the *Yiddish*-reader as strange: as if one were to spell English "boy" as "boi," which could be justifiable as *a* phonetic representation, but is strange, alienating, and simply inaccurate orthographically. The same is true in Birnbaum's use of the impossible, non-existent ו with umlaut as the transliteration of /ü/ in *grüeȝen,* or the inaccurate or misleading transliteration of Middle High German /ȝ/ as Old Yiddish sadhe (Mhg. /ȝ/ ≠ [ts]) in the same word. Again one could contend that Birnbaum is simply transliterating /ü/ strictly – one symbol substitution with diacritics, and since / ¨ / does not exist in Hebrew, one must choose a symbol to represent it; a sensible choice would obviously be / ¨ /. But we can only approve his strict transliteration as a scholarly exercise of twentieth-century linguistics. If, however, Birnbaum wishes us to understand it as a possibility for the medieval treatment of Roman-alphabet material to be rendered into the Hebrew alphabet – or rather as the refutation of the claim of such a possibility - then his argument cannot be taken seriously.[70] If we conceive of a scribe transposing an entire Roman-alphabet, Middle High German text into a Hebrew-alphabet, Old Yiddish text, then we cannot at the same time conceive of this scribe as so ignorant of the grapho-phonemic systems of both Middle High German and Old Yiddish as to produce יקה/יכה from "ich."

His whole argument is an attempt to deny the possibility of impossibilities and irrelevancies, for the threat to his pro-Yiddish position comes rather from those who propose that Old Yiddish texts are *transcribed* from Roman-alphabet, Middle High German texts. It initially seems thus that his argument misses the point entirely. But as the article progresses, it becomes clear that his is an unexpected argument indeed. The system of transcription proposed here rejects Middle High German as its *telos*: "we cannot transpose O.Y. texts into the M.H.G. system of spelling. What we have to do is express the O.Y. system in Roman characters" (p. 22). He notes the immense difficulty of this project, especially with respect to vowels, and concedes that Middle High German phonology must be utilized, "albeit with great caution."[71] In opposition to Weinreich and Shmeruk, Birnbaum favors Roman transposition over a Hebrew-alphabet text in order to preserve the Yiddish character of the text and avoid an automatic transposition by the reader of the text into normalized Middle High German.[72] This fear is in itself rather surprising, for it presupposes (just as do the blatantly anti-Yiddish, Germanistic reviews) that the audience of such texts is by definition composed of readers of Middle High German who are so conversant with that language that Old Yiddish texts, *even if* (or according to Birnbaum: *especially if*!) in Hebrew, would automatically be read as if normalized Middle High German.

Despite the sometimes quite substantial differences in their arguments, Weinreich, Shmeruk, and Birnbaum all sound important notes of dissent against the prevailing practice of the appropriation of Old Yiddish language and literature by medieval German studies via transliteration/transcription. Weinreich and Shmeruk oppose transposition in general, while Birnbaum clings to the concept of an interpretation-free transposition. The arguments against transposition are sound, but have, historically, carried little weight among Germanists. There have been two reasons for this failing: first, the topos of accessibility, which posits a Germanistic inability to read a Hebrew-alphabet text; second, since the text is said to be German already, a Hebrew-alphabet edition of it is viewed as a deliberate obscuring of the tradition and an attempted affirmation of the text's pretense of inaccessibility and alterity. Birnbaum's argument for transposition is somewhat less consistent than Weinreich's and Shmeruk's against, since he must necessarily make significant use of determinant linguistic evidence drawn from Middle High German in order to construct his system of transposition – despite the fact that he rejects that linguistic form from the outset as the target language of the transposition. In the proposals of Weinreich/Shmeruk and Birnbaum there is thus the recurring problem of the double-bind inherent in the conflict of center and margin: the marginal element is simultaneously "inaccessible" to the center and (but/although) already centralized. The editor of the center must then simply perform a mechanical task on the text in order to render it accessible, while the editor of the margin attempts either to retain the essential aspects of marginality (Birnbaum) or to center the marginal in a new constellation and thus eliminate that marginality (Weinreich/Shmeruk).

The most important attempt to publish Old Yiddish texts in a diplomatic, Hebrew-alphabet edition, which thus affirmed the principles expressed by Weinreich (and later by Shmeruk) was the second full-scale edition of the Cambridge codex in its entirety, by Eli Katz. Its purpose "is to make available for study" the texts of the codex (p. 4) without burdening the edition with unnecessary interpretive problems.[73] Katz had obviously profited from the reviews of Fuks' edition, other publications on the codex, and not least from Fuks' edition itself, all of which contributed to the result that his edition is in most respects superior to Fuks'. It includes only a single, Hebrew-alphabet diplomatic edition, with no facsimile, transposition, or translation; the introduction is comprehensive especially in linguistic matters, and the textual apparatus includes all previous variant readings.[74] Thus in order to propose his edition as one which makes the texts accessible, despite the existence of Fuks' edition and despite his own lack of a Roman transposition,[75] Katz must conceive of a very different audience from that served by Fuks.

His editorial practice is rather strictly diplomatic: he avoids emendations and conjectures on lacunae and rejects the practice of Roman transcription/transliteration:

> I believe that any attempted Latin-letter transcription other than a symbol for symbol transliteration is prejudicial to the objective study of the phonological system. Such a transliteration, however, presents to the scholar a *Schriftbild* which is easily as forbidding as the original script ... The scholar who wishes to devote himself to serious study of the MS must be prepared to master the Jewish alphabet. (p. 22).

Katz is skeptical of the attempted reconstruction of precise phonetic values of the text's graphemes, for "to attempt precise phonetic descriptions of the phones represented would, of course, be impossible. We can at most concern ourselves with distinctions and similarities among sounds" (p. 41).

Often there is no internal evidence to support the proposition of various phonetic realizations of a given grapheme, and thus they rest on external evidence from an "approximate knowledge" of both Middle High German dialects and cotemporal Hebrew graphophonemic usage (or subsequent documented developments in Yiddish phonetics), neither of which is precise, and quite often neither of which suffices to decide a particular case. Thus he does suggest approximate values in a rather detailed analysis (pp. 23-52), but he does not take these suggestions as conclusive (or even polemical) evidence for or against any identification of language. He notes that identification of vowel length is moot (p. 42), but some internal evidence is present in the manuscript in the absence of rhyme between pairs of words which are, in their Middle High German cognate forms, contrasting long/short minimal pairs. The front rounded vowels known from Middle High German are not present in the manuscript, as rhyme analysis demonstrates: e.g. שׂונא/קרונא.[76] There is evidence of a graphematic distinction between [s]/[z][77] and [f]/[v]. In general, Katz finds the orthographic system to be "of striking consistency," and while it demonstrates some acquaintance with Roman-alphabet, Middle High German scribal practice, it "readily departs" from it when it conflicts with the traditional usage of Hebrew-alphabet scribal practices (pp. 51-52).

In his grapho-phonemic analysis, Katz often uses terms such as "corresponds to" or "cognate with" in order to identify relationships between Old Yiddish and Middle High German,[78] but he sees no more than a relationship between, never an identity of the two languages. He notes nevertheless that the morphology of the text's language exhibits virtually no deviations from that of Central German (p. 53).

For typographical reasons (p. 22) Katz cites the text in his introduction and apparatus in transliteration.[79] Since he adheres to the strict principles of transliteration, his transliterated text citations are often all but illegible: e.g., *#?rqljngn'* (p. 32). His analysis of the grapho-phonemic system (pp. 23-52) is remarkable in the context of Old Yiddish studies for its lack of polemic, but despite the fact that he denies the possibility of identifying the precise grapho-phonemic correspondence, his suggestions of "approximate phones" is by definition just as interpretive as those of Ganz/Norman/Schwarz, Marchand/Tubach, or Matenko/Sloan. Katz's distinction from them is of paramount importance, however. While they take their posited phones as definitive and print them *as* their edition (Marchand/Tubach without even supplying a transcription table), Katz maintains a clear distinction between his introductory grapho-phonemic interpretation and the text. He does not reject interpretation or deny its legitimacy, but rather more convincingly demonstrates the necessity of it by at least distinguishing its most radical operation in such editions (i.e., grapho-phonemic interpretation) from the diplomatic edition.[80] Thus despite his generally pro-Yiddish stance, he does not attempt to transform the text into a demonstrably Yiddish form. In the context of the double-stranded "tradition" of Old Yiddish studies – Yiddishistic and Germanistic – his exclusively Hebrew-alphabet text is a tacit but quite graphic argument for the Jewish and perhaps even Yiddish nature of the text.[81]

While Katz is thus at worst only implicitly ideological in this respect, the next major edition of a text from the Cambridge codex, Ganz/Norman/Schwarz's edition of *Dukus Hurnt*, is by far the most transparently ideological in its editorial policy of any thus far treated, for as discussed in chapter two above, the constituent parts of the edition, the excision of the one "Germanistic" text from the manuscript, the disciplinary alignment of the series in which the edition appeared, its theoretical form, the name*s* assigned to the language, and the lack of (and denial of the importance of) a Hebrew-alphabet text all contribute to a prejudicial edition.

Ganz justifies the edition by invoking the accessibility topos, remarking that it was Fuks' service, "die Handschrift bekannt und wenn auch nur unzulänglich, zugänglich gemacht zu haben." ("to have made the manuscript accessible, even if incompetently," p. 3). The fact that they have been able to read more than Fuks and generally also more than Katz, who is cited only in the bibliography, absolves them, Ganz contends, of any duty to justify the new edition.[82]

In Ganz's earlier examination of *Dukus Hurnt*,[83] the pattern of editorial ideology is already established. He remarks that texts of non-Semitic languages written in the Hebrew alphabet are doomed to be reconstructed, since only approximate representation is possible. In his analysis of grapho-phonemics (p. 55), he takes Middle High German as his basis for no compelling argumentative reason, but "for the sake of convenience," perhaps simply because by the time of his article, such had become standard practice.

Schwarz's contribution to the collaborative edition, on the grapho-phonemic problems of the text, illustrates essentially the same editorial principles which the edition itself manifests. The main tenets of his method were discussed at length above, in connection with his identification of the language as German, a decision which predetermines the course of his editorial efforts. In addition to the disturbing aspects of this guiding ideological principle, another basic problem with Schwarz's editorial method arises specifically out of his performance of the task of transliteration/transcription, of paramount importance for an edition in Roman: it is especially problematic that he discounts the importance of comparative graphophonemic analysis of manuscript evidence from *Dukus Hurnt* and other relevant documents from the period.[84]

The edition itself consists of a transliteration and a transcription. The purpose of the transliteration is specified: "diese rein mechanische Umsetzung ermöglicht es dem Leser, die Hs. ohne Mühe zu rekonstruieren" ("this purely mechanical transposition enables the reader to reconstruct the manuscript without difficulty," p. 21). Despite the identification of the dialect as Central German, the editors note that the text presented is not a transcription into this[85] or any other individual dialect, nor into normalized Middle High German, but is rather "[eine] Umschrift in ein Schriftbild, das dem mittelalterlichen Deutsch angepaßt ist" ("a transposition into a script/form, that has been accommodated to medieval German," pp. 20-21). The meaning of this enigmatic term, "medieval German,"[86] unique as the name of the language of a single, extant text, is not explained by any of the editors, even though its spectrum of significations could range from "Old High German" of the eighth century to "Middle Low German" of the fifteenth, with all the geographical and developmental stages in between. Since it is unclear what this "medieval German" is, or whether it is more than a construct by the editors, one does not and cannot know what was actually involved in the philological editorial process by which the editors accommodated the text of the manuscript to this unknown linguistic model. The language of the edited text is certainly not Old (High or Low) German, nor is it Low German of any period. In fact it looks very similar to Middle High German, though, as Schwarz claims, it is not (at least not fully) "normalized." The claims that the editors present the text as non-normalized, undefined "medieval German" that is uninfluenced by any dialect, implies a certain mechanical, unbiased objectivity on their part, but the presentation of this text is, as is always the case with critical editions, rather more a matter of editorial *production*.

In Schwarz's actual graphemic and phonemic analyses, one gains at least a hint of his otherwise obscure, ill-defined method, and the degree of interpretation required by the method becomes clear: he uses the Hebrew alphabet and its traditional orthographic system as the basis of his analysis of the consonants, while in the analysis of the vowels, Middle High German serves as the basis (cf. p. 23). Here it is necessary to know which of the various extant Middle High German*s* Schwarz uses, for he has already rejected dialect forms and normalized Middle High German. What remains if one rules out both the language of the manuscripts and the literary standard, constructed by nineteenth-century philologists? The answer is found in the analysis itself, where Schwarz recurringly cites the Middle High German grammars and historical grammars of Paul/Mitzka, Moser, Weinhold, and Behaghel, that is, the grammars of standard, normalized Middle High German. While this general practice is not in itself *necessarily* prejudicial (since they are, despite their faults, the most comprehensive grammars available), Schwarz's particular use of them reveals his interpretive program, especially the formulation employed in citing Middle High German material: "Das mhd. Wort *menigîn* kommt im *Horant* 4mal in drei verschiedenen Schreibungen vor" and "Mhd. *ich* wird immer *ikh*" (p. 33). The macron indicating vowel length in *menigîn* is part of normalized Middle High German, but is rarely found in Middle High German manuscripts. When it is said that a Middle High German word occurs in this text (and it is so expressed for almost all words cited by Schwarz), the implication is that the language of the text is not "mitteldeutsch" or a colorless medieval German, but normalized Middle High German. In the second case, it seems that the Middle High German wird *ich* has become something other than *ich* in the text. In fact, however, the cited /kh/ is merely Schwarz's transliteration of Hebrew kaph, which he identifies as Middle High German /ch/ (p. 36). But here it is not a matter of phonological change, for /ich/ does not *become* /ikh/ at all. There is in fact no *ich* until Schwarz introduces it.[87] Although the editors do not ostensibly transcribe the Ashkenazic script into Roman-alphabet, normalized Middle High German orthography, Schwarz analyzes the grapho-phonemic system of the text on the basis of that model.[88]

The conclusions Schwarz draws from his phonetic analysis are disappointing, since they are not related to, but programmatically isolated from the analyzed text, and thus they present yet another example of the school of interpretation that views early Yiddish texts as useful only for the information they might yield on the history of the German language: e.g., the distinctions between voiced and unvoiced [s]/[z] and [f]/[v] demonstrate that this alternation had already taken place in fourteenth-century *German* (p. 74). In general, Schwarz's analysis adds little to Katz's and Weissberg's studies of the grapho-phonemic system of the manuscript. The edition itself is, however, not as arbitrary as Schwarz's introductory essay could lead one to believe, although there are major practical and theoretical problems: e.g., קוניק is transliterated *qwniq* but transcribed *kunik*, and thus the edition is *not* strictly normalized Middle High German, despite Schwarz's use of that dialect as the basis of his analysis.[89]

Most important is perhaps the question: What purpose and what audience does the transliteration serve? The unique *ad hoc* system is illegible for Yiddishists, Germanists, scholars of Judaic studies, for general medievalists, the educated layman, in short for everyone who might be interested in the text: who could recognize the monstrosity *qwniq* as any known form of "medieval German?" Such transliteration seems rather to benefit the editors, for by this means they have ostensibly fulfilled their duties to the "original" and even tried to make it "accessible." The reader, however, does not benefit and turns his eyes to the "medieval German" of the facing page and reads on.

The reviews of Ganz/Norman/Schwarz often address the problem of audience and accessibility. After an insightful critique of certain aspects of the edition, Rosenfeld concedes that the editors have made the poem accessible in scholarly form.[90] Stopp (p. 463) also notes that the edition makes further research possible.[91] Weissberg on the other hand castigates the editors for their omission of the Hebrew-alphabet original, "which cannot in any way be justified" ("Zur Stellung," p. 391). Rauh and Paucker claim that the edition is superior to Fuks since it offers a transcription of the text in addition to a transliteration.[92] Paucker praises the editors for their transliteration of the text, which, he inexplicably claims, *replaces* the photographic facsimile of Fuks' edition! He further claims that this edition is the "definitive text," by means of which the editors have made the work "accessible to Germanists" (p. 275). This Germanistic note is sounded relatively more often in reviews of this edition than of others, probably due to its character and placement: edited by well-known Germanists, written in German, and published in a renowned series of medieval German texts. This attitude is also illustrated by Rauh's extraordinary remark: "Besonderen Dank verdient es, daß dieser in England konzipierte Band in deutscher Sprache erscheint" ("it deserves especial thanks that this volume, conceived in England, was published in German," pp. 159-160). One must suppose that the reasons for her pleasure in the fact of German-language publication relate to Rauh's wish to use the edition in "Seminarübungen," i.e., in courses in medieval *German* literature, in German universities. She despairs, however, at the price of the edition, which will prevent its use in such classes.[93] Strangely, Weissberg ("Zur Stellung," p. 393) also approaches the edition with an exclusively Germanist perspective, such that he even appends a list of tasks remaining for Germanists to perform on this text.[94]

Kaplowitt claims that this "critical edition truly worthy of the name" makes the text accessible to the student of both medieval German literature and the history of the German language (p. 538).[95] The restriction of the audience of such texts obviously has great significance – especially when done post-factum by a reviewer. Thus Kaplowitt blithely labels Birnbaum's paleographic examination for the sake of dating the manuscript "superfluous," since the manuscript is itself dated,[96] and "marginal" since the edition is "patently designed for Germanists" (p. 538). Kaplowitt ascribes to the "ignorant Germanist" theory and thus wishes to spare the Germanist such esoteric – and non-Germanistic – subjects as Hebrew paleography. His paragraph on Birnbaum's essay is replete with patronizing, value-laden terminology: "...short piece entitled 'Die Schrift,' ... begins by informing us ... proceeds to convince us ... one cannot help wondering what the point of such a procedure is" (p. 538). With his lack of understanding of the importance of the original manuscript and script in the preparation of an edition, it is little wonder that Kaplowitt does not understand the point of Birnbaum's essay.

This disciplinary (cultural) prejudice becomes even clearer in Kaplowitt's comments on the text itself. He remarks that the editor's transcription presents "a legible form of medieval German" (p. 542). Does he imply thus that other forms of medieval German are illegible, or only other kinds of editions, such as those of the manuscript, a facsimile, or a diplomatic edition? If the latter, then illegible for whom? Obviously he again has the putatively ignorant Germanist in mind. The transliteration, he patronizingly notes, "enables those who are so inclined" to reconstruct the manuscript text (p. 542), a task for which he sees no purpose. Kaplowitt finally notes that despite the fact that the editors did not transpose the edition into normalized Middle High German (the implied ideal form of such an edition), "the text can be read easily in its present form by anyone who has acquired a basic knowledge of Middle High German" (p. 542). The possible existence of interested readers beyond this group is not admitted by Kaplowitt, and even this group is thought to be extremely limited in its scope of interest and competence.

Stopp on the other hand praises Ganz/Norman/Schwarz for rejecting a transposition of the text into normalized Middle High German, as suggested by Fourquet and executed by Roelly.[97] He also notes here instances of the editors' deviations from their stated procedure toward a transcription into normalized Middle High German.[98] Schröbler (pp. 73-74) claims that the transliteration is meticulous and accurate and the transcription is "ein Text, der so gut ist, wie er angesichts der besonderen Lage der Überlieferung sein kann" ("a text that is as good as it can be, in view of the special circumstances of the textual tradition," p. 74).[99]

Walter Röll's review is the most relevant to the present topic and deserves detailed treatment here because of its insightful analysis and its own inherent ideology.[100] His general evaluation – that this edition provides a solid basis for research – resembles that of other reviewers. He goes on to note, however, that only with and on the basis of this edition will the majority of Germanists begin to work with the text (p. 269). This statement is obviously double-edged: 1) Germanists for some reason have generally ignored *Dukus Hurnt* up to this point, due mainly to 2) the lack of an edition suitable for them.

The assumed objectivity of the editors in not attempting to construct any particular dialect of "medieval German" in their transcription is recognized and identified by Röll as mere pretense and illusion, since editorial interpretation is constantly necessary, as for instance, in choosing between *uch* and *och* and *moge* and *muge*, each pair of which is represented identically in the manuscript (p. 272). The transliteration is, according to Röll, "quite incomprehensible for the normal user" because of a technical error: the difference between the transliteration and the transcription is too great (indicative of the massive amount of interpretation on the editors' part) and additionally, the transliteration in this form is "no more legible than the original in Hebrew letters, without special study" ("ohne spezielle Studien nicht lesbarer als das in hebräischen Buchstaben geschriebene Original," pp. 272-273).

The basic problem, according to Röll, is that the editors lost sight of the fact that the transliteration was to be "a German-language text for Germanists" ("ein deutschprachiger Text für Germanisten," p. 273), a proposal that invites criticism on many levels – how so is the text *prima facie* a German text? Why is the edition for Germanists exclusively or even primarily? And what requirements does such a purpose impose on the editors? Röll posits two conditions for transliterations: transparency of the symbolic system and easy legibility of the transliterated text (p. 273). The illegibility of this transliteration stems not just from the general problems of interpretation and considerations of convenience in the transliteration process, but also, according to Röll, from the fact that the editors forgot their Germanistic audience and "use an unnecessarily alien orthography, namely that common in Oriental studies or English" ("verwende[n] unnötigerweise fremde, nämlich in der Orientalistik oder im Englischen übliche Schreibweisen," p. 273). He notes specifically the use of *q* for *k*, *kh* for *ch*, *s* for *z*, *z* for voiced *s*, *w* for ו (signifying /u/ü/o/ö/ but never /w/).

In each case, Röll is arguing for a transliteration system based on the orthographic rules of modern German, as opposed to the system used by the editors, which has some of its elements in common not just with Judaic Studies and English (?) as Röll claims, but also with other transpositions of (Old and) Modern Yiddish. While one could certainly argue that especially the latter transliteration methods have often been avowedly, militantly anti-German (orthographically, if not otherwise), and are thus indeed "alien" to German, could such an influence from Yiddish Studies in the transliteration of this text not be seen as appropriate? However one might answer that question, with respect to Ganz/Norman/Schwarz's edition, one would have to agree with Röll in principle, since the use of a "non-German" transliteration orthography in this profoundly Germanizing edition is incongruous, confusing, and thus perhaps ultimately in fact inappropriate for its intended audience.

Röll suggests an alternate form of transposition, the problem with which is that it is not strictly, or even freely, transliteration, but rather a mixture of transliteration and transcription: he notes that Ganz/Norman/Schwarz use *kh* for the monograph כ and *w* for the digraph וו and thus suggests further exceptions, such as the distinction between vocalic and diacritical (i.e., initially, to indicate initial vowel) or final א; since א, ע, י and ו are, with "characteristic restrictions," vowels, they should be transliterated with vowels. He praises the editors for making so few emendations, but criticizes many of those made as unnecessary (partial list, p. 273, n. 14). Nothing would have been worse than too "critical" an *editio princeps*, he claims (p. 273); he obviously means too radically emended. But why does he call this edition an *editio princeps*, since he knows of the editions by Fuks (which he calls "die erste Veröffentlichung" four pages earlier) and Katz? Are they simply not *editions* in his view?

Seemingly in response to the pedagogical needs of the discipline as also conceived by Rauh, Röll informs the reader, that (apparently) he is preparing a comprehensive word index and a critical edition of *Dukus Hurnt* with commentary for use in "Übungen" and as a basis for literary studies; this proposed edition is itself based on the Ganz/Norman/Schwarz edition, but will offer "einen noch übersichtlicheren Text" (p. 274 and n. 15), i.e., one still more "accessible" to students and literary (as opposed to linguistic?) scholars. Röll sounds the recurring note of the ignorant Germanist topos. His critical edition in "legible" transcription with major emendations on the basis of metrics and rhyme, and further analysis of literary parallels, has never appeared in full,[101] but it has been cited in the published studies by Röll/Gerhardt and Caliebe.

In attempting to come to terms with an edition that has been labeled the "standard," one must also deal with the general concept of a standard edition, insofar as that concept presupposes an institutional, academic audience. In the case of Ganz/Norman/Schwarz's hyper-Germanistic, traditionally philological edition in the Altdeutsche Textbibliothek series, the intended audience is rather clearly defined from the outset. For any other conceivable potential audience, such an edition would have been an utter failure, as in fact theirs has been for the actual more broadly defined audience of this literature. If one evaluates the success of their edition in terms of their own (and others') claims of its making the text accessible to both literary and linguistic scholars, then the edition has been a resounding failure, for only one major study of the poem has appeared since their edition, and it cited the text in Röll's construction.[102]

Yet with the publication of Ganz/Norman/Schwarz's *Dukus Horant*, it was not the case that editorial activity ceased. Rather it simply entered another stage: that of the hyper-positivistic editions, which proclaimed their all but absolute objectivity. The first such work was Hakkarainen's edition of the whole of the Cambridge codex, followed later by Althaus' edition of the Lion Fable from the same codex. In such cases, stated editorial principles are few, since the editors claim to engage in little textual manipulation, but the effects of their ideologies and their undying rage for order and objectivity are of great importance in determining the final form of the edited texts.

By the time of Hakkarainen's edition, a tradition of topoi associated with the genre of publications on the Cambridge codex had become well established, one of which was the expression of gratitude to Fuks for making the Cambridge codex accessible. Thus Hakkarainen claims that Fuks is not to be roundly condemned, because after all, "it is thanks to him that the Cambridge manuscript was (re)gained at all by Germanistic scholarship" ("ihm gebührt der Dank dafür, daß die Cambridger Hs. der germanistischen Forschung überhaupt (wieder)gewonnen wurde," I, 5). At the same time, however, the texts were apparently not yet actually accessible, for the ideal edition and thus Hakkarainen's goal is one "without any interpretation by the editor" ("ohne irgendwelche Interpretation seitens des Herausgebers," I, 5), so that scholarship might finally have a reliable text on which to base further study (I, 14). The editor's main task is the decipherment (*Entzifferung*) of the manuscript, a task that he claims is, by means of his edition, "in essence complete" (I. 14).

The basic principles of his edition are reducible to one (with its concomitant qualifications): to give an exact representation of the text in Roman transliteration. He chose Roman rather than Hebrew, because, he claims, the audience of the edition cannot be expected to know the Hebrew alphabet, because printing problems are fewer and the expense less with the Roman alphabet, and because no advantage was to be had with the Hebrew alphabet with respect to exactitude (I, 25). He also fears that any step beyond transliteration toward transcription leads the editor into the realm of interpretation, which opposes his basic conception of the editor's task. Furthermore, transcription requires a better understanding of the grapho-phonemic system of the language than we possess at present. Only a version in normalized Middle High German (*Mhd. Normalsprache*) parallel to a transliteration would be acceptable – but such a version would no longer be a transliteration or even a transcription, but a translation (*Übersetzung*, I, 25). He claims that such a text would be more easily readable than a transliteration, but the accuracy of even this seemingly unassailable generalization again depends on one's conception of audience. Hakkarainen's conception becomes clear in the next sentence, when he suggests that Germanists and others who can read Middle High German will have no trouble in constructing a Middle High German version on the spot as they read the transliteration. Since Hakkarainen in fact offers only a transliteration, we can understand this statement as a preliminary response to potential critics of his "illegible" edition. The response is, interestingly for questions of audience, directed to the concerns of Germanists – i.e., he acknowledges that the transliteration is difficult, but proposes that if one knows Middle High German, then one can read it as if it were that language. He presents his present work as a detailed linguistic study, which he posits as a prerequisite to any edition that can present the language of the texts "at least approximately" ("wenigstens annähernd," I, 26). Obviously he sees this next editorial step as a transcription, with an indication of vowel phones.[103]

In the second volume of his edition, Hakkarainen attempts to contrast the phonemic system of the texts (based on the graphemic system) with *both* Old Yiddish and Middle High German. He thus implies, on the one hand, that the text is neither the one nor the other, and on the other hand (without any supporting analysis) that the grapho-phonemic systems of Old Yiddish and Middle High German are distinct *and* already well-defined, and thus susceptible to contrastive analysis. But at the end of the volume, after the completion of the phonemic and graphemic analyses, i.e., at the point where one could reasonably expect conclusions of some kind, Hakkarainen can do no more than deny the possibility of determining the relationship between the graphemic and phonemic systems (II, 116). Despite this conclusion, however, he attempts a reconstruction of the phonetic shape of the first forty-eight lines of *Dukus Hurnt* (II, pp. 136-137).

Caliebe's review of Hakkarainen's first volume contributes

almost as much to the present topic as did Hakkarainen himself.[104] He speaks directly to the topos of accessibility in a variety of senses: he laments the inaccessibility of Katz's edition, since it is only available on microfilm (p. 140);[105] and, in not so many words, also laments the inaccessibility of Hakkarainen's edition, since it does not include a transcription that would identify the dialect and language of the manuscript (p. 140). In this respect, he prefers Ganz/Norman/Schwarz's text, since it has been formatted stanzaically and accommodated to medieval German. The first reason for the preference is clearly noted – "without preparatory studies and a parallel Middle High German text, this transliteration [is] no more legible for the Germanist than an edition in Hebrew letters" ("diese Transliteration [ist] ohne Vorstudien und einen parallel gedruckten mittelhochdeutschen Text für den Germanisten nicht lesbarer als ein Abdruck in hebräischen Lettern," p. 140). From this statement and the general tenor of Caliebe's remarks, it is clear that he sees these texts only in terms of their relevance to medieval German studies. His point concerning legibility is well taken, however, but has implications beyond that argumentative point – transliteration into Roman is "illegible" and thus unusable and superfluous. Caliebe's argument is for the primary importance of transcription, perhaps supplemented by a Roman transliteration; one could just as easily and more logically conclude from his premises and argument that a *Hebrew* transliteration and Roman transcription would be at least as useful. Here one might also note the ideological nature of Caliebe's argument – how can he propose any analysis of language and dialect – as the most important goal of the investigation – on the basis of an edition that has been "accommodated to medieval German"? Obviously only if he has already ideologically identified the text as such, as he (and obviously Ganz/Norman/Schwarz) had done.

The second reason for his preference for the Ganz/Norman/Schwarz text is the stanzaic format, the lack of which in Hakkarainen's edition he suggests makes the analysis of metrics and rhyme, and thus a determination of language and dialect, impossible. This seems to be another instance of the "ignorant Germanist" topos – denying that the Germanist has the ability to discern metrics and rhyme without a text printed in stanzaic format. Caliebe even implies (p. 141) that Hakkarainen had failed in his duty as an editor, due to his refusal to emend on the basis of metrical considerations, formulaicity, and topoi used. He claims that these editorial tasks are expected in a critical edition and implies that Hakkarainen's edition suffers from their absence. Ultimately, however, practically all of

Caliebe's criticism of Hakkarainen's edition is misdirected, misleading, and irrelevant, for Hakkarainen's stated purpose is to produce a diplomatic edition, i.e., an edition that manipulates neither the language of the text through "accommodation to medieval German," nor the manuscript format. Hakkarainen generally understands what a diplomatic edition is; Caliebe does not.[106]

Caliebe's misunderstanding continues in his discussion of Hakkarainen's transliteration system. He criticizes the edition for not distinguishing between consonantal and (various) vowel values of ו (Hakkarainen transliterates consistently as /v/), i.e., the phonetic values Caliebe posits in order to transform the language into Middle High German. He further calls for a uniform system of transliteration that corresponds to the "phonetic facts" (*lautliche Gegebenheiten*, p. 141) of the manuscript. Again we must note the naive conception of "fact" in this complex area where the only fact is that of constant interpretation and contingency. Caliebe concludes by outlining the primary task of further scholarship: "The next task must be a Middle High German text that has been accommodated to the phonetic and metrical conditions of the manuscript" ("Die nächste Aufgabe müßte ein den lautlichen und metrischen Verhältnissen der Handschrift angepaßter mittelhochdeutscher Text sein," p. 141). In the context of Caliebe's argument, this would indeed be the next logical step; but for no other reason could such a creation have any value.

Murdoch's review treats the problems somewhat differently than does Caliebe.[107] He accepts Hakkarainen's justification of the edition, that no satisfactory edition of the whole manuscript yet exists (p. 441). The problems with previous editions are summarized: it is noted that Fuks' edition has many problems; Katz's edition is rejected outright, since it is in Hebrew alphabet only, is unpublished, and is based on ultra-violet photographs and not the manuscript (p. 442); Ganz/Norman/Schwarz only include half the manuscript in their edition (i.e. the one text, *Dukus Hurnt*); other partial editions are transcribed into normalized Middle High German, "the validity of which is questionable" (p. 442). Murdoch goes on to argue for the advantages of a Hebrew square script transcription of the text over a Roman transliteration: "Could the technical difficulties (i.e., in printing) be overcome, however, there would be certain advantages in a Hebrew-character text such as those attempted by Fuks and Katz. Transcription is not without its problems, and a Hebrew-character text would, after all, be closer to the actual form of the MS." (p. 442). Even so, Murdoch considers an accurate transliteration text a prerequisite to an interpretive critical edition. He also gives a brief excurse on transliteration systems, noting that Hakkarainen's system resembles that of Ganz/Norman/Schwarz, but more closely approximates the IPA system. Some problems remain, such as /צ/ as /ts/, ע as /e/ (despite the fact that it represents various vowels, according to Murdoch and Schröbler's review of Fuks, cited here by Murdoch), although Hakkarainen uses neutral symbols for א and ו. The "technical difficulties" that Murdoch hints might be at the root of the omission of a Hebrew-alphabet text must certainly be taken into account: it is quite simply very expensive to have the text typeset. But Fuks did it. Why not Ganz/Norman/Schwarz or Hakkarainen? It was obviously not important enough to their conception of the text and the editors' task.

Mader agrees rather more with Caliebe than Murdoch, especially with respect to the ignorant Germanist topos: he rejects Hakkarainen's decision against transcription, "because a transcription would make literary investigations noticeably easier" ("denn für literarische Untersuchungen wäre eine Transkription eine spürbare Erleichterung") than using Hakkarainen's transliteration which is, in its turn, said to be easier than a text in Hebrew script.[108] Surprisingly, he predicts (p. 723) that Hakkarainen's edition will be of great aid in the preparation of critical editions of all or part of the manuscript – eight years after the critical edition by Ganz/Norman/Schwarz! Obviously Mader does not consider that edition "critical" or at least not sufficiently so.

In his review Lindgren states a preference for more objectivity than even Hakkarainen pretends to.[109] His acceptance of Hakkarainen's transliteration as definitive is phrased in a such way that the manuscript itself is marginalized and becomes superfluous – "Only now do we know what is actually found in the manuscript" ("Erst jetzt wissen wir, was in der Handschrift tatsächlich steht," p. 724). He nevertheless would have preferred diacritical marks instead of digraphs for /pf/ and /ts/ (since they are monographs in the Hebrew alphabet) and less use by Hakkarainen of his knowledge of the text's content to decide graphemic problems (pp. 724-725). He finds Hakkarainen's phonemic analysis somewhat less satisfactory, but still praises the work (volumes one and two) for providing the basis for further research into the relations of graphemic and phonemic systems in *Middle High German* (p. 726). The general premises of the review are thus apparently at cross purposes: a wish for still less interpretation on the editor's part and an *a priori* assumption that the texts, even with respect to their graphemic system – in the Hebrew alphabet – and its relation to the phonemic system, are not only simply Middle High German, but that the grapho-phonemic system of the Hebrew-alphabet manuscript can be of aid in Middle High German *graphemic* analysis!

Birnbaum's review is quite brief; he praises Hakkarainen's work in general and hopes for more from him.[110] As noted earlier, he agrees that there is no gain in accuracy if the texts are printed in Hebrew script, and even goes on to contend that there are even advantages to the Roman version, for if the Old Yiddish text is given in the original alphabet, there is a danger that it will simply be transposed by readers into "standardized Middle High German" (p. 102).[111] He continues with an ambiguous adversative: "but the visual impact of words such as the following may draw their attention to the real problem and make them appreciate the difference between transliteration and transcription: *mngm', uuld'...*" It is not clear what Birnbaum's meaning is here – could he be implying that a transcription would be preferable to a transliteration? Or is the "real problem" to which he alludes that a transcription is necessarily interpretive? One might generally tend to favor the latter possibility, for Birnbaum has done perhaps more work on the theory and practice of transposition than any other scholar of Old Yiddish. In the headnote to the bibliography of texts in transcription in *Yiddish: a Survey and Grammar* (p. 342), he notes that satisfactory transcription is extremely rare, since the distinction between transcription and transliteration is rarely understood, and they are usually mixed; some use standard Middle High German for Old Yiddish and a Germanized system or simply German for modern texts. He then astutely remarks:

> It is a mistake to try and "make things easier" for the layman or even for the student of German/Germanic philology. To do so only blurs and obscures the facts and problems, or blinds him to their existence.

The second of the major projects in "objective" editing, Althaus' edition of the lion fable, deals in great detail with the problems of editing Old Yiddish texts and thus also with audience, accessibility, and alphabet. He begins his discussion with the observation that four attempts have been made historically to represent spoken German in writing: the Runic (seventh century), Roman (eighth century), Hebrew (thirteenth-fourteenth century) and shorthand (seventeenth century) alphabets (p. vii). His *a priori* decision that Old Yiddish texts are German is thus at work even from the opening page of his study. He further claims that the Roman alphabet offered a "Plenarsystem," while the Hebrew alphabet offered only a "Defektarsystem" for the representation of Middle High German (p. vii). It is unclear what he means by classifying the Roman alphabet as a "Plenarsystem" in representing, one would assume, Old High German in the eighth century. Only a passing acquaintance with the chaotic state of orthography in the earliest texts, and with the persistent problems of, for instance, umlaut representation even as late as the early modern period, is necessary to question how "sufficient" the Roman alphabet was. After the initial generations of orthographic pioneers, however, the alphabet was adapted to the point that a "norm" in a sense was established, as is necessarily the case with each such attempt to represent a language with an alphabet not designed for it. The same is true of the use of the Hebrew alphabet for Old Yiddish in the high Middle Ages. As the studies of Weissberg and especially Katz have shown, there is an orthographic system to be discerned even in the orthographically seemingly most chaotic of early Yiddish texts.[112] To put this situation into context: this chaos in Old Yiddish seems hardly more pronounced than, for instance, that found in the Old High German translation of Isidor of Seville's *De fide catholica contra Iudaeos*: is *chiquhedan* or *uuootnissa* or *euuuih* any more transparent phonetically and phonemically than *Dukus Hurnt*'s גון or הורנט or ורוון; in the latter case, certain phonemes are ostensibly underdetermined and in the former they are everything but that. The correspondence between the graphemic representation of the language in the translation of Isidor and its contemporary pronunciation is difficult to determine – especially if one attempted to adhere to Althaus' notion of a Roman *Plenarsystem*, i.e., sufficient graphemes exist and are interpretable within that system – an interpretation of any of these three examples on the basis of anything remotely resembling Latin grapho-phonemics would produce, one must assume, pure nonsense, and a strictly German grapho-phonemic system has not been extrapolated from the Isidor tradition.

Althaus further prefaces his study with an overview of what he sees as the three stages in the editorial history of the Cambridge manuscript (pp. 21-23). The initial period was that of translations or proposed translations into normalized Middle High German by Lévy, Fourquet, and Roelly. He views such translations as attempts to recover the lost archetype, albeit attempts that are ultimately misguided, since it is at least as likely that this text was orally transmitted among the Jews after having been borrowed from medieval German Christian culture. Thus there may well have never been a normalized Middle High German version. These translators do not admit such a possibility nor even conceive of its relevance. Althaus compares the results of such translation attempts to those found elsewhere in Germanic studies (p. 22) – the Frings/Schiebs translation of Heinrich von Veldeke's *Eneide* into a constructed Old Limburg dialect (in 1964-65) and the Krogmann translation of the *Hildebrandslied* into an invented "Lombardic" (in 1959), and thus they are to be classed among the most embarrassing of pseudo-philological excesses. The second phase is characterized by Fuks' edition, which offers no transcription or Middle High German version, but rather only two transliterations, since Fuks viewed the manuscript as a Jewish cultural document that would be visually, interpretively, and ideologically transformed into a Christian document if presented in Middle High German (Fuks, ed., I, pp. xxvi-xxix). The third stage came in reaction to Fuks and produced numerous types of editions: 1) Hebrew square script transliteration (Katz), 2) Roman transliterations (Hakkarainen and Ganz/Norman/Schwarz), 3) critical editions with considerations of metrics, in Hebrew transliterations (lacking except for *Yosef Hatsadik*, cf. Trost), 4) critical editions with considerations of metrics in Roman transposition (the unpublished edition of *Dukus Hurnt* by Röll et al.), and, 5) Roman transcription (most others).

The point of Althaus' brief history is to demonstrate that no critical edition of the various poems based on a determination of the graphemic inventory had been done, except in the case of *Yosef Hatsadik*. The editions in category five were based partly on graphematic analysis, partly on the "inspiration" of the editors (p. 23). He rejects Hakkarainen and Birnbaum's notion that an edition in the Hebrew alphabet has no advantages, and even lists three advantages: Hebrew is more loyal to the original in a general sense; Hebrew is more legible than transliterations;[113] and if the text is in Hebrew, it is easier to compare the text to others with the same graphic inventory and similar graphic norms (p. 24).

Althaus' edition thus includes a Hebrew square script transliteration, a Roman transliteration and a "critical edition" of the poem in Hebrew and in Roman (pp. 8-19). The critical edition consists of a reprint of the transliteration with divisions into lines, punctuation, and five emendations (listed, p. 18). He also offers a "Konstruktion und Edition des Textes" (pp. 210-218), which is, according to his pervasive and obscurantist jargon, a transcription and nothing more than an edition of the text in quasi-normalized Middle High German. The edition in Roman is justified, he claims, because it 1) makes comparisons of Middle High German and Hebrew-Middle High German texts possible; 2) makes conclusions about structural laws of graphemic systems possible; 3) reveals linguistic processes in Middle High German; 4) makes conclusions about textual history possible (pp. 208-209). He condemns Wolf's transcription of the lion fable as too much a transliteration and thus unreadable (pp. 208-209), but his own is in fact hardly more legible. His transcription is generally normalized Middle High German, with few exceptions. He even doubles consonants, includes his "proven" umlauts (see above, chapter two), and makes the text look very German with his /ch/ for כ and /ck/ for ק.

Althaus' method in fact differs little from those of his predecessors, the primary distinction being in his use of obscure terminology and his tediously repetitive insistence on his own objectivity and methodological rigor. He maintains that no identification of the language and dialect can be attempted until the graphemic system of the manuscript has been defined and the phonemic system extrapolated from the defined graphemic system. He accuses his predecessors of the opposite procedure – of having projected their phonemic identification onto the graphemes as their point of departure (p. 42). Yet even in his preface he assumes that the Hebrew graphemic system used in this text, just as the Roman system used for Middle High German texts, was based on the medieval German "Phonemsprache" (p. vii), the implication being that his text in the Hebrew alphabet either *was* essentially German, or if not, at least its writing system was based on some form of spoken German. Althaus does not specify what form of Middle High German he conceives of as appropriate here. He later maintains, however, that despite the fact that normalized Middle High German is no more than a scholarly construct, it can nonetheless be legitimately used for comparative purposes (p. 69). One wonders what comparative *grapho-phonemic* analysis could possibly profit from the use of this artificial, nineteenth-century scholarly dialect of Middle High German.

Thus it comes as no surprise that Althaus later – in the midst of his analysis of graphs, that is before he could, according to his own criteria, deem it methodologically defensible to speak of phonetics/phonemics – takes Middle High German as the underlying, somehow merely disguised language of the text, for he notes without comment (p. 59) that seven Hebrew vowel graphemes *have to* correspond to twenty-four Middle High German vowels, some few of which (he lists them in *phonetic* transcription) are not represented by Hebrew graphemes, and others of which are diphthongs, but are represented only by Hebrew monographs.[114] Althaus consistently uses Middle High German as the basis of his analysis: e.g., p. 62, where a text form is expressed simply as a contraction of a Middle High German word:

"'אִים (xim') kontrahiert aus mhd. *in deme*"; and p. 87: "Anstelle von mhd. *ei* wird in der LF in initialer und medialer Position יי geschrieben" ("in place of Middle High German *ei*, יי is written in initial and medial position in the lion fable") – as if *ei* were actually to be expected in the Hebrew alphabet text. Despite these frequent slips in his methodological mask, Althaus maintains the pretense of objectivity, such that he goes to great lengths to present an argument concerning the relationship of the language of the text to Middle High German – i.e., the relationship which his initial assumption had already defined and from which his entire analysis had derived; even so, the only "objective" conclusion that Althaus can draw (and express) from his tortuous argument is that "der Text einer Sprachnorm angehört, die zu mhd. Sprachnormen in einer bestimmten Beziehung steht."[115] On the one hand, this conservative conclusion is to be praised; on the other, it is only a prelude to less well-founded conclusions.

Thus already in the analysis of the graphemic system – which, according to Althaus is all-important as an objective, pre-phonemic/pre-phonetic stage of the investigation, in fact a *sine qua non* of any legitimate conclusions – one finds that the identification or postulation of graphemic-phonemic identities is one of the most important, if not the only, means of defining the graphemic system. This actual method is followed throughout, even to the point of positing the eight umlauted vowels and diphthongs characteristic of normalized Middle High German, despite the fact that these supposed vowels are represented in the manuscript by the same graphemes as their un-umlauted counterparts (chart, p. 128; discussion, pp. 127-130), and despite the fact that Althaus clearly notes in his text both that the manuscript does not distinguish among long, short, umlauted or un-umlauted /o/ and /u/ (p. 129) and that even Middle High German manuscripts are notoriously unsystematic in representing the posited umlauts of the normalized language (p. 130; i.e., the umlauts that modern scholars would like to find in the manuscripts but most often do not).

His concern for methodological rigor is admirable, but it often seems misdirected and almost naive. For instance, he informs the reader that a certain amount of first-stage decoding is necessary and legitimate in the analysis of such a text: e.g., the researcher does not expect ב = ⟨m⟩ or ע = ⟨r⟩ (p. 70). For the reader who has even a basic knowledge of the Hebrew alphabet, the point is obvious and unnecessary,[116] and for the reader without that knowledge – i.e., for all other readers – it is indecipherable. Even so, the fact that Althaus feels compelled to include such an explanation is interesting, as is his formulation as well: "On the basis of the position and function that the graphs of the Hebrew script take in the system of Hebrew graphemes, conclusions concerning the positions and functions in the graphemic system of Middle-High-German-graphemic-Hebrew are possible. It is, for example, not to be expected that beth corresponds with ⟨m⟩, ayin with ⟨r⟩" ("Von der Position und Funktion, die die Graphe der hebr. Schrift im System der hebräischen Grapheme einnehmen, sind Schlüsse auf Positionen und Funktionen im Graphemsystem der MhdGraHeb möglich. Es ist zB. nicht zu erwarten, das ב mit ⟨m⟩, ע mit ⟨r⟩ ... korrespondiert," p. 70). In other words, he is in fact admitting here to the necessity of active interpretation even in the ostensibly innocuous act of transposition. But at the same time, the lack of an agent (for instance, Althaus) in his passive formulations disguises that admission; and even if the reader does take note of the admission, he is not likely to call Althaus' objectivity into question here, since the graphemic point at issue is so painfully obvious as to trivialize the entire process. Althaus does not, however, concede the slightest necessity for the researcher's interpretation in other cases – where the issues are all but obvious: e.g. in the prefatory remarks to his critical edition (p. 210) he introduces the linguistic term, "Null-grapheme," which are printed in the edition in cursive. As (mis-)used here, the term signifies a *phoneme* assumed by the editor to be present in the text, despite its graphemic (i.e., actual) absence from the text – that is, the editor conjectures a letter where there is none. The introduction of this concept here ostensibly gives the editor no more latitude in emending the text than he has by definition as an editor of a text which has an unconventional system of vowel representation, but its existence as a nameable and named editorial "category" does invest the editor's emendations with an aura of scholarly legitimacy and in fact empowers him to interpret at will. Althaus does not address this issue, but does distinguish these particular alterations of the text in kind from editorial emendations *per se*, which are dealt with separately in the introduction. They are, however, indistinguishable in the edition, since both are printed in cursive.

The result of 157 pages of this method leads to Althaus' table of graphemic-phonemic correspondences: despite the fact that the Hebrew alphabet is a "defective graphemic system" in representing the language of this text, as he claims, Althaus manages to identify all vowel phonemes of the text, and, not surprisingly, this inventory is all but identical to that of normalized Middle High German (there are three exceptions, all perfectly explicable as Middle High German dialect forms, pp. 158-159). Thus after the interminable analysis (which was conditioned and wholy determined by his preconception that the language was Middle High German), Althaus, like most of his predecessors, comes to the conclusion that the language is Middle High German. His pose of objectivity remains, however, and he does not even specify in his conclusion that he has identified the language.

Nevertheless he does at least admit at this point the relevance of Middle High German evidence for determining the provenance and date of the text (p. 176). The analysis of these problems further demonstrates the general weakness of Althaus' study, since in identifying the specific phonetic qualities of vowels pertinent to determining their dialect affiliation, he simply refers to earlier sections of the book as the authority for such identification; those sections do not, however, provide any evidence, but are rather simply the initial mention of this putative identity (pp. 199-201). Here he also appeals to the authority of the Paul/Moser/Schröbler's standard grammar of normalized Middle High German, which, one would have to admit, is legitimate *in the context of his study*, since he has tacitly identified the language as Middle High German all along. He can then identify the dialect of the text as South Thuringian of ca. 1300. As he admits, his conclusion does not differ from those of Röll/Gerhardt and Neumann, but he hastens to add that his is based on evidence, while theirs were methodologically faulty (p. 202).

The final section of the study is a critical edition of the text in Roman transcription, and the text is, as one would expect, simply normalized Middle High German (with some few transliteration symbols, e.g. *ʃ* = *š*). His edition (as his identification of provenance and date) does not differ appreciably from those of his predecessors. Nor could one expect it to do so, since in fact his method of arriving at the edition is also essentially the same as theirs, although he strives at every point to obscure that fact. One wonders why such an edition was necessary. It contributes nothing to the advancement of scholarship in the field.

The excesses of the positivistic project in Old Yiddish textual editing did not go unopposed, as has been noted above, in the discussion of the reviews of Hakkarainen's edition. In Manfred Caliebe, the anti-positivists gained a rather cogent spokesman.[117] His adamantly pro-Germanistic ideology of textual editing and audience generally resembles those of Ganz/Norman/Schwarz, in that he conceives of the audience as one consisting primarily of Germanists whose great interest in Yiddish studies developed after World War II: "the new impulses in Yiddish research find their origin precisely in Germanistic, which is not surprising, since it provides the specialized preparation in linguistic and literary research for solid scholarly work with Yiddish on a large scale" ("die neuen Ansätze der Jiddischforschung gehen gerade von der Germanistik aus, was nicht verwunderlich ist, da diese in Sprach-und Literaturwissenschaft das fachliche Rüstzeug für eine solide wissenschaftliche Beschäftigung mit dem Jiddischen im großen Umfang bietet," "Zur Problematik," p. 52). This viewpoint is also characteristic of Caliebe's study of *Dukus Hurnt*. In the foreword he claims that the work has been "accessible" to a sizable reading public since 1964 ("seit 1964 einem größeren Leserkreis zugänglich," p. 5). Thus he either ignores or chooses to label inaccessible the editions by Fuks and Katz. His reasons are not specified, but one can, on the basis of the general tenor of his approach, speculate that the single-alphabet edition by Katz and the absence of a normalized Middle High German version in Fuks' edition, the presence there of two versions in the Hebrew alphabet, the English language introduction, the Dutch publisher, and the pro-Yiddish editor all contribute to its "inaccessibility," as opposed to the "accessible" Tübingen edition with its German introduction and publisher, absence of a Hebrew-alphabet text, presence of a Roman transliteration and Middle High German transcription, edited by three Germanists, and published in Germany. Later, however, he betrays a disconcerting ignorance of Fuks' edition: "In addition to a facsimile of the manuscript and a modern German table of contents which he did not write, L. Fuks has given only a reprint in Hebrew letters, which is unsuitable for a thorough study of the text by Germanists" ("L. Fuks hat neben einem Faksimile der Handschrift und einer, nicht aus seiner Feder stammenden, neuhochdeutschen Inhaltsangabe nur einem Abdruck in hebräischen Buchstaben gegeben, was für eine gründliche Bearbeitung des Textes durch Germanisten ungünstig war," *Dukus Horant*, p. 10). Fuks' edition additionally has a Roman transliteration (the very type of version that would, according to Caliebe, make the edition more accessible), *but* in fact no modern German table of contents; instead it contains a modern German *translation*. One wonders how Caliebe could make such an error, until one checks his footnote reference here to Röll's review of Ganz/Norman/Schwarz,[118] the relevant passage of which is remarkably similar to Caliebe's: "doch stand die Tatsache, dass Fuks neben einem Faksimile und einer ungenauen neuhochdeutschen Prosafassung (die nicht aus seiner Feder stammt) nur einen Abdruck in hebräischen Buchstaben gab, und die Unsicherheit des Textes einer weitergehenden Erforschung durch Germanisten entgegen" (p. 269). Caliebe's paraphrase of Röll at points even goes as far as (unacknowledged) quotation. One wonders then why he changes Röll's "prose version" to "table of contents" – if he did not know Fuks' edition himself, then he should have at least taken Röll's word for it, if he could not inform himself by examining the edition. But then one must also question why Röll denies the presence of the Roman transliteration in Fuks' edition – which is in fact one of the major sticking points for both him and Caliebe[119] in their notions of the inaccessibility to Germanists.

The Tübingen edition which Caliebe so praises over Fuks established "a basis for Germanists . . . on which further research can build" ("für den Germanisten eine Arbeitsgrundlage . . . auf der die weitere Forschung aufbauen kann," p. 11). Even this edition, however, is not the ultimate tool of the Germanist, for Caliebe notes that Röll's planned critical edition will give "a still more easily surveyable text" ("einen noch übersichtlicheren Text"), which he cites in his study. Caliebe's major criteria for an acceptable critical edition of *Dukus Hurnt* include a consideration of metrics and rhyme – both conceived strictly in terms of a posited Middle High German base text – and stanzaic structure: in other words, a hyper-Germanistic edition which outdoes even Ganz/Norman/Schwarz. His requirement of a more accessible text explains his rejection of Hakkarainen's edition, since its avowed purpose is not to produce a text that reveals the language and dialect of the text.[120] Caliebe lets fall the magic comparison – Hakkarainen failed to produce a text that is more legible for the Germanist than the Hebrew-alphabet original (p. 13). In contrast to Hakkarainen's edition, Althaus' of the lion fable is praised as exemplary for its production of a text on the basis of an analysis of the graphic inventory (p. 14, n. 24a). The results of this edition have already been treated above.

The extremities of Hakkarainen and Althaus' positivistic stance essentially exhausted this school of textual editing in Old Yiddish, just as the excesses of Marchand's work had put an end to a previous stage of research and editing. But at the same time, a new editorial methodology was developing, which has brought about a second transformation of the editorial paradigm, but which in some senses returns the focus to a topic similar to that of the first stage of scholarship on Old Yiddish: the significance of these literary documents as *cultural* documents. These two stages are distinguished, however, by the fact that now the texts are not viewed as German literature disguised in the Hebrew alphabet, but as *Jewish* literature that participates – in its own unique way – in the tradition of European literature of the Middle Ages. The editorial principles are essentially a hybrid of various ideological positions, combining some aspects of both the Germanistic and Yiddishist programs. Although its theoretical principles do seem to offer a new paradigm, in practice it still bears many of the traditional problems of Yiddish textual editing, and in fact there is no strict uniformity of editorial principles and ideology among this group of editors. A consideration of the implications of the interdisciplinary and intercultural approach characteristic of these scholars forms the subject of the following chapter.

FOUR

The New Paradigm(s)

THE MOST RECENT approach to the research problems in Old Yiddish studies is still in its initial stages of development; it redefines the problem in its entirety and for the first time proposes a new primary question. The old question – Old Yiddish or Middle High German? – is recognized as, or at least treated as an aporia, a question that distorts the object of study and distracts from what have been or what have become more important scholarly concerns. This approach has not abandoned the essential dichotomy of previous analyses, nor does it reject all or even most of the information and insights accumulated by studies of the first two ideological stages. Rather, it attempts to reformulate the question to take into account the broader cultural contexts of the literary documents under investigation. No longer do mere word counts, discussions of German versus Jewish motifs, and graphemic-phonemic correspondences dominate. Instead scholars have turned their attention to the cultural conditions of literary production and reception, and to the establishment and utilization of various available literary traditions.

On the other hand, however, in dealing with the text *per se*, that is, in determining how to present the text in an edition, these scholars differ among themselves widely in their practices, displaying the traditional duality of solutions to the problems of representing Old Yiddish texts: both Roman transcriptions into Middle High German and Hebrew-alphabet editions of the texts. This dichotomy surprisingly (due to the otherwise generally "enlightened" views of those favoring transcription) reflects the disciplinary and/or cultural affiliations of the scholars involved. Chief among these scholars are Maks Weinreich, Lajb Fuks, Khone Shmeruk, Walter Röll, Manfred Caliebe, Wulf-Otto Dreeßen, and Erika Timm.[1]

As was discussed at the beginning of chapter two above, Maks Weinreich was a staunch defender of the strictly pro-Yiddish ideology, both in naming all stages of the language and (seen in his response to Marchand) in adamantly opposing all Roman transposition of texts. His ideological program developed along consistent lines throughout his long scholarly career, culminating in his monumental study, *Geshikhte fun der yidisher shprakh*, which is, in one sense, an extended treatise on the necessity of dealing with all periods of Yiddish language and literature as integral elements of an inevitably discrete and independent – not to say isolated – Yiddish cultural life, summed up in the concept of *yidishkayt*. He rarely deals specifically with the processes and mechanisms of medieval literary production and transmission, but his general argument consistently adheres to the notion that texts produced by and for a Jewish community and transmitted by that community through its traditional methods of textual transmission can only be dealt with in terms of the larger cultural context of that community. To extract a text or texts from that context – through identification of the text's language as German, through Roman transposition of the text, through an interpretive focus on that extant text's cultural background as other than Jewish, is to misrepresent the text and the culture that produced it.

Weinreich nevertheless never attempts to deny the multi-cultural nature of (medieval) Jewish culture, as the example of his analysis of Yiddish as a fusion language clearly demonstrates: the language itself is a product of various stages of fusion of numerous linguistic determinants (Germanic, Semitic, Slavic, and Romance), but that "product" is, at any given period of development, necessarily an independent system in itself. The culture as a whole, just as the language and literary corpus of the culture, selects (as it were), adapts, and integrates elements which were theretofore external and alien. The linguistic similarity of Old Yiddish to Middle High German does not thus render the former simply a sub-class of the latter; nor can a literary text whose theme was borrowed from German (or French or Hebrew) into Yiddish be considered other than a Yiddish literary text.

Weinreich's scholarly oeuvre can thus in one sense be seen as a career-long quest to de-marginalize (Old) Yiddish language (and thus by extension also Yiddish culture) and establish it as a discrete, independent entity, recognized as functioning as the center of its own structure. Early in his career he was one of the co-founders of YIVO, which centers Yiddish culture as has no other institution before or since; in his four-volume history of the Yiddish language, written in Yiddish, he has provided an example of and a monument to this centering. In this respect, the work of Lajb Fuks and Khone Shmeruk is quite similar, but here the implications of the broadly culturally-based pro-Yiddish ideology become somewhat more concrete, for Fuks and Shmeruk's work has been of a much more "practical" tendency.

In addition to the Cambridge codex, Fuks has published editions of the *Shmuel-bukh* and the *Melokhim-bukh.*[2] In thus publishing three of the major works of Old Yiddish literature, Fuks' editorial practice has also become a force with which to reckon in Old Yiddish studies. After the edition of the Cambridge codex, he has moved more and more in the direction of Maks Weinreich's dictum that the transposition of Old Yiddish texts into Roman in any form is "detrimental." The extent to which this is the case is clearly demonstrated in his publication of Falk's edition of *Shmuel-bukh,* which the original editor had planned for three separate publications designed for three distinct modern audiences: 1) a critical edition of the Augsburg *editio princeps* (in the Hebrew alphabet); 2) a partial critical edition in normalized Middle High German, with accompanying Hebrew alphabet text; 3) a full edition in Roman, normalized Middle High German, without critical apparatus. Fuks argues in his preface that a facsimile of the *editio princeps* is a necessary complement to Falk's critical notes and is more useful for scholarly purposes than any *Idealtext* in a form of Middle High German (*Schmuel-buch,* I, xii). Thus he prints *no* text other than the facsimile in the Hebrew alphabet!

In the "Vorbemerkung" to his own edition of *Melokhim-bukh,* Fuks contends that it is only by means of facsimile editions that Old Yiddish scholarship can be duly served, since editions in Middle High German distort the evidence and give the impression that Old Yiddish literature is somehow *German* literature *(Melokhim-bukh,* I, "Vorbemerkung," n.p.). Fuks' editions are thus significant for at least two reasons: 1) he makes available to the scholar/reader the texts in the "actual" form, or at least in the form closest to the manuscript, i.e., photographic facsimiles;[3] and 2) by means of this radical (in comparison to the tradition of Old Yiddish editions) practice, he has evoked quite different responses from the Old Yiddish editorial community, especially Shmeruk and Dreeßen.

Shmeruk has published an edition – in the Hebrew alphabet –

of *Yosef Hatsadik* (discussed above, chapter three) and has been active in a large-scale project to make available on microfilm many early Yiddish texts, and in his review of Fuks' facsimile edition of *Melokhim-bukh*, his editorial ideology is clearly revealed, for he praises the edition for establishing "a solide un tsuganglekhe base" for Old Yiddish studies.[4] That is, he extols the accessibility of the text – that is edited and published exclusively in a Hebrew-alphabet facsimile – not just to a "wider circle of readers and scholars," but "far jedn farinteresirtn"! (Shmeruk, rev., p. 209). Thus he intimates that all interested readers by definition and without further comment can read the text in the Hebrew alphabet, thus radically modifying the accessibility topos of Old Yiddish studies.

The necessary affiliation of Old Yiddish texts with medieval Jewish culture has thus been established by the work of Weinreich, Fuks, Shmeruk, and others, but another branch of Old Yiddish scholarship has recently begun to take further steps to investigate the place of these documents in the medieval Jewish cultural context. Many questions remain: why was, for instance, *Dukus Hurnt*, adapted into Yiddish, while other works were not? What conditions in medieval Jewish society "encouraged" the adaptation and integration of particular non-Jewish literary works? What was the audience of such works? What elements in the Jewish community functioned as patrons? What were the conditions of the artists themselves?[5] It has been from another, rather unexpected, quarter that such questions have been addressed in recent years: by a (primarily) post-World War II generation of German scholars of Germanistic orientation.[6] That disciplinary orientation makes itself felt at all times and determines many aspects of the work of these scholars, but is nevertheless not nearly so dominant as was the case in earlier periods (and is even now the case among non-German Germanists, such as Marchand and Lockwood).

The contributions of Walter Röll to the discussion of early Yiddish deal with problems of name and language only obliquely, since his primary orientation has been toward literary analysis. As one of the staunchest promoters of Yiddish studies in post-war Germany, however, he has furthered the development of the field through the encouragement of numerous students and young scholars. His ideological position is, as is the case for most of the Trier School, difficult to classify. In 1967, he noted that the Cambridge codex contains no linguistic features which would allow one to call it anything but Middle High German,[7] and his text citations from *Dukus Hurnt* are in a transcribed construction, the principles of which he pointedly declines to elucidate; its form is generally that of normalized Middle High German, although he claims it is "weitgehend neutral" (p. 518).[8] In his article on *Dukus Hurnt* in *Kindlers Literaturlexikon*, he calls the text "mhd." in Hebrew letters;[9] and in his response to and complement of Weissberg's article on the consonant inventory of the manuscript, he identifies manuscript readings with their normalized Middle High German forms.[10] Eight years after "Literarische Einordnung," however, Röll calls the codex "die älteste bekannte Sammlung jiddischer literarischer Texte"[11] and details several linguistic features in the texts which identify them as Yiddish (especially pp. 66-68). His articles in *Kindlers Literaturlexikon* on "Abraham" ("Awroham Owinu," I, 573) and "Gan Eden" (II, 1069) identify the poems as Old Yiddish.

At the end of his foreword to the special volume of *Zeitschrift für deutsche Philologie* which he edited and which is devoted to Yiddish studies, Röll remarks: "Finally a technical note. The transposition of Yiddish and Hebrew texts is not uniform. I have attempted, at least for older Yiddish texts, to achieve a certain measure of uniformity. I hope that the historically conditioned lack of uniformity on this point, which reflects the international nature of this field, does not contribute to the confusion."[12] It is obvious from this statement that he is not unaware either of the problems arising out of any transposition, especially those of early Yiddish texts or of the multiple systems of transposition used throughout the world in order to deal with these problems. Why then does he consider it necessary to mask those problems and the solutions by the various contributors by means of his imposed *Konvergenz*, especially when he already assumes that this problem in general is confused, for he fears a further "contribution" to the confusion via his standardization?

His work on *Dukus Hurnt* and Old Yiddish in general is thus of a dual nature: while accepting the language and literature in general as phenomena of Jewish culture, he initially favored an implicit usurpation of at least *Dukus Hurnt* for the German tradition by means of his transcription of that text into Middle High German for the purpose of a critical edition. The fact that he abandoned this transcribed edition must, however, figure significantly in any evaluation of his general role in the study of Old Yiddish.

In his monograph on *Dukus Hurnt*[13] Manfred Caliebe concentrates on the text as a literary document, and thus conclusions about his interpretation of the language must be drawn on the basis of his practice and a few oblique remarks. He cites the text in Röll's normalized Middle High German construction, and thus for him the text *is* simply Middle High German. He offers no justification for this choice other than that it is "übersichtlicher" ("more easily surveyed," p. 11) than previous editions, i.e., one must assume, according to the customary signification of this and similar terms concerning "accessibility," closer to standard German. Caliebe's analysis of the text as a literary document is, however, not nearly so characteristically pro-Germanistic and anti-Yiddishistic as one might expect on the basis of his identification of the language. Even so, Caliebe concentrates almost exclusively on the Germanic literary tradition at work in the text, which is certainly the dominant one in this particular text. He deals with it in great detail, but in doing so, he treats the adapter's alterations of that tradition for his Jewish audience somewhat too summarily, thus misrepresenting their significance.

Caliebe's published response to Helmut Dinse's study of Yiddish is perhaps even more important in evaluating Caliebe's work than his own monograph. Here he does deal specifically with the problem of the names of Yiddish.[14] He rejects Dinse's denial of the name "Jiddisch" to West Yiddish (which Dinse calls "Jüdisch-deutsch").[15] Dinse justifies his claim on the basis that "Jüdisch-deutsch" is completely based on Middle High German dialects (Dinse, p. xxii; Caliebe, p. 53). But immediately prior to this argument, Dinse had maintained that both West Yiddish and East Yiddish had the same origin. Caliebe points out that if one wishes to justify the name "Jüdisch-deutsch" for West Yiddish alone, the more legitimate argument would be that West Yiddish remained in contact with German and thus did not develop as independently as did East Yiddish (p. 53; this is not, however, Caliebe's argument). He also criticizes Dinse's unfounded dating of the origin of Yiddish to the transitional period between Middle High German and New High German, which Dinse apparently derived from a misreading of Birnbaum;[16] and thus Dinse anachronistically joins the ranks of the assimilationists who saw Yiddish as a mere corruption of modern German without a pre-sixteenth-century history. The same is true with respect to his notion of the development of Yiddish as a function solely of the religion of the Jews, ignoring, as Caliebe points out, the significant factors of economics and geographical location (Caliebe, p. 52; Dinse, p. xx). Caliebe's evaluation of Dinse's work presents another example of the "dangerous/difficult" topos of Yiddish studies: "with publications such as this, Yiddish studies will continue to have difficulty gaining recognition as a scholarly discipline. A book like this one does more harm than good."[17]

The work of Wulf-Otto Dreeßen is scrupulously researched and informed and is characterized by its attention to the historical and ideological problems inherent to the field of Old Yiddish studies. Dreeßen's publications deal with a variety of topics in Old Yiddish, especially as they seek to reformulate the dominant question.[18] He notes, for example, that the problem of the (name of the) language of the texts is not merely one of terminology, but of great significance for further questions of analysis.[19] Like Maks Weinreich, he addresses the problem of the use of Hebrew vs. Germanic words in texts as a matter of style and register, and not one of significance in identifying the language as Middle High German or Old Yiddish: the Hebrew word usually being of a more formal, restricted register and thus appropriate only in certain textual contexts.[20] The use of a Germanic word for which there is also an available Hebrew word appropriate to the stylistic context is often due to narrative demands on characterization: the poet tends to place the Germanic rather than the Hebrew word in the mouth of the non-Jewish character ("Synonymik," p. 66). The entire question of Hebrew word counts is rejected by Dreeßen since, as had been pointed out earlier by Weinreich, legitimate analysis of non-Yiddish vs. Yiddish lexemes must also take into account all Germanic words used in non-German semantic functions (p. 67; e.g., *lernen* "to study the Talmud").

The entire problem of Middle High German vs. Yiddish as the dominant question of Old Yiddish studies is viewed by Dreeßen as an outmoded relic of the nineteenth-century romantic notion of literary history as a history of national literatures, a method which has all but disappeared from recent literary criticism, but has strangely remained current in Yiddish studies ("Rezeption," p. 116). The legitimate problem is thus not one of German vs. Yiddish language, but rather one of the production and reception of literary works in German vs. Yiddish. These latter texts, whatever their linguistic identity, whatever the origin of their motifs, whatever the percentage of the Hebrew versus Germanic lexical components (even those allegedly transcribed/transliterated from Roman into Hebrew) must be dealt with as Jewish literature in the context of that subset of society, since that is where such texts functioned as literature.[21] The essence of this approach may be illustrated by its attention to the facts of textual "intention," reception, and text transmission.

In his article on the concept of midrashic vs. biblical epic, he points out that the thesis advanced by Marchand and Howard that the sources of a literary text must be exclusively Jewish in order for it to be designated Yiddish makes no more sense than, for instance pointing to the Babylonian origin of the Mordkhe/Esther story and suggesting that the Esther texts of both the Deutscher Orden and the medieval Jews belong exclusively to Babylonian literature.[22] One must look closer at the "intention" of the poems and their audience and reception. As it turns out, these Jewish texts in fact do not have the Bible as a source, but rather use midrashim, which were not accessible to Christian writers; such texts can hardly be considered "German" in any regard, since both their source and their audience were Jewish.

These texts were not transmitted in the medieval period via the Christian institutions of literacy – the medieval monastic and cathedral scriptoria, the libraries of royalty, or the urban patriciate. Rather, one finds them, for instance, in the Cairo Genizah. The mechanisms of their transmission were Jewish: they were written by Jews in the Hebrew alphabet[23] in the Jewish community for a Jewish audience.[24] What sense does it make to treat them as culturally German, despite any linguistic affinities between the language of these documents and Middle High German? Here we have to do with documents of cultural significance, and the *Sitz im Leben* must be determined in the case of each text.[25] The constitution of these texts thus can reveal much about the literary and cultural traditions of medieval Jewry in central Europe, about cross-cultural currents, and about the nature and purpose of the earliest extant vernacular literary production in Ashkenazic culture. Dreeßen thus emphasizes that to deal with these texts as purely linguistic data is to utterly misunderstand and misrepresent their significance. He designates them *altjiddisch*.

When one turns to a consideration of Dreeßen's editorial policy, however, one finds it anything but consistent with his general interpretive strategy. He has, for instance, responded to Fuks' later principles and practice in great detail and from quite a different perspective.[26] He notes that scholars are in general still not in agreement about the ultimate value of facsimile editions and remarks further that if Old Yiddish texts are to gain the interest of Germanists that is due them, "die Schriftschranke [muß] überwunden werden" ("the barrier of the script [must] be surmounted," *Doniel*, II, 1). In isolation, this statement could be interpreted to mean either that the texts must be edited in Roman, or that Germanists must learn the Hebrew alphabet. Dreeßen's approach is, however, a strictly practical one, specifically in terms of Germanistic research, for he notes that Fuks' editions of *Melokhim-bukh* and *Shmuel-bukh* in Hebrew-alphabet facsimiles drew little attention from Germanists, while the edition in Roman of *Dukus Hurnt* by Ganz/Norman/Schwarz significantly intensified the study of that text.[27] And thus, he argues, Old Yiddish texts should be printed in Roman.

Dreeßen's guiding principles are to present a single text, in Roman, that, unlike Hakkarainen's (relatively) strict transliteration, is "legible" and "kontrollierbar," that is, a strictly accurate representation of the manuscript text (via the edited text itself and its critical apparatus), which the reader could check against the manuscript. Among the consequences of such an edition is that a facsimile (and indeed the manuscript?) becomes superfluous, as Dreeßen/Müller in fact claim.[28] Dreeßen justifies his use of Roman with two philological arguments: vowels can be differentiated more precisely in Roman than in the original;[29] and for scholars, especially those concerned with German or Dutch texts, the edition in Roman is more accessible, and it would be a mistake to deny these Germanists access to the texts and thus prevent their participation in the scholarly dialogue, simply for the sake of the preservation of the text in the original alphabet (*Akedass*, p. 5).

As noted, however, Dreeßen and Müller do nevertheless include a facsimile volume in their edition of *Doniel* and justify (and restrict) the value of facsimiles in some detail.[30] Their justifications are significant, but at the same time they reveal what slight value the original text has in their estimation for the scholarly uses of the edition. And in contrast to Dreeßen's reasons for a Roman edition, the reasons for a facsimile are "cultural": facsimiles are valuable in the study of the history of early printing (especially with respect to the *Doniel* text); they enhance the "legibility" of the Hebrew-alphabet text over a Roman version for many of the modern readers of Old Yiddish literature: they are manifestations of the historical significance of the Hebrew alphabet as the vehicle of Yiddish literature. Transcriptions are by definition scholarly constructs, necessarily fraught with interpretation; unlike the language itself, which in its essence embodies a blending of its Judaic and German components, the *study* of Yiddish is still far removed from such a melding, and thus an edition with both a Hebrew-alphabet *and* a Roman-alphabet text is appropriate (*Doniel* II, 3-4). The facsimile is thus viewed simply as an adjunct to the edition in Roman, for the convenience of part of the audience, but not as an essential part of the edition; its inclusion is due in large part (as the editors note) to recent technical developments which render facsimile editions financially feasible, and not to its value as a research resource or to recognized scholarly need.

Dreeßen also addresses a recurring point in editorial prefaces: that there must be two types of editions of Old Yiddish texts – one for linguistic research, and one for literary scholars. One can normally classify extant editions according to these two categories, usually dependent on whether the edition is in transliteration (for linguists) or transcription (for literary scholars and general readers). The assumptions regarding these two types of editions are, in simplified form: the linguist does not need a "legible" text, since his/her primary concern is not reading, but minute linguistic analysis. Also, if the Roman version of an Old Yiddish text is a strict enough transliteration to allow a "reconstruction" of the original, then the linguist need have no recourse to the original Hebrew-alphabet text. The literary scholar on the other hand needs first and foremost a "legible" text that will allow fluent reading of the text.[31]

Dreeßen's principles raise a number of problems. If the linguist using the edition has no knowledge of the Hebrew alphabet, he is always at the mercy of the editor's accuracy and consistency, for he cannot himself "reconstruct" the original nor even check the accuracy of the edition (that is, the text is in fact not "kontrollierbar"). On the other hand, the literary scholar, who it is assumed also has no knowledge of the Hebrew alphabet, must rely on a text that is not only in Roman, but has been sufficiently manipulated such that it is "fluently legible."

In principle there can be few objections to Dreeßen's projection of an ideal edition (which he by no means claims to have produced) that meets the needs of both linguistic and literary scholars by being "legible" and "kontrollierbar." In practice, however, editions of Old Yiddish texts have traditionally fulfilled few of Dreeßen's requirements, and while his own editions are dramatic improvements over his forbears – primarily because he is quite aware of the many ideological pitfalls to which such editions are subject and makes a point of addressing these problems – they suffer from many of the same problems as those that plagued his predecessors. He chooses, for instance, to take as an orthographic model for transcription a "historically-given orthographic system," for the sake of the audience's convenience in reading. The chosen system is that of the "nächst verwandte Sprache," i.e., German, and the details of the system are generally adopted from Staerk-Leitzmann's system of transcription into a form of early New High German (*Akedass*, pp. 72-73). The assumption here is that the audience is by definition German.[32] Thus while claiming that the texts in question are Yiddish, not German, Dreeßen's intended audience is strictly German(ists), and his edition is conditioned by (the putative needs of) that intended audience; thus he transcribes the Old Yiddish text into Early Modern German, an edited form which, he nevertheless contends, renders the need and value of the original text negligible.

Erika Timm has published three major studies of Old Yiddish. In her analysis and edition of *Beria and Simra*, Timm treats the text as a work of Old Yiddish literature (so designated, even from p. 1), and a participant in the Jewish and specifically Yiddish literary tradition.[33] Her study of the lion fable of the Cambridge codex is similar in its purpose, but more interesting in the present context, since it deals with a text that has been subject to a variety of interpretations of its language and cultural origins. She deals with the text in its cultural context and in relation to the literary tradition*s* both prior and subsequent to its composition.[34] She never addresses the question of the language of the text, except to note (p. 157) that the poet had a good understanding of the German literary tradition, such that he could even turn this knowledge to good phraseological use in *his own* composition. The implication is that the poem is Old Yiddish, but it remains an implication, since Timm's purpose is to deal with the complexities of the *literary* traditions at work in this widespread fable. In doing so, she demonstrates that the text of the Cambridge codex participated in a Jewish literary tradition as a mediate text between a Hebrew and later Yiddish version, i.e. this text functioned as an available text in the Jewish and specifically Yiddish literary tradition. In dealing with this text as a literary work (in a manner similar to that suggested by Dreeßen), she draws conclusions that seem much more important ultimately than the primarily linguistic concerns of the positivists.

Timm's editorial practice exhibits the same inconsistency with her general interpretive strategy as does Dreeßen's. Since her transcription and editorial principles are in large part derived from those of Dreeßen, it is not surprising in her edition of *Beria und Simra* that she makes the same general assumptions of audience identity as he had.[35] She addresses the problem of audience directly in *Beria and Simra* and notes that most recent Germanistic interest in Old Yiddish has been directed to linguistic rather than literary problems, due in large part, she maintains, to the obstacle of the Hebrew script, which hinders the literary scholar from achieving the *Ganzheitseindruck* necessary for literary scholarship and attainable only through fluency in reading. Thus, with a bow to the importance of the Hebrew script for Jewish culture,[36] she concludes that since an edition is accessible to the largest possible number of readers only when it is presented in their orthography, then her audience will be more numerous and can better profit from the edition if it is constructed in a Roman-alphabet edition according to German orthographic rules (p. 2). Thus she does not ascribe to the ignorant Germanist theory altogether, since she does not insist on Germanists' ignorance of the Hebrew alphabet, but only suggests that they read the Roman alphabet with more ease, and texts in German orthography still more fluently.[37] As to her last point – that a Roman-alphabet version will reach a larger public – I am very skeptical. Those who do not know the Hebrew alphabet constitute a very small portion indeed of the audience of Old Yiddish.

Also like Dreeßen, Timm is quite aware of the historical and ideological problems associated with her subject, as becomes clear in the reflective and problematic question she poses regarding the potential audience: "finally one may pose the question as to what audience an edition appearing in Germany can address today" ("schließlich wäre zu fragen, welchen Leserkreis heute eine in Deutschland erscheinende Ausgabe ansprechen kann.") In its formulation, the question shows that the problem is perceived in a restricted way – is the fact of publication in Germany relevant because of publication in the German language and the consequent restrictions on its reading public? The effect on the potential audience due to the cataclysmic history of Germany and Jewry in the present century? Or simply the needs of a Germanistic audience? The question is not formulated so specifically.

Timm's Roman-alphabet version is executed on Dreeßen's hybrid system of transliteration/transcription principles. She lists its advantages as follows: 1) it allows for an accurate reconstruction of the original and thus makes use of the original superfluous for scholarly purposes (linguistic and literary); 2) it reduces the double edition of original or transliteration *and* transcription to a single text; 3) it makes possible a consideration of the phonetic system, insofar as it is determinable;[38] 4) it seeks to reach the largest possible audience, in that its transliteration/transcription system is based on the orthographic tradition of the audience. These are the four guiding principles of reconstruction, economy, interpretation and utility.

These principles are all compromises, as are, of course, all editorial principles when put into practice, but here the normal bounds of editorial compromise are stretched rather wide. The first principle is, as noted above in discussing Dreeßen's work, questionable on principle; the second is irrelevant: the question is more legitimately not just how many texts the edition includes, but rather how many are necessary for the purposes of the edition. Principle three is hard to interpret, but seems to make the claim that such a transliteration/

transcription is more revealing of the phonetic system than is a mere transcription. Principle four illustrates the cliché of robbing Peter to pay Paul: if the orthographic tradition of a linguistically unified audience is indeed as important as Timm claims, then by transforming the text into German orthography she alienates all non-speakers and non-native speakers (and readers) of German.[39]

The third of Timm's major publications is her *Habilitationschrift*, which as originally conceived was to be a "linguistic commentary" to her edition of *Beria and Simra*, including a justification of the system of transposition.[40] When this commentary appeared a decade-and-a-half after the edition, it was no longer merely a justification of the transposition, but had rather grown into a comprehensive six-hundred-page analysis of the grapho-phonemic system of Old and especially Middle Yiddish. No other published study on this topic, however that topic has been conceived and constructed, bears any comparison to Timm's monumental achievement.[41]

In such a study it is not surprising that Timm justifies her designation of the language. She designates early Yiddish texts *Jiddisch*, even though, as she notes, "their graphemic systems reveal no clear phonetic distinctions from coterritorial varieties of German" (p. 357). As a result of Weinberg's attempt to rehabilitate the term "Jüdischdeutsch," she justifies her usage. The justification is based on a uniform view of the field: it is more appropriate to designate the languages of the western and eastern dialects as West and East Yiddish than as Judeo-German (in the West) and Yiddish (in the East); and likewise it is more appropriate to designate the western idiom of whatever period, from whatever scientific perspective, uniformly as Yiddish rather than as Yiddish in one context and Judeo-German in another (p. 358). Further, she argues for Yiddish as the appropriate designation for the earliest documents of the idiom for much the same reason as those which have led to the distinctive nomenclature German-Dutch. Despite the strictly German*ic* identity of Dutch (with slight admixture of non-Germanic loan words, of course), there is no reason to subsume it or its history under that of German; how much less so is that the case with Yiddish, which has Germanic as only one of its components.

Generally on early Yiddish, Timm notes that the language is to be seen as part of a Yiddish linguistic continuum and not as a linguistically easily identifiable entity in opposition to cotemporal German, except in its transmission via the Hebrew alphabet (p. 385); not until the late Middle Ages does Yiddish literature contain a substantial Hebrew component (pp. 385-386); the independence of Yiddish appears more clearly in vocabulary than in grammar, since it seems to be here that a conscious attempt was made to profile the group language and distinguish it from that of those exterior to the group (p. 386). By 1500, according to Timm (p. 386), Yiddish has achieved such a measure of independence, that no one denies its linguistic integrity; here she, like Birnbaum and Weinreich before her, is obviously substituting prescription for description, still in the pro-Yiddish cause, as it were.

Timm's study was originally announced as a linguistic commentary, which, by means of an explanation of the Dreeßen/Timm system of transposition, would justify her "editorial procedure,"[42] and this is in fact the main focus of the investigation. The first quarter of the study maintains an at times almost maddeningly scrupulous empiricism, for she initially assumes the intellectual pose of extreme positivism, which pretends to begin an investigation without knowledge of any aspect of its object. She holds the pose well, so well in fact that she easily outdoes even the arch-positivists, Hakkarainen and Althaus. In the course of this first part of her study, all material not directly derived from her study is enclosed in brackets, to set it off from "objectively obtained" information.[43] The practice is at first tedious indeed for the reader, who must work through the thirty-five densely detailed (and methodologically exasperating) pages of the graphetic analysis in order to discover that the symbols used to write the texts under examination are based on a principle of "ausdrucksseitig-subsyllabischer Segmentation," that is, an alphabetic script. Not until five pages later is this script finally identified as "varieties of the Hebrew alphabet," the letters of which can thus legitimately be transliterated into square script and called by name.

The same fanatically positivistic method is then applied to the graphemic system. Proceeding according to both established and innovative linguistic methods, Timm attempts to identify vowel vs. consonant graphs, but ultimately abandons much of her fictive principle of 'internal analysis' (*Immanenzprinzip*), since the material will not yield results via this method (p. 59); graphemic analysis without concomitant phonemic analysis is "wenig ergiebig" ('hardly profitable,' p. 67), and ultimately causes insurmountable problems in phonetic/phonemic analysis, so that she declares a rigorously empirical method unsuitable for such analysis and abandons it.

Her own pose of the purely objective scientist who begins with a *tabula rasa*, is after all only a pose, and Timm has clearly identified it as such at the very outset and periodically also reminds the reader of the ficticity of this pose of facticity (e.g., p. 40). Thus it seems, but only seems, that Timm leads us around in hyper-positivistic circles as Hakkarainen and Althaus had done, whereas in fact her ultimate purpose is, by means of an uncompromisingly strict application of its principles, once and for all to demonstrate that this scientifistic approach to grapho-phonemic analysis (in early Yiddish) is fruitless. Or, as she more entertainingly suggests, if the scholar submits to peer pressure to exclude all non-linguistic data from the investigation, then s/he condemns her/himself to a "pseudo-detectivistic state of consciousness" *(pseudodetektivische Bewußtseinslage)*, which in the long run can only hinder all empirical scholarship. She thus abandons such principles and provides as much ancillary contextual information as is necessary in order to interpret the 'internal' evidence (p. 59).

With this abandonment of the principle of a strict empiricism, she as a consequence also denies the possibility of realizing one of the ideals of structuralist historical linguistics: performing synchronic analysis independent of diachronic analysis, which, if successful, would reduce diachronic analysis to a mere catalogue of the relationships among various synchronic stages (p. 75).

A further consequence of the abandonment of the principle of internal analysis is the perceived need for a language of comparison exterior to that of the texts. Timm chooses normalized Middle High German as the most appropriate such language. She notes that while normalizations are welcome as a standard of citation, caution must be exercised in the use of the Middle High German normalizations of the Lachmann school and the Hebrew normalizations of the Massoretic tradition (p. 77), and normalized Middle High German should be replaced by non-normalized forms wherever the latter offer more exact information (p. 75). Nonetheless, she makes consistent use of normalized Middle High German in the remainder of the study, for in her apology (not to say defense) of the practice, she claims that in general there is no viable alternative,[44] and in the case of Middle High German, non-normalized forms carry no more exact information (as here defined) than do normalized ones, since Middle High German presents no cases of phonemic merge not also present in Yiddish. Thus the use of normalized texts (apparently even in phonetic/phonemic analysis) is justified, she claims.

Timm identifies the primary purpose of her study as "einen möglichst großen Teil der Untersuchungseinheit hinsichtlich der Verteilung der einzelnen Graphien ausschließlich mit Hilfe graphematischer oder (zu erschließender) phonematischer Bedingungen – also ohne Nennung einzelner Lexeme bzw. morphemischer oder sonstiger Kategorien – zu beschreiben." (p. 82). The conclusions Timm draws from her detailed analytical study take up almost 150 pages (pp. 357-499); the chapter is dense, well-argued, scrupulously researched and documented, constantly informative and often even entertaining. The rich data base on which she draws allows her to confirm many important suppositions by previous scholars and to add important new theses of her own.

What ultimately results is, despite her qualification of her achievement (p. 89), a "Lautlehre" of Middle Yiddish, especially in its larger context of historical West Yiddish. It is a monumental undertaking and, the present critique notwithstanding, a comparably monumental achievement. As with all undertakings and achievements of this magnitude, it is not without its problems, but Timm's literary and linguistic sophistication and astoundingly wide reading in theoretical linguistics, Germanic linguistics, Judaic studies, and Old and Middle Yiddish primary texts, and her long experience in conducting advanced seminars in early Yiddish language and literature inform the study throughout.

Perhaps the best indication of the effects of ideology on textual studies is to analyze illustrative examples of textual editing. Thus manuscript readings of three texts and editorial readings will be presented and commented on here. The first is from the lion's fable from the Cambridge codex.[45]

Ms.: איין פ̆ערט שלוק אין מיט ליקן דש / בגונדא אין זירא ארש̆ריקן
Fuks 1: איין פ̆ערט שלוק אין מיט ליקן דש / בגונדא אין זירא ארשריקן
Althaus 1: איין פ̆ערט שלוק אין מיט ליקן. / דש בגונדא אין זירא ארש̆ריקן,
Katz: איין פ̆ערט שלוק אין מיט ליקן. דש / בגונדא אין זירא ארש̆ריקן
Fuks 2: 'iin ṗert slvk 'in mit likn ds / bgvnd' 'in zir' 'rsrikn.
Hakkarainen: ˀiin pfert slvk ˀin mit likn . ds / bgvndˀ ˀin zirˀ ˀršrikn.
Althaus 2: ein phërt sluk in mit lẹcken. / d*as* begund*e* in ʃẹr*e*
*e*rschrẹck*en*.
Althaus 3: xiiń ṗyrt slvq xiń mit liqń. / ds bgvndx xiń zirx xršriqń.
Wolf: ein fert schluk in mit leken, / das begund in ser arschreken.
Trost: ein pfert schluc in mit lẹcken / das begunde in sẹre erschrecken.

Fuks' Roman transliteration is in the case of this line rather strict, and as such it is a relatively accurate rendering of the original text. The same can be said of Althaus' Roman transliteration, which indicates final consonant graphemes with an acute accent, while Fuks omits this information. All three Roman transliterations represent א with a "neutral" (i.e., ostensibly noninterpretive) symbol: Fuks = /'/,

Althaus = /x/, Hakkarainen = /ʔ/. Otherwise Hakkarainen's transliteration is inconsistent, since he interprets פֿ as /pf/. Althaus and Fuks represent this grapheme with /p̆/ and thus imitate the Hebrew-alphabet original. Hakkarainen and Althaus interpret שֿ as [sh] and ש as [s]; Fuks does not distinguish between them (nor even note that the former is in the MS.). The transcriptions by Wolf, Althaus, and Trost are constructions of (or better – translations into) a putative Middle High German form, as Wolf and Trost's transcription of ש as /sch/ or /ss/ as "appropriate," Trost's פֿ = /pf/, and Althaus' positing of /ẹ/ and /c/ before *k* in *lecken* and *erschrecken*, indicate. As such these transcriptions are perfectly legible – for the medieval Germanist, that is.

The problem of accessibility arises here not just with respect to the varying systems of transposition, but also with respect to simple "legibility": e.g., א, which *could* be interpreted as some realization of the phonemes [a], [o], or perhaps even [ə] (in addition to its function as indicator of initial vowel), is represented as /x/, /ʔ/ and /'/ by Althaus, Hakkarainen, and Fuks, respectively. Such transliterations render the line all but illegible for the reader, especially when they contain (as they do here) similarly problematic rendering such as ק = /q/, ו = /v/, פֿ = /p/, יי = /ii/, etc.[46] The question is, of course, do transliterations need to be "legible," are they to be *read* at all, or do they rather simply supply the raw data for linguistic analysis? If the latter is the case, as the editors of type three claim, then for what kind of analysis, to what end, and for what audience? Certainly no transliteration such as Althaus', Hakkarainen's or Fuks' can either easily or legitimately be used as raw data for phonetic, phonemic, graphemic, or any other kind of analysis, since they already quite obviously present the *results* of interpretive acts. For as Althaus' choice of /p̆/ and /š/ demonstrates, he is engaged in more than mere "objective" transliteration: these symbols indicate the editor's *interpretation* of the phonetic value of the graphs פֿ and שֿ as [pf] and [sh], in the tradition of phonetic transcription. It seems then that one has only the choice between Althaus/Hakkarainen/Fuks' "manipulative illegibility" and Katz's "authentic illegibility."

The second text sample is from *Dukus Hurnt*, in the same manuscript.[47]

Ms.: דער שטולצא קוניק איטנא גינק מיט / אין אוף דש מיר
Fuks 1: דער שטולצא קוניק איטנא גינק מיט / אין אוף דש מיר
Katz: דער שטולצא קוניק איטנא גינק מיט / אין אוף דש מיר
Fuks 2: der stvlž̊' kvnik 'itn' gink mit / 'in 'vf ds mir.

Hakk.: der stvlts? kvnik ?itn? gink mit / ?in ?vf ds mir.
GNS 1: d^{c}r stwlṣ’ qwniq ’itn’ ginq mit / ’in ’wf ds mir.
GNS 2: dër śtolze kunik Etene gink mit in uf daś mer.
Marchand: Der stolze kunec Etene ginc mit in uf das mer.
Fourquet: Der stolze künec Eten gienc mit in ûf das mer.

In this second text, the problems noted above with respect to Fuks’ and Hakkarainen’s transliterations are again evident. The transliteration of the line in the standard edition by Ganz/Norman/Schwarz is so alien as to be even more illegible than Althaus’ of the first text: ע = /^{c}/, צ = /ṣ/, ק = /q/, ו = /w/, א = /’/. Their transcription is essentially a construction in Middle High German, as are also the renderings by Fourquet and Marchand, the latter in fact so radically transformed as to be “fluent” normalized Middle High German; Fourquet goes so far as to supply the macrons with which nineteenth-century philologists provided Middle High German texts (rarely with manuscript evidence).

The last sample, from the *Akedas Yitskhok*, is intended to show that not just “objective” transliteration and Middle High German transcription (that is, both ostensibly neutral and anti-Yiddish transcription) can be ideological, but that “pro-Yiddish” editorial practice can be such as well.[48]

Ms.: אזו גינג איר דיא נשמה אויז מיט וויינן אונ׳ זויפצן
Matenko: azo ging ir di(e) n^{e}šama oiz mit uuiinn̥ un’ züftn̥.
Dreeßen: aso̊ ging ir di’ nšoma ou*s* mit wainėn uṅ süfzėn.
Birnbaum: azọọ ging ir di nyśoomy ous mit vaainyn un’ züfcyn.

The renderings by Matenko/Sloan and Dreeßen seem relatively innocuous, but even so their interpretations are obvious: וו becomes /uu/ or /w/, and ז is rendered as /z/ or /s/, according to the demands of modern Yiddish and modern German usage, respectively. In general Matenko/Sloan often modernize the text to conform to modern Yiddish: e.g., they read אויז as *oiz*, as in modern Yiddish. But the most clearly ideological edition of this text is Solomon Birnbaum’s *ad hoc* transcription system, which is another manifestation of Birnbaum’s long-time struggle against the modern Lithuanian dialect as a standard.[49] Ultimatively it also results in a text at least as illegible as Althaus’, Ganz/Norman/Schwarz’s, or, of course, the Hebrew-alphabet text.

With the exception of Katz’s and Shmeruk’s editions, some

aspects of the editions by Fuks, and quite different aspects of the work by the "Trier School," the state of Old Yiddish studies has been chaotic indeed, especially in the field of textual editing: if several editors can conceivably transform the same manuscript text into exemplary specimens of, for example, archaic modern standard Yiddish, Middle High German, or early modern German, simply via their respective editorio-ideological principles, then these editions are little more than rather curious examples of flights of academic fancy. With the exceptions of those editions that include facsimiles, it is still necessary, after more than a century of scholarly activity in the field (especially intensive in the last thirty years), to consult the manuscripts or microfilm of the manuscripts for *every* text for every scholarly purpose, simply because the editions (especially those in Roman) are so unreliable.

If accessibility is one of the main goals of textual editing, then the Old Yiddish project has thus far generally failed, for it has not produced text editions for an identified and identifiable *existent* audience. Rather, most editions seem to have been used to propagate the editors' interpretive (and most often ideologically conceived) answers to some basic questions concerning the history of the Yiddish language in general: when did it arise, at what point was it independent of its Germanic determinant,[50] and what was the phonetic system of this Germanic language spoken by the medieval Ashkenazim? Such questions are legitimate and of great significance in Old Yiddish studies, and the contributions by editors of Old Yiddish texts to answering them have been pioneering and often valuable. The necessary objection to their editorial practice is not that their efforts have been interpretive, but rather that their interpretive programs have been incorporated into, and even constituted, their *editorial* projects to the extent that the manuscript text is irrecoverably lost behind an ideologically determined façade.

Thus, for whatever reasons the existing genres of Old Yiddish text editions have arisen, it would be useful now to expand the pioneering efforts of those few editors who have published facsimile editions of the early texts, so that they are *accessible* to scholars in their extant form. Diplomatic editions would of course also be helpful, as would critical editions: as long as they were editions in the Hebrew alphabet. Interpretation of these texts would naturally follow, by the editors and others, many of whom would most likely make use of Roman alphabet transliteration in their text analysis; but these interpretations should be kept separate from the editions *per se* as much as possible, much as Fuks' Cambridge codex edition, Katz's introduction and text and Dreeßen/Müller's *Doniel.* Such facsimile, diplomatic, and critical editions in the Hebrew alphabet would not, by virtue of their use of the Hebrew alphabet, be free of ideology and interpretation, especially in their apparatus (no edition of any kind can be), – since interpretive decisions are necessary and expected here, nor would they solve all or even most textual or literary critical problems inherent in the texts, for that would not be their more realistically conceived purpose. Instead they would seek simply to make these legitimate scholarly concerns "accessible," by stripping away the artificial, false problems with which previous editors have overlaid them.[51]

There may be two important objections raised against the present thesis. First that it is in itself no more than a disgruntled objection to the definition of "diplomatic edition," as conceived by those editors with whose theses I disagree; that is, that my proposal is simply that such texts should be presented rather as *I* see them, for I have already denied the possibility of anything approaching pure objectivity ("as the reading I sees it") in any editorial enterprise. The objection is not altogether refutable. The editorial policy I recommend is obviously, but consciously, also ideological; it denies pure objectivity, but proposes a quite *practically,* pluralistically conceived compromise: that diplomatic editions in the Hebrew alphabet are *relatively* less misleading, less ideological, less interpretive, and less subjective than those editions that either 1) purport to be purely objective while imposing the entirety of their cultural ideologies on the manuscript text even before the text has been made accessible to the scholarly audience in a (to use Dreeßen's misused term) *controllable* form, thus presenting the results of that ideological manipulation *as the text itself*; or 2) even if a facsimile or Hebrew-alphabet transliteration is included, pretend that their Roman transposition and commentary is no more than an inevitable consequence of a rigorous investigation of that text.

Perhaps an example will best illustrate the point. Without access to the *Yosef* text in facsimile or diplomatic transliteration, Marchand/Tubach's edition is, for the uninformed reader (which is in fact their intended audience), a brilliant and inspiring revelation of as-yet-undiscovered scholarly vistas and a *newly discovered* literary corpus within the disciplinary purview of medieval German studies. For the informed reader (or the reader who happens to come to this edition via Shmeruk's edition), Marchand/Tubach is one of the most insidiously ideological, even irresponsible theses in the recent history of Germanistic. By contrast, Shmeruk's edition, not wholly without interpretation and editorial manipulation, is nonetheless in principle and in practice free of the kind and magnitude of ideology that makes Marchand/Tubach a disciplinary embarrassment. Had Marchand/Tubach's article followed the publication of an edition such as Shmeruk's and dealt with the ideologically-based distinctions between the two editions, or included a diplomatic Hebrew-alphabet transliteration or facsimile itself and then appended the same ideological interpretation as that found in their actual article, the problems with the article would have been far fewer. For even if this hypothetical article had been identically worded, it could not have purported to be anything but an interpretation. At least one might hope that such would have been the case.[52]

The necessary second objection to the present thesis is that it is elitist, since it proposes that Old Yiddish text editions *per se* must necessarily be printed in the Hebrew alphabet, which would render them *in*accessible to all those who do not read the Hebrew alphabet fluently. But compared with the present chaos, I would counter that it could be only an improvement, for Althaus' and Schwarz's Roman transliterations and even Birnbaum's transcription are in the end hardly less "illegible," scarcely more accessible than is the Hebrew-alphabet original, even for someone who does not know that alphabet, since in order to be able to make sense of these editions, the reader will have to learn the Hebrew alphabet *and* learn to interpret the editions in light of their interpretations of that alphabet. Second, the "legible" transcriptions are so-called (by Germanists) because they are in essence *translations* into normalized Middle High German, hardly accessible to a non-specialist audience, and certainly not to be taken seriously as *editions* of Old Yiddish texts. For the sake of accessibility to a wider, perhaps even non-specialist audience, a translation should perhaps accompany Old Yiddish text editions, but this translation should be into a modern language, not into an artificial medieval language of which there are no modern (and perhaps were no medieval) native speakers. In any case, it is a bit too ironic to make a knowledge of normalized Middle High German a prerequisite for the reader of Old Yiddish literature.

Finally, to return to the problem posed at the outset of the study: what is the audience of Old Yiddish? It is not the general reading public, nor is it exclusively or even primarily medieval Germanists, as one might assume from the *intended* audience as identified by many editors' remarks, but rather the audience consists of Yiddishists, both professional and amateur (in the best sense), but Yiddishists nonetheless, in that they are simply interested in Yiddish.

They are of various nationalities, educational backgrounds, disciplinary affiliations and native languages, and are united perhaps only by their interest in Old Yiddish.

On the other hand, since most editors of Old Yiddish texts assume that medieval Germanists are their primary audience and since they design their editions ostensibly with that audience in mind, then perhaps it is time for medieval Germanists to begin to protest the expressed and implied criticism of their resourcefulness, paleographical skills, and interest in subjects not by definition their areas of specialization. It is implied, for instance, that they are irresponsible if they do not take a major interest in this Old Yiddish/Germano-Judaic/Hebrew-German/Jewish-German/*Jüdisch-deutsche/judéo-allemande* literature, since it is for all intents and purposes nothing but medieval German. They are constantly patronized for their putative inability to read the original texts, since they are written in the Hebrew alphabet and for their inability to learn that alphabet. They are expected to base their studies, linguistic and literary, on editions that have miraculously transformed these (for them) hermetically obscure, inaccessible documents into (for them) familiar Middle High German without the least suspicion of the pure objectivity of the editorial principles or the text edition itself, on which they are to base their own "scholarly" arguments.

The premise that medieval Germanists have no access to Old Yiddish texts due to the alien alphabet is as provincial as it is insulting: whoever can deal with the myriad linguistic and paleographical problems of Old and Middle High German manuscripts, with excruciating complexities of language in Wolfram or the Old High German Isidor, with the textual problems of the *Hildebrandslied* or the *Nibelungenlied*, can this person, so trained, not also learn the Hebrew alphabet, *if* s/he has interest in Old Yiddish texts? We do not insist on presenting the medieval Germanist – who after all was not born with his/her knowledge of Gothic and Old Saxon (or even the Roman alphabet) – with laundered texts for scholarly use, so why should the Yiddishist be offered Middle High German translations of Old Yiddish texts as the "standard" editions?

Among the predictable consequences of the "pro-Germanistic" project is the fact that Germanists in general continue to ignore Yiddish, medieval and modern. And why should they not – it is unpleasant to be constantly reprimanded for one's putative scholarly incapacity. One might in the end also ask who these Germanists might be to whom Old Yiddish texts so desperately need to be rendered accessible, as if it were a holy cause? Those Germanists (and non-Germanists) who *are* interested in Yiddish texts have revealed themselves in sizable numbers through their more or less informed reviews, articles, and monographs. To take the work on *Dukus Hurnt* as an example, probably as many studies have been published on the work as all but a few other works of medieval literature during the past thirty years. An excellent example of the way this false problem is constructed may be taken from Dreeßen/Müller's edition of *Doniel* in two volumes: one with the Hebrew-alphabet text and one with the Roman transposition. The purpose of dividing the work into two volumes was to accommodate the audience – libraries and those with scholarly interest could buy both volumes, others (Germanists, students in medieval German classes, etc.) only the Roman transposition. This plan is certainly an advance over the dictatorial editorial choice to simply print the edition in Roman and force the scholar still to consult the manuscript for any and all purposes. The results of the considerate publication in two volumes are interesting and amusing, however, for according to the publisher, the two volumes are in fact selling at the same rate, as a set, despite the added cost of the Hebrew-alphabet volume (personal communication from Dr. Dreeßen). The actual audience of Old Yiddish is, quite simply, not the world of Germanistic (certainly not as narrowly and insultingly conceived by many Germanistic Yiddishists), nor even a sizable portion of that rather small group. Instead it consists of people interested in Yiddish and able (or at least willing to become able) to work with the texts in the original.

The relationship between editor and reader in the sub-field of Old Yiddish studies has only in rare cases not been dominated by the editors' ideological power plays; in spite of their protests to the contrary, these editors have freely exercised their editorial power to determine to an astounding degree, if not absolutely, what form the actual text has, that the much maligned, putatively ignorant Germanistic readers finally hold in their hands. More deplorable still is the fact that the non-Germanistic reader must also make do with these same "editions".

But let us take another tack here and return to the audience of Old Yiddish texts, defined simply as those who have an interest in such texts, both professional Yiddishists and others whose interest comes most likely as an adjunct to their primary fields of endeavor in Romance or Germanic languages and literature, or Art History, Judaic Studies, Folklore, or the History of Religion, as is most often the case with amateur Yiddishists. If these interested parties do not already know the Hebrew alphabet, then as a result of their interest in the subject, they can certainly be expected to take the few hours necessary to learn it, since, as they will certainly already know, that is in fact how the literature and language have been transmitted to us, and thus the Hebrew-alphabet text is *the* evidence for all scholarly debate. And finally they will learn the Hebrew alphabet since it is, quite simply, in the long run, necessary to decipher the several dozen equally "illegible" systems of transposition already in existence.[53] Perhaps the future propagation of such systems could be halted or at least slowed, were Yiddishists to begin to conceive of each other as intelligent, critical scholars.

Then the work on more relevant problems of literary and linguistic significance in the field of Old Yiddish studies could be continued and even given a broader base; and as a result it would become somewhat less marginalized. Most studies of Old Yiddish language and literature have taken as their starting points (whether intentionally or not) an issue related to the *origin* of the language and/or literature and proceded to define the object of study on that basis in order to analyze the so-constructed object: e.g., in the primary categories of research – that Old Yiddish was simply Middle High German and its literature Middle High German literature, or that the language was already specifically Jewish as its inception and was thus the fountainhead of modern Yiddish language, literature, and Ashkenazic culture in general. In their search to define proposed origins, each of these schools in the end must base its argument on the identity of the most basic component element of the language: the grapho-phonemic system. The solution to this problem is, however, neither the foundation nor the culmination of potential research in the field. After a century-and-a-half of the most concentrated linguistic research to be found in any subdiscipline, we still have, for instance, relatively little definitive knowledge of Middle High German dialects, yet other kinds of literary, cultural and even linguistic research continues unabated. I do not wish to argue that Old Yiddish grapho-phonemics is of no interest or value, but rather that it is merely of little relevance to the larger context, and it certainly need not be viewed as the basis of all research. The Old Yiddish grapho-phonemic 'question' may remain undecided for the moment and even for the decade without grave consequences for the field. Both the pro-and anti-Yiddish theses proceed from the same kind of nationalistic ideology, and thus they are, from the point of view of contemporary literary criticism, obsolete. But it is more than mere critical fashion which ousts them from their position of dominance; it is also their inability to "explain" any more about Old Yiddish than they already have (attempted). Neither of the theses is without value; both have contributed to our present understanding of the literary documents under discussion, of their linguistic nature, of their socio-cultural contexts. But especially with respect to this latter complex of problems, their contributions have been slight, and it has become clear in recent decades that precisely this area of inquiry is of paramount importance *as a foundation* of analyses of other basic topics in (medieval) literary criticism.

For if Old Yiddish participates in some aspects of medieval European culture and is to participate in modern scholarship on that period, then it too must be susceptible to modern scholarly interests, methods, and study. The fact that the study of Old Yiddish has in general methodologically lagged behind its sister disciplines is perhaps explainable on the basis of its cultural history. It is therefore not surprising that there has been only a single "vulgar Marxist" reading and one "close reading" of a work of Old Yiddish literature, no structural(ist) studies, only a few fledgling attempts at *Rezeptionsgeschichte* and oral-formulaic compositional study, and no deconstructive or feminist readings.[54] While there is no compelling necessity for such studies specifically and thus no reason to advocate their "production" now as part of a future program of Old Yiddish studies, some reorientation of the priorities of Old Yiddish might well serve to render it more "accessible" and of interest to a wider scholarly and student audience, simply by means of making it somewhat more relevant to their studies in their own particular fields: Old Yiddish studies might be drawn into the realm of twentieth-century literary scholarship.

TRANSCRIPTION/TRANSLITERATION SYSTEMS

	F1	F2	K1	K2	G1	G2	Hak	Alt1	Alt2	Mat	Tim	GG1	GG2	L1	L2	B1	B2	B3	B4	B5	B6	How	D	FOY
א	ʼ	•	ʔ	•	•		ʔ	×	•	•	•	ʼ	•	ʔ	•	ʼ	•	ʼ	•	ʼ	•	@	•	9
בּ	b	b	b	b	b	b	b	b	b/v	b/v	b	b	b	b	b/p	b	b	b	b	b	b	b	b/v̄	b
בֿ	v̄/f	v̄/f	ƀ	v	v̄	v	b̄	b̄			v̄	ḇ	v	v	f	b̆	ʌ	v	v	ḇ	v	b	v̄	b̄
ג	g	g	g	g/ɣ•	g	g	g	g	g	g	g	g	g/ng	g	g/k	g	g	g	g	g	g	g	g	g
ד	d	d	d	d	d	d	d	d	d	d	d	d	d	d	d/t	d	d	d	d	d	d	d	d	d
ה	h	h	h	h	h	h	h	h	h	h	h•	h	h/ch	h	h/e	h	h	h	h	h	h	h	h/e	h
ו	v/f	•	v	•	•	•	v	v	•	•	•	v	•	w	•	u̯	•	v	•	v	•	v	•	v
ז	z	z	z	z	z	s	z	z	s	z	s/s̱	ż	s	z	z/s•	z	z	ż	s	z	z	z	s	z
ח	ḥ	ḥ	×	•	ḥ	ḥ	ḥ	×	h		ḥ	ḥ	ch			ḥ	ḥ	ḫ	ch	ḥ	ḥ	ḥ	·ḥ	×
ט	t	t	t	t	t	t	t	t	t	t	t	t	t	t	t	ṭ	t	t	t	ṭ	t	t	t	t
י	ı	•	j	•	•	•	i	i	•	•	•	j	•	y	•	i̯	•	j	•	y	•	i	•	y
כּ	×		k	k/χ•	kh	ch	×	k̇	[illegible]	×	c	ch	ch	kh	ch/k	k	×	k	k	k	×	×/x̣	c/ch	k
כֿ		kh						k̄			ch	c̱ẖ				×		ch	ch					k̄
ך	×	kh	ḱ	χ	kh	ch	×	ḱ	h/ch	×	ch	ch	ch		ch	k/x	×	ch	ch	K	×	x·	ch	ḱ
ל	l	l	l	l	l	l	l	l	l	l	l	l	l	l	l	l	l	l	l	l	l	l	l	l
מ	m	m	m	m	m	m	m	m	m	m	m	m	m	m	m	m	m	m	m	m	m	m	m	m
ם	m	m	ḿ	m	m	m	m	ḿ	m	m	m	m	m	m	m	M	m	m	m	M	m	m	m	ḿ
נ	n	n	n	n	n	n	n	n	n	n	n	n	n	n	n	n	n	n	n	n	n	n	n	n
ן	n	n	ń	n	n	n•	n	ń	n	n	n	n	n	n	n	N	n	n	n	N	n	n	n	ń
ס	•		σ	s	s̀	ś	ś	σ			s̀	ś	ś	s	s	s		s	ṡ	•		ṣ	s̀	σ
ע	e	e/ē	ʕ	ɛ/E	•	•	e	y	ä/ë	•	•	e	ɛ	ʕ	e/ö•	ʿ	•	e	•	ʿ	•	e	•	ʕ
פּ	p	p	p	p	p	p	p	p	p	p/f	p	p	p	p	p	p	p	p	p	p	p	p	f/p	p
פֿ	f	f	p̄	f	f̄	f	f	p̄	f		p̄/f	f	f	f	f	p̄	f	f	p	p̄	f	f	f	p̄
פ·	p	p	ṗ	p	ṗ	p	ṗ	ṗ	p															
פ̌	p̌	p•	p̈	pf	p̌	pf	pf	p̌	pf/ph							p̌	p̌			p̌	pf			
ף	f	f	ṕ	f	f	f	f	ṕ	f		f	f	f			P	f	f	f	P̄	f	ρ/r̃		ṕ
צ	ż	ż	c	ts	ṣ	z	ts	c	z/tz	ts	z	z	z	ts	z	ṣ	c	z	z	ṣ	c	c	z	c
צ̌	ž	tsh•	c̈	tʃ	ṣ̌	tsch	tš	č	tsch											ṣ̌	ć			
ץ	ż	ż	ć	ts	ṣ	z	ts	ć	z/tz	ts	z	z	z	ts	z	Ṣ	c	z	z	ṣ	c	c	z	ć
ק	k	k	q	k	q	k	k	q	k/c	k	k	k	k	k	k	q	k	k	c/k	q	k	k	k	q
ר	r	r	r	R•	r	r	r	r	r	r	r	r	r	r	r	r	r	r	r	r	r	r	r	r
ש	s	s	s	s	s	ś	s	s	s/z	s/š	•	s	ś/sch	š	•	•	ṡ	Ś	•	s	s	s	•	s
שׂ								·s										Ś						·s
שׁ								s·										Ś						s
ש̌	š	sh	s̈	ʃ	š	sch	š	š	sch			s				š	š			š	ś			
ת	ṭ	ṭ	Θ	t	ṭ	t	ṭ	Θ			ss/th	ṭ	ś					t	t				ss/t	Θ
ת̄								Θ̱								t		s̄	ṡ			Θ		Θ̄
וו	vv	w/au		•	•	•			•	uu	•		w	ww	w	u̯u̯	•		w/u	vv	•		•	
יי	ıı	ei		je/ei	•	•			•	ii	•		ei	yy	•	i̯i̯	ai		i	yy	ai		•	
וי	vı	eu/ue		iu	•	•			•	•	•			wy	•	u̯i̯	•			vy	•		•	

• = discussion in following commentary

Appendix

Notes on Transliteration/Transcription Systems

Some of the editors/commentators here cited do not propose a transcription system *per se* (e.g., Katz), but their proposal of phonetic/phonemic equivalents of the Hebrew graphs is here presented as such for comparative purposes, nonetheless. An empty block in the chart indicates: 1) the Hebrew graph is not found in the particular text edited, 2) digraphs are represented as their component monographs, 3) the text does not employ diacritical marks to differentiate base graphs, or, 4) the editor does not distinguish the graph in the edition.

Fuks

F1: Transliteration.[1] Fuks' use of the terms "transcription" and "transliteration" is somewhat confusing: "transcription" in the layman's sense of copying the manuscript, which yields the Hebrew square script *transliteration* of the Ashkenazic cursive original; his "transliteration" designates the Roman transliteration of the Hebrew square script transliteration. Fuks viewed his task as a mechanical one of "replacing the Hebrew characters by characters derived from the European writing system" (I, xxxvi). His comments on preserving the "semiologic system" must be interpreted as referring to a strict symbol-for-symbol transliteration, as his examples seem to demonstrate: כ = /x/ (instead of, perhaps, /ch/ or /kh/), שׂ = [š] (instead of /sh/ or /sch/).[2] In keeping with his attempt to avoid interpretation, the editor chose the "neutral" symbols /'/, /v/ and /ı/ for א, ו, and י respectively; he nevertheless expands abbreviations (he calls them "apocope"[3]) in אונ׳ = /'vnd/, with underlining of the expansion. He omits ט from the table, presumably because the graph is rare; he claims it is used in only two foreign words ("sapir" and "balsamen,"

I, xxxv), which is inaccurate: it is also used in יוסף and סליק. As a transliteration, Fuks' system (I, xxxvii) calls for comment on several points. In several cases, his concept of a strict transliteration is not preserved: both בֿ and ו may be rendered by /f/; finals are not distinguished from non-finals; פֿ and פ are not distinguished.[4]

F2: Transcription.[5] Interestingly, before Fuks discusses his system of objective transliteration, eschewing all interpretation ("We shall leave that to the philologists," I, xxxvii), he includes a two-and-a-half page note on "orthography," which is in fact a brief but full-scale interpretation of the grapho-phonemic system of the manuscript, complete with a table of grapho-phoneme correspondences (I, xxxiv-xxxvi). Here Fuks' inadequate expertise as a linguist naturally becomes even more obvious than elsewhere in his introduction where he attempts to avoid such topics. His procedure is in principle essentially the same as that of his linguist colleagues in their analyses of Old Yiddish grapho-phonemic systems, for he assumes a Middle High German basis for the phonemic system: וו is, without further comment, assumed to represent [au] in /kvvfn/:/kaufen/. His discussion of such points that require precision is exasperating in the same way as that of his later colleagues – e.g., "often the vowel 'o' is used instead of 'a' or 'â,' which already in the 13th century had become rounded (*haar* – hor; *hat* = hot; *apfel* = opfel)." (I, xxxv). His table does not list a possible representation of /â/; one might conjecture that with "o" he means ו and with "a" he means א, since in each case he maintains in his list that these are among the phonemes represented by those graphemes.

His transcription system proposes the following phonetic values for "vowel graphs":[6]

א	[a/ô/ō/e]
ו	[v/f/û/u/ū/ō/o/oe]
י	[i/î/ī/ê/j]

צֿ and צׂ are identified as "zade + shin" (I, xxxiv). The transcription of פֿ is given in the table as [p] but identified as "pe – fe" and on the following page is identified as "pf."

Katz

K1: Transliteration.[7] Katz does not discuss his system of transliteration *per se*, since it is used only in the introduction and notes, while his edition is in the Hebrew alphabet. The system of transliteration is presented only in tabular form (p. vi). He claims that it is the same as Uriel Weinreich's standard system, elucidated in the first volume of *The Field of Yiddish*, but he adds פֿ = /p̈/, צ̇ = /č/ and ש̇ = /s/,[8] substitutes without noting it /j/ = י for Weinreich's /y/.

K2: Proposed Phonetic Values.[9] Katz discusses the orthography and phonology of the texts in this separate chapter of the introduction, where he attempts to identify the phonetic value of the graphs to the extent possible, and notes that such an identification cannot be precise (p. 41). His evidence comes primarily from correspondences between the orthography of the manuscript and the phonetics of Middle High German cognates. Thus Katz too makes use of Middle High German in determining the phonetic value of the graphs, just as had his predecessors and as would subsequent scholars. He distinguishes himself from them, however, in that he never attempts to identify the language of the manuscript with Middle High German, nor even to imply that the suggested phonetic values are necessarily to be taken as more than possibilities ("presumed phones," p. 41). The form of his inquiry can be illustrated by an example. After suggesting that י had the approximate phonetic realizations [i:], [i], [e:], [E] (pp. 36-37), he then notes: "There is no positive evidence, for example, that #*j* [sc. י] actually represents the four vowel sounds assigned to it. But knowledge of the High German dialects of the period would lead to such an expectation as would knowledge of subsequent phonological developments in Yiddish" (p. 41). He further notes that there are no front rounded vowels indicated in the manuscript, characteristic of both Central German and Yiddish; vowel length is moot and the proposed long vowels here rest on negative evidence of the absence of rhyme (pp. 41-42).

Suggested phonetic values of "vowel graphs":

א [∅/ə/a/ɔ]
ו [v/ɔ/o/o:/u/u:]
וו [w/wu/ou/uo]
י [j/i:/i/e:/e/E]
ע [ɛ/E]

Comments on other graphs:

ג medial [γ]
ה initial [hɛ], medial [ɛh]
ק medial [χ]
ר alveolar trill, "for convenience in presentation" (n. 90)

Ganz/Norman/Schwarz[10]

G1: Transliteration.

G2: Transcription. The consonants are listed and analyzed in the order of the Hebrew alphabet[11]; the vowels in the order and according to the posited values of Middle High German vowels; in rationalizing that convoluted discussion, one derives the following table of transliteration and phonetic values of "vowel graphs":

ו	/w/	[v/u/o/ou]
י	/i/	[j/e/i]
יי	/i, ii/	[j/ei]
וו	/ww/	[w/ou/u/uw/oi/w]
א	/', ∅/	[a/e]
ע	/ʿ/	[ë]
∅	∅	[e]
וי	/wi/	[ui/oi]

Hakkarainen

H: Transliteration.[12] Since Hakkarainen strives to avoid all interpretation and sees his transliteration as mechanical, he offers little in the way of justification of his system, but does list five guiding principles: 1) traditional phonetic value of the Hebrew graphs; 2) suitability with respect to the graphemic system of the Cambridge manuscript; 3) the phonemic value of Hebrew graphs in this manuscript – "das phonemische System der Hs. also"; 4) IPA; 5) the ease of legibility and typographical simplicity and clarity. He concedes that these principles in themselves indicate that the grapho-phonemic and even phonetic systems have already been predetermined before the analysis.[13] In indicating the strength of the manuscript evidence for any particular reading, he distinguishes between three stages of "legibility": "lesbar," "undeutlich lesbar," and "kaum oder nicht lesbar," the distinctions among which he admits are "fluid" and depend "on subjective judgments." Conjecture is limited primarily to "letters of a partially legible word, as well as obviously certain rhyme words"; any more conjecture would eliminate the text as the "objective basis of further investigations of the language and content"; correction of scribal error is confined to the apparatus. He cites transliterated readings of other scholars/editors in his own transliteration system, while transcriptions are cited in the form given the text by the other scholar.

IPA symbols are used for א, זֿ, כ, פֿ, צ; IPA ʃ for ש is not used, but rather /š/, and צ̆ is thus /tš/; the common transliteration of ע as ʕ is rejected here in favor of /e/, "since ayin is exclusively a vocalic graph for various *e*-sounds in our manuscript." Final and non-final forms are not distinguished. Hakkarainen also concedes that his transliteration *per se* breaks down in the double graphs /pf/, /ts/ and /tš/ (II, 26-28).

In his second volume, Hakkarainen also deals with the graphophonemic relations and on pp. 121-135 details these relations. On the basis of this system, he transcribes the first forty-eight lines of *Dukus Hurnt* (pp. 136-137).

Althaus

Alt1: Transliteration.[14] His practice is a hybrid of usages: he insists on the legitimacy, even necessity of the Hebrew-alphabet text, but ultimately, subtly, and ideologically denies its Yiddishness. He explains his system of transliteration on pp. 56-57 and maintains that the transliteration of Hebrew to Roman is in principle not a problem, if one holds to a strict one-to-one replacement of symbols; in this way the original is reconstructable. He establishes five principles for the transliteration: 1) one graph corresponds to one graph; thus monographs are represented by monographs and digraphs by digraphs; 2) finals are distinguished from non-finals, which he unnecessarily (in this context) divides into the categories "Initial- und Medialgraphe" (p. 56), by an acute accent, i.e., n/ń; 3) diacritics are preserved unchanged from the manuscript; 4) misinterpretations are hindered by transliteration of א with /x/ and ע with /y/, "beides in Anlehnung an die graphetische Struktur der Quadratschriftgraphe" (p. 57). Obviously Althaus is attempting to deal here with the common problem of the probable multiple phonetic significations of the two graphs and how to represent them: Birnbaum had already objected to Hakkarainen's use of /i/ for י and /e/ for ע (rev. of Hakkarainen, p. 102), simply because they look too familiar and thus could lead to misinterpretation. Althaus avoids this problem, but goes to the other extreme in taking the actual shape of the Hebrew graphs as determinant in choosing a transliteration symbol. With this practice, there would be no need to transliterate at all, if it were possible to preserve the shape of the Hebrew letters in Roman. Ultimately, however, this is merely another false problem, stemming from the "ignorant Germanist" topos: if one tells one's readers (in a transliteration table) that, for instance, /i/ and /e/ are the *transliteration* symbols for י and ע respectively, then there is no reason for them to interpret /i/ and /e/ as [i] and [e], and the use of, for instance, /x/ for א is no less than exasperating, leading to such monsters as /xlx/ for אלא and /xvnvvxvnx/ for

אונוואונא (pp. 61-62). Such transliterations are in fact useless for both Yiddishists and Germanists and indeed all conceivable readers. 5) The transliteration system should, according to Althaus, be simple, logical, and produceable on a typewriter, which seems hardly a reasonable requirement, since languages are neither simple nor logical, nor, as Althaus must surely know, are typewriter keyboards uniform in the symbols they include: this is especially an impossible demand, when one is addressing an international scholarly audience, which uses the full spectrum of extant keyboards; this problem shows little sign of being solved by the present generation of word processors, since programs still go their own separate ways, with generally only a bow to the ASCII system (which is in itself inadequate to the needs of both textual editor and linguist).

Despite Althaus' generally pro-German ideological position, as discussed above, in chapter two, he denies that the text can be "decoded" on the basis of Middle High German, but rather only on the basis of Hebrew.[15] The decoding of the graphemes must proceed without native informants,[16] and one is thus forced to do some first-stage decoding: i.e., interpretation of possible grapho-phonemic correspondences.

Notes to transliteration:

χ – as IPA [χ]

In the transliteration chart, Althaus distinguishes between ש = / ˙s/ as "sin mit Punkt" and ש = /s˙ / as "schin mit Punkt" without explanation of the distinction; he also enigmatically notes: "Die Opposition von ש und ש ist durch ש und שׂ ersetzt" (p. 61).[17] In general "non-German" /q/ for ק, /θ/ for ת, /p̌/ for פֿ, etc. His goal is strict transliteration.

Alt2: Transcription.[18] Althaus' transcription of the text (pp. 210 ff.) is based on his proposed identification of the grapho-phonemic relations, through which the Middle High German phonemic system is discovered to be a mirror of Old Yiddish phonemics.

א [a/â]
ו [o/ö/u/ü/â/ô/oe/û/iu/uo/üe/v]
י [e/i/æ/ê/î/ie/j]
ע [ä/ë]
וו [ou/öu/w]

יי [ei]
וי [iu/üe]
∅ [a/ë/â/e]

Matenko/Sloan[19]

Mat: Transcription. Although they call their system "transliteration" (pp. 44-45), it is in fact a transcription, since they attempt to distinguish various phonetic values of both vowel and consonant graphs (pp. 44-46). Modern Yiddish plays a major role in determining their interpretation of graphemes: ו = [u]; they transcribe *kumn̥*, not *komn̥* and *zun* not *zon* since "it seems to have been the prevailing form among Yiddish speaking groups from a very early time so that it is the rule today in the more conservative Lithuanian Yiddish. . ." (p. 47, no. 9 & 13).[20] Omitted from their table are ר (/r/ in their transposition) and final graphs.

Suggested phonetic values of "vowel graphs":

א [å/a/e (mute final ‹ Mhg. /e/)/ø (pre-vocalic initial)]
ו [o/u/consonantal u = Mhg /v/]
וי [oi/ö/ü]
י [i/ei/consonantal i]
יי [ii]
ע [e]
וו [uu, "for Mhg. /w/"]
∅ [a]

Timm

Timm: Transcription.[21] Timm's system is arranged in list form (generally) alphabetically according to the Roman alphabet; German orthographic features predominate: כֿ = /ch/, וו or וי = /au/, יי = /ei/, צ = /z/, but ש = /sch/, ש = /ß/. Timm lists two distinct transcriptions for non-final פֿ = /p̄/ and /f/ (p. 6). Vocalic values are conjectured and printed in the edition, with justification to follow in the linguistic commentary (p. 7).

/s/ = ז pre-vocalic and ש pre-consonantal and final
/s/ = ז pre-consonantal and final
/ś/ = ש in Hebrew-Aramaic words
/š/ and /sch/ = ש
/ß/ = ש, pre-vocalic
/ss/ = ת, in Hebrew-Aramaic words

Phonetic values of "vowel graphs":

א [a/o/']
∅ [ȧ/ ė]
וו [au/w]
וי [au/ö/ou/öu/ü]
יי [ai/ei]
יֵ [ê]
ע [e]
י [e̊/i/j]
ה [*e*/h]
ו [o̊/u/v]
ויי [öu]
וֻ [ü]

Guggenheim-Grünberg[22]

GG1: Transliteration ("Zeichengetreue Umsetzung").

GG2: Transcription. She notes (p. 233, n. 1) that in ambiguous cases of vowel quality, the modern German values are used in the edition.

Phonetic values of "vowel graphs":

א [a/o/ĕ (final)]
ו [v/u/ü/o/ö/uo/ĕ]
י [j/i/ei/ie/e/ĕ]
∅ [a/ĕ]
ע [ɛ]
יי [ei]

Lockwood[23]

L1: Transliteration ("Umschrift").

L2: Transcription ("Lautwert"). He posits devoiced final ב, ג, and ד; ש = שׂ as [s/z/ʃ]; ז = [s/z].

Phonetic values of "vowel graphs":

א [ø/a/o/u (?)/au (?)]
ו [u/o/a (?)/ü (?)/eu (?)/f]
וי [au/i/ü (?)]
י [i/ü (?)/unstressed e/j]
יי [ei/eu (?)]

ע [e/ö (?)]
וו [w]

Birnbaum

Solomon Birnbaum has devoted considerable attention to the problems associated with the transposition of both early and modern Yiddish text into Roman.[24] Birnbaum's 1932 article, "Das älteste datierte jiddische Schriftstück" is interesting for a number of reasons. It deals with an Old Yiddish transcription from Roman into Hebrew of a Central German text. Thus Birnbaum can at least attempt to determine the phonetic value of the Middle High German graphemes transliterated by the Hebrew graphemes (pp. 13-22). Whether this attempt is successful is, of course, a more complicated problem than Birnbaum lets on, but the evidence for a dialect resembling Central German is considerable (p. 13) if one accepts the legitimacy of the methodology: the dialect of the Hebrew-alphabet transcription differs little from that of the original (p. 13), and thus the Hebrew graphemes render the phonetics represented by the original Roman graphemes rather exactly, and thus one can also identify the Yiddish phonetics rather well. Obviously there is a lot of speculation involved here, especially since 1) the original Roman-alphabet document does not survive, 2) the Central German dialect of the period is not known in enough detail to determine precisely the phonetic value of Roman graphemes in Central German, and 3) the phonetic value of Hebrew graphemes are even less well known. Birnbaum is obviously not on firm methodological ground here.

B1: Transliteration.[25] This system is presented briefly in the note, listing (in Hebrew-alphabet order) *only* the Roman transliteration symbols, which leads to confusion in at least one case: it seems in the note that ך = /X/, while in the *transcription* table (p. 26), the transliteration is again given, but here as /K/; perhaps the appended comment explains this inconsistency: "undecided whether palatal or velar." Birnbaum remarks (p. 23, n. 12) that in the system proposed in his 1932 article "there were some unnecessary M.H.G. signs." ש is represented by /s̊/ in n. 6, but /š/ in the table (p. 26). פּ = /p̄/ and פֿ = /p̌/ are listed in the table (pp. 25-26) but not in the note (p. 21).

B2: Transcription.[26] The transcription system is based on Central German dialect characteristics (p. 24), since, as he contends, the specimen text here presented ("Abraham") displays primarily features of that dialect (with some admixture of Upper German features). The transcription is thus predetermined: the text is judged to be phonetically primarily Central German, and is thus transcribed phonetically into Central German.

Phonetic values of “vowel graphs”:

א [ø/e]
∅ [a/aa]
יי [ai]
וו [au/öu/û/ʌ̈]
י [é/éé/i/ii/î]
ו [o/oo/ô/ö/öö/u/uu/û/ü/üü/ʌ]
ע [è/èè]
וי [üü/ü̂][27]

B3: Transliteration.[28]

B4: Transcription. ש is transcribed as [s̊/ś/sch].[29]
Phonetic values of “vowel graphs”:

א [ō/ô/ĕ/ø]
ו [v/ô/ō/o/u/û/ū/ü/ǖ/oe]
י [i/î/ī/e̊[30]/ê]
ע [e/ē]

Remaining vowels are included in the chart.

B5 (Transliteration) and B6 (Transcription) differ relatively little from B1/B2, since they appear in Birnbaum's revised version of “Old Yiddish or Middle High German,” reprinted in his *Yiddish: A Survey and Grammar.*[31]

Phonetic values of “vowel graphs” (B6):

א [ø/e]
∅ [a/aa/e]
יי [ai]
ע [é/éé]
י [ẹ/ẹẹ/i/ii/î]
ו [o/oo/ọọ/ö/ọ̈ọ̈/u/uu/ü/üü/v]
וו [ou/öu/w/u]
וי [üü/ü̂]

Howard

How: Transliteration.[32] Howard calls the system “transkribiert,” although it is obviously a rather strict transliteration; vowel points are also included in his system. כ = /x/,כּ = /x̹/; נ̊ = /n̊/, ן̊ = /*n̊*/.

Dreeßen

D: Transcription.[33] שׁ and שׂ are not distinguished by diacritical marks, and thus Dreeßen transcribes /ש/ as /s/ß/ś/š/sch/ depending on the situation (see pp. 99-100).

Phonetic values of "vowel graphs":

א	[a/unstressed final e/o/ø]
∅	[a̍/e̍/o̍]
וי	[aa/ö/ü/ou]
יי	[ai/ei]
ע	[a/ẹ]
י	[unstressed e/e̊/i/j/ê]
יֵ	[ê]
ה	[final e]
ו	[o̊/u/v]
ויי	[öu]
וו	[w]

Uriel Weinreich

FDY: Transliteration.[34] Weinreich notes three conditioning factors on transcription systems of Yiddish and Hebrew that frequently conflict: "1) readability of transcribed forms without ambiguity as to the sound value of the Latin letters; 2) definite correspondence of the transcribed form with the Jewish graphic form where the latter is significant for etymological or other purposes; 3) accommodation of existing habits, good or bad, of libraries and bibliographers" (p. vi). These considerations obviously bear on the audience. The written forms whose pronunciation is not clear are in general simply transliterated, and decoding is left to the reader; thus pre-nineteenth-century forms are rendered in transliteration, identified as such by a preposed musical "natural" sign: ♮. The reason given for this practice is the inadequate state of knowledge of early Yiddish phonetics, especially with respect to vowels. The transliteration system is characterized by three features: 1) strict one-to-one transliteration; 2) Roman consonant letters for Hebrew letters, Roman vowel letters for Hebrew vowel points; 3) diacritics in transliteration correspond exactly to the use in the original, except that the acute accent designates final consonant variants.[35]

Notes

Preface

1. And other opportunities certainly do exist: there are formal courses at numerous colleges and universities in the area, courses offered by the Workmen's Circle, meetings of the Culture Club and regular but informal meetings of other groups. I was actually approaching the language from a different direction, but even so, the preceding depiction of my initially unsuccessful attempt to find tutors should by no means be taken as disparagement of the Yiddish-speaking community of Los Angeles. Rather, it has become clear that I was, not surprisingly for a beginner, initially simply looking in all the wrong places for what I was seeking.

2. E.g. Siegmund Wolf, *Jiddisches Wörterbuch* (Mannheim 1962), p. 9.

3. My aim is at least to map out some of the causes for confusion in the field, and not to add still more, as Maks Weinreich feared might result from any "Mitwirkung von Laien und Dilettanten" (in his "Studien zur Geschichte und dialektischen Gliederung der jiddischen Sprache," Part 1: "Geschichte und gegenwärtiger Stand der jiddischen Sprachforschung," 3 vols. Diss. Marburg 1923, III, p. 155).

4. In *Germanische Dialektologie. Festschrift Walther Mitzka zum 80. Geburtstag,* L.E. Schmitt, ed., (Wiesbaden 1968), I, 224-263.

5. Dovid Katz, "On Yiddish, in Yiddish and for Yiddish: 500 Years of Yiddish Scholarship," in *Identity and Ethos: A Festschrift for Sol Liptzin on the Occasion of his 85th Birthday,* Mark H. Gelber, ed., (New York/Bern/Frankfurt 1986), 23-36; the epigram to the present study is from p. 23.

6. The 3-volume 600-page dissertation has never been published, and as far as I have been able to ascertain exists in three copies in the world: Weinreich's own photostat, now in the YIVO library in New York; the Marburg copy; and a photostat made by Professor Erika Timm (Trier) in the early 1970s. Yet this comprehensive history of Yiddish scholarship seems hardly dated sixty-five years after completion. I am presently engaged in editing the work for publication from Weinreich's personal copy, complete with his copious revisions.

Chapter 1

1. Joseph S. Roucek, "A History of the Concept of Ideology," *Journal of the History of Ideas* 5 (1944), 479-488.

2. There is certainly no need to castigate Roucek for putative naiveté or ideological "corruption" here, for he, like each of us, is a product of his own environment, and his article a product of the times. When his article appeared in 1944, the concrete manifestations of ideologies – scientific ideology and ideological science – were all too apparent in the destructive forces that were physically turning Europe and the Pacific into a shambles and destroying the very fabric of historical culture in those areas and the world; but it was only a matter of a few months until this mythic and myopic oversimplification of the good Allies vs. the evil Axis powers was finally and irrevocably shattered in Dresden and in Hiroshima, when science in its (according to Roucek's view) pure, non-ideological (i.e., U.S.) form – as opposed to the perverse inhumanity of Nazi-science as a handmaiden to genocide – would finally be defrocked and present incontrovertible and un-ignorable evidence not that it had now entered, but rather that it had always been, a part of the realm of politics, racism and ideology.

3. James D. Watson, *The Double Helix* (New York: Athenaeum, 1968). Thomas Kuhn, *The Structure of Scientific Revolutions* (Chicago: University of Chicago Press, 1962).

4. "Le mythe est un parole ... le mythe est un système de communication, c'est une forme ... des limites historiques," Roland Barthes, *Mythologies* (Paris: du Seuil, 1957), p. 215; this and all other translations throughout the book are my own.

5. This generation of further *signifiants* resembles Peirce's notion that the relation of the Representamen and the Object generate a further Object, which is involved in its own triadic semiotic structure, which then can generate another Object, *ad infinitum.* See Charles Sanders Peirce, "Logic as Semiotic: The Theory of Signs," in *Philosophical Writings of Peirce*, Justus Buchler, ed., (New York: Dover, 1955), 99-100.

6. "Le mythe est une parole dé-politisée. Il faut naturellement entendre: politique au sens profond, comme ensemble des rapports humains dans leur structure réelle, sociale, dans leur pouvoir de fabrication du monde; il faut surtout donner une valeur active au suffixe *de-*; il représente ici un mouvement opératoire, il actualise sans cesse une défection" (p. 252).

7. Terry Eagleton, *Literary Theory: An Introduction* (Minneapolis: University of Minnesota Press, 1983), 14-15.

8. "Die in vorliegender Arbeit meist nur im negativen Sinn angedeutete Bestimmung folgt aus der Schwierigkeit, den unabdingbaren Gegenbegriff der 'Wahrheit' prozeßhaft und zeitadäquat, d.h. ohne dogmatische Fixierung

– schon dies ein wesentlich ideologischer Aspekt – zu fassen. Um dennoch nicht selbst den Anschein der gerügten Beobachterneutralität und Universalskeptik zu erwecken, versuche ich hier, abstrakt und summarisch einige Hauptkomponenten des Ideologischen anzugeben: 1. gesellschaftliche Legitimationsfunktion im Interesse herrschender Gruppen zum Trost der Beherrschten; 2. den Zweifel ausschließende affirmative Versteinerung historisch gewordener, überlieferter und bestehender Verhältnisse zu selbstverständlichen, ewigen Naturwesen; mithin auch: paralysierendes, anachronistisches Beharren auf dem Ungleichzeitigen, den 'Ablagerungen überwundener Epochen' (Brecht); 3. 'gesellschaftlich notwendiges falsches Bewußtsein' (Marx) oder zur Zwangsvorstellung kollektivierte 'Rationalisierung' verstreckter Willensziele, Surrogat für den wissenschaftlichen 'Indikativ' im 'unbewußten Optativ' (Freud); in beiden Fällen also auch (die Wahrheit des Bedürfnisses symptomatisch ausdrückendes) richtiges Abbild falscher Wirklichkeit; 4. Spaltung des unauflöslichen Zusammenhangs theoretischer und praktischer Tätigkeit und Absonderung des 'reinen Geistes' von den sozialen Bedingungen seiner Existenz; 5. Kompromisstopik zur tröstlichen Verschleierung leidvoller, aber austragbarer gesellschaftlicher Widersprüche," Peter von Moos, *Mittelalterforschung und Ideologiekritik: Der Gelehrtenstreit um Héloise* (Munich: Fink, 1974), 129-130.

9. Karl Mannheim, *Ideology and Utopia* (New York 1936), p. 244.

10. Especially with respect to the study of Old Yiddish, few of these terms are relevant, since there has been little attention to the subject by scholars of any critical affiliation except the historico-philological school. And here too one may see a fact of ideological importance – why is the subject ignored by scholars of these newer modes of criticism? Or, rather, why do critics interested in Old Yiddish partake only of the older modes of criticism? An exception is the growing tendency in the "Trier School" toward a recasting of the basic problems in Old Yiddish in terms of *Rezeptionsgeschichte*.

11. Gayatri Spivak, "Explanation and Culture: Marginalia," *Humanities in Society* 2 (1979), 201-221.

12. Spivak is, however, utterly aware of this self-reflective double-bind and recognizes it as being itself formative and deformative of the "subject" of her essay: that is (one of) her point(s). Roucek seems blissfully unaware of the whole critical problem, due to his inability to perceive his own argument as anything other than "objective" analysis.

13. Cf. Michael Ryan, *Marxism and Deconstruction: A Critical Articulation* (Baltimore: Johns Hopkins, 1982), p. 48 on Marx's notion of "relations," and the Hegelian idea of interrelation.

14. This move will become a focus of my discussion later, in the analysis of Sander Gilman's concept of *Jewish Self-Hatred* (Baltimore: Johns Hop-

kins, 1985), and especially of the German vs. Yiddish debate.

15. Citation by Spivak, 205-206, of Freud, *The Standard Edition of the Complete Psychological Works of Sigmund Freud*, translated by James Strachey (London 1964), XXII, 116-117.

16. Ref. from Spivak: Rich's address to Smith College in 1979, published in *Ms.* (September 1979), p. 43.

17. As a colleague of sorts once expressed it to me, with utter seriousness.

18. She also notes the prevailing nineteenth-century usage of the term in the sense: "an unquestioningly accepted system of ideas that takes material shape in social action."

19. One might note here that this view of language = culture is a typically "Western," logocentric perception of the value of language and its place in culture. And as such, it is certainly relevant to the object of Gilman's study (and my own), since this view of language was the prevailing one in the periods under investigation and obviously the most relevant, given the kind of evidence adduced: texts.

20. The marginality of this group was, however, again only relative, for these white male slave-holders who led the movement, founded the republic, and wrote the U.S. Constitution, in doing so immediately centered themselves and protected and institutionalized their interests.

21. The penchant for transliteration/transcription into Roman by editors of Old Yiddish texts is a further, powerful sign of this same denial of Yiddish.

22. Nor was it often even mentioned as a member of the "extended family" of Germanic languages, including English, Dutch, Norwegian, etc. Its existence was simply ignored, despite the fact that in terms of its number of speakers, it (before the Holocaust) ranked third among Germanic languages, behind only English and German. Interestingly, however, this tendency was reversed, when it became politically expedient to do so (a prime example of the protean nature of ideology): before and during World War I there were attempts by Germans to appropriate Yiddish as a German dialect, for the purpose of political influence in Poland against Russia. See esp. Zosa Szajkowski, "The Struggle for Yiddish during World War I: The Attitude of German Jewry," *Leo Baeck Institute Yearbook* 9 (1964), 131-160.

23. As will be discussed in more detail later, this particular brand of the self-other bipolarity is forced even onto the use of the alphabet, for very often the contrast drawn between the alphabets used is not between the Hebrew and Roman alphabet, but between the Hebrew and "German"/ "*Deutsch*," terms which designate no existent alphabet, but which, one must assume, are used to signify the Roman/*lateinisches* alphabet in the code of

German "national language." Strangely, however, this terminology occasionally appears even where one cannot assign its significance to this ideology: e.g., Gilman, p. 124.

24. See esp. Gilman, p. 81 on this point.

25. See esp. Gilman, *Jewish Self-Hatred*, 22-67.

26. On the various pro-and anti-Yiddish political movements within the Ashkenazic community, see Emanuel S. Goldsmith, *Architects of Yiddishism at the Beginning of the Twentieth Century: A Study in Jewish Cultural History* (Rutherford: Farleigh Dickinson University Press, 1976), 45-69.

27. Also adopted into Yiddish as *zshargon.*

28. This characterization of Yiddish is still common in contemporary criticism, even among ostensibly pro-Yiddish scholars. On the general problem, see Gilman, 77, 113 & 155 ff.

29. On supplementality, see esp. Jonathan Culler, *On Deconstruction: Theory and Criticism after Structuralism* (Ithaca: Cornell University Press, 1982), 102-106.

30. Of course scattered university degrees, and even secondary school courses, do exist in a number of countries around the world, especially in the United States, Israel, and the Federal Republic of Germany. On the institutionalization of Yiddish, see also Klaus Cuno's article which analyzes in detail relevant and practical considerations in instituting the study of Yiddish in the Federal Republic on both secondary and university level. After some discussion, he concludes that the most advantageous university affiliation would be within Germanistik, as long as Yiddish is not viewed as a marginal dialect, obscured by an intimidating script-barrier (which, he maintains, can be eliminated by, for instance, Timm's transposition system). Second, one must guard against viewing Yiddish as fossilized Middle High German, and thus attention must be directed not just to early Yiddish (implying that early Yiddish is, apparently, no more than fossilized Middle High German); "Die Beschäftigung mit dem Jiddischen und der Kanon der Wissenschaften," *Auseinandersetzung um jiddische Sprache und Literatur. Jüdische Komponenten in der deutschen Literatur – die Assimilationskontroverse*, Walter Röll and Hans-Peter Bayerdörfer, eds., vol. 5 of *Kontroverse, alte und neue. Akten des VII. Internationalen Germanisten-Kongresses, Göttingen 1985*, ed. Albrecht Schöne (Tübingen 1986), 94-103.

31. An exception is in the rapidly growing Yiddish-speaking Hasidic community, which in demographic terms makes Yiddish a currently expanding language.

32. On the official Israeli attitude toward Yiddish, see [Florence] G[uggengeim]-G[rünberg], "Jiddisch in Israel unerwünscht, in New York

aber anerkannt," *Der Sudentendeutsche*, Hamburg, 24 July 1954; and esp. Shikl [Joshua A.] Fishman, "Vos ken zayn di funktsye fun yidish in Yisroel?" *Yidisher kemfer* (New York, April 1974), 40-46.

33. On the development of Yiddish studies, see Maks Weinreich's dissertation, "Studien zur Geschichte und dialektischen Gliederung der jiddischen Sprache," part 1: "Geschichte und gegenwärtiger Stand der jiddischen Sprachforschung," 3 vols., Diss. Marburg 1923, and more recently, Hans-Peter Althaus, "Die Erforschung der jiddischen Sprache," in *Germanische Dialektologie. Festschrift Walther Mitzka zum 80. Geburtstag*, L. E. Schmitt, ed., (Wiesbaden 1968), I, 224-263 and "Jiddistik: Umriß einer Wissenschaft," *Emuna* 2 (1967), 248-256.

34. e.g., Yisroel Tsinberg [Israel Zinberg], *Altyidishe literatur fun di eltste tsaytn biz der haskole-tkufe*, vol. 6 of *Di geshikhte fun der literatur bay yidn*, 2nd ed. (Vilna 1933).

35. Some of the problems can be seen simply in the variety of modern languages in which individual scholars and teams publish the results of their research: James Marchand has written in both English and German for his intended audience of Germanists: review of L. Fuks, *The Oldest Known Literary Documents*, in *Word* 15 (1959), 383-394 and "Einiges zur sogenannten "jiddischen Kudrun'," *Neophilologus* 45 (1961), 55-63 [published in the Netherlands]. Jean Fourquet aimed for a similar audience via French: "Ernest-H. Lévy et le Dukus Horant," *Études germaniques* 14 (1959), 50-56. Perhaps most revealing are the publications by Lajb Fuks himself, the director of the Amsterdam Rosenthaliana, who sought an audience of Yiddishists, Germanists, and "friends of Yiddish"; he published very similar articles on the "discovery" of the Cambridge Codex in both English and Yiddish: "The Oldest Literary Works in Yiddish in a Manuscript of the Cambridge University Library," *Journal of Jewish Studies* 4 (1953), 176-181 and "Der eltster literarisher dokument in yidish," *Yidishe kultur* 16 (1953), 30-35. His edition of the codex, published in Holland with both an English and a Yiddish title page, attempted to appeal to a wide audience, in that it included a photographic facsimile of the text, a transliteration from the Ashkenazic cursive into Hebrew square script, another into Roman, a modern *German* translation and a general introduction in English (in which his primary argument for Yiddish as the language of the text is based on an example of Dutch-German dialectology). How does one begin to define the audience sought by such an edition? At the same time, however, one should not go to the extreme of positing clearcut answers to all such questions in all cases for the other medieval European national literatures. Even here there are cross-cultural, multi-audience publications: e.g., the most comprehensive study of the fragment of the Old English heroic poem, *Waldere*, is the brilliant study – in Italian – by the German scholar, Ute Schwab, *"Waldere": Testo e Commento* (Messina 1967). One of the standard grammars of Middle English is Fernand Mossé's *Manuel de l'anglais du moyen age, des origines au XIVe siècle* (Paris

1945) [normally cited, however, in its English translation by James A. Walker, *A Handbook of Middle English*, 5th ed. (Baltimore 1968)]. But even here the parallel is not complete. The first book is intended for Italian, the second for French, university students of English literature. Old Yiddish literature can have, in the present circumstances, no such wide, institutionalized, extranational audience – it does not even have such a *national* one!

Chapter 2

1. "Jiddisch," *Encyclopaedia Judaica* (Berlin 1932), IX, p. 112; here he claims that terms such as "Jüdisch-deutsch" and "Judendeutsch" had for all practical purposes disappeared from use, having been replaced by "Jiddisch."

2. Maks Weinreich, *Geshikhte fun der yidisher shprakh* (New York 1981), I, 331. On the historical names of Yiddish, see also the discussion by Yankef Shatski, "Vegn di nemen far yidish," *Yivo-bleter* 8 (1935), 148-154.

3. "Yidish iz gevorn der koyleldiker nomen fun der gantser shprakh," *Geshikhte*, I, p. 331.

4. Cf. also Weinreich, *Geshikhte*, I, 328 on Birnbaum's primary responsibility for this change in fashion, although he was not the first to use the term (cf. Werner Weinberg on its usage by Porges, Weill, and Mieses: "Die Bezeichnung Jüdischdeutsch: eine Neubewertung," *Zeitschrift für deutsche Philologie* 100 (Sonderheft *Jiddisch* 1981), 263-264.

5. A Paucker, rev. of Peter Ganz, Frederick Norman and Werner Schwarz, eds., *Dukus Horant*, in *German Life and Letters*, n.s. 21 (1968), p. 274.

6. Hans-Peter Althaus, *Die Cambridger Löwenfabel von 1382: Untersuchung und Edition eines defekten Textes* (Berlin 1971), 31-32; and also Wulf-Otto Dreeßen, "Zur Rezeption deutscher epischer Literatur im altjiddischen: Das Beispiel "'Wigalois' – 'Artushof'," in *Deutsche Literatur des späteren Mittelalters - Hamburger Kolloquium 1973*, W. Harms and L. P. Johnson, eds., (Berlin 1975), p. 116.

7. Nor was it the first time that Weinreich had advanced this argument; cf. his article, "Yidish," in *Algemayne entsiklopedie. Yidn B.* Paris 1940, col. 23-90.

8. I do not seek to define this ill-conceived, ill-defined, Romantic term here, since I intend it in all its various vague and often even unjustifiable senses.

9. The Yiddish term coined under the influence of anti-Yiddish terms in other languages.

10. Thus even in the names used, there is a kind of appropriation of the margin by the center, for the language is neither *nomin*ally marginal, nor purely central: it is a hybrid, with the center's designation as the base and the margin's as a qualifier; the language is 'German' in some sense, but *not* in the only true, real, important sense, for it is ultimately not German without qualification. It is still marginal, although now annexed by/to the center.

11. Weinreich's analysis of the *fusion* nature of Yiddish is the most precise linguistic formulation of this complex problem in Yiddish linguistics: see *Geshikhte*, II, 261-320.

12. On the theoretical underpinnings of the notion of "national language," see esp. Wolfgang Pfaffenberger, *Blütezeiten und nationale Literaturgeschichtsschreibung: Eine wissenschaftsgeschichtliche Betrachtung*, Europäische Hochschulschriften 353 (Frankfurt 1981), 48-54.

13. Leo Landau, *Arthurian Legends; The Hebrew-German Rhymed Version of the Legend of King Arthur*, Teutonia 21 (Leipzig 1912), xxii-xxiii.

14. M. Grünbaum, "Die jüdischdeutsche Literatur in Deutschland, Polen und Amerika," in J. Winter and A. Wünschen, eds., *Geschichte der poetischen, kabbalistischen, historischen und neuzeitlichen Litteratur der Juden*, vol. 3 of *Die jüdische Litteratur seit Abschluß des Kanons* (Trier 1896), p. 533.

15. "Bloße Unterhaltungslektüre ... ohne allen ethischen Werth, und natürlich auch ohne allen sittlichen Einfluß, sie sind also entfernt nicht mit den Erzeugnissen der eigentlichen und originell-autochthonen jüdischdeutschen Litteratur zu vergleichen. Zur jüdischen Litteratur gehören sie keineswegs, und es ist die Frage, ob sie zu jüdisch-deutschen gehören," 536. In his general, layman's history of Yiddish literature, Max Waxman, renders much the same verdict, although with less polemic and generally fewer pejorative terms: Old Yiddish literature is superficial, non-intellectual, and of little value as literature, since it was intended to be mildly amusing for its female audience. Old Yiddish literature is blamed 1) for being merely translation of Hebrew literature; but also 2) for *not* being a translation of Hebrew literature, but a literature comprised of frivolous, secular, non-Jewish topics. See his "Judaeo-German Literature," 613-665 in *A History of Jewish Literature*, vol. II: *From the Twelfth Century to the Middle of the Eighteenth Century*, 2nd ed. (New York 1943).

16. Gustav Karpeles, *Jewish Literature and Other Essays* (Philadelphia 1895), p. 47.

17. Karpeles, *Jewish Literature*, 184; cf. also Karpeles, "Die Jüdischdeutsche Literatur," in *Geschichte der jüdischen Literatur* (Berlin 1886), II, p. 1001, where he claims that pre-sixteenth-century Judeo-German literature is not "Jüdisch-deutsch" but merely German.

18. Leo Wiener, *A History of Yiddish Literature in the Nineteenth Century* (New York 1899; 2nd ed., with a new introduction by Elias Schulman, 1973). Wiener's work deals with a later period of Yiddish literature, but, typically, he also includes a prefatory discussion of the language and its history. Cf. Maks Weinreich, "Studien zur Geschichte," III, 113-114 on Wiener.

19. Wiener also attempts this same identification of the culture of Jews and co-territorial populace in the culture of the Sephardic Jews in medieval Spain! Cf. Elias Schulman's introduction to Wiener's book, esp. p. x, on Wiener's "assimilationist" attitude: he notes that German was the language of Wiener's home, and that as a child, Wiener's son did not even know that he was Jewish.

20. Maks Weinreich calls Landau's preface "vortrefflich gearbeitet," but also explains in detail how Landau's name for the language is inappropriate and how the edition is problematic, since it is in transcription (Studien zur Geschichte," III, 115-117 & 131, and below, chapter 3).

21. See esp. below, chapter 3 on the consequences of this practice for Landau's editions.

22. Landau gives Süßkind of Trimberg as an example, in *Arthurian Legends*, p. xxiv; cf. also Wiener, p. 3, on Süßkind.

23. This is an example of the once common Romantic notion of the "birth" of a literature. In general Landau's knowledge of the production of and conditioning factors governing medieval literature is very limited. He denies, for instance, that the literature of the "Germanic or Teutonic nations" dates back as far as that of the Romance nations, and thus betrays an ignorance of Old High German, Old Norse, and Old English literature, and generally any knowledge of the nature of the development of vernacular literature in the Romance languages. Or is it just that he means *Latin* when he writes "Romance," and if so, does he assume that a lack of written documents of Germanic literature from the period before the seventh and eighth centuries is evidence of a lack of literature itself? Landau's naiveté evokes many such questions. But one must keep in mind that he is a pioneer in the field of Old Yiddish studies (as he himself notes, p. vii) and could not benefit from more recent critical developments in medieval studies and in oral-poetry theory, which have revised many of the nineteenth-century philological notions that he held. Nonetheless, he is obviously not particularly well informed about the literary-critical status quo of his own time.

24. M. Pines, *Die Geschichte der jüdischendeutschen Literatur*, trans. Georg Hecht (Leipzig 1913), p. 9. The French original, *Historie de la litterature judéo-allemande* (Paris 1911), was unavailable to me. Weinreich ("Studien zur Geschichte," III, 112-113) notes the amazing success of this book via translation, but also refers to the review by Bal-Dimjen [N. Shtif] in *Pinkes* I, 313-348, which demonstrates clearly that the book is beneath all

criticism with respect to its treatment of early Yiddish. Weinreich simply notes that the book is the most accessible of its kind, and thus, since of no scholarly value, the most misleading.

25. Pines generally calls the language "jüdischdeutsch" and maintains it is "reines Deutsch" from its earliest appearance in Rashi's glosses (1040-1105) on Hebrew texts. At one point, however (p. 6), he calls the language "jiddisch" in quotation marks, which one assumes, according to his own criteria (just noted), would indicate that the term is inappropriate without further definition. He does not further define it.

26. He does not explain, however, how this theory can account for the numerous Hebrew expressions in the text which he edits, a text for which he proposes a Middle High German source (p. lxv ff.), which of course had no Hebrew component.

27. Wiener, p. 14. Even so, he generously absolves speakers of Judeo-German of any responsibility for their "*intentional* neglect of grammatical rules" (my emphasis).

28. He cites Dick's use of German in his Yiddish as a means to "lead his people to German culture."

29. His discussion deals almost exclusively with lexical borrowings, and all but ignores syntactic and morphological influences from Hebrew and Slavic. He simply remarks for instance that the syntax of Yiddish resembles English more than it does German.

30. "Diese[s] jüdisch-deutsch[e] Jargon ... deutsches Sprachgut ... das man hier so lange hat unbenutzt verwildern lassen ... dessen einziges Gesetz die Willkur gewesen zu sein scheint ... Wenn man von Flexion spricht, so darf man doch nicht an bestimmte grammatische Formen denken, die in dieser Mischsprache vielmehr nachlässig durcheinandergeworfen sind," *Geschichte*, p. 1002.

31. Cf. for instance, Karpeles, p. 100.

32. Edward Sapir, "Notes on Judeo-German Phonology," *Jewish Quarterly Review*, n.s. 6 (1915-1916), 231-266, here, p. 232.

33. Especially Steinschneider's bibliographical work in *Serapeum* (see the bibliography for full references).

34. Generally rendered as *evreiskii iazik* or *evreisko-nemetskii iazik* by C.C. Vermel in the Russian translation, *Istoria evreiskoi literatury* (Moscow 1913), see esp. 14-17; and *yudish-daytsh* by Baal Makhshoves in his profoundly *daytshmerish* Yiddish translation, *Di geshikhte fun der yudisher literatur* (Warsaw 1911).

35. Felix Perles, "Zur Erforschung des Jüdisch-Deutschen," *Beiträge*

zur Geschichte der deutschen Sprache und Literatur 43 (1918), 296-309.

36. Hecht: *jüdisch*, p. 14; Vermel: *idish*, p. 15; Baal Makhshoves: *yudish*, p. 19.

37. Again, however, one must recall Wiener's temporal context: the Singers, for instance, had not yet appeared on the scene of modern Yiddish literature, but Mendele and Sholem Aleikhem had.

38. On the Tshernovits conference, see esp. Joshua A. Fishman, "The Tshernovits Language Conference and the "Rise of Yiddish'," *International Journal of the Sociology of Language*, 24 (1980), 43-73; and Goldsmith, *Architects of Yiddishism*, 183-221, with extensive bibliography, and most recently Dovid Katz, "On Yiddish, in Yiddish and for Yiddish: 500 Years of Yiddish Scholarship," in *Identity and Ethos: A Festschrift for Sol Liptzin on the Occasion of his 85th Birthday*, Mark H. Gelber, ed., (New York/Bern/Frankfurt: Peter Lang, 1986), 23-36.

39. Robert Holub, *Reception Theory: A Critical Introduction* (London: Methuen, 1984), p. 2.

40. On YIVO, see esp. most recently the jubilee volume of *Yivo-bleter*: "Lekoved fuftsik jor Yivo," *Yivo-bleter* 46 (1980), esp. the essays by Abraham [Arcadius] Cahan, "Der derekh fun Yivo in sayn vilner tkufe," 9-21 and Mordkhe Schaechter, "Dem Yivos yidish-oyftu: roshiprokimdike observatsies un sakhaklen tsu a yubl-date," 192-228.

41. Among others, Maks Weinreich and Solomon Birnbaum, two of the foremost scholars of Yiddish, are of course exceptions to this last statement, but since their long and productive scholarly careers have spanned several periods of twentieth-century Yiddish studies - and even shaped the course of the discipline itself - and Birnbaum is even now still actively at work in the field, their work will be treated in detail later in the study.

42. Maks Erik, *Di Geshikhte fun der yidisher literatur, fun di eltste tsaytn biz der haskole-tkufe, fertsnter-akhtsnter jorhundert, mit bilder un melodies* (Warsaw 1928); and *Vegn altyidishn roman un novele* (Warsaw 1926). Erik's books are replete with problems, both methodological and informational - inaccurate citations, mistaken identifications, etc. They are thus typical of all early, pioneering, full-scale philological studies of a literature. See Yankef Shatski's review of Erik's *Vegn altyidishn roman*, in *Pinkes* 1 (1928), 274-279.

43. *Geshikhte*, p. 8 [there is a pagination error: following p. 9 the numbering again reverts to p. 8 and continues from there; the present reference is to the second p. 8]. Cf. also Moritz Güdemann, *Geschichte des Erziehungswesens und der Cultur der abendländischen Juden während des Mittelalters* (Vienna 1880; repr. Amsterdam 1966), vol. I, chapter iv: "Geistiger Zustand der deutschen Juden während des Zeitraumes vom 9. bis zum 12.

Jahrhundert," 107-126. Yitskhok Shiper, in his critique of Erik's *Geshikhte* claims that Erik assumes an identity of Christian and Jewish language and culture in twelfth-and thirteenth-century Germany and thus contradicts himself in calling the literature of his study "yidish," in "Problemen fun der altyidisher literatur-geshikhte," *Yivo-bleter* 7 (1934), p. 41. Shiper designates it "yidish-taytsh" or "taytsh-yidish," a translation of "Jüdisch-deutsch," in "Kultur-geshikhtlekher fon fun der yidisher literatur," *Yivo-bleter* 8 (19350, p. 53.

44. Cf. also Erik, *Geshikhte*, 29-202.

45. Cf. Shatski's review of *Vegn altyidishn roman*, p. 274.

46. *Vegn altyidishn roman*, p. 24; cf. Shatski's critique, p. 275.

47. Moses Gaster, "Yiddish Literature of the Middle Ages," in *Essays by Divers Hands*, Transactions of the Royal Society of Literature, n.s. 7 (Oxford 1927), p. 109.

48. "Yiddish Literature," 109-110. Somewhat earlier Gaster makes the intriguing statement that since the Jews were generally literate and commonly used the Hebrew alphabet for writing non-Hebrew languages, many European languages may have been recorded in writing in the Hebrew alphabet before they were in the Roman.

49. Yisrael Tsinberg, *Geshikhte fun der literatur bay yidn*, vol. 6: *Altyidishe literatur fun di eltste tsaytn biz der haskole-tkufe*, 2nd ed. (Vilna 1933; repr. New York 1943).

50. *Geshikhte*, p. 55 on rabbinical/pilpulistic literature, and p. 110 on the style of the Yiddish Pentateuch translation by M. Adam.

51. *Geshikhte*, 23-24; Leopold Zunz, *Die Gottesdienstlichen Vorträge der Juden*. Berlin 1832; 2nd ed. Frankfurt 1892, 438-441; 2nd ed. 453-455.

52. Jechiel Bin-Nun [Fischer], *Jiddisch und die deutschen Mundarten* (Tübingen 1973).

53. German is generally the guiding grapho-phonemic norm in his study. Yiddish citations whose pronunciation is known are transcribed accordingly (in the orthography of modern German, however). Yiddish citations from periods before the pronunciation can be determined are, however, cited in an "accommodation to modern German" (p. 13).

54. N. Siskind, "Betrakhtungen vegn der geshikhte fun yidish," *Yidishe shprakh* 13 (1953), 97-108.

55. Without clearly enunciating it or following up on it, he touches on an important point here: to seek a single, unified Old Yiddish language is as misdirected as it is to attempt to identify existing Old Yiddish documents with any single Middle High German dialect, since the Old Yiddish dialects are by definition mixtures.

56. He makes this claim without evidence of any kind. He particularly abhors the method of the philological *gribler*, Erik and Weinreich, and thus his evidence consists exclusively of an appeal to the *lebensgefil* of the literary works themselves, i.e., the works that he posits, but which are not extant. He deems this "evidence" sufficient (in fact much more so than the philological data compiled by Erik and Weinreich) to date the non-extant texts.

57. A. A. Roback, *The Story of Yiddish Literature* (New York 1940).

58. While Roback's arguments can hardly be taken as important contributions to the field, since they lack all evidence (he is, after all, quite consciously and deliberately writing a book for a popular, not a scholarly audience), at least this last one is similar to the argument advanced and instructively (even if not always convincingly) championed with linguistic and sociological evidence by Solomon Birnbaum during the last six decades. See below on Birnbaum's thesis.

59. It is, however, only fair to note that there has been no dearth of such speculation not only by popularizers and translators of the poem, but also by scholars, such that during the past two centuries a library of speculations on this subject and most other aspects of this fragmentary text has been produced. Roback is thus not alone in such conjecture.

60. Yudl Mark, *Di geshikhte fun der yidisher literatur* (New York 1943), 5-6.

61. *Mitteilungen aus dem Arbeitskreis für Jiddistik.*

62. Franz J. Beranek, "Die Erforschung der jiddischen Sprache," *Zeitschrift für deutsche Philologie* 70 (1947/1948), 163-174.

63. One is amazed by the formulation of this explosive statement in a construction that implies that cosmic forces, not Nazis, were responsible for the murder of the Jews: "...wegen der unseligen Rolle, die das Verhängnis dem deutschen Volke beim Niedergang des Jiddischen aufgelastet hat..."

64. S. Lastik, *Di yidishe literatur biz di klasiker* (Warsaw 1950). The implications for audience identification and didactic purpose are intriguing indeed. The author's application of putatively Marxist principles is manifested in 1) the castigation of previous "bourgeois" studies of Yiddish literature, among them those by Tsinberg, Shiper, Erik, Shtif, Prilutzki, whose works are characterized by "an idealistiker, birgerlekh-yidistiker tsugang tsu dem problem" (p. 4); and 2) a denial of value to all Yiddish literature which he cannot re-form into his conception of "folks-literatur"; especially is this the case with religious texts.

65. With the exception, of course, of Weinreich's more elaborate and ultimately better-argued and -supported argument concerning the two *styles* of the First Literary Language of Yiddish: the horizontal and vertical languages. Cf. Weinreich, "History of the Yiddish Language: The Problems and

Their Implications," *Proceedings of the American Philosophical Society* 103 (1959), 563-570.

66. Again one must be aware that there are a number of exceptions to this generalization, among them, again, certainly Weinreich and Birnbaum.

67. This change in the *content* of Old Yiddish literature must also be kept in mind when evaluating the work of these early scholars: they obviously cannot be faulted for not knowing what was still undiscovered or inaccessible.

68. There are some notable exceptions, of course, e.g., Nathan and Solomon Birnbaum, great champions of Yiddish on two fields, neither of whom were native speakers of the language.

69. This aspect of centering, as "on, in and for" Yiddish is the subject of Dovid Katz's article, "On Yiddish, in Yiddish and for Yiddish: 500 Years of Yiddish Scholarship," for through the production of encyclopedias, plays, medical treatises, etc. in Yiddish, the language and linguistic culture receives the right to its own phonology, dialectology, literary history, folklore, etc.

70. The research sections were: history, philology and literature, economics and statistics, psychology and education; cf. esp. Sol Lipztin, "YIVO," in *Encyclopaedia Judaica* (New York 1971), XVI, 837-839.

71. Solomon Birnbaum, "Old Yiddish or Middle High German?" *Journal of Jewish Studies* 12 (1961), 19-31.

72. Cf. P.E. Kahle's study, *The Cairo Genizah* (Oxford 1959) and Chaim Ginninger, "A Note on the Yiddish Horant," in *The Field of Yiddish* 1, Publications of the Linguistic Circle of New York 3 (New York 1954), 275-277 on the history of the manuscript since its rediscovery.

73. S. Roelly, "Essai de reconstitution en moyen haut-allemand normalisé d'un texte en strophes ... *Dukus Horant*," Diss. Paris 1960. See esp. Jean Fourquet, "Ernest-H. Lévy et le Dukus Horant," *Études germaniques* 14 (1959), 50-56 and Ginninger's "A Note," and S. Birnbaum's review of Fuks' edition, in *Biblioteca Orientalis* 16 (1959), 50-52 on the involvement of both Lévy and D. S. Blondheim with the codex and on Fuks' misrepresentation thereof (cf. Blondheim, *Les parlers judéo-romans et la Vetus Latina* (Paris 1925), pp. lxxv ff.). Birnbaum calls Fuks to account for maligning especially Lévy in this regard: "...he ... goes on to criticize both these scholars unjustly. It is absurd to say that Lévy did not recognize the importance of the MS for Yiddish language and literature; it was not his fault that he did not live to publish the edition he was preparing" (rev. of Fuks, ed., p. 50, n. 3), The manuscript of Lévy's planned edition was lost after his death in 1940.

74. L. Fuks, "The Oldest Literary Works in Yiddish in a Manuscript of the Cambridge University Library," *Journal of Jewish Studies* 4 (1953), 176-181; "On the Oldest Dated Work in Yiddish Literature," *The Field of*

Yiddish 1, Publications of the Linguistic Circle of New York 3, Uriel Weinreich, ed., (New York 1954), 267-274; "Der eltster literarisher dokument in yidish," *Yidishe kultur* 16 (1953), 30-35; the edition: *The Oldest Known Literary Documents of Yiddish Literature (c. 1382),* 2 vols. (Leiden 1957).

75. Fuks here quotes W. G. Hellinga, "Principes linguistiques d'édition des textes," *Lingua* 3, p. 302.

76. Cf. Fuks, "The Oldest Literary Works," p. 178, where he asserts that the manuscript is "Yiddish in the sense that it is transliterated in Yiddish [sc. Hebrew] script, not that its language is Yiddish."

77. Cf. also on this point, Fuks, "On the Oldest Dated Work," p. 268.

78. He supplies a personal anecdote as support for his view: despite the fact that the speech of the inhabitants on each side of the Dutch-German border is indistinguishable, those in Holland perceive their language to be Dutch, not German (I, xxvi-xxvii).

79. Cf. especially Maks Weinreich's *Geshikhte* and the analysis of his work below. The particular nature of a language and its history can hardly be comprehensively analyzed solely as a linguistic phenomenon, unless one includes sociological and historical factors as a part of one's definition of linguistic analysis; one would be tempted to claim that such factors are of more than usual importance in the analysis of Yiddish as a fusion language.

80. And not just because Fuks can offer nothing but anecdotal evidence. His summary of the history of the names used by speakers of Yiddish for their own language (I, xviii-xxiv) is also without relevance for his argument: Rashi's use of "loshn Ashkenaz" and the pre-eighteenth-century use of "taytsh" need not indicate the speakers' perception of their language as either identical to or different from German; it *could* have been such, but a detailed analysis of these terms *in contrast* to those used at those times specifically to denote the German language would be necessary in order to prove anything. Fuks does not offer such evidence. See below on Marchand's interpretation of this point and Weinreich's response.

81. He had "saturated" the market: see, for instance, Frederick Norman's "Remarks on the Yiddish Kudrun," *Journal of Jewish Studies* 5 (1954), p. 86, for a sense of the impatience with which the edition was awaited.

82. Cf. for example, K. Habersaat, in *Biblica* 39 (1958), p. 527, who calls *Dukus Hurnt* "das Hildebrandslied"!

83. H. Beim, "Tsushtayer tsu der forshung fun eltstn yidishn manuskript," *Yidishe shprakh* 20 (1960), p. 10.

84. "*shlekht* – dos letste vort iz dos mhd. 'sleht,'" p. 14.

85. J. Carles, "Un fragment judéo-allemand du cycle du *Kudrun*," *Études germaniques* 13 (1958), 348-351: cf. "le jongleur juif" (p. 349), "le poete juif" (p. 350).

86. S. Birnbaum, "The Age of the Yiddish Language," *Transactions of the Philological Society* (1939), 31-43.

87. Leonard Forster, *"Dukus Horant," German Life and Letters* 11 (1958), 276-285.

88. Cf. esp. p. 281: the problem of both Wate and Hagen hailing from Greece; p. 282: the poem is characterized as a "debased" *Spielmannsepos.*

89. Gottfried von Straßburg, *Tristan*, Peter Ganz, ed., Deutsche Klassiker des Mittelalters, n.s. 4 (Wiesbaden 1978), II, p. 50.

90. Forster's interpretations are in general rather inconsistent and arbitrary: e.g., Hurnt's assurance of Hilde that he is happily married and is seeking her hand for his king and not for himself is taken by Forster as direct evidence for the claim that Hurnt wishes to take Hilde for himself, and that he in fact does so in the lost conclusion of the poem (p. 283).

91. Ingeborg Schröbler, "Zu Fuks' Ausgabe der ältesten bisher bekannten Denkmäler jiddischer Literatur," *Zeitschrift für deutsches Altertum* 89 (1959), p. 136. Thus the use of "jiddisch" in the title of her review is most likely no more than the reviewer's paraphrase of Fuks' title, not an indication of her own view of the matter.

92. Peter F. Ganz, rev. of Fuks, *The Oldest ... Documents*, in *Journal of Jewish Studies* 8 (1957), p. 248.

93. One must assume he means normalized Middle High German.

94. Ganz refers here to Birnbaum's articles: "Das älteste datierte Schriftstück in jiddischer Sprache," *Beiträge zur Geschichte der deutschen Sprache und Literatur* 56 (1932), 11-22 and "Umschrift des ältesten datierten jiddischen Schriftstücks," *Teuthonista* 8 (1932), 197-207; on which see chapter 3.

95. Peter Ganz, "*Dukus Horant* – An Early Yiddish Poem from the Cairo Genizah," *Journal of Jewish Studies* 9 (1958), 47-62.

96. Although it is of seminal importance, he does not specify here what he means by "German": which dialect or dialects, whether vernacular or literary.

97. He notes, however, that this language is represented in some surviving texts.

98. And since the poem is "certainly not the production of a Jewish minstrel" (p. 58).

99. Werner Schwarz, "Einige Bemerkungen zur jiddischen Gudrun," *Neophilologus* 42 (1958), 327-332.

100. For this reason he makes the linguistically naive claim that by dating this text, scholars could determine the date of the beginning of the Yiddish language (p. 328).

101. A hidden assumption is present here: does he mean Old Yiddish or modern Yiddish? If Old Yiddish (which alone would be relevant here), then which specific texts are meant (since little concerning the entire problem of Old Yiddish vs. Middle High German can be taken for granted), and how does he distinguish them from Middle High German? He assumes that there are solid criteria for identifying those manuscripts (here unnamed) as Old Yiddish that could also be applied to the Cambridge codex.

102. One would wonder for what purpose this might be the case, if Yiddish and German were, as he maintains, already distinct; one might further wonder what the "German" word *tifle* means.

103. In *Word* 15 (1959), 383-394.

104. James Marchand and Frederic C. Tubach, "Der keusche Josef; Ein mitteldeutsches Gedicht aus dem 13.-14. Jahrhundert. Beitrag zur Erforschung der hebräisch-deutschen Literatur," *Zeitschrift für deutsche Philologie* 81 (1962), 30-32.

105. Rev., p. 384 and "Josef," p. 30: "hebräisch-deutsch" = "deutsche[] Literaturwerke in hebräischen Schriftzeichen" ("German literary works in the Hebrew alphabet"). Marchand and Tubach also claim that "Yosef" is a "Transliteration oder Quasi-Transliteration aus dem deutschen" ("transliteration or quasi-transliteration from German," p. 36). One must assume that they mean from the *Roman* [German term = *lateinisches*] alphabet here, since there is no "German alphabet." Or are they simply confused about the terminology of their topic: one can translate, but hardly transliterate from one language (*Deutsch*) to another. Cf. Fuks' parallel naming of the Hebrew alphabet as "Yiddish," noted above; this usage clearly manifests the operative ideologies in each case.

106. Some Hebrew alphabetic tables were copied into Latin manuscripts during various periods of the Middle Ages – as a representation of the most ancient of the *tres linguae sacrae* – and in practically no such cases is there any evidence for the slightest knowledge of the Hebrew language or scribal practice beyond these crude alphabetic tables; such knowledge was not common among Christians until the early modern period.

107. "[Er] war sich bewußt, daß sein 'ältestes datiertes jiddisches Schriftstück' eigentlich deutsch war" ("Josef," p. 31, n. 5); reference to S. Birnbaum, "Umschrift des ältesten datierten jiddischen Schriftstückes," *Teuthonista [Zeitschrift für Mundartforschung]* 8 (1832), 197-207.

108. N. Süsskind, "Das Shmuel-Bukh," Diss. New York University 1941, p. 162; Erik, *Geshikhte*, pp. 58 f. and 128; Maks Weinreich, *Bilder fun der yidisher literatur-geshikhte* (Vilna 1928), 100-104.

109. See Maks Weinreich's discussion of the early names and their various significations, in "Old Yiddish Poetry in Linguistic and Literary Research," *Word* 16 (1960), 100-118.

110. Marchand uses the term "Negro English."

111. He then cites Kurath, *A Word Geography of the Eastern United States* (Ann Arbor, 1949), p. 6, to give his anecdote the semblance of scholarly authority.

112. One might argue that it is not legitimate to attach so much significance to a very brief and merely illustrative anecdote, or to criticize Marchand's general argument on this basis, and I would agree to a certain point. However, it seems that uninformed, chauvinistic, and anecdotal generalizations – whether clothed in scientific garb or not – need not be propagated, and certainly have no place in the scholarly forum.

113. Rev., p. 387.

114. Marchand/Tubach (p. 33) cite Yudl Mark, "A Study of the Frequency of Hebraisms in Yiddish: Preliminary Report," *The Field of Yiddish*, Uriel Weinreich, ed., (New York 1954), 24-48, and Florence Guggenheim-Grünberg, "The Horse Dealers' Language of the Swiss Jews in Endingen and Lengnau," pp. 50 f. in the same volume, according to whom modern Yiddish has 5% Hebrew vocabulary, and Old Yiddish had an even higher percentage. See below on Marchand/Tubach's misinterpretation of Mark and the difficulty of using descriptive data as prescriptive, especially in such cases, in which stylistic register plays such an important role in the use and avoidance of learned and non-learned vocabulary.

115. As this criterion is actually applied by Marchand, however, it demands that the themes be *solely* from Jewish sources, with no non-Jewish sources either extant or conceivable. If the material appears elsewhere only in Jewish sources, then the text is "Jewish," but not necessarily Yiddish, which depends on the text's satisfying the strictly linguistic criteria. Such is also the case with respect to the extra-linguistic conditions 4 & 5, also explained in "Josef," 33-34.

116. In "Josef" (p. 33), it is specified that the relevant Yiddish dialects are post-1500. *Kinigyn*, an example of a lexeme often noted by defenders of Old Yiddish as a specifically Yiddish word, is rejected by Marchand (in "Three Basic Problems in the Investigation of Early Yiddish," *Orbis* 9 (1960), p. 40) since it is formed on a typically German pattern of word formation (although this is not one of his criteria) of which he cites several illustrations – none of them involving the word *kinigyn* and none of them typical of Yid-

dish texts. The only other example of this particular word in a *German* text that Marchand can cite is from Munich, Cod. Hebr. 347, a text written in the Hebrew alphabet. Thus Marchand attempts to prove the specific German (and specifically non-Yiddish) character of a word found in a Hebrew-alphabet text by citing its use in another "purely German" text that is also written in the Hebrew alphabet and is, beyond the bounds of Marchand's ideology, thus also susceptible to identification as Yiddish. This circularity does not seem to bother Marchand, so sure is he of his quest. Thus he can even conclude this part of his argument by making the statement: "To cite it [*kinigyn*] and like words as Yiddish developments is to ignore the evidence of the German background of Yiddish" (p. 40). Dare one point to his ignoring the Jewish (and perhaps Yiddish) background of these "German" texts that he cites?

117. He notes the first two omissions, but not the last.

118. In his rev. of Fuks, ed., p. 387, n. 16. One hopes that "Josef" is not the promised article, since its premise of a Roman-alphabet, Christian source was devastatingly refuted even as it was advanced, for the poem contains a Hebrew acrostic, which one would hardly find in a Roman-alphabet, German poem. See below.

119. Cf., however, Eli Katz, "Six Germano-Judaic Poems from the Cairo Genizah," Diss. U.C.L.A. 1963, 48-52, on the consistent system of traditional orthography employed in the manuscript, in the context of which the use of double consonants can only be seen as isolated exceptions (in identifiable graphemic environments, *within* the context of the Hebrew-alphabet text) and thus hardly significant enough to deny the otherwise clearly Jewish character of the orthographic system. Cf. also Dov Sadan's argument that the "numerous verbatim agreements between the Yiddish poem ['Paradise'] and the Hebrew prototype" are more important in assigning the poem to a Jewish poet than Marchand's proposal of doubled consonants as evidence against that proposal: in "The Midrashic Background of the 'Paradise' – Its Implication for the Evaluation of the Cambridge Yiddish codex (1382)," *Field of Yiddish* 2, Uriel Weinreich, ed., (London 1965), 254-255, n. 8.

120. Cf. the similar claim in "Three Basic Problems," 37-38; here he also demands that no one not thoroughly grounded in Middle High German and Early New High German and their dialects be allowed to edit early Yiddish texts. This admonition resembles Siegmund Wolf's claim that anyone who wishes to work with Yiddish texts must know Middle High German, Hebrew, Polish, and perhaps one additional Slavic language (*Jiddisches Wörterbuch*, Mannheim 1962), p. 9). One might respond that it would most likely be more relevant, in the first case, to demand that editors of Old Yiddish texts be thoroughly grounded in early Yiddish (which as a scholarly tool would profit from a knowledge of medieval German as a relevant, ancillary field). And in the second case, would it not be better for the aspiring Yiddishist to learn Yiddish instead of, say, Polish?

121. James W. Marchand, "Einiges zur sogenannten 'jiddischen Kudrun,'" *Neophilologus* 45 (1961), 55-63.

122. Khone Shmeruk, "The Hebrew Acrostic in the Yosef Hatsadik Poem of the Cambridge Yiddish Codex," *Michigan Germanic Studies* 3 (1977), 67-81. The acrostic had already been noted by A. M. Haberman in his review of Fuks' ed., "Ktav-hayad hakadum beyoter biyehudit-ashkenazit," in *Hapo'el hatsa'ir* 29 (24 December 1957), 20-21, ignored by Marchand/Tubach.

123. On this linguistic usage, Shmeruk refers to Weinreich, "Old Yiddish Poetry," 109-112. Surprisingly, considering the general tenor of his analysis of the other poems, Shmeruk concurs with Marchand's proposal of a German-language, Roman-alphabet source for *Dukus Hurnt*, from which the poem was transcribed into the Hebrew alphabet (pp. 76 & 80).

124. "Hebräisch-teutsch," p. 101, n. 3.

125. See below, chapter 4.

126. Birnbaum makes a similar argument, but without Weinreich's very precise and insightful terminology, when he notes that Old West Yiddish and Middle High German "overlapped" to some degree, but that the "language of non-literary texts is often highly Judaised, unlike, for instance that of our MS. [i.e. the Cambridge codex]. This fits into what we know of the relation between spoken and written language in general": "Old Yiddish or Middle High German?" *Journal of Jewish Studies* 12 (1961), p. 21. See also Joséf Weissberg's remarks on the variation in the use of Hebrew in Yiddish literary texts, depending on the given literary theme: "Bemerkungen zu den Artikeln von J. W. Marchand," *Zeitschrift für deutsche Philologie* 85 (1966), p. 99. He also argues that the reduction of the problem to one of Old Yiddish vs. Middle High German is extreme and illegitimate, since *Dukus Hurnt*, for instance, is written in a consciously conceived and executed literary register, which he nonetheless – in apparent contradiction of his thesis – designates typical of Middle High German poetry (101-102); in passing he also calls the vowels of the text Middle High German vowels expressed with the Hebrew alphabet: "ein ... System hebräischer Zeichen zur Widerspiegelung der ... mittelhochdeutschen Vokale" (p. 103). Cf. also Peter Ganz, "An Early Yiddish Poem," discussed above, on the distinction between literary and colloquial style.

127. Similar to the distinction among, for instance, Middle High German courtly literary style, the style of the mystics, translations from Latin philosophical works, etc.: all "literary," but each of a different register. In Old Yiddish such distinctions are made clear in the stylistic difference in the preface vs. text of sixteenth-century prose novels, adapted from German: the text of the novel is a highly stylized close translation/paraphrase, and thus greatly influenced by the German original; the prefaces, on the other hand, are origi-

nal compositions in a more colloquial Yiddish and are thus more closely related to (even modern) colloquial Yiddish in morphology, syntax, and lexicon. Cf. Birnbaum, "Two Problems," p. 69 on this topic.

128. Weinreich's term is *shmelts-shprakh,* see his discussion of the concept in *Geshikhte,* II, 261-320.

129. Weinreich refers (p. 109, n. 24) on this concept to B. Axelson, *Unpoetische Wörter. Ein Beitrag zur Kenntnis der lateinischen Dichtersprache* (Lund 1945); cf. also Weinreich, *Geshikhte,* I, 318-320. See, however, also Erika Timm's critique of Weinreich's use of Axelson's theory here, since in Yiddish vs. Hebrew (unlike in Axelson's work), the contrastive exclusion is of one entire component of the language; in Timm, *Graphische und phonische Struktur,* p. 375, n. 44.

130. Cf. Weinreich's fuller treatment of this point in *Geshikhte,* II, 322-323, especially on *taytsh* as Yiddish or German and the eighteenth-century distinction between them in Yiddish through the use of the contrast *galkhes* with *our language [undzer shprakh - biloshenu].*

131. Weinreich also lists examples of other features (p. 112).

132. Cf., however, "Josef," p. 33: "von 1500 an."

133. Landau for instance claims that the Esther paraphrase is Hessian ("A Hebrew-German (Judeo-German) Paraphrase of the Book of Esther of the Fifteenth Century," *Journal of English and Germanic Philology* 18 (1919), 501-502), and contends that *Vidvilt* is Central German (*Arthurian Legends,* p. lxiv).

134. Cf. on this point Weinreich, "Prehistory and Early History of Yiddish: Facts and Conceptual Framework," *The Field of Yiddish,* Uriel Weinreich, ed., Publications of the Linguistic Circle of New York 3 (New York 1954), 74-75.

135. He actually posits the existence of Yiddish from the beginning of Jewish settlement in the Rhineland, ca. A.D. 1000, "Prehistory," p. 75; cf. also "Old Yiddish Poetry," p. 108.

136. Weinreich notes Landau's letter to Sainéanu in 1902, where this point is also discussed; the correspondence is cited by Chaim Ginninger, "Di korespondents A. Landoy - L. Saineanu," *Yivo-bleter* 13 (1938), 275-300.

137. Birnbaum notes that Yiddish would never have developed as an independent language without the determinative, group-forming influence of the Jewish religion ("Two Problems," p. 67, n. 4). Weinreich formulates this idea somewhat differently and the distinction is, I think, significant: for him it is the entirety of Jewish civilization, for which his all-encompassing term is "yidishkayt." To put it in more general terms, it is the Jews' particular background that prevents them from simply adopting the language and cul-

ture *per se* of a new country ("Prehistory," p. 100). This topic, the historical "cause" of the origin of Yiddish, although it can only be noted here, has been the subject of much attention throughout the history of the study of Yiddish.

138. This ideologically charged warning contrasts well with Marchand's caveat that it would be "disastrous" to view such texts as Old Yiddish.

139. "Es hängt nicht allzuviel davon ab, welche Benennung wir einer Sache beilegen, sofern wir uns über den Inhalt des Terminus geeinigt haben," "Studien zur Geschichte und dialektischen Gliederung der jiddischen Sprache," Part 1: "Geschichte und gegenwärtiger Stand der jiddischen Sprachforschung," 3 vols. Diss. Marburg 1923, I, p. 3.

140. "Der für seine [des jüdischen Volkes] Sprache einzig passende Ausdruck," I, 4-9.

141. As was done in Russian, *jevrejski jazyk*, as opposed to the term for Hebrew, *drevne-jevrejski jazyk* (Weinreich's transcription).

142. "Germanistik ... [zieht] mit Recht das Jiddische in ihren Forschungskreis ein" (Diss., I, p. 65).

143. In *Indogermanica, Festschrift Wolfgang Krause* (Heidelberg: Winter, 1960), 145-165.

144. "Für den Freund der altdeutschen Dichtung," p. 145. He remarks, for instance, that *Dukus Hurnt* scarcely has epic characteristics and is subliterary *(unterliterarisch*, p. 162).

145. "Ich gebe den Text in lateinischen Buchstaben und setze die nicht geschriebenen Vokale und Konsonanten hinzu. In den sonstigen Zitaten aus der Cambridger Hs. schreibe ich die Wörter in normalisiertem Mhd." (p. 146, n, 5).

146. It is of course to be expected that Neumann reaches the same conclusions concerning the language of these texts as he did in his analysis of *Dukus Hurnt*, since here too he analyzes the rhymes in his normalized Middle High German construction.

147. The invidious nature of Neumann's preconceptions and how they insinuate themselves into even the ostensibly most innocuous "matters of fact" is well illustrated here: when the poem in question is given a title in the manuscript tradition and the early printed editions it follows the general form of "[Ayn shen mayse fun] kenig artis hof." Modern scholars have renamed it *Vidvilt* [often spelled in Germanized orthography (also true of some of the later prints and adaptations): *Widuwilt*] for its protagonist. Neumann tacitly changes the title to that of an earlier Middle High German poem, which almost certainly played a role in the prior tradition of the tale that led to *Vidvilt*, but according to recent research probably did not serve

as a direct source of that poem, which is in fact quite a different poem indeed, in form, content, and structure. Thus, just as ideology plays a role in the process of assigning a name to the language, here too, even in naming the poem, ideology is at work, for Neumann manages to make the Yiddish work an insignificant appendage to German literature, not even worthy of retaining its own title.

148. Joséf Weissberg, "The Vowel System of MS Cambridge T-S10 K 22 Compared with Middle High German," *Journal of Jewish Studies* 14 (1963), 37-57; "Das Konsonantensystem des "Dukus Horant' und der übrigen Texte des Cambridger Manuskripts T.S. 10. K. 22, verglichen mit dem Mittelhochdeutschen," *Zeitschrift für Mundartforschung* 32 (1965), 1-40.

149. In "Konsonanten," p. 1, he claims that the texts are Middle High German and that the manuscript is the oldest example of Middle High German written in the Hebrew alphabet. In this article he also maintains that the dialect of the texts is primarily Upper German, with some Central German features.

150. In "Konsonanten," 2-3, he even denies that any identification of the language or dialect is possible, since too little is known about Old Yiddish and Middle High German dialects. As just noted, however, he had already identified both language and dialect only a page earlier.

151. He argues that the orthography of the manuscript points to the later development of an orthographic system in Yiddish and is thus important for the history of the Yiddish language ("Konsonanten," p. 5).

152. Weissberg commits an error here which is rather common in studies of Old Yiddish, based on a transliterated/transcribed text: after having transposed the text into the Roman alphabet, which in itself involves the scholar in a morass of interpretive decisions (or more often simply in the execution of his *a priori* assumptions), then that transposed "text" is taken as the basis of analysis and as an absolute guarantor of meaning in all senses. Only in this way can Weissberg (and other scholars) seriously maintain, as an informed linguistic argument, for instance, that *jar* as opposed to *jur/jor* does not occur in the text.

153. See below on the editions by Hakkarainen and Althaus.

154. Eli Katz, "Six Germano-Judaic Poems from the Cairo Genizah," Diss. U.C.L.A. 1963. The edition, completed as a dissertation, has never been published as such and has thus never achieved widespread use among scholars. Even so, it is the definitive edition of the codex.

155. "Because of their connotations, implicit and explicit" – primarily as they developed in the school of the Wissenschaft des Judentums (p. 73, n. 21).

156. In his article, "Old Yiddish or Middle High German," Birnbaum simply proposes that since Yiddish had begun at some indeterminate time, perhaps even as far back as the ninth-century settlements of Jews in the Rhineland, then one must posit the beginnings of the language at the time of that settlement. Thus by the time the Cambridge codex was written down, Yiddish had already had a 500-year history, and the language of the manuscript can hardly be called anything but Yiddish. Katz rightly points out that this is a case of *petitio principii* (p. 12).

157. Unlike the terms, "Hebrew-German" and "Judeo-German," "Germano-Judaic" as a term signifies a language primarily Jewish, with some German attributes, since its determinant is "Judaic," not "German," and only its qualifier is "Germano". Thus the "Jewishness" of the language is not merely a marginal qualification of the basically German linguistic strata, but is itself centered.

158. Here one does note a slip in Katz's otherwise impeccable methodological mask, for what does he mean by "Yiddish" of this period?

159. Cf. Marchand's rev. of Fuks' ed. of the Cambridge codex, p. 188; Marchand/Tubach, "Josef," p. 36; Ganz, "An Early Yiddish Poem," p. 56; Neumann, "Sprache und Reim," p. 148.

160. Peter Ganz, Frederick F. Norman and Werner Schwarz, eds., *Dukus Horant*, Altdeutsche Textbibliothek, Ergänzungsreihe 2 (Tübingen 1964).

161. Whose informed and scholarly interests, I hasten to add, also extend to other fields.

162. Thus a brief excurse on the edition in general is in order here, since its constitution bears greatly on the topic of the name of the language. Further analysis of the edition as such will be deferred to chapter 3.

163. Cf. Josėf Weissberg, "Zur Stellung der altjiddischen Literatur in der Germanistik," *Zeitschrift für deutsche Philologie* 91 (1972), p. 390, who criticizes the editors for excising *Dukus Hurnt* from its manuscript and treating it in isolation, without taking into account the significance of its presence in a collection of texts, especially in this particular collection, which is unique in kind among surviving medieval manuscripts.

164. Ganz/Norman/Schwarz, "Zu dem Cambridger Josef," *Zeitschrift für deutsche Philologie* 82 (1963), p. 86.

165. Interestingly, and typically, the fourth edition of B. Symons's edition of *Kudrun* by Bruno Boesch, which appeared in the ATB in the same year as did the edition of *Dukus Hurnt* devotes almost a full page to the latter text, but without once mentioning even the possibility of its being Yiddish, of its transmission via the Hebrew alphabet, or of the existence of questions of linguistic or cultural identity; in fact the only point worth the editor's men-

tion is that *Dukus Hurnt* had no textual or *sagengeschichtlicher* value in *Kudrun* scholarship (xvii-xviii).

Recent editors of the series have, however, become more responsive to twentieth-century advances in methods of textual criticism, especially since B. Wachinger has assumed the position of chief editor of the series.

166. With respect to the latter possibility, one would wonder why: the number of texts readily available on microfilm, the modern scholar's new medium of preliminary manuscript research, was not yet as great as it is now (esp. from the Jewish Studies Microfiche Project, directed by Khone Shmeruk), but that is not to say that microfilm (or the manuscripts themselves) were inaccessible. At any rate, it is unsettling that the editor analyzes grapho-phonemic relations either based on edited texts (rather than manuscripts) or not at all.

167. Are not the Greek, Cyrillic, and even Runic alphabets also European? The standard German term for the Roman alphabet is "das *lateinische* Alphabet." Cf. Ganz/Norman/Schwarz, "Zu dem Cambridger Joseph," p. 86: "deutsche Buchstaben" (twice); Schwarz, "Prinzipielle Erwägungen zur Untersuchungen der Cambridger Handschrift T.-S. 10. K. 22," *Zeitschrift für Mundartforschung* 33 (1966), p. 142: "deutsche Buchstaben" contrasted with the Hebrew alphabet.

168. At this point it is perhaps already useful to begin to put the critique of this edition into context by posing a general question: conceivably the alphabet used, the inclusion of the text in a Jewish collection, and the Jewish adaptations of the themes of this poem are, from the editors' perspective, all merely aspects of a textual disguise; but would it not be enlightening for the reader and helpful to other scholars to be shown why all these factors are thought irrelevant, before the process of violent excision of the "actual" text begins, especially in the "standard edition"?

169. Ingeborg Schröbler concurs that the dialect is Central German (review, in *Germanistik* 7 (1966), p. 73). Kaplowitt calls it simply "Middle High German" and notes that Schwarz's argument is convincing for "late Middle High German" (review, in *Journal of English and Germanic Philology* 65 (1966), p. 538); Joséf Weissberg, "Zur Stellung," p. 391, points out that the Upper German features seem to outweigh the Central German, a position he argues in greater detail in "Bemerkungen zu den Artikeln von J. W. Marchand," *Zeitschrift für deutsche Philologie* 85 (1966), 106-110. Walter Röll denies that a specific identification of the dialect is possible, since the text contains a mixture of Upper, Central, *and* Low German features (review, in *Studi Medievali*, ser. 3/7 (1966), p. 272).

170. In order to proceed in an unbiased manner, it is also necessary, he maintains, to work with as exact a transposition (*Umschrift*) as possible ("Prinzipielle Erwägungen," p. 141). One might well ask why the original, in which all information is immediately available, is not to be preferred, at least

at this stage of the investigation, even if it were necessary in the end to publish the edition as a transposed text for the sake of the unlettered (in the Hebrew alphabet) Germanistic audience. But to use a transposed text as the basis of analysis is utterly indefensible as textual scholarship, especially if the transposition is not strict transliteration.

171. See especially Rauh's review of the edition, in *Euphorion* 60 (1966), p. 159, on the redundancy, disorganization, and lack of coordination of the essays.

172. He locates the origin of the poem in "Mitteldeutschland" (p. 30), an obscure term of geography (especially linguistic geography), to say the least, and especially unclear with reference to the fourteenth century, but certainly consistent with Schwarz's identification of the dialect as "mitteldeutsch." He further specifies the provenance by noting that the literary relations of the poem point to the Rhineland (p. 130).

173. This is the closest the editors come to associating the language with "Yiddish"; the name is never used with reference to *Dukus Hurnt* in the entire course of their study, and thus the editors do not deal with one of the most important questions of their time in any fashion, except by tacitly assuming an answer to the unexpressed question.

174. Norman claims (77-78) that the Jewish features of *Dukus Hurnt*, (reduced to *tifle*, the substitution of *juden* for *junger* in the Crusader song, and the title of the poem), are later additions to the original poem. Even if that were the case, are they not, nonetheless, at least "Jewish coloring" of the actual extant text, i.e. of *Dukus Hurnt*, ostensibly the text about which Norman is writing?

175. The phrase is actually: "*nicht mehr* rein deutsch" (my emphasis), thus implying in Haskalah fashion that Jews originally spoke "pure German" before corrupting it into Yiddish.

176. Norman cites Landau, p. 75, n. 1, but not Marchand, with whose arguments he may not want to be associated.

177. The lists of gems and Pentateuch readings, text no. 6 of the manuscript, are never dealt with by Ganz/Norman/Schwarz (nor is their significance for the cultural context of the manuscript), although they are at least listed by Ganz in his outline of the contents of the manuscript (p. 6).

178. Presumably he means "normalized" (*normalisiertes*) Middle High German. Lachmann commonly used the term *Normalmittelhochdeutsch* for the *langue*, as it were, that he visualized; other scholars have sometimes followed this usage. Most commonly nowadays, however, the term *normalisiertes Mittelhochdeutsch* is used to designate both this idealized *langue* (if still so conceived) and those actual occurrences of it that do not conform to it except through the good offices of sympathetic editors. *Normal*

Mittelhochdeutsch, on the other hand, is at least a rarity to be added to these editors' list of abnormal and undefined terms: "normal" as opposed to "abnormal" Middle High German.

179. Whether or not this is Norman's intent, the assumption would be accurate, since probably no one, whether Christian or Jewish, poet or craftsman, in the Middle High German period, spoke the literary language as a native speaker.

180. With reference not to the fuller treatments by Shmeruk and Haberman, but only to Ganz/Norman/Schwarz's own article "Zu dem Cambridger Joseph," where reference is made to Haberman; nor does he mention Marchand/Tubach's elaborate attempts to argue for a German origin for this poem, although they were instrumental in eliciting Shmeruk's detailed refutation on the basis of the acrostic, perhaps again to avoid association with Marchand/Tubach's argument.

181. His formulation is a patronizing, sarcastic barb for those scholars who argue for Jewish authorship of the poem: " ...sie [sc. die zarte Musikempfindsamkeit] ... spricht nicht *gerade* für einen jüdischen Autoren" [the delicate musical sensibility ... does not *exactly* speak for a Jewish author," (my emphasis of the emotive particle)]. Paucker (review, in *German Life and Letters*, n.s. 21 (1968), 274-275) concurs with Norman's dismissal of Jewish authorship, since he argues that the queen need not be viewed as the typically Jewish wifely handmaiden, and that the mercantile atmosphere need not be exclusively Jewish, and otherwise "Jewish coloring" is scanty. Here again the Marchandian principle of "Jewishness' is applied: evidence for any pro-Jewish or pro-Yiddish (as opposed to pro-Middle High German) argument is tacitly required to be "exclusively Jewish" in order to have any weight; otherwise the evidence is invariably dismissed as irrelevant. And in these cases only the clichés of Gentile views of "Jewish" culture seem to have been considered relevant as signs of that culture: the prohibition of pork, female subservience, and the dominance of a mercantile mentality.

182. This tone seems to be Norman's characteristic method of denying "Jewish coloring" of any kind; for when he rejects the theory of the origin of *Dukus Hurnt* in an urban ghetto, he patronizingly cajoles Hermann Menhardt, one of the theory's proponents, for his inability to think for himself, since he simply "allowed himself to be persuaded by Colditz," p. 130, n. 90.

183. Weissberg astutely notes that the editors deny *Dukus Hurnt* any literary value due to their arbitrary valorization of the heroic epic as the most important literary genre of the period. From their perspective then, *Dukus Hurnt* is naturally "unterliterarisch" ("Zur Stellung," p. 391).

184. See esp. 130-131 of the edition for an example of the rhetoric that results from such a method.

185. This is especially true with respect to Norman's speculations on the literary prehistory of *Dukus Hurnt,* particularly in his apparently total lack of acquaintance with the vast and informative scholarly literature on oral poetry, which has in recent years (even before the publication of this edition) re-oriented almost all studies of medieval literature, especially of the genre with which Norman here deals. He nevertheless still faults the poet for his "poverty" (*Armut*) of rhyme and vocabulary, and repetitions of words and phrases (listed, 87-89); i.e., for precisely those kinds of devices that modern critics would treat as characteristic of some stage of the oral tradition.

186. Inexplicably, U. Rauh maintains that the editors summarize everything published up to that time on *Dukus Hurnt* [rev. of Ganz/Norman/Schwarz, eds., *Dukus Horant*, in *Euphorion* 60 (1966), p. 159]. Michael Curschmann's brief comment, on the other hand, is much more to the point and in its double-edged but gracious understatement, all the more telling: their bibliography (xii-xiii), which consists of only twenty-two items and fifteen reviews of Fuks' edition, contains fifteen citation errors [Michael Curschmann, *Spielmannsepik: Wege und Ergebnisse der Forschung von 1907-1965, mit Ergänzungen und Nachträgen bis 1967* (Stuttgart 1968), discussion of *Dukus Hurnt*, 41-45 & 102-108].

187. The assumption on her part being that it has been proven that this language is "a linguistic form of German."

188. Schwarz's discussion of the letter makes no such claim (38-42), but provides evidence which could be interpreted in precisely the opposite way (he does not do so): ח contrasted with ח̇ represents a contrast not present in Middle High German and thus a sound not in Middle High German, it could thus be interpreted as evidence for Yiddish, but probably should not be, since it is too slight to support an argument, certainly not Rauh's self-contradictory one.

189. Cf. also H. Rosenfeld's review of the edition on this point, in *Deutsche Literaturzeitung* 87 (1966), p. 126.

190. For instance: Schmitt's article, listed by Rauh on p. 163 as appearing in "Zs.f.Mafg.," an abbreviation not included in her list; " ZfMf" is, however, present in the list (p. 164); both refer to the same journal: *Zeitschrift für Mundartforschung.* "Beiträge," a recurrent journal in her bibliography is not identified, although there are numerous journals whose titles begin with this word. One might object – but *we* all know that "Beiträge" obviously refers to "PBB" [which is itself rather a confusing abbreviation, since the journal's title was in fact never "Paul und Braunes Beiträge"]; but if that is in fact so "obvious," then why identify abbreviations at all? Obviously because a multi-disciplinary audience is interested in the study of these texts.

191. H. Stopp, review of Ganz/Norman/Schwarz, eds., in *Zeitschrift für deutsche Philologie* 86 (1967), p. 458. Paucker also notes this difficulty in his

review of the edition, but nevertheless calls the text a "'Yiddish' *Dukus Horant*" and asserts that since the text presents an early stage in the formation of the Yiddish language, designating it either Yiddish or Middle High German is "largely a matter of terminology," and thus Yiddish scholars may legitimately claim the text as an "Ancient or Old Yiddish text," since there is necessarily a distinction between literary and vernacular language [*German Life and Letters*, n.s. 21 (1968), p. 274]. As we have already seen, the "matter of terminology" has been made one of the primary questions of scholarship in this field. In discounting this topic's importance, Paucker is reflecting the editors' lack of attention to it.

192. Cf. also Rosenfeld, rev. p. 126, on this point.

193. Röll's methodological acuity, demonstrated in his other contributions to the field as well, may also appear here in slightly ironic form: Norman's positing of the existence of a non-extant text for which there is also no external evidence seems by definition "irrefutable."

194. See, for instance, Rosenfeld's explication of "Wate the Greek" (p. 127), which had caused Norman so much difficulty.

195. But not so surprising that it is merely a variation on one of the existing names. Colditz, "Das hebräisch-mittelhochdeutsche Fragment vom 'Dukus Horant,'" *Forschungen und Fortschritt* 40 (1966), 302-306.

196. As, apparently, he himself had done six years earlier, in his article, "Das jiddische Fragment von Herzog Horand."

197. Friedrich C. B. Avé-Lallemant, *Das deutsche Gaunerthum in seiner socialpolitischen, literarischen und linguistischen Ausbildung*, 3. Theil (Leipzig 1862), p. 52.

198. He refers here to their article, "Süßkind von Trimberg, der jüdische Minnesänger," *Literaturblatt des Orients* 10 (7 March 1840), p. 146 f.

199. Regardless of the term's neutrality, it is interesting to note that the exigencies of the developing nomenclature of Yiddish and the process of naming itself have now forced the creator of a new name to add an English translation to his German coinage, perhaps due to the undeniable influence of "Hebrew-German" on the name "Hebrew-Middle High German."

200. He refers here also to Hermann Menhardt, "Regensburg, ein Mittelpunkt der deutschen Epik des 12. Jahrhunderts," *Zeitschrift für deutsches Altertum* 89 (1958), 271 ff.; "Zur Herkunft des "Dukus Horant,'" *Mitteilungen aus dem Arbeitskreis für Jiddistik* 2 (1961), 33-36; and Weissberg, "Konsonanten."

201. Michael Curschmann, *Spielmannsepik*, especially 41-45 and 102-107 on *Dukus Hurnt*.

202. Siegfried Colditz, "Das jiddische Fragment von Herzog Horand in seinem Verhältnis zum Gudrunepos und dem König Rother," *Mitteilungen aus dem Arbeitskreis für Jiddistik* 2 (1960), p. 24.

203. Strangely, this particular tendency, which is quite pronounced in Althaus' edition of the Cambridge lion fable is all but absent from his other studies.

204. Heikki J. Hakkarainen, *Studien zum Cambridger Codex T.-S. 10. K. 22*; 1: *Text* (Acta Universitatis Turkuensis, ser. B, vol. 104; Turku 1967), 2: *Graphemik und Phonemik* (Acta, ser. B, vol. 174, 1971), 3: *Lexicon* (Acta, ser. B., vol. 182, 1973).

205. "I use this designation since we quite obviously have to do here with a manuscript that 1) was written by Jews and 2) whose language is substantially German. It should be understood only in this sense." He refers back to this footnote in his identification of the language as German (I, p. 16, noted above), thus providing a strange example of his use of authority and evidence: for his second generalization, he refers back to the initial occurrence in his study of the identical, unsupported generalization.

206. One might question whether it would ever under any conditions be legitimate to ignore the context of documents to be analyzed. Cf. Röll's review, in *Germanistik* 13 (1972), p. 101, on the illegitimacy of treating these differing texts together without discrimination.

207. B. Murdoch claims that Hakkarainen generally succeeded in his attempt at pure objectivity and "mechanical" transposition (in his review of Hakkarainen's edition, in *Modern Language Review* 65 (1970), p. 443). See also, however, Erika Timm's critique of Hakkarainen's inconsistent empiricism, that is, his constant interpretation in the face of his denial of all interpretation; *Graphische und phonische Struktur des Westjiddischen unter besonderer Berücksichtigung der Zeit um 1600* (Tübingen 1987), pp. 59-61.

208. The extremes to which one may be led by protestations of objectivity may be seen in Hakkarainen's third volume, which he calls a "Lexikon," although it is in fact merely a computer concordance of various features in the texts, still in such "undigested" form that Röll [review, *Germanistik* 15 (1974), p. 351] even comments on the absurdity of Hakkarainen's refusal to do more than "describe," never deigning to actually analyze. But in fact there is in the "description" and selection of that which is to be described obviously already a kind of implicit analysis and interpretation.

209. Obviously one should not understand the actual order of presentation in any study as a chronologically-ordered record of the progress of the study, but the importance of placement here is just as obvious: the guiding principle cannot but be stated early on, although not itself a subject of the study.

210. In comments on specific word forms, his practice is also revealing, for he follows the standard Germanistic practice of equating lemmata with Middle High German: e.g. "'kvng' (= mhd. künegin)" (I, p. 22, n. 31).

211. "Hebrew appears in the 'German' text in isolated words, which have the character of a foreign word and designate specifically Jewish concerns, as well as in several purely Hebrew words – detached from the 'German' text – at the end of the individual sections of the manuscript ... In general one remarks that Hebrew words and Hebrew language are very rare in the manuscript."

212. B. Lindgren, Review of Hakkarainen, *Neuphilologische Mitteilungen* 73 (1972), p. 724.

213. One wonders nonetheless about the significance of the added phrase in the first term, "in Hebrew script," for in its qualification of the initial noun, it implies that it is possible for "Judeo-Middle High German" texts to be written in an alphabet other than Hebrew, i.e. Roman, but still be *Judeo*-Middle High German, that is, still (somehow recognizably?) different from Middle High German *per se*.

214. Hans-Peter Althaus, *Die Cambridger Löwenfabel von 1382; Untersuchung und Edition eines defekten Textes* (Berlin 1971).

215. Or both. See below, chapter 3 on his editorial practice.

216. In his article, "Die Erforschung der jiddischen Sprache," in *Germanische Dialektologie. Festschrift Walther Mitzka zum 80. Geburtstag*, L. E. Schmitt, ed., (Wiesbaden 1968), I, 224-226, Althaus notes without further discussion that Yiddish did not develop until the High Middle Ages, and that Jews were conscious of speaking German, since they called the language "tajtsch," thus again attempting to employ a simple argument based on this complicated semantic complex that Weinreich had already refuted some time before.

217. Respectively: "mittelhochdeutsche Phonemsprache christlicher Sprachbenutzer," "mittelhochdeutsche Phonemsprache jüdischer Sprachbenutzer," "mittelhochdeutsche antiqua-orientierte [i.e. Roman-alphabet] Graphemsprache," "mittelhochdeutsche quadratschriftorientierte [i.e. Hebrew square script] Graphemsprache," *Die Cambridger Löwenfabel*, p. 68.

218. Apparently, according to his use of the term, "medieval German spoken language," p. vii.

219. Compare Katz's usage of the term "zero grapheme," however, in reference to initial, non-vocalic א (31-32).

220. Guggenheim-Grünberg, "Zur Umschrift deutscher Mundarten des 14./15. Jahrhunderts mit hebräischer Schrift," *Zeitschrift für Mundartforschung* 24 (1957), 229-246.

221. Arnold Paucker, "Yiddish Versions of Early German Prose Novels," *Journal of Jewish Studies* 10 (1959), 151-167; cf. also his "The Yiddish Versions of the German Volksbuch," Diss. Nottingham 1959.

222. Maks Weinreich also notes that the influence of the German printing industry and developing tradition on Yiddish printing was so strong that, for instance, "umlaut" is represented in the Yiddish *Brantshpigl* of 1676, although it was not to be found in other Yiddish works of the period (*Geshikhte*, I, p. 52).

223. W. B. Lockwood, "Die Textgestalt des jüngeren Hildebrandliedes in jüdisch-deutscher Sprache," *Beiträge zur Geschichte der deutschen Sprache und Literatur* (Halle) 85 (1963), 432-447.

224. John A. Howard, "Bemerkungen zu einem Aspekt altjiddischer Literaturgeschichte," *Archiv für das Studium der neueren Sprachen und Literaturen* 215 (1978), 1-20.

225. In his articles on the "Bärmuttersegen," he simply assumes the language to be Middle High German and refers to the texts as "hebräisch-deutsche Handschriften," or Middle High German "in hebräischen Buchstaben verfaßt" [sic], "Der Bärmuttersegen wiederentdeckt," *Zeitschrift für deutsches Altertum* 108 (1979), p. 252; "Der Bärmuttersegen – Ein mittelhochdeutscher Spruch," *Colloquia Germanica* 12 (1978), p. 214; cf. also the assumption of German as the language of Hebrew-alphabet chapbooks (including *Vidvilt* under this generic rubric!), in "A Little Known Version of *Til Eulenspiegel*," *Amsterdamer Beiträge zur älteren Germanistik* 15 (1980), 127-142.

226. This same usage is also the rule in "The Bodleian *Fortunatus*," *Yiddish* 6 (1985), 15-20.

227. For a recent defense of the *Spielmann* theory and rejection of the relevance of the oral poetry theories for this poem, see Kurt Ruh, "Epische Literatur des deutschen Spätmittelalters," *Neues Handbuch der Literaturwissenschaft*, vol. 8, *Europäisches Spätmittelalter*, ed. Willi Erzgräber (Wiesbaden 1978), 117-118; but also Dreeßen, "Midraschepik," p. 97 on necessary principles of a critique of the *Spielmann* theory.

228. Later in the article he also claims that Yiddish developed into mutually incomprehensible dialects even in neighboring ghettoes, and cites as proof Jacob Maarsen's remarks in the preface to his translation of Boccaccio (1710), that it was difficult to make oneself understood to all Jews. At the very least, it is difficult to see Howard's causal connection here.

229. I. Abrahams, *Jewish Life in the Middle Ages* (New York 1896), p. 359.

230. As opposed, he inexplicably contends, to Weinreich's claim that

it signifies Yiddish; Weinreich rather analyzes in great detail exactly how and why such claims are virtually impossible to support, since the use of this terminology is so complex.

231. It would be interesting to know what he understands as the "standard".German of the late seventeenth century.

232. Siegmund Wolf, *Jiddisches Wörterbuch* (Mannheim 1962).

233. He is, apparently, speaking of Modern Yiddish here.

234. Werner Weinberg, "Die Bezeichnung Jüdischdeutsch: eine Neubewertung," *Zeitschrift für deutsche Philologie* 100 (Sonderheft *Jiddisch* 1981), 253-290.

235. Table 3 ostensibly lists those who used *Jüdischdeutsch* to designate only West Yiddish (258-259), but actually includes some writers/scholars who used the term to mean Yiddish in general (e.g., Waxman, Karpeles); table 4 lists Jews who used the term to mean East Yiddish as well (259-260).

236. "Yidish" in the *Algemayne entsiklopedie, Yidn B*, Paris 1940, col. 31; he rather sarcastically refers to Weinreich as a person "der ja ein großer Namengeber war," referring to Weinreich's work on the concepts of whole and merged Yiddish, fusion language, and the vertical and horizontal styles.

237. *Tsum yidishn vokalizm*, Warsaw 1920, p. 159 index.

238. *Die jiddische Sprache*, Berlin/Vienna 1924, p. xv.

239. "Jiddisch," *Enc. jud.*, col. 119.

240. "Einen Aspekt des früheren Idioms der deutschen Juden auf sich selbst bezogen und nicht als Teil einer größeren historischen, philologischen oder geographischen Einheit" (p. 277).

241. Percy Matenko and Samuel Sloan, "The Aqedath Jiṣḥaq; A Sixteenth Century Epic," in *Two Studies in Jewish Culture* (Leiden 1968), 1-70.

242. See below, chapter 3 on Matenko/Sloan's editorial method.

243. With the obvious exception of the rebuttals of Marchand by Weinreich and Shmeruk, who were not bound by the ideological restrictions of this particular conception of Old Yiddish studies. While their major publications have already been dealt with as they relate especially to Marchand, the ideological implications of their work will be treated below in chapter 4, since it is actually in the context of a radically different paradigm of Yiddish studies that their work belongs.

Chapter 3

1. John M. Manly and Edith Rickert, eds., *The Text of the Canterbury Tales, Studied on the Basis of All Known Manuscripts*, 8 vols. (Chicago 1940). Helmut de Boor, ed., *Das Nibelungenlied*, 21st ed. rev. by Roswitha Wisniewski (Wiesbaden 1979).

2. F. N. Robinson, ed., *The Works of Geoffrey Chaucer*, 2nd ed. (Boston 1957). R. M. Lumiansky, trans., *The Canterbury Tales* (New York 1954).

3. Or perhaps in this case, it would be necessary to cite directly from the pertinent manuscript.

4. For up to the present no one has apparently conceived of a significant audience for popular or student editions or paperback translations of Old Yiddish literature, as there is in a restricted sense, for instance, for Old English and even Old Norse literature.

5. Hans-Peter Althaus, *Die Cambridger Löwenfabel von 1382; Untersuchung und Edition eines defekten Textes* (Berlin 1971), 31-32.

6. Cf., for instance, Theodor Frings and Gabriele Schiebs, eds., *Henric van Veldeken: Eneide*, 2 vols. Deutsche Texte des Mittelalters 58-59 (Berlin 1964-1965); or Willy Krogmann, *Das Hildebrandslied in der langobardischen Urfassung hergestellt* (Berlin 1959).

7. The decision concerning the identity of the language resembles to a certain extent the principle of the traditional editorial problem of archetypes, in that it, too, attempts to reproduce in the editor's conception the state of the text closest to the original. But in Old Yiddish studies this desire to move back to an "original," whatever that may be, is ultimately not as important as the will to make the text accessible to the modern audience, conceived in terms of the *necessity* of its access to and interest in Old Yiddish.

8. That is, until recently, when a tendency toward more accuracy in textual editing has developed, giving rise to more stringently diplomatic texts, perhaps reflecting a final, belated positivistic influence on textual criticism.

9. Whether one happens to be an adherent of this group or not, one must be aware that the edited text in the Roman alphabet, transformed and printed as if it were Middle High German, is in and of itself powerful concrete "evidence" after the fact (for the audience) for the editors' argument that the text *is* Middle High German. The same caveat applies equally, of course, to the ideological implications of the actual printed texts of editions of type two, which tacitly, graphically "argue" for the text's identity as Yiddish.

10. Cf. Fuks, *The Oldest . . . Documents*, I, p. xxxvii, who claims to present the text "as the reading eye sees it"; and Hakkarainen, *Studien*, I,

13-14: "Fragen, die die Sprache und den literarischen Inhalt der Hs. berühren, bleiben in diesem Teil meiner Studien völlig ausgeklammert. Hier kommt es nur darauf an, die Hs. zu entziffern und eine zuverlässige Grundlage für die weiteren Untersuchungen zu schaffen, deren Hauptgewicht überhaupt in der Zukunft auf der sprachlichen (linguistischen) und der literarischen Seite liegen muss." ("Questions touching on the language and literary content of the manuscript are completely excluded from this part of my study. Here it is only a matter of deciphering the manuscript and producing a reliable basis for further research, whose primary emphasis in the future must be in the first instance on the linguistic and literary aspects.")

11. In more recent times, "assimilationism" is more abstract, more easily subsumable under the rubric of central usurpation/annexation of the margin, than under the rubric of "evangelical" assimilationist propaganda.

12. Max Waxman, "Judaeo-German Literature," in *A History of Jewish Literature*, vol. II: *From the Twelfth Century to the Middle of the Eighteenth Century*, 2nd ed. (New York 1943), 613-665. Such practices, when consistent, can be taken as indicators of ideology. For a number of reasons, however, they tend to appear even where least expected: e.g., Gilman cites an article by Maks Weinreich, giving its title in English and the name of the journal in German, although the article, its title, and the name of the journal are all Yiddish (p. 409, n. 79); sometimes such orthographic substitutions occur even as (Germanistic-intrained) proofreading oversights, as in my own article in *The German Quarterly* 59 (1986), p. 199, n. 1.

13. The choice of the Lithuanian dialect of modern Yiddish as the standard is, however, in itself not without ideological implications: the controversy concerning the establishment of a basis for a modern standard Yiddish orthography and pronunciation shows little sign of resolution even today. The Lithuanian dialect was proposed as the standard not just because of its relative similarity to German (in part by staunch assimilationists), but also because of the *relative* concentration of Yiddish intellectual endeavor in the geographical regions where that dialect was spoken, which gave rise to institutions of the intellect that then attempted to standardize the "home" dialect: cf. for instance the generally Lithuanian usage of YIVO publications, and especially the attempt at prescriptive, educational propagation of this dialect via Uriel Weinreich's elementary Yiddish textbook, *College Yiddish* (beyond all ideological concerns, the book is nonetheless without question the best language learning tool for the beginning student of modern Yiddish). The southern dialect, although it counted more speakers, was thus generally denied the prestige of being the "standard," despite the efforts of many champions of that dialect, chief among them being Solomon Birnbaum (who learned Yiddish only in adulthood). See especially the discussion of the problem of a linguistic standard by Mordkhe Schaechter, "Four Schools of Thought in Yiddish Language Planning," *Michigan Germanic Studies* 3 (1977), 34-66; and "Dem Yivos yidish-oyftu: roshiprokimdike observatsies un sakhaklen tsu a yubl-date," *Yivo-bleter* 46 (1980), 192-228. Schaechter's

own recently published textbook of Yiddish, *Yidish tsvay: a lernbikhl far mitndike kursn/Yiddish II: A Textbook for Intermediate Courses* (Philadelphia: Institute for the Study of Human Issues, 1986), attempts to de-emphasize the North-South conflict by adopting a specificist approach: see *Yidish tsvay,* "Hagdome," p. ix and "Preface," vii-viii [not identical]. This North-South conflict yields yet another instance of marginalization: for within the Yiddish-speaking community (which was itself marginalized by the non-Jewish center), there is yet another projection of alterity, such that the language of speakers of the southern dialect of Yiddish was labeled non-standard and provincial. The phenomenon of marginalization apparently knows no limits.

14. *Arthurian Legends*, p. vii. Due to his definition of the language (cf. chapter two above) as Hebrew-German, the relevance of Yiddish language and literature is an ideological impossibility. This is yet another example of the prescriptive marginalization of the literature by making it so radically Other that it is inaccessible except to the initiated.

15. Cf. also Landau's edition of *Esther,* where in his discussion of orthography, he takes Middle High German as the basis for the determination of the value of the Hebrew graphemes (p. 498-502). He also notes that Wagenseil's edition of *Vidvilt* includes a transliteration into German (*Arthurian Legends*, p. lxv); i.e., here one finds the same confusion of transliteration/translation and alphabet/language, that characterized Marchand and Schwarz's terminology, as noted above in chapter 2.

16. *Arthurian Legends*, p. xxii.

17. He does, however, at least mention the fact of the Hebrew alphabet's use in the text, p. xlix.

18. For the editor apparently need not be ruled by a text written by an author/scribe whose grammatical proficiency was so slight. One might nevertheless forgive the author of *Vidvilt* for a number of reasons – one of which is that he, like many Middle High German authors as well, had no access to nineteenth-century grammars of normalized Middle High German.

19. Jechiel Bin-Nun [Fischer], *Jiddish und die deutschen Mundarten* (Tübingen 1973), p. 13.

20. Franz J. Beranek, "Die Erforschung der jiddischen Sprache," *Zeitschrift für deutsche Philologie* 70 (1947-1948), 163-174.

21. For some inexplicable reason, Wolf, like Marchand/Tubach and Schwarz, calls the Roman alphabet "deutsch" (e.g., p. 18 and passim).

22. On the other hand, in *Vegn altyidishn roman un novele* (Warsaw 1926), he does not modernize the language.

23. Chaim Ginninger, "A Note on the Yiddish Horant," in *The Field of Yiddish*, vol. 1 (New York 1954), 275-277.

24. Percy Matenko and Samuel Sloan, "The Aqedath Jiṣḥaq; A Sixteenth Century Epic; with Introduction and Notes," in Percy Matenko, *Two Studies in Jewish Culture* (Leiden 1968), 1-70, plus 10 facsimile plates.

25. Wilhelm Gesenius, *Hebräische Grammatik*, rev. ed. by E. Kautsch (Leipzig 1902), p. 23 f.

26. Uriel Weinreich, *College Yiddish*, 4th ed. (New York 1965).

27. Although it is in practice much less troublesome than it initially sounds, simply because of the predominance of the first two categories and also, of course, because transliteration systems for modern Yiddish simply do not suffice for the ambiguous graphemic system of medieval Yiddish.

28. Is this an indication that even Matenko/Sloan are not immune to the Middle German bias, despite their generally pro-Yiddish stance?

29. Yet in the mere act of editing the manuscript, Fuks demonstrates that he holds the text to be important enough to be made accessible to some audience, and he does so with some pride, for he claims, albeit without grounds, that Lévy and Blondheim, who had known of the manuscript a generation earlier, did not recognize the manuscript as such and thus did not see fit to make it accessible (ed., II, 171, n. to p. 40, 1.15). See above in chapter 2, especially Birnbaum's adjustment of Fuks' skewed depiction of the roles of Lévy and Blondheim.

30. But perhaps one need not speculate too wildly here; as is often the case in such matters, circumstances may well have played a more significant role than well-planned scholarly intentions – the simple availability of a German rather than English translation (or translator) at the moment when the edition is conceived or the publisher consents to include a translation often decides such questions. It is also of interest, in light of the recurring demands for team editions, noted also by Fuks, that his edition is in fact the result of a joint effort with other scholars, although the contributions of the others is not unambiguously acknowledged, and Fuks' name alone appears on the title page as editor: H. Beem and M. Klein are responsible for (much/all of?) the modern German translation (II, 3, note); W. G. Hellinga was responsible for the summary discussion of language and dialect identity (I, p. xxviii, n. 1); J. A. Huisman wrote the section on metrics (I, p. xxxii, n. 2).

31. Not so surprisingly, neither do the editors of types one and two, but the case of Fuks' edition is historically a unique one, since it presents the scholarly world with a corpus of texts which literally transformed the field of Old Yiddish studies by providing it with a body of texts which not only predated anything even remotely so substantial, but also, in *Dukus Hurnt*, provided a text which forced a final showdown between the pro- and anti-Yiddish forces by engaging a wide range of Germanistic/Yiddishist interests.

32. Cf. also Schwarz's "ein europäisches System" (Ganz/Norman/Schwarz, eds., *Dukus Horant*, 16-17).

33. Ganz, rev. of Fuks, ed., *The Oldest . . . Documents*, in *Journal of Jewish Studies* 8 (1957), 246-247.

34. Birnbaum, "Das älteste datierte Schriftstück in jiddischer Sprache," *Beiträge zur Geschichte der deutschen Sprache und Literatur* 56 (1932), 11-22 and "Umschrift des ältesten datierten jiddischen Schriftstücks," *Teuthonista [Zeitschrift für Mundartforschung]* 8 (1932). 197-207.

35. Leonard Forster, rev. of Fuks, ed., *The Oldest . . . Documents*, in *German Life and Letters*, ns 11 (1958), 276-285.

36. Solomon Birnbaum, rev. of Fuks, ed., *The Oldest . . . Documents*, in *Bibliotheca Orientalis* 16 (1959), p. 52.

37. G. Schramm, rev. of Fuks, *The Oldest . . . Documents*, in *Göttingische Gelehrte Anzeigen* 212 (1958), p. 212.

38. His transcription method demonstrates that the three "languages" are identical: for normalized Middle High German, he transcribes ו as /o/ in *brot*, /u/ in *und*, /uo/ in *guotem* and /v/ in *vröuden*; in the "Yiddish" transposition, he transliterates ו as /u/ in *burgaeres*, /o/ in *kemnote*, /uo/ in *suoch*, as /v/ in *vindet*, /ü/ in *dürftec* and /e/ in *helfe*.

39. Rev. of Fuks, *The Oldest . . . Documents*, in *Neophilologus* 42 (1958), 328 & 332.

40. Schwarz, rev. of Fuks, p. 330; the system by Birnbaum cited here is that described in "Die Umschrift des Jiddischen," *Teuthonista [Zeitschrift für Mundartforschung]* 9 (1933), 90-105.

41. Which, one must conclude, means that *his own* edition of *Dukus Hurnt* abdicated its "primary editorial responsibility," since it presented no Hebrew text.

42. They never published such an edition; their publication contained only *Dukus Hurnt*.

43. Ingeborg Schröbler, rev. of Fuks, *The Oldest . . . Documents, Zeitschrift für deutsches Altertum* 89 (1959), 141-142.

44. "Wer es unternimmt, einen solchen Text der wissenschaftlichen Welt zugänglich zu machen, sollte sich der Verantwortung bewußt sein, die damit verbunden ist und die um so größer ist, als sehr verschiedene Disziplinen an einer solchen Ausgabe interessiert sind. Die vorliegende Ausgabe, ohne Zweifel hervorgegangen aus innerer Anteilnahme an Geschichte und Kultur des Judentums, ist philologisch unzulänglich." (p. 162).

45. J. Carles, "Un fragment judéo-allemand du cycle de Kudrun," *Études Germaniques* 13 (1958), p. 351.

46. Fourquet, "Ernest-Henri Lévy," p. 55. S. Roelly, "Essai de reconstitution en moyen haut-allemand normalisé d'un texte en strophes . . ., Dukus Horant," Thesis Paris 1960. Cf. also on that edition, J. Carles, *Le poème de Kudrun. Étude de sa matière* (Paris 1963), p. 232, n. 1. The edition has never been published.

47. James Marchand, rev. of Fuks, *The Oldest . . . Documents. Word* 15 (1959), p. 391.

48. James Marchand, "Three Basic Problems in the Investigation of Early Yiddish," *Orbis* 9 (1960), p. 34.

49. For he denies that there are theoretical problems (p. 34).

50. i.e., one could extrapolate, it is necessary for editors of Old Yiddish texts to know the history of the German language, but not Yiddish, not Hebrew paleography, etc. It is doubtful that Marchand would make such an explicit argument, but it is nonetheless significant that he does not see fit at least to note these further requirements of his ideal editor, especially in this article that is so given to list compilation.

51. James W. Marchand, "Einiges zur sogenannten 'jiddischen Kudrun,'" *Neophilologus* 45 (1961), p. 60.

52. For he envisions their responsibility in the study of these texts to be of great moment – insofar as it would aid Germanistic analysis of the texts.

53. James Marchand and Frederic C. Tubach, "Der keusche Joseph," *Zeitschrift für deutsche Philologie* 81 (1962), 30-52.

54. Erik, *Geshikte*; Wiener, *A History*; M. Pines, *Histoire*; Maks Weinreich, *Bilder fun der yidisher literatur-geshikhte* (Vilna 1928); Yitskhok Shiper, "Kultur-geshikhtlekher fon fun der eltster yidisher literatur," *Yidishe Welt* (Vilna 1928).

55. E.g.: "Für *s* steht außer einmal (Zeile 29: *ovvjgt swiget*), *s*" (p. 39). Here one *can* distinguish transliteration from transcription: *ovvjgt* must be transliteration, otherwise samekh would never be represented by such a confusing symbol as *o*.

56. Perhaps one could justify the use of such incongruities for the sake of simplicity (or reducing printing costs), if (and only if) the system of transposition had already been defined precisely. But in the present case, the use of Roman qua Hebrew is simply irresponsible.

57. Even in their citation of other scholars' work, they are imprecise: in 1.64 of their text (ms. p. 36), they read "kopte" and note: "Fuks liest *kvpe*,

aber auf der Photographie steht deutlich *p* (d.h. *kop'*)" (p. 41). To be accurate, however, Fuks transliterates קופא and *kvp'* and translates *Schalen*; no *kvpe* is found in Fuks. Their implied correction of Fuks' *p* to *p* is also confusing, but their putative correction of Fuks' alleged *e* (actually /'/) to /'/ is irresponsible, as is their apparent transliteration (i.e., direct, uninterpreted mechanical replacement of Hebrew with Roman) of ו as *o*, implying that Fuks' transliteration as *u* is inaccurate, and not simply a different interpretation. After all is said and done, they also add a non-existent *t* to their reading, indicating, one must assume, that they posit an omitted grapheme in the manuscript.

58. They cite, for instance, the manuscript by folio, but identify the folio as "page" (sc. "S."): e.g. "S. 6-b" is either p. 12 or fol. 6v.

59. John A. Howard, "Der Bärmuttersegen – Ein mittelhochdeutscher Spruch," *Colloquia Germanica* 12 (1978), p. 214.

60. John A. Howard, "A Little Known Version of *Til Eulenspiegel*," *Amsterdamer Beiträge zur älteren Germanistik* 15 (1980), 127-129.

61. "Der Bärmuttersegen," p. 227, which he nonetheless calls a *Transkription*. His transliteration system is also used in his analysis of the *Fortunatus* chapbook, "The Bodleian *Fortunatus*," *Yiddish* 6 (1985), 15-20.

62. John A. Howard, "Der 'Bärmuttersegen' wiederentdeckt," *Zeitschrift für deutsches Altertum* 108 (1979), 252-258.

63. W. B. Lockwood, "Die Textgestalt des jüngeren Hildebrandliedes in jüdisch-deutscher Sprache," *Beiträge zur Geschichte der deutschen Sprache und Literatur* (Halle) 85 (1963), 433-447.

64. Khone Shmeruk, "The Hebrew Acrostic in the Yosef Hatsadik Poem of the Cambridge Yiddish Codex," *Michigan Germanic Studies* 3 (1977), 67-81.

65. The "stout defender" referred to is Wulf-Otto Dreeßen, in his edition of *Akedas Yitskhok: Akedass Jizḥak; Ein altjiddisches Gedicht über die Opferung Isaaks; mit Einleitung und Kommentar kritisch herausgegeben*, Diss. Hamburg, Hamburger Beiträge zur Geschichte der Juden 2 (Hamburg 1971).

66. Max Weinreich, "Old Yiddish Poetry in Linguistic-Literary Research," *Word* 16 (1960), p. 116.

67. As will be discussed further below, the failings of the Ganz/Norman/Schwarz and Hakkarainen editions generally support this claim.

68. Solomon Birnbaum, "Old Yiddish or Middle High German?" *Journal of Jewish Studies* 12 (1961), 19-31.

69. Some of the forms he uses differ in the 1961 version and its revision, published in *Yiddish: A Survey and a Grammar*, p. 308; both forms are cited here, in chronological order.

70. Transliteration such as Birnbaum suggests here (as illegitimate) is practically unknown from the Middle Ages, occurring only occasionally, for instance, in the transposition of isolated Greek words into Roman by scribes who knew little Greek.

71. On his various systems of transposition as they have developed over the decades, see the appendix.

72. As he claims would be the result, in his rev. of Hakkarainen, *Studien*, in *Journal of Jewish Studies* 20 (1969), p. 102.

73. Obviously, as has been noted before, there are interpretive problems even in a strictly diplomatic edition, of which Katz is quite aware; cf. in the headnote to the critical apparatus: "Matters of interpretation are, *for the most part*, not touched upon" (p. 164, italics mine).

74. Katz prints these variant readings in the orthography (i.e. transliteration/transcription system) used by the scholars cited.

75. And finally also despite the fact that his edition is a U.S. dissertation, which are not as a matter of course published; the lack of a published version of Katz's edition has led to the recurring characterization of it as "inaccessible," despite the availability of U.S. doctoral theses on microfilm.

76. This lack of umlaut is also characteristic of Central German dialects, as Katz notes, p. 43.

77. Which can be taken as evidence against Marchand's proposal of a Roman-alphabet source of the manuscript, since such a distinction is not possible in the Roman-alphabet, Middle High German source envisioned by Marchand (p. 50). Other evidence against Marchand's theory is also adduced. Consonant doubling, which Marchand takes as indicative of a Roman-alphabet, Middle High German source, is in fact very rare in the manuscript: only seventeen occurrences, in only ten separate words, all but three of which occurrences are found in the Abraham poem, and all involve the graphemes ל, נ, and ר when they follow ע or י. This practice seems to indicate a familiarity with Roman-alphabet scribal practice, but does not indicate a Roman-alphabet source, for that would not account for the infrequency of the practice or the environmental consistency of it (p. 48). The spellings of the terms for Egypt and Spain, also taken by Marchand as evidence for a Roman-alphabet source, are more likely orthographic representations of Yiddish words derived from the Romance determinant of Yiddish, and thus in fact argue in favor of a Hebrew-alphabet source (p. 49).

78. Birnbaum's practice is similar in "Old Yiddish or Middle High German." Katz also cites cognate material from the standard grammars of Middle High and early modern German.

79. Transliteration table, p. vi. The system is essentially that of Uriel

Weinreich, in *The Field of Yiddish* (New York: Linguistic Circle of New York, 1954), vii-viii, the major distinction being Katz's use of /j/ and Weinreich's use of /y/ for י. On transposition systems, see the appendix below.

80. He for example also treats posited textual "defects" in the critical apparatus and does not print them as conjectural readings in the text itself.

81. Just as an edition in transposed Middle High German is "evidence" for the text's being Middle High German.

82. Cf., however, Röll's review of Ganz/Norman/Schwarz (p. 274), where it is noted that Fuks not infrequently reads more than they do. Katz's dissertation appeared in the year before their edition and was probably not available on microfilm until soon before their edition went to press.

83. Peter Ganz, "Dukus Horant. An Early Yiddish Poem from the Cairo Genizah," *Journal of Jewish Studies* 9 (1958), p. 53.

84. Cf. esp. 15-17 of the introduction to the edition and above in chapter 2.

85. One wonders, if the dialect *is* Central German, why the editors would have to *do* anything to the text in order to present it as such.

86. While it is true that the traditional terms, such as Old High German, Middle Low German, etc., have rightfully fallen out of favor in recent decades, due to their imprecision, their replacement by this even less precise term is hardly an improvement.

87. This is a clear example of the "false problem" created by editors of texts in transliteration/transcription, who then use that transposed text as the basis of their justification of the principles of the transposition.

88. And as noted above in chapter 2, Norman even cites the texts in "normale[m] Mittelhochdeutsch" (cf. p. 76).

89. There are, however, numerous textual emendations which accommodate the text toward an implied *telos* of normalized Middle High German; on this problem, see below on reviews of the edition.

90. H. Rosenfeld, rev. of Ganz/Norman/Schwarz, eds., *Dukus Horant, Deutsche Literaturzeitung* 87 (1966), p. 129.

91. H. Stopp, rev. of Ganz/Norman/Schwarz, eds., *Dukus Horant, Zeitschrift für deutsche Philologie* 86 (1967), p. 463.

92. U. Rauh, rev. of Ganz/Norman/Schwarz, *Euphorion* 60 (1966), p. 159; A. Paucker, rev. of Ganz/Norman/Schwarz, *German Life and Letters*, n.s. 21 (1968), p. 274.

93. Yet another twist to the accessibility topos.

94. Even so, he generally cites Old Yiddish texts in the Hebrew alphabet, when he analyzes the grapho-phonemic system; significantly, however, in his two articles for the traditional Germanistic journal, *Zeitschrift für deutsche Philologie*, only Roman is used; see bibliography for references.

95. S. J. Kaplowitt, rev. of Ganz/Norman/Schwarz, *Dukus Horant, Journal of English and Germanic Philology* 65 (1966), p. 538.

96. Thus he either misunderstands or misrepresents the problems of dated manuscripts: whether the date is that of the extant manuscript, a previous copy, or the original composition, etc.

97. H. Stopp, rev. of Ganz/Norman/Schwarz, eds., *Dukus Horant*, in *Zeitschrift für deutsche Philologie* 86 (1967), p. 459.

98. Cf. also Rosenfeld's comments [rev., p. 127] on the editors' addition of letters (especially /e/) when they are not present in the manuscript and are even opposed by metrical considerations. He nevertheless remarks that the editors' meticulous transcription is "über jede Kritik erhoben" (p. 126).

99. Ingeborg Schröbler, rev. of Ganz/Norman/Schwarz, *Dukus Horant*, in *Germanistik* 7 (1966), 73-74.

100. Walther Röll, rev. of Ganz/Norman/Schwarz, eds., *Dukus Horant*, in *Studi Medievali*, 3rd ser. 7 (1966), 269-275.

101. See below in chapter 4 on Professor Röll's reasons for abandoning this project.

102. Manfred Caliebe, *Dukus Horant*, Philologische Studien und Quellen 70 (Berlin 1973).

103. The fact of the Hebrew alphabet is very much present in Hakkarainen's edition (as opposed, for instance to Landau's): in his transliteration table, table of paleographic letter types, and consistent transliteration, from which one could indeed "reconstruct" the original.

104. Manfred Caliebe, rev. of Hakkarainen, *Studien*, in *Wirkendes Wort* 20 (1970), 139-141. Unfortunately, this and other reviews were written before the appearance of Hakkarainen's second volume, in which much material was included, for the "omission" of which he was castigated in reviews of volume one.

105. Does availability only on microfilm constitute *in*accessibility? especially at present, when much preliminary manuscript research is done via microfilm.

106. This he also demonstrates in his castigation of Hakkarainen for not including all editors' variant readings in his apparatus, so that the reader

can convince him/herself of the editor's advance over his predecessors (p. 141). It seems hardly the task of the diplomatic editor to provide readers with this tool – serious scholars and even reviewers who work with complex textual traditions and even single manuscript texts with complex editorial problems are accustomed to consulting all significant editions in addition to the manuscript. Caliebe seems to require a variorum edition from Hakkarainen. Nevertheless Hakkarainen does in fact note *many* variant editorial readings in his apparatus. On a practical level, one must remark that there is no need for any editor to propagate the erroneous readings of his/her forbears.

107. B. Murdoch, rev. of Hakkarainen, *Studien*, in *Modern Language Review* 65 (1970), 441-444.

108. F. Mader, rev. of Hakkarainen, *Studien*, in *Neuphilologische Mitteilungen* 73 (1972), p. 722.

109. B. Lindgren, rev. of Hakkarainen, *Studien*, in *Neuphilologische Mitteilungen* 73 (1972), 724-726.

110. Solomon Birnbaum, rev. of Hakkarainen, *Studien*, in *Journal of Jewish Studies* 20 (1969), 101-103.

111. One recalls that Hakkarainen (I, 25-26) made a similar (positively valued) suggestion about his readers' ability to construct a Middle High German version while reading his transliteration.

112. Joséf Weissberg, "The Vowel System . . . ," *Journal of Jewish Studies* 14 (1963), 37-51 and "Das Konsonantensystem . . . ," *Zeitschrift für Mundartforschung* 32 (1965), 1-40; Katz, *Six Germano-Judaic Poems*, see above.

113. This is perhaps the first instance of a scholar's positing the superior *legibility* of Hebrew over the many transliteration systems, although others before him had noted that Hebrew was no less legible than some transliterations.

114. Caliebe praises Althaus for this use of Middle High German as the norm for his analysis, as opposed to Hakkarainen, who, Caliebe claims, works strictly "textimmanent" (rev., in *Wirkendes Wort* 24 (1974), p. 288).

115. "The text belongs to some linguistic norm which stands in a certain relationship to Middle High German" (p. 67).

116. As if one were to say that we assume in editing, for instance, an English language text that /b/ should not be interpreted as [m].

117. Manfred Caliebe, "Zur Problematik von Gesamtdarstellungen jiddischer Literaturgeschichte in deutscher Sprache; Bedenken, Berichtigungen und Ergänzungen zu Helmut Dinse, 'Die Entwicklung des jiddischen Schrifttums im deutschen Sprachgebiet,'" *Wirkendes Wort* 27 (1977), 51-66 and *Dukus Horant* (Berlin 1973).

118. Walther Röll, rev. of Ganz/Norman/Schwarz, eds., *Dukus Horant*, in *Studi Medievali*, 3rd ser. 7 (1966), 269-275.

119. At this point we need not ask why Caliebe denies this: he is simply "citing" Röll.

120. Hakkarainen's second volume appeared too late to be treated in Caliebe's study.

Chapter 4

1. I loosely group Röll, Caliebe, Dreeßen, and Timm together as a "Trier School" (only Röll and Timm are actually in Trier), although their publications are by no means uniform in matters of methodology. There does seem to be a unifying tendency, however, at least in general ideological alignment, although even here there is sometimes a wide divergence; Althaus (also in Trier), for instance, would probably also have to be assigned to the group. Thus my use of the designation "Trier School" is appropriate only in a restricted sense, but it is still more than a mere term of convenience. Naming is indeed a problem! Gabriele L. Strauch's dissertation, "Dukus Horant: Doch ein jiddisches Epos," Wisconsin 1984, presents its examination of "Majoritäts- und Minoritätsgeschichts- und -literaturschreibung" as a novel approach; but in imputing the role of definitive *textual* critic to Fuks she is simply wrong, in taking Caliebe's literary study and Ganz/Norman/Schwarz's edition as the bases of her study she is hardly 'progressive,' and in ignoring the work of Dreeßen, Timm, Shmeruk and the corpus of Yiddish-language research literature, she undermines her own protracted vindication of the integrity of medieval Jewish culture. It is a well-intentioned attempt, run afoul of its limitations.

2. Edited with critical notes by Felix Falk, published posthumously with a preface by Fuks, *Das Schmuelbuch des Moshe Esrim Wearba*, 2 vols., Bibliotheca Rosenthaliana 1 (Assen: van Gorcum, 1961); Lajb Fuks, ed., *Das altjiddische Epos Melokim-buk*, 2 vols.: 1. *Einleitung und Faksimile der* editio princeps, *Augsburg, 1543*. 2. *Hebräische und aramäische Quellen, textkritischer Apparat, und Glossar* (Assen: van Gorcum, 1965).

3. The value of the facsimile of the Cambridge codex in his edition is severely limited due to its not having been photographed under ultra-violet light, as noted by Marchand in his review of the edition (p. 384, n. 5; see above, chapter 3).

4. Shmeruk, rev. of *Melokhim-bukh*, "Di naye editsye funem altyidishn 'Melokhimbukh,'" *Di goldene keyt* 59 (1967), p. 208.

5. Some of these questions were, of course, occasionally addressed, but not as the primary focus of study.

6. There is in general a tendency among German-language scholars toward a more intimate acquaintance with and use of the interpretive methods of reception theory/*Rezeptionsgeschichte* than is the case especially among British and North American scholars, perhaps simply due to the fact that the first comprehensive methodological program of reception theory, as a radical, almost revolutionary interpretive strategy, grew out of the political upheaval of the 1960s in Germany, articulated by Hans-Robert Jauß and Wolfgang Iser. This method has so permeated subsequent German literary scholarship – and university training in literary disciplines – that it has become an essential, almost unconscious standard of contemporary German literary scholarship, in much the same way that New Criticism became (and generally still retains its place as) the dominant mode of unconscious "non-ideological" criticism in the twentieth-century Anglo-American tradition. On the German school of reception theory, see the insightful overview by Robert C. Holub: *Reception Theory: A Critical Introduction* (London: Methuen, 1984).

7. Walter Röll and Christian Gerhardt, "Literarische Einordnung des sogenannten 'Dukus Horant,'" *Deutsche Vierteljahrsschrift für Geistesgeschichte und Literaturwissenschaft* 41 (1967), p. 517.

8. Röll's text citations are from his critical edition, prepared over a number of years, with the participation of several of his students, as a collective propaedeutic project in editing and emendation, especially on the basis of metrical considerations. Caliebe also cites from this unpublished, mimeographed critical edition in his monograph, *Dukus Horant*. Röll announced his intention to publish a critical edition of the poem as early as 1966 (in his rev. of Ganz/Norman/Schwarz, p. 274, n. 15). The edition never appeared, and Professor Röll has since abandoned the project, due to the subsequent appearance of Hakkarainen's edition and his own growing dissatisfaction with the necessarily arbitrary methods of textual emendation. The method was invaluable as a practical, hands-on, pedagogical tool of philological training in advanced seminars, but was ultimately too subjective to stand under the rigor of scholarly investigation [information from personal communication with Professor Röll].

9. Walter Röll and Rolf Eckart, "Dukus Horant," *Kindlers Literatur-Lexikon* (Zurich 1964), II, 1691-1692. He also remarks that it is unclear whether the author of *Dukus Hurnt* was Jewish.

10. Walter Röll, "Zum Konsonantensystem der Cambridger Handschrift," *Zeitschrift für Mundartforschung* 33 (1966), 144-146.

11. "The oldest known collection of Yiddish literary texts," in Röll's, "Zu den ersten drei Texten der Cambridger Handschrift von 1382/1383," *Zeitschrift für deutsches Altertum* 104 (1975), p. 54.

12. "Zuletzt noch eine technische Bemerkung. Die Umschrift jiddi-

scher und hebräischer Texte ist uneinheitlich. Zumindest für ältere jiddische Texte habe ich versucht, ein gewisses Maß an Konvergenz zu erreichen. Ich hoffe, die geschichtlich bedingte Uneinheitlichkeit in diesem Punkt, in der sich die Internationalität der Forschung spiegelt, trägt nicht zur Verwirrung bei." (Röll, "Vorwort," *Zeitschrift für deutsche Philologie* 100 (Sonderheft *Jiddisch* 1981), p. 3).

13. Manfred Caliebe, *Dukus Horant*, Philologische Studien und Quellen 70 (Berlin 1973).

14. Helmut Dinse, *Die Entwicklung des jiddischen Schrifttums im deutschen Sprachgebiet* (Stuttgart 1974); Caliebe, "Zur Problematik von Gesamtdarstellungen jiddischer Literaturgeschichte in deutscher Sprache; Bedenken, Berichtigungen und Ergänzungen zu Helmut Dinse, "Die Entwicklung des jiddischen Schrifttums im deutschen Sprachgebiet," *Wirkendes Wort* 27 (1977), 51-66.

15. W. Weinberg, *Die Reste des Jüdischdeutschen* (Stuttgart 1969), p. 14 also wishes to replace "West Yiddish" with "Jüdisch-deutsch," since, as he claims; 1) it is not a real language; 2) the term is much younger than the language and thus inappropriate; 3) "Jüdisch-deutsch" is the customary term in grammars, dictionaries, etc. His reasons thus bear a striking resemblance to those of the Haskalah ideological position.

16. Caliebe, p. 53; Dinse, p. xxv; Birnbaum, "Jiddisch," *Encyclopaedia Judaica*, IX, p. 115.

17. "Es [wird] die Jiddistik mit dieser Art Veröffentlichung weiter schwer haben ..., eine anerkannte Wissenschaft zu werden. Ein Buch wie dieses stiftet mehr Schaden als Nutzen" (p. 64).

18. See bibliography for complete list of Dreeßen's relevant publications.

19. Dreeßen, "Zur Rezeption deutscher epischer Literatur im Altjiddischen: Das Beispiel 'Wigalois' – 'Artushof,'" *Deutsche Literatur des späteren Mittelalters – Hamburger Kolloquium* 1973, Wolfgang Harms and L. Peter Johnson, eds., (Berlin 1975), p. 116.

20. Dreeßen, "Zur altjiddischen Synonymik," *Trierer Beiträge: Fragen des älteren Jiddisch*, H.-J. Müller & Walter Röll, eds., (Trier 1977), p. 63.

21. He notes that *adaptations* of German texts into Hebrew-alphabet, Yiddish-language versions certainly exist from the Middle Ages, but there are no early examples of German merely transliterated into Hebrew ("Rezeption," p. 166).

22. Wulf-Otto Dreeßen, "Midraschepik und Bibelepik: Biblische Stoffe in der volkssprachlichen Literatur der Juden und Christen des Mittelalters im deutschen Sprachgebiet," *Zeitschrift für deutsche Philologie* 100 (Sonder-

heft *Jiddisch* 1981), 81-82. Cf. also Barbara Könnecker's critique and qualification of Dreeßen's term *Midraschepik*: the narrative structure of works such as *Shmuel-bukh* are not accounted for by midrashic models, but rather derive from the structures of non-Jewish heroic epic. See Könnecker, "Zum literarischen Charakter und der literarischen Intention des altjiddischen Schmuelbuchs," in *Auseinandersetzung um jiddische Sprache und Literatur. Jüdische Komponenten in der deutschen Literatur – die Assimilationskontroverse*, Walter Röll and Hans-Peter Bayerdörfer, eds., vol. 5 of *Kontroverse, alte und neue. Akten des VII. Internationalen Germanisten-Kongresses, Göttingen 1985*, Albrecht Schöne, ed., (Tübingen 1986), 3-12.

23. Dreeßen remarks that the use of the Hebrew alphabet is not decisive of language *per se*, but does nonetheless clearly show that very specific reception-decisions have been made before writing the text down ("Midraschepik," esp. 93-96).

24. Robert G. Warnock argues similarly that *Vidvilt* shows adaptations specifically for the sake of a Jewish audience, and thus this Old Yiddish text is an example of late medieval Jewish intellectual life, in "Wirkungsabsicht und Bearbeitungstechnik im altjiddischen 'Artushof,'" *Zeitschrift für deutsche Philologie* 100 (Sonderheft *Jiddisch* 1981), 98-109. His suggestion that the text was intended to be read aloud for wedding audiences – based on the inclusion of wedding motifs and hints of marriage in the text – is somewhat far-fetched. He refers to the first adaptation (early fifteenth century) as "Dieser, sagen wir, jiddische Grundtext . . . ," in "Frühneuzeitliche Fassungen des altjiddischen 'Artushofs,'" *Auseinandersetzung um jiddische Sprache und Literatur. Jüdische Komponenten in der deutschen Literatur – die Assimilationskontroverse*, Walter Röll and Hans-Peter Bayerdörfer, eds., vol. 5 of *Kontroverse, alte und neue. Akten des VII. Internationalen Germanisten-Kongresses, Göttingen 1985*, Albrecht Schöne, ed., (Tübingen 1986), 13-19.

25. He sees this kind of analysis as particularly important in the revision of the notion of *Spielmannsepos* and its application to Old Yiddish literature ("Midraschepik," p. 97).

26. See esp. his ed. of *Akedas Yitskhok*, 4-5, and his collaborative edition, with Herman-Josef Müller, *Doniel: Das altjiddische Danielbuch nach dem Basler Druck von 1557*, Litterae 59, 1-2 (Göppingen 1978), II, 1-4.

27. Albeit with the myriad problems deriving from the editors' presentation of the text in both transliteration and transcription, he notes. And it is not the case that the edition by Ganz/Norman/Schwarz spawned a great number of new studies, but primarily only reviews.

28. *Doniel* II, p. 2. They also note the irony of such a statement in the preface to a facsimile edition.

29. The necessary qualification here is, of course, that only the vowel's quality *as interpreted and posited by the editor* can be more precisely defined.

30. Dreeßen does not include a facsimile in his edition of *Akedas Yitskhok*; perhaps for "legitimate" reasons, however: the edition was his published dissertation [Hamburg 1970], and the added expense of a facsimile would probably not have been attractive to a publisher (nor to the doctoral candidate). Additionally, Matenko/Sloan's edition had already published a facsimile.

31. In each case, however, the "ignorant Germanist" topos is determinative: the Hebrew-alphabet text is by definition inaccessible to linguists, literary scholars, and indeed almost the entirety of the conceived audience. But in any case that text, the Hebrew-alphabet text, is deemed not just inaccessible, but also inessential, inconsequential, supplemental, incidental, and replaceable.

32. Shmeruk's assumption, noted above, that texts in the Hebrew alphabet are accessible to *all* interested parties resembles the character of Dreeßen's assumption, but would seem a more logical conclusion even for Dreeßen, since in his view too, the texts in question are Yiddish, not German.

33. Timm, "Beria und Simra; Eine jiddische Erzählung des 16. Jahrhunderts," *Literaturwissenschaftliches Jahrbuch*, ns. 14 (1973), 1-94.

34. Timm, "Die 'Fabel vom alten Löwen' in jiddistischer und komparatistischer Sicht," *Zeitschrift für deutsche Philologie* 100 (1981, Sonderheft), 109-170.

35. She also cites Dreeßen's *Akedass* as the authority for her transcription system: Erika Timm, ed., "Beria und Simra," p. 3.

36. "In no way do I underestimate the constitutive function of the Hebrew script for Jewish culture, especially of the Diaspora" ("Ich verkenne keineswegs die konstitutive Funktion der hebräischen Schrift für die jüdische Kultur besonders der Diaspora," p. 2).

37. But by the same logic they also generally read their native language better than any other, but that hardly justifies presenting any given text from a related language in the 'orthography' of that native language *as if* that resulting text were a text edition.

38. She does note that such a transcription requires both transliteration and interpretation (p. 3).

39. Another concession to the German reader is the inclusion of Middle High German correspondences in the table of vowels, which are only to serve as "orientational aid for readers . . . , who are familiar with the reading of Middle High German texts" ("Orientierungshilfe für Leser . . . , die mit der Lektüre mhd. Texte vertraut sind," p. 3).

40. Erika Timm, *Graphische und phonische Struktur des Westjiddischen*

unter besonderer Berücksichtigung der Zeit um 1600, Hermaea: Germanistische Forschungen, n.s. 52 (Tübingen 1987). Cf. "Beria und Simra," p. 7: "im einzelnen muß die Rechtfertigung dieses Verfahrens dem sprachlichen Kommentar vorbehalten bleiben."

41. One might nonetheless mention the three other studies that attempt similar tasks for a restricted number of texts (briefly characterized by Timm, pp. 2-3): B. Korman, *Die Reimtechnik der Esther-Paraphrase Cod. Hamburg 144. Beitrag zur Erschließung des altjiddischen Lautsystems*. Diss. Hamburg 1930; J. L. Haines, *Proto-Yiddish and the History of Yiddish Phonology: the Front Rounded Vowel Phonemes*. New York 1975; Manfred Gernot Heide, *Graphematisch-phonematische Untersuchungen zum Altjiddischen: Der Vokalismus* (Bern 1974).

42. Although in the context of my own evaluative perspective and Timm's avowed (*and* practiced) anti-empirical view of interpretation as a scholarly activity, it would hardly be accurate to designate her comprehensive linguistic analysis merely a justification of her edition. It certainly is that, but only incidentally; and its structure, style and tone of presentation, its length, depth and period of incubation indicate that it is an unashamed work of interpretive scholarship, not a mere catalogue of data.

43. "Wir gehen zunächst von dem Grundsatz aus, Schriftsystem, phonisches Korrelat und Inhalt unserer Texte seien uns unbekannt. Aussagen, die weder unmittelbar aus dem Material noch aus (Quasi-)Universalien abgeleitet sind, erscheinen in eckigen Klammern." (p. 23).

44. She blithely dismisses the option, "durch Dick und Dünn einer Handschrift zu folgen." (p. 78, n. 158).

45. Cambridge T.-S. 10. K. 22, p. 37, 11. 11-12 (facs. Fuks, *The Oldest . . . Documents*, vol. I); Fuks: Hebrew (1) and Roman (2) transliterations, *The Oldest . . . Documents*, II, p. 74; Katz: transliteration, "Six Germano-Judaic Poems," p. 116; Hakkarainen: transliteration: *Studien*, I, p. 73; Siegmund A. Wolf: transcription, *Jiddisches Wörterbuch* (Mannheim 1962), p. 35; Althaus I: transcription, *Die Cambridger Löwenfabel*, p. 9; Pavel Trost: transcription, "Zwei Stücke des Cambridger Kodex T-S 10. K. 22," *Philologica Pragensia* 4 (1961), p. 19.

46. But on the other hand, were the transliterations to attempt to account for the possible vocalic values of the graph and be "legible," they would cease to be transliterations.

47. Cambridge T.-S. 10. K. 22, p. 50, 11. 215-216 (facs. Fuks, *The Oldest , , , Documents*, vol. I); Fuks: Hebrew (1) and Roman (2) transliterations, *The Oldest . . . Documents*, II, p. 100; Katz: transliteration, "Six Germano-Judaic Poems," p. 129; Hakkarainen: transliteration, *Studien*, I, p. 86; Ganz/Norman/Schwarz: transliteration (1) and transcription (2), *Dukus Horant*, 150-151; James Marchand: transcription, rev. of Fuks, *The Oldest . . . Docu-*

ments, in *Word* 15 (1960), p. 391; Jean Fourquet: transcription, cited by Chaim Ginninger, "A Note on the Yiddish Horant," in *The Field of Yiddish*, Uriel Weinreich, ed., (New York: Linguistic Circle of New York, 1954), p. 277.

48. Paris, BN, hebr. 589, fol. 129v; stanza 73, 4 (facs. Matenko/Sloan, "The Aqedath Jiṣḥaq"); Matenko/Sloan: transliteration, "The Aqedath Jiṣḥaq," p. 66; Wulf-Otto Dreeßen: transcription, *Akedass Jizḥak*, p. 141; Solomon Birnbaum: transcription, *Yiddish: A Survey and Grammar* (Toronto 1979), p. 158.

49. Certainly that struggle is to the point when dealing with Old Yiddish texts, since any influence exercised on their transposition by modern Lithuanian dialect is by definition illegitimate. But here we can also perhaps see the ultimate point of Birnbaum's denying the necessity of the Hebrew-alphabet original: even more of a threat than that readers will simply read the Hebrew alphabet text as if Middle High German (which seems rather unlikely) is the probability that they will read it as if it were *standard* modern Yiddish. In his unique system of transcription, which is as "non-German" *and* "non-Lithuanian Yiddish" as conceivable, that is not even a remote possibility.

50. It is independent of its Germanic determinant even now? Yiddish has certainly continued to borrow terms from German (as have so many other languages, depending on prevailing Zeitgeist and ascendent Weltanschauung), and in some sense German has even served as a "hidden standard"; see esp. Mordkhe Schaechter, "The 'Hidden Standard': A Study of Competing Influences in Standardization," in *Field of Yiddish* III, M. Herzog, ed., (The Hague 1969), 284-304.

51. On the notion of "false problems" of textual criticism arising from editorial ideology (with specific reference to humanistic editions of ancient Latin and Greek texts), see E. J. Kenney, *The Classical Text: Aspects of Editing in the Age of the Printed Book* (Berkeley 1974), 1-20. Editions in the Hebrew alphabet would conform to many of the basic principles of edition type three, as discussed above in chapter 3, especially in presenting the text (as nearly as possible) "as the reading eye sees it." Even with only this simple requirement, however, there are numerous problems, as Fuks discovered in his transliterations of the manuscript text. Perhaps Katz's edition comes closest to achieving this ideal of the basic edition.

52. But Althaus' edition may undermine even that hope, for despite the fact that he prints a Hebrew-alphabet diplomatic text and Roman transliteration, and only then, on the basis of his protracted ideological argument, does he present his Middle High German construction, his pretense to objectivity attempts to obscure his ideological intent.

53. Or if their interest in Yiddish does not dictate that they work with

the text "in the original," then they need to be supplied with translations.

54. Some few strictly linguistic studies of Old Yiddish have made use of contemporary linguistic methodologies.

Appendix

1. Fuks, ed., *The Oldest . . . Documents*, I, p. xxxvii.

2. Fuks' linguistic naiveté is demonstrated here also in his exasperatingly imprecise terminology, which often obscures his meaning: /s/ represents a "lisping sound"; the Roman alphabet is a "European writing system"; ש is a "diacritical symbol" (I, p. xxxvi).

3. Which he cannot mean, since his restoring of these final phonemes would thus constitute a much greater conjecture, interpretation, and manipulation of the text than mere expansion of abbreviations. In addition, one would have to question the legitimacy of attempting to restore syllables lost by apocope.

4. /ıı/ = ײ and /vı/ = ױ are redundant in the chart, since the transliteration of each symbol accounts for the combination.

5. Fuks', ed., *The Oldest . . . Documents*, I, p. xxxiv: "Orthographic Rules."

6. The term refers to those graphs to which scholars normally assign both vowel and consonantal values. Only those are listed here which do not fit into the table above.

7. Katz, *Six Germano-Judaic Poems*, p. vi.

8. In each case, both Hebrew and Roman have diaresis not hachek, but the Hebrew characters of the text so transliterated have hachek. This is most likely simply a typographical constraint in Katz's typescript.

9. Katz, ed., 23-52.

10. The transliteration and transcription systems are discussed simultaneously by Schwarz in his introductory essay to the edition, *Dukus Horant*, 24-74.

11. ן is not listed, but a comment is added to the effect that it does not differ phonetically from כ (p. 49), thus implying, one must assume, that for instance ס which is listed on the previous page *does* differ from מ.

12. Hakkarainen, *Studien*, I, 27-30.

13. "Dass dadurch der graphemischen, phonemischen und phonetischen Deutung des graphischen Systems einigermassen vorgegriffen wird,

lässt sich nicht vermeiden. Das kann und darf aber unvoreingenommenem weiterem Studium der Hs. nicht in Wege stehen." (I, 27-28).

14. *Die Cambridger Löwenfabel,* p. 65 chart.

15. Even so, at this point, he makes the ludicrously "objective" discovery that "Dennoch kann die Hypothese aufgestellt werden, daß der Text einer Sprachnorm angehört, die zu mhd. Sprachnormen in einer bestimmten Beziehung steht" (p. 67). This hypothesis is possible due to the graphemic identity of some transliterated words of the text with their Middle High German counterparts.

16. Noted, almost lamented, recurringly: pp. 67, 70, etc.

17. Could this confusion simply be the result of unfortunate, but understandable proofreading errors, by means of which the points were omitted?

18. Althaus, *Die Cambridger Löwenfabel,* 158-159.

19. Matenko/Sloan, *Aqedath Jis̥ḥ̥aq,* 44-46.

20. Cf. also p. 53, stanza 25, l. 3 - *tifniš,* and note 11: "This MHG. ending "nisse" is transliterated as "niš," because this pronunciation seems to have become universal in Yiddish at an early period."

21. Erika Timm, "Beria und Simra," 5-7.

22. Florence Guggenheim-Grünberg, "Zur Umschrift . . . , p. 230, n. * and 230-236.

23. W. B. Lockwood, "Die Textgestalt des jüngeren Hildebrandliedes in jüdisch-deutscher Sprache," *Beiträge zur Geschichte der deutschen Sprache und Literatur* (Halle) 85 (1963), 434-438.

24. See the bibliography in his *Yiddish: A Survey and a Grammar,* 330-331, for references to his own publications on transposition, as well as scholarly responses to his systems.

25. S. Birnbaum, "Old Yiddish or Middle High German?" p. 21, n. 6.

26. S. Birnbaum, "Old Yiddish or Middle High German?" 25-30.

27. As is clear from the list, and noted (p. 26) by Birnbaum, vowel length is expressed by circumflex and by doubling the vowel; yet since he transcribes with two differing symbols, he must posit a phonetic distinction between them; he does not explain that distinction.

28. B3 and B4 from: "Das älteste datierte Schriftstück in jiddischer Sprache," *Beiträge zur Geschichte der deutschen Sprache und Literatur* 56 (1932), p. 12; essentially the same system is used in his article appearing in *Teuthonista* 8 (1932), 197-207, with the exceptions of וֹ = [ô], ץ = *z*, and ש =

/ś/. In general it seems that the many distinctions between Hebrew-alphabet graphs depend in the transcription on the contrast between italics and Roman and might well lead to confusion.

29. In his *Teuthonista* article, p. 207, n. 1, he clarifies the usage of these three symbols: /ṡ/ = [s], /sch/ = [ʃ], /ś/ is used when it is impossible to determine whether the signification is [s] or [ʃ].

30. The transcription system employed in *Teuthonista,* p. 206 differs from this system only in the representation of ׳ as [ė].

31. Solomon A. Birnbaum, *Yiddish: A Survey and a Grammar* (Toronto 1979), 110-111.

32. John A. Howard, "Der Bärmuttersegen - Ein mittelhochdeutscher Spruch," *Colloquia Germanica* 11 (1978), p. 227 and "Der 'Bärmuttersegen' wiederentdeckt," *Zeitschrift für deutsches Altertum* 108 (1979), p. 255, where italicized graphs are underlined.

33. Wulf-Otto Dreeßen, *Akedass Jizḥak*, 69-103. His system is essentially that adopted by Timm.

34. Uriel Weinreich, "Preface," *The Field of Yiddish*, vol. 1 (New York: Linguistic Circle of New York, 1954), vii-viii; he notes the influence of S. Birnbaum's 1932 article in *Teuthonista* on the development of this system.

35. Dageš, šurek, mappik are represented by a dot over the transliteration symbol; vowel points are represented by superscripts.

Bibliography

Abrahams, Israel. *Jewish Life in the Middle Ages.* 2nd ed. London 1932.

Agus, Irving, A. "The Language Spoken by Ashkenazic Jews in the High Middle Ages." In *Joshua Finkel Festschrift.* Sidney B. Hoenig, ed. New York 1974, 19-28.

Althaus, Hans-Peter. "Die Jiddische Sprache. Eine Einführung," *Germania Judaica* 4 (1965), 1-24 & 7 (1968), 1-24.

—— Rev. Fuks, ed., *Melokim-buk.* In *Germania Judaica* 5 (1966), 25-27.

—— "Die Cambridger Löwenfabel von 1382." In *Forschungsinstitut für deutsche Sprache. Jahresbericht 1966.* Marburg 1967, 19-21.

—— "Die Erforschung der jiddischen Sprache." In *Germanische Dialektologie. Festschrift Walther Mitzka zum 80. Geburtstag.* L. E. Schmitt, ed., Wiesbaden 1968, I, 224-263.

—— "Jiddistik: Umriß einer Wissenschaft," *Emuna* 2 (1967), 248-256.

—— *Die Cambridger Löwenfabel von 1382; Untersuchung und Edition eines defekten Textes.* Berlin 1971.

—— "Die Kunst der Paraphrase. Otto F. Best über das Jiddische," *Zeitschrift für Dialektologie und Linguistik* 41 (1974), 318-337.

—— Rev. of Birnbaum, *Yiddish.* In *Germania Judaica* 5 (1966), 25.

Avé-Lallemant, Friedrich C. B. *Das deutsche Gaunerthum in seiner socialpolitischen, literarischen und linguistischen Ausbildung.* 3. Theil. Leipzig 1862.

Axelson, B. *Unpoetische Wörter. Ein Beitrag zur Kenntnis der lateinischen Dichtersprache.* Lund 1945.

Beim, H. "Tsushtayer tsu der forshung fun eltstn yidishn manuskript" [rev. of Fuks, ed., *The Oldest . . . Documents*]. *Yidishe shprakh* 20 (1960), 9-16.

Beranek, Franz J. "Die Erforschung der jiddischen Sprache," *Zeitschrift für deutsche Philologie* 70 (1947/1948), 163-174.

—— "Neues zur jiddischen Gudrunhandschrift," *Mitteilungen aus dem Arbeitskreis für Jiddistik* 1 (1956), 49-52.

—— "Jiddisch." In *Deutsche Philologie im Aufriß*. Wolfgang Stammler, ed. 2nd ed. Berlin 1957, I, 1955-2000.

—— "Zur Geschichte des jiddischen Vokalismus," *Zeitschrift für Mundartforschung* 32 (1965), 260-274.

Berliner, A. *Aus dem Leben der deutschen Juden im Mittelalter.* Berlin 1900.

Best, Otto F. *Mameloschen. Jiddisch - Eine Sprache und ihre Literatur.* Frankfurt 1973.

Bin-Nun [Fischer], Jechiel. *Jiddisch und die deutschen Mundarten.* Tübingen 1973.

Birnbaum, Solomon A. [Shloyme Birnboym/Salomo Birnbaum]. *Praktische Grammatik der jiddischen Sprache.* Vienna/Leipzig 1915.

—— "Transkriptsies fun yidish," *Filologishe shriftn* 3 (1929), 485-496.

—— "Jiddische Sprache." In *Jüdisches Lexikon.* Berlin 1929, III, 269-278.

—— "Umschrift des ältesten datierten jiddischen Schriftstückes," *Teuthonista [Zeitschrift für Mundartforschung]* 8 (1932), 197-207.

—— "Das älteste datierte Schriftstück in jiddischer Sprache," *Beiträge zur Geschichte der deutschen Sprache und Literatur* 56 (1932), 11-22.

—— "Jiddisch," *Encyclopaedia Judaica* (Berlin 1932), IX, 112-127.

—— "Die Umschrift des Jiddischen," *Teuthonista [Zeitschrift für Mundartforschung]* 9 (1933), 90-105.

—— "The Age of the Yiddish Language," *Transactions of the Philological Society* (1939), 31-43.

—— "Two Problems of Yiddish Linguistics." In *The Field of Yiddish.* Vol. 1. Uriel Weinreich, ed., New York 1954, 63-72.

—— Rev. of Fuks, *The Oldest . . . Documents.* In *Bibliotheca Orientalis* 16 (1959), 50-52.

—— "Old Yiddish or Middle High German?" *Journal of Jewish Studies* 12 (1961), 19-31.

—— Rev. of Hakkarainen, *Studien*, I. In *Journal of Jewish Studies* 20 (1969), 101-103.

—— *Yiddish: A Survey and a Grammar.* Toronto 1979.

Blondheim, D. S. *Les parlers judéo-romans et la Vetus Latina.* Paris 1925.

Bräuer, Rolf. *Literatursoziologie und epische Struktur der deutschen "Spielmanns"- und Heldendichtung.* Berlin 1970.

Cahan, Abraham [Arcadius]. "Der derekh fun Yivo in sayn vilner tkufe," *Yivo-bleter* 46 (1980), 9-21.

Caliebe, Manfred. "Dukus Horant. Studien zu seiner literarischen Tradition." Diss. Kiel 1970; revised & publ. as *Dukus Horant.* Philologische Studien und Quellen 70. Berlin 1973.

—— Rev. of Hakkarainen, *Studien,* I. In *Wirkendes Wort* 20 (1970), 139-141.

—— Rev. of Althaus, *Die Cambridger Löwenfabel.* In *Germanistik* 13 (1972), 103-104.

—— Rev. of Dreeßen, ed., *Akedass.* In *Germanistik* 13 (1972), 111.

—— Rev. of Althaus, *Die Cambridger Löwenfabel* and Hakkarainen, *Studien,* II & III. In *Wirkendes Wort* 24 (1974), 286-289.

—— Rev. of Heide, *Untersuchungen.* In *Germanistik* 17 (1976), 92-93.

—— "Zur Problematik von Gesamtdarstellungen jiddischer Literaturgeschichte in deutscher Sprache; Bedenken, Berichtigungen und Ergänzungen zu Helmut Dinse, "Die Entwicklung des jiddischen Schrifttums im deutschen Sprachgebiet," *Wirkendes Wort* 27 (1977), 51-66.

Carles, J. "Un fragment judéo-allemand du cycle de Kudrun" [rev. Fuks, ed., *The Oldest . . . Documents*]. In *Études Germaniques* 13 (1958), 348-351.

—— "Le poème de Kudrun," *Publications de la faculté des lettres et sciences humaine de l'université de Clermont-Ferrand,* ser. 2/16 (1963), 231-241.

—— *Le poème de Kudrun. Étude de sa matière.* Paris 1963.

Colditz, Siegfried. "Das jiddische Fragment von Herzog Horand in seinem Verhältnis zum Gudrunepos und dem König Rother," *Mitteilungen aus dem Arbeitskreis für Jiddistik* 2 (1960), 17-24.

—— "Studien zum hebräisch-mittelhochdeutschen Fragment vom 'Dukus Horant' (c. 1382)." Diss. Leipzig 1964.

—— "Das hebräisch-mittelhochdeutsche Fragment vom 'Dukus Horant,'" *Forschungen und Fortschritt* 40 (1966), 302-306.

Cormeau, Christoph. "Die jiddische Tradition von Wirnts *Wigalois,*" *Zeitschrift für Literaturwissenschaft und Linguistik* 8 (1978), 28-44.

Cuddihy, John Murray. *The Ordeal of Civility: Freud, Marx, Lévi-Strauss, and the Jewish Struggle with Modernity.* New York 1974.

Cuno, Klaus. "Die Beschäftigung mit dem Jiddischen und der Kanon der Wissenschaften." In *Auseinandersetzung um jiddische Sprache und Literatur. Jüdische Komponenten in der deutschen Literatur – die Assimilationskontroverse.* Walter Röll and Hans-Peter Bayerdörfer, eds., Vol. 5 of *Kontroverse, alte und neue. Akten des VII. Internationalen Germanisten-Kongresses, Göttingen 1985.* Albrecht Schöne, ed., Tübingen: Niemeyer, 1986, 94-103.

Curschmann, Michael. *Spielmannsepik: Wege und Ergebnisse der Forschung von 1907-1965, mit Ergänzungen und Nachträgen bis 1967.* Stuttgart 1968.

Dinse, Helmut. *Die Entwicklung des jiddischen Schrifttums im deutschen Sprachgebiet.* Stuttgart 1974.

Dinse, Helmut and Sol Liptzin. *Einführung in die jiddische Literatur.* Stuttgart 1978.

Dreeßen, Wulf-Otto, ed. *Akêdass Jizḥak; Ein altjiddisches Gedicht über die Opferung Isaaks; mit Einleitung und Kommentar kritisch herausgegeben.* Diss. Hamburg. Hamburger Beiträge zur Geschichte der Juden 2. Hamburg 1971.

—— Rev. of *The Field of Yiddish.* Vol. 3. in *Germanistik* 12 (1971), 236-237.

—— "Die altjiddische Bearbeitung des Barlaam-Stoffes," *Zeitschrift für deutsche Philologie* 93 (Sonderheft 1974), 218-233.

—— "Zur Rezeption deutscher epischer Literatur im Altjiddischen: Das Beispiel 'Wigalois' - 'Artushof,'" *Deutsche Literatur des späteren Mittelalters – Hamburger Kolloquium 1973,* Wolfgang Harms and L. Peter Johnson, eds., (Berlin 1975), 116-128.

—— Rev. of Dinse, *Die Entwicklung.* In *Anzeiger für deutsches Altertum* 86 (1975), 162-166.

—— "Jiddische Drucke vor 1800. Hilfen für den Umgang mit einem neuen Quellenverzeichnis," *Zeitschrift für deutsches Altertum* 105 (1976), 310-317.

—— "Die altjiddischen Estherdichtungen: Überlegungen zur Rekonstruktion der Geschichte der älteren jiddischen Literatur," *Daphnis* 6 (1977), 27-39.

—— Rev. of Dinse/Liptzin, *Einführung*. In *Germanistik* 19 (1978), 1096-1097.

—— "Midraschepik und Bibelepik: Biblische Stoffe in der volksprachigen Literatur der Juden und Christen des Mittelalters im deutschen Sprachgebiet," *Zeitschrift für deutsche Philologie* 100 (Sonderheft *Jiddisch* 1981), 78-97.

—— "'Akedass Jizchak' ('Bindung Isaaks')." In *Die deutsche Literatur des Mittelalters. Verfasserlexikon*. 2nd ed. by Kurt Ruh. Berlin 1977, I, 95-97.

—— "Eisek der Schreiber." In *Die deutsche Literatur des Mittelalters. Verfasserlexikon*. 2nd ed. by Kurt Ruh. Berlin 1980, II, 433-434.

—— "'Ben ha-melech weha-nosir' ('Königssohn und frommer Asket')," In *Die deutsche Literatur des Mittelalters. Verfasserlexikon*. 2nd ed. by Kurt Ruh. Berlin 1978, I, 686-687.

—— "Doniel." In *Die deutsche Literatur des Mittelalters. Verfasserlexikon*. 2nd ed. by Kurt Ruh. Berlin 1980, II, 205-206.

—— "'Joßef ha-zadik' (*der gute Joßef*, Str. 1, 2)." In *Die deutsche Literatur des Mittelalters. Verfasserlexikon*. 2nd ed. by Kurt Ruh. Berlin 1983, IV, 878-880.

—— "Zur altjiddischen Synonymik" In *Fragen des älteren Jiddisch. Trierer Beiträge*, Sonderheft 2. Hermann-Josef Müller & Walter Röll, eds., Trier 1977, 63-67.

Dreeßen, Wulf-Otto and Hermann-Josef Müller, eds. *Doniel: Das altjiddische Danielbuch nach dem Basler Druck von 1557*. Litterae 59, 1-2. Göppingen 1978.

Eckart, Rolf and Walter Röll. "Dukus Horant." In *Kindlers Literatur-Lexikon*. Zurich 1974, II, 1691-1692.

Erik, Maks [Zalmen Merkin]. *Vegn altyidishn roman un novele*. Warsaw 1926.

—— "Bletlekh tsu der geshikhte fun der elterer yidisher literatur," *Tsaytshrift* 1 (1926), 173-178.

—— *Di Geshikhte fun der yidisher literatur, fun di eltste tsaytn biz der haskole-tkufe, fertsnter-akhtsnter jorhundert, mit bilder un melodies*. Warsaw 1928.

—— *Etiudn tsu der geshikhte fun der haskole*. Minsk 1931.

—— "Inventar fun der yidisher shpilman-dikhtung," *Tsaytshrift* 2/3 (1928) (Institut far vaysruslendisher kultur, Minsk), col. 545-558.

Falk, Felix. "Die Bücher Samuelis in deutschen Nibelungenstrophen des XV. Jahrhunderts," *Mitteilungen der Gesellschaft für jüdische Volkskunde* (1908), 95-116 & 129-150.

—— *Mélanges bibliographiques sur les livres de Samuel en strophes de Nibelungen.* Leipzig 1909.

—— ed. [posth.; L. Fuks, ed.]. *Das Schmuelbuch des Mosche Esrim Wearba; Ein biblisches Epos aus dem 15. Jahrhundert; Einleitung und textkritischer Apparat.* Assen 1961.

Fishman, Joshua A. [Shikl]. "The Tshernovits Language Conference and the 'Rise of Yiddish,'" *International Journal of the Sociology of Language*, 24 (1980), 43-73.

—— "Vos ken zayn di funktsye fun yidish in Yisroel?" *Yidisher kemfer* (New York, April 1974), 40-46.

Forster, Leonard. "Dukus Horant" [rev. of Fuks, ed., *The Oldest . . . Documents*]. In *German Life and Letters* 11 (1958), 276-285.

Fourquet, Jean. "Ernest-H. Lévy et le Dukus Horant" [rev. of Fuks, ed., *The Oldest . . . Documents*]. In *Études Germaniques* 14 (1959), 50-56.

Frakes, Jerold C., "Critical Ideology in Old Yiddish Studies: The Names of Old Yiddish," *Yiddish* 6 (1985), 5-14.

—— "Audience, Accessibility, and Ideology; On Editing Old Yiddish Texts," *The German Quarterly* 59 (1985), 187-202.

Friedrichs, Theresia. "Zu 'Fleré Blankéfleré.'" In *Fragen des älteren Jiddisch. Trierer Beiträge*, Sonderheft 2. Hermann-Josef Müller & Walter Röll, eds., Trier 1977, 68-73.

Fuks, Layb [Leo]. "Der eltster literarisher dokument in yidish," *Yidishe kultur* 16 (1953), 30-35.

—— "The Oldest Literary Works in Yiddish in a Manuscript of the Cambridge University Library," *Journal of Jewish Studies* 4 (1953), 176-181.

—— "On the Oldest Dated Work in Yiddish Literature," *The Field of Yiddish* 1. Publications of the Linguistic Circle of New York 3. Uriel Weinreich, ed., New York 1954, 267-274.

—— ed. *The Oldest Known Literary Documents of Yiddish Literature (c. 1382).* 2 vols. Leiden 1957.

—— "Die jiddische Literatur." In *Die Literatur der Welt in ihrer mündlichen und schriftlichen Überlieferung.* Wolfgang von Einsiedel, ed., Zurich 1964, 101-109.

—— *Das altjiddische Epos Melokim-buk; 1. Einleitung und Faksimile der editio princeps. Augsburg 1543.* 2. *Hebräische und aramäische Quellen, textkritischer Apparat und Glossar.* Assen 1965.

Ganz, Peter F. Rev. of Fuks, *The Oldest . . . Documents.* In *Journal of Jewish Studies* 8 (1957), 246-249.

—— "*Dukus Horant* - An Early Yiddish Poem from the Cairo Genizah," *Journal of Jewish Studies* 9 (1958), 47-62.

Ganz, Peter, Frederick Norman and Werner Schwarz. "Zu dem Cambridger Josef," *Zeitschrift für deutsche Philologie* 82 (1963), 86-90.

—— eds. *Dukus Horant.* Altdeutsche Textbibliothek, Ergänzungsreihe 2. Tübingen 1964.

Gaster, Moses. "Yiddish Literature of the Middle Ages." In *Essays by Divers Hands,* Transactions of the Royal Society of Literature, n.s. 7. Oxford 1927, 104-131.

Gerzon, J. *Die jüdisch-deutsche Sprache.* Diss. Heidelberg 1902. Cologne 1902.

Gesenius, Wilhelm. *Hebräische Grammatik.* Rev. ed. by E. Kautsch. Leipzig 1902.

Gilman, Sander. "The Flight of the Hero: Modalities of Reception in Yiddish Fiction," *Colloquia Germanica* 4 (1976), 336-52.

—— *Jewish Self-Hatred.* Baltimore 1985.

Ginninger, Chaim [Khaym]. "Sainéan's Accomplishments in Yiddish Linguistics." In *The Field of Yiddish* 1. Publications of the Linguistic Circle of New York 3. Uriel Weinreich, ed., New York 1954, 147-178.

—— "A Note on the Yiddish Horant." In *The Field of Yiddish* 1. Publications of the Linguistic Circle of New York 3. Uriel Weinreich, ed., New York 1954, 275-277.

—— "Di korespondents A. Landoy - L. Saineanu," *Yivo-bleter* 13 (1938), 275-300.

Goldsmith, Emanuel S. *Architects of Yiddishism at the Beginning of the Twentieth Century: A Study in Jewish Cultural History.* London 1976,

Grünbaum, M. *Jüdisch-deutsche Chrestomathie.* Leipzig 1882; repr. Hildesheim 1969.

—— "Die jüdischdeutsche Literatur in Deutschland, Polen und Amerika." In J. Winter and A Wünschen, eds. *Geschichte der poetischen, kabbalistischen, historischen und neuzeitlichen Litteratur der Juden.* Vol. 3 of *Die jüdische Litteratur seit Abschluß des Kanons.* Trier 1896, 533-623.

Güdemann, Moritz. *Geschichte des Erziehungswesens und der Cultur der abendländischen Juden während des Mittelalters.* 3 vols. Vienna 1880; repr. Amsterdam 1966.

Guggenheim, Siegfried. "Die Gudrunsage. Mittelhochdeutsch, jüdischdeutsch oder jiddisch? Und ein Brief von Karl Wolfskehl," *Allgemeine Wochenzeitung der Juden in Deutschland* (30 April 1954).

Guggenheim-Grünberg, Florence. "The Horse Dealers' Language of the Swiss Jews in Endingen and Lengnau." In *The Field of Yiddish.* Uriel Weinreich, ed., New York 1954, 48-62.

—— "Die Sprache der Zürcher Juden im 14. Jahrhundert: Deutsch oder Jiddisch?" *Israelitisches Wochenblatt für die Schweiz,* no. 21a. 25 May 1954.

—— "Zur Umschrift deutscher Mundarten des 14./15. Jahrhunderts mit hebräischer Schrift," *Zeitschrift für Mundartforschung* 24 (1957), 229-246.

—— "Sprachen und schrieben die Zürcher Juden jiddisch zu Ende des 14. Jahrhunderts?" In *Fragen des älteren Jiddisch. Trierer Beiträge,* Sonderheft 2. Hermann-Josef Müller & Walter Röll, eds., Trier 1977, 2-3.

G[uggenheim]-G[rünberg, Florence]. "Jiddisch in Israel unerwünscht, in New York aber anerkannt," *Der Sudetendeutsche,* Hamburg, 24 July 1954.

Haberman, A. M "Ktav-hayad hakadum beyoter biyehudit-aškenazit," in *Hapo'el hatsa'ir* 29 (24 December 1957), 20-21.

Habersaat, Karl [Carlo]. "Repertorium der jiddischen Handschriften," *Revista degli Studi Orientali* 29 (1954), 53-70 & 30 (1955), 235-249.

—— Rev. of Fuks *The Oldest Known Literary Documents.* In *Biblica* 39 (1958), 526-527.

—— "Beitrag zur Chronologie der datierten jiddischen Handschriften (1307-1619)," *Mitteilungen aus dem Arbeitskreis für Jiddistik* 2 (1960), 117-118.

—— "Prolegomena zum Repertorium der jiddischen Handschriften," *Zeitschrift für deutsche Philologie* 81 (1962), 338-348.

—— "Materialien zur Geschichte der jiddischen Grammatik," *Orbis* 11 (1962), 352-368.

—— "Zur Geschichte der Jiddischen Grammatik. Eine bibliographische Studie," *Zeitschrift für deutsche Philologie* 84 (1965), 419-435.

Hagen, Friedrich Heinrich von der. "Die romantische und Volks-Litteratur der Juden in Jüdisch-Deutscher Sprache," *Phil.-hist. Abhandlungen der königl. Akademie der Wissenschaften.* Berlin 1954, 1-11.

—— "Süßkind von Trimberg, der jüdische Minnesänger," *Literaturblatt des Orients* 10 (7 March 1840), 146 f.

Hakkarainen, Heikki J. *Studien zum Cambridger Codex T.-S. 10. K. 22*; 1: *Text.* Acta Universitatis Turkuensis, ser. B, vol. 104, 1967. 2: *Graphemik und Phonemik.* Acta, ser. B, vol. 174, 1971. 3: *Lexikon.* Acta, ser. B., vol. 182, 1973.

Heide, Manfred Gernot. *Graphematisch-phonematische Untersuchungen zum Altjiddischen: Der Vokalismus.* Bern 1974.

Howard, John A. "Hebrew-German and Early Yiddish Literature: Survey of Problems." Diss. University of Illinois. 1972.

—— "Bemerkungen zu einem Aspekt altjiddischer Literaturgeschichte," *Archiv für das Studium der neueren Sprachen und Literaturen* 215 (1978), 1-20.

—— "Der Bärmuttersegen - Ein mittelhochdeutscher Spruch," *Colloquia Germanica* 12 (1978), 211-232.

—— "Der Bärmuttersegen wiederentdeckt," *Zeitschrift für deutsches Altertum* 108 (1979), 252-258.

—— "A Little Known Version of *Til Eulenspiegel,*" *Amsterdamer Beiträge zur älteren Germanistik* 15 (1980), 127-142.

—— "The Bodleian *Fortunatus,*" *Yiddish* 6 (1985), 15-20.

Hruby, K. Rev. of Dreeßen, ed. *Akêdass.* In *Judaica* 28 (1972), 44-45.

Joffe, Judah A. [Yuda A. Yofe], ed. *Elia Bachur*'s *Poetical Works.* Vol. 1. New York 1949.

—— "Dating the Origin of Yiddish Dialects." In *The Field of Yiddish.* Publications of the Linguistic Circle of New York 3. Uriel Weinreich, ed., New York 1954, 102-121.

Kahle, P. E. *The Cairo Genizah.* Oxford 1959.

Kaplowitt, S. J. Rev. of Ganz/Norman/Schwarz, eds. *Dukus Horant.* In *Journal of English and Germanic Philology* 65 (1966), 537-542.

Karpeles, Gustav. "Die Jüdisch-deutsche Literatur." in *Geschichte der jüdischen Literatur.* Berlin 1886, II, 1000-1029.

—— *Jewish Literature and Other Essays.* Philadelphia 1895.

Katz, Dovid. "On Yiddish, in Yiddish and for Yiddish: 500 Years of Yiddish Scholarship," in *Identity and Ethos: A Festschrift for Sol Liptzin on the Occasion of his 85th Birthday*, Mark H. Gelber, ed., New York/Berne/ Frankfurt: Peter Lang, 1986, 23-36.

Katz, Eli. "Six Germano-Judaic Poems from the Cairo Genizah." Diss. U.C. L.A. 1963.

Kisch, Guido. *The Jews in Medieval Germany: A Study of their Legal and Social Status*. Chicago 1949; repr. New York 1970.

Könnecker, Barbara. "Zum literarischen Charakter und der literarischen Intention des altjiddischen Schmuelbuchs." In *Auseinandersetzung um jiddische Sprache und Literatur. Jüdische Komponenten in der deutschen Literatur – die Assimilationskontroverse*. Walter Röll and Hans-Peter Bayerdörfer, eds., Vol. 5 of *Kontroverse, alte und neue. Akten des VII. Internationalen Germanisten-Kongresses, Göttingen 1985*. Albrecht Schöne, ed., Tübingen: Niemeyer, 1986, 3-12.

Kroes, H. W. J. "Ducus Horant een jiddische Kudrun?" [Rev. of Fuks., ed., *The Oldest . . . Documents*]. In *Duitse Kroniek* (1959), 89-93.

Landau, Leo. *Arthurian Legends; The Hebrew-German Rhymed Version of the Legend of King Arthur*, Teutonia 21. Leipzig 1912.

—— "A Hebrew-German (Judeo-German) Paraphrase of the Book of Esther of the Fifteenth Century," *Journal of English and Germanic Philology* 18 (1919), 497-555.

—— "A nisht-bakanter yidish-daytsher nusekh fun der Artus-legende," *Filologishe shriftn* 1 (1926), 129-140.

Lastik, S. *Di yidishe literatur biz di klasiker*. Warsaw 1950.

Leviant, C. *King Artus: A Hebrew Arthurian Romance of 1279*. Assen 1969.

Lindgren, B. Rev. of Hakkarainen, *Studien*, I & II. In *Neuphilologische Mitteilungen* 73 (1972), 724-726.

Linn, I. "Widwilt, Son of Gawain." Diss. New York University 1942.

Liptzin, Sol. "YIVO." In *Encyclopaedia Judaica*. New York 1971, XVI, 837-839.

—— *A History of Yiddish Literature*. New York 1972.

Lockwood, W. B. "Die Textgestalt des jüngeren Hildebrandliedes in jüdisch-deutscher Sprache," *Beiträge zur Geschichte der deutschen Sprache und Literatur* (Halle) 85 (1963), 433-447.

Lowenstein, Steven M. "The Yiddish Written Word in Nineteenth Century Germany," *Leo Baeck Institute Yearbook* 24 (1979), 179-192.

Lotze, H. "Zur jüdisch-deutschen Literatur," *Archiv für Literaturgeschichte* 7 (1970), 90-101.

Mader, F. Rev. of Hakkarainen, *Studien*, I. In *Neuphilologische Mitteilungen* 73 (1972), 721-723.

Maitlis, Jacob M. [Yankev Meytlis]. "Die altjiddische Volksliteratur des 16.-18. Jahrhunderts," *Deutsche Universitätszeitung* 13 (1958), 107-108.

—— "Alt-yidishe epishe literatur," *Zukunft* 72 (1967), 13-17.

—— "Akedas Jizchok." *Kindlers Literatur-Lexikon*. Zurich 1965, I, 320-321.

Marchand, James. Rev. of Fuks, ed., *The Oldest . . . Documents*. In *Word* 15 (1959), 383-394.

—— "Three Basic Problems in the Investigation of Early Yiddish," *Orbis* 9 (1960), 34-41.

—— "Einiges zur sogenannten 'jiddischen Kudrun,'" *Neophilologus* 45 (1961), 55-63.

Marchand, James and Frederic C. Tubach. "Der keusche Josef; Ein mitteldeutsches Gedicht aus dem 13.-14. Jahrhundert. Beitrag zur Erforschung der hebräisch-deutschen Literatur," *Zeitschrift für deutsche Philologie* 81 (1962), 30-52.

Mark, Yudl. *Di geshikhte fun der yidisher literatur*. New York 1943.

—— "A Study of the Frequency of Hebraisms in Yiddish: Preliminary Report." In *The Field of Yiddish*. Uriel Weinreich, ed., New York 1954, 24-48.

—— "Yiddish Literature." In *The Jews: Their History, Culture, and Religion*. L. Finkelstein, ed., 3rd ed. New York 1966, II, 1191-1233.

Matenko, Percy and Samuel Sloan. "The Aqedath Jiṣḥaq; a Sixteenth Century Epic; with Introduction and Notes." In Percy Matenko. *Two Studies in Jewish Culture*. Leiden 1968, 1-70, plus ten facsimile plates.

Menhardt, Hermann. "Regensburg, ein Mittelpunkt der deutschen Epik des 12. Jahrhunderts," *Zeitschrift füt deutsches Altertum* 89 (1958), 271-274.

—— "Zur Herkunft des 'Dukus Horant,'" *Mitteilungen aus dem Arbeitskreis für Jiddistik* 2 (1961), 33-36.

Mieses, M. *Die Entstehungsursachen der jüdischen Dialekte*. Vienna 1915.

Minis. Cola. Rev. of Fuks, ed., *Melokimbuk*. In *Neophilologus* 54 (1970), 196-198.

Minkoff, N. B. "Old Yiddish Literature." In *The Jewish People Past and Present*. New York 1952, III, 145-164.

Müller, Hermann-Josef. "Zur Edition des altjiddischen 'Donielbuchs.'" In *Fragen des älteren Jiddisch. Trierer Beiträge*, Sonderheft 2. Hermann-Josef Müller & Walter Röll, eds., Trier 1977, 57-62.

Murdoch, B. Rev. of Hakkarainen, *Studien*, I. In *Modern Language Review* 65 (1970), 441-444.

Neumann, Hans. "Sprache und Reim in den judendeutschen Gedichten des Cambridger Codex T.S.10.K.22," in *Indogermanica, Festschrift Wolfgang Krause*. Heidelberg: Winter, 1960, 145-165.

Norman, Frederick. "Remarks on the Yiddish Kudrun," *Journal of Jewish Studies* 5 (1954), 85-86.

—— "Early Yiddish Literature" [Rev. of Fuks, ed., *The Oldest . . . Documents*. In *The Jewish Chronicle*, 21 February 1958.

Ott, Norbert. "Die Bilderlosigkeit jiddischer Handschriften: Zur Frage von Gebrauchssituation und Anspruch jiddischer Literatur anhand ihrer Überlieferung." In *Fragen des älteren Jiddisch. Trierer Beiträge*, Sonderheft 2. Hermann-Josef Müller & Walter Röll, eds., Trier 1977, 42-45.

Paper, Herbert H. "An Early Case of Standard German in Hebrew Orthography." In *The Field of Yiddish*. Uriel Weinreich, ed. Publications of the Linguistic Circle of New York 3. New York 1954, 143-146.

Paucker, Arnold. "The Yiddish Versions of the German Volksbuch," Diss. Nottingham 1959.

—— "Yiddish Versions of Early German Prose Novels," *Journal of Jewish Studies* 10 (1959), 151-167.

—— Rev. of Ganz/Norman/Schwarz, eds. *Dukus Horant*. In *German Life and Letters*, n.s. 21 (1968), 274-275.

Perles, Felix. "Zur Erforschung des Jüdisch-Deutschen," *Beiträge zur Geschichte der deutschen Sprache und Literatur* 43 (1918), 296-309.

Petsch, Robert. Rev. of Landau, ed., *Arthurian Legends*. In *Archiv für das Studium der neueren Sprachen Literaturen* 132 (1914), 174-181.

Pfaffenberger Wolfgang. *Blütezeiten und nationale Literaturgeschichtsschreibung: Eine wissenschaftsgeschichtliche Betrachtung*. Europäische Hochschulschriften 353. Frankfurt 1981.

Pinès, M. *Histoire de la litterature judéo-allemande*. Paris 1911; German trans. by Georg Hecht, *Die Geschichte der jüdischdeutschen Literatur*. Leipzig 1913; Russian trans. by C. C. Vermel, *Istoria evreiskoi literatury*. Moscow 1913; Yiddish trans. by Baal Makhshoves: *Di geshikhte fun der yudisher literatur*. Warsaw 1911.

Piquet, F. Rev. of Landau, ed., *Arthurian Legends*, In *Revue critique d'histoire et de la litérature* 76 (1913), 427.

Rauh, Ursula. Rev. of Ganz/Norman/Schwarz, eds., *Dukus Horant*. In *Euphorion* 60 (1966), 154-164,

Roback, A. A. *The Story of Yiddish Literature*. New York 1940.

Robinson, F. N., ed. *The Works of Geoffrey Chaucer*. 2nd ed. Boston 1957.

Röll, Walther. "Die Abenteuer einer Handschrift. Das deutsche Heldenepos vom 'Dukus Horant' liegt wieder vor" [rev. of Ganz/Norman/Schwarz, eds., *Dukus Horant*, In *Die Welt*, 12 February 1965.

—— Rev. of Ganz/Norman/Schwarz, eds., *Dukus Horant*. In *Studi Medievali*, 3rd ser. 7 (1966), 269-275.

—— "Zum Konsonantensystem der Cambridger Handschrift," *Zeitschrift für Mundartforschung* 33 (1966), 144-146.

—— "Das älteste datierte jüdisch-deutsche Sprachdenkmal; Ein Verspaar im Wormser Machsor von 1272-1273," *Zeitschrift für Mundartforschung* 33 (1966), 127-138.

—— Rev. of Hakkarainen, *Studien*, I & II. In *Germanistik* 13 (1972), 101-102.

—— Rev. of Hakkarainen, *Studien*, III. In *Germanistik* 15 (1974), 351.

—— "Zum 'Sefer ha-Gan' Jizḥaks ben Elieser." In *Fragen des älteren Jiddisch. Trierer Beiträge*, Sonderheft 2. Hermann-Josef Müller & Walter Röll, eds., Trier 1977, 35-41.

—— "'Gan Eden' ('Das Paradies')." In *Die deutsche Literatur des Mittelalters. Verfasserlexikon*. 2nd ed. by Kurt Ruh. Berlin 1980, II, 1069-1070.

—— "'Awroham Owinu' ('Unser Vater Abraham')." in *Die deutsche Literatur des Mittelalters. Verfasserlexikon*. 2nd ed. by Kurt Ruh. Berlin 1977, I., 573-574.

—— "Zu den ersten drei Texten der Cambridger Handschrift von 1382/1383," *Zeitschrift für deutsches Altertum* 104 (1975), 54-68.

—— "Vorwort." In *Zeitschrift für deutsche Philologie* 100 (Sonderheft *Jiddisch* 1981), 2-3.

—— Rev. of Birnbaum, *Yiddish*. In *Zeitschrift für deutsche Philologie* 102 (1983), 466-469.

Röll, Walter and Christoph Gerhardt, "Zur literarischen Einordnung des sogenannten 'Dukus Horant,'" *Deutsche Vierteljahrsschrift für Geistesgeschichte und Literaturwissenschaft* 41 (1967), 517-527.

Roelly, S. "Essai de reconstitution en moyen haut-allemand normalisé d'un texte en strophes . . . *Dukus Horant*," Diss. Paris 1960.

Rosenfeld, Helmut. "Die Kudrun – Nordseedichtung oder Donaudichtung," *Zeitschrift für deutsche Philologie* 81 (1962), 289-314.

—— "Der Dukus Horant und die Kudrun von 1233," *Mitteilungen aus dem Arbeitskreis für Jiddistik* 2 (1964), 129-134.

—— "Die Namen der Heldendichtung, insbesondere Nibelung, Hagen, Wate, Hetel, Horand, Gudrun," *Beiträge zur Namenforschung* n.s. 1 (1966), 231-265.

—— Rev. of Ganz/Norman/Schwarz, eds., *Dukus Horant*. In *Deutsche Literaturzeitung* 87 (1966), 126-129.

Roucek, Joseph S. "A History of the Concept of Ideology," *Journal of the History of Ideas* 5 (1944), 479-488.

Ruh, Kurt. "Epische Literatur des deutschen Spätmittelalters." *Neues Handbuch der Literaturwissenschaft*. Vol 8. *Europäisches Spätmittelalter*. Willi Erzgräber, ed., Wiesbaden: Akademische Verlagsgesellschaft Athenaion, 1978, 117-118.

Sadan, Dov. Rev. of Fuks, ed., *The Oldest . . . Documents*. In *Maḥanaim* 33 (1957), 25-28.

—— "The Midrashic Background of the 'Paradise' – Its Implication for the Evaluation of the Cambridge Yiddish codex (1382)." In *The Field of Yiddish* 2. Uriel Weinreich, ed., London 1965, pp. 253-262.

—— "Der eltster gram in yidish," *Di goldene keyt* 47 (1963), 157-159.

Sapir, Edward. "Notes on Judeo-German Phonology," *Jewish Quarterly Review*, n.s. 6 (1915-1916), 231-266.

Schaechter, Mordkhe [Shekhter]. "The 'Hidden Standard': A Study of Competing Influences in Standardization," in *Field of Yiddish* III, M. Herzog, ed., (The Hague 1969), 284-304.

—— "Four Schools of Thought in Yiddish Language Planning," *Michigan Germanic Studies* 3 (1977), 34-66.

—— "Dem Yivos yidish-oyftu: roshiprokimdike observatsies un sakhaklen tsu a yubl-date," *Yivo-bleter* 46 (1980), 192-228.

—— *Yidish tsvay: a lernbikhl far mitndike kursn/Yiddish Two: A Textbook for Intermediate Courses.* Philadelphia: Institute for the Study of Human Issues, 1986.

Scholz, Manfred Günter. *Hören und Lesen. Studien zur primären Rezeption der Literatur im 12. und 13. Jahrhundert.* Wiesbaden 1980.

Schramm, G. Rev. of Fuks., ed., *The Oldest . . . Documents*, in *Göttingische Gelehrte Anzeigen* 212 (1958), 211-221.

Schröbler, Ingeborg. "Zu L. Fuks' Ausgabe der ältesten bisher bekannten Denkmäler jiddischer Literatur" [rev. of Fuks., ed., *The Oldest . . . Documents*]. In *Zeitschrift für deutsches Altertum* 89 (1959), 135-162.

—— Rev. of Ganz/Norman/Schwarz, eds. *Dukus Horant.* In *Germanistik* 7 (1966), 72-72.

—— Rev. of Fuks., ed., *Melokim-buk.* In *Germanistik* 8 (1967), 578-79.

Schüler, Meier [Meïr]. "Die hebraeische Version der Sage von Arthur und Lanzelot aus dem Jahre 1279," *Archiv für das Studium der neueren Sprachen und Literaturen* 127 (1909), 51-63.

—— "Beiträge zur Kenntnis der alten jüdisch-deutschen Profanliteratur." In *Festschrift zum 75-jährigen Bestehen der Realschule mit Lyzeum der Israelitischen Religionsgesellschaft.* Frankfurt 1928, 89-132.

Schulman, Elias. *Sephath yehudith ashkenazith we-saphrutah.* Riga 1913.

Schwarz, Werner. "Einige Bemerkungen zur jiddischen Gudrun" [rev. of Fuks, ed., *The Oldest . . . Documents.* In *Neophilologus* 42 (1958), 327-332.

—— "Notes on Formulaic Expressions in Middle High German Poetry." In *Mediaeval German Studies Presented to Frederick Norman.* London 1965, 60-70.

—— "Die weltliche Volksliteratur der Juden." In *Miscellanea Mediaevalia.* Veröffentlichungen des Thomas-Instituts an der Universität Köln. P. Wilpert, ed., Vol 4: *Judentum im Mittelalter.* Berlin 1966, 72-91.

—— "Prinzipielle Erwägungen zur Untersuchungen der Cambridger Handschrift T.-S. 10. K. 22," *Zeitschrift für Mundartforschung* 33 (1966), 138-144.

Shatski, Yankef [Jacob/Jakob Shatzky]. Rev. of Erik, *Vegn altyidishn roman.* In *Pinkos* 1 (1928), 274-279.

—— "Vegn di nemen far yidish," *Yivo-bleter* 8 (1935), 148-154.

Shiper, Yitskhok. "Problemen fun der altyidisher literatur-geshikhte," *Yivo-bleter* 7 (1934), 36-46.

—— "Kultur-geshikhtlekher fon fun der yidisher literatur," *Yivo-bleter* 8 (1935), 44-60.

—— "A yidisher libe-roman fun mitl-elter; tsu-shtayern tsu der geshikhte vegn dem oyf-kum fun 'Maase Brie ve-Zimre," *Yivo-bleter* 13 (1938), 232-245.

Shmeruk, Chone [Khone]. "Di naye editsie funem alt-yidishn 'Melokhim-bukh'" [rev. of Fuks, ed., *Das altjiddische Epos*]. In *Di goldene keyt* 59 (1967), 208-215.

—— "Yiddish Literature." In *Encyclopaedia Judaica*. New York 1971, XVI, col. 798-833.

—— "Die alt-yidishe literatur; eyre on-haybn un primere kontaktn," *Pinkos far der forshung fun der yidisher literatur und prese* 3 (1976), 1-80.

—— "The Hebrew Acrostic in the Yosef Hatsadik Poem of the Cambridge Yiddish Codex," *Michigan Germanic Studies* 3 (1977), 67-81.

Shtif, N. [Nahum]. "Ditrikh fun Bern; yidishkayt und veltlekhkayt in der alter yidisher literatur," *Yidishe filologie* 1 (1924), 1-11 & 112-122.

—— "Loshn ashkenaz, taytsh," *Yidishe filologie* 1 (1924), 386-388,

—— *Di eltere yidishe literatur; literarishe khrestomatie mit an araynfir und erkleyrungen tsu yedn shrayber.* Kiev 1929.

Siskind, Nusn. [Nathan Süsskind]. "Das Šmuel-Bukh." Diss. New York University 1941.

—— "Betrakhtungen vegn der geshikhte fun yidish," *Yidishe shprakh* 13 (1953), 97-108.

—— "Alt-yidish und mitl-yidish," *Yidishe shprakh* 29 (1969/70), 43-64.

Spivak, Gayatri. "Explanation and Culture: Marginalia," *Humanities in Society* 2 (1979), 201-221.

Stackmann, Karl. "Die Stellung des 'Dukus Horant' in der Geschichte der Hildessage." In *Kudrun*. Ed. Karl Bartsch. 5th ed. by K. Stackmann. Wiesbaden 1965, lxxiv-lxxvii.

Staerk, W. and A. Leitzmann. *Die jüdischdeutschen Bibelübersetzungen von den Anfängen bis zum Ausgang des 18. Jahrhunderts.* Frankfurt 1923; repr. Hildesheim 1977.

Steinschneider, Moritz. "Jüdischdeutsche Literatur," *Serapeum* (Leipzig 1848/1849/1864/1869; repr. Jerusalem 1961).

Stockwell, Robert P. Rev. of *The Field of Yiddish* 1. In *Language* 32 (1956), 374-384.

Stopp, H. Rev. of Ganz/Norman/Schwarz, eds., *Dukus Horant*. In *Zeitschrift für deutsche Philologie* 86 (1967), 457-463.

Strauch, Gabriele L. "*Dukus Horant*: Doch ein jiddisches Epos." Diss. Wisconsin 1984.

Strauss, Raphael. "Was Süsskind von Trimpberg a Jew?" *Jewish Social Studies* 10 (1948), 19-30.

Symons, B., ed. *Kudrun*. 4th ed. by Bruno Boesch. Tübingen: Niemeyer, 1964, xvii-xviii.

Szajkowski, Zosa. "The Struggle for Yiddish during World War I: The Attitude of German Jewry," *Leo Baeck Institute Yearbook* 9 (1964), 131-160.

Thiel, Erich J. "Zur Cambridger jiddischen Gudrunhandschrift," *Mitteilungen aus dem Arbeitskreis für Jiddistik* 1 (1956), 34-36.

Timm, Erika. "Beria und Simra; Eine jiddische Erzählung des 16. Jahrhunderts," *Literaturwissenschaftliches Jahrbuch*, ns. 14 (1973), 1-94.

—— "Jiddische Sprachmaterialien aus dem Jahre 1290; Die Glossen des Berner kleinen Aruch." In *Fragen des älteren Jiddisch. Trierer Beiträge*, Sonderheft, 2. Hermann-Josef Müller & Walter Röll, eds., Trier, 1977, pp. 16-34.

—— "Die 'Fabel vom alten Löwen' in jiddistischer und komparatistischer Sicht," *Zeitschrift für deutsche Philologie* 100 (Sonderheft *Jiddisch* 1981), 109-170.

—— "Zur jiddischen Fabelliteratur des 16. Jahrhunderts," *Proceedings of the Eighth World Congress of Jewish Studies*. Jerusalem 1982, 159-164.

—— "Jehoschua." In *Die deutsche Literatur des Mittelalters. Verfasserlexikon*. 2nd ed. by Kurt Ruh. Berlin 1983, IV, 511.

—— *Graphische und phonische Struktur des Westjiddischen unter besonderer Berücksichtigung der Zeit um 1600*. Tübingen 1987.

Trost, Pavel. "Hebrejsky' rukopis nemecké špilmanské basně" [rev. of Fuks, ed., *The Oldest . . . Documents*]. In *Časopis pro moderni filologii* 2 (1959), 112.

—— "Zwei Stücke des Cambridger Kodex T-S 10. K. 22," *Philologica Pragensia* 4 (1961), 17-24.

—— "Noch einmal zu Josefslegende des Cambridger Kodex," *Philologica Pragensia* 5 (1962), 3-5.

—— "Glosse zu den Erzväterlegenden des Cambridger Kodex," *Mitteilungen aus dem Arbeitskreis für Jiddistik* 2 (1964), 152-153.

Tsinberg, Yisroel [Israel Zinberg]. "Der kamf far yidish in der alt-yidisher literatur," *Filologishe shriftn* 2 (1928), 69-106; trans: "A Defense of Yiddish in Old Yiddish Literature," *YIVO Annual of Jewish Social Science* 1 (1946), 283-293.

—— "Oys der alt-yidisher literatur," *Filologishe shriftn* 3 (1929), 173-184.

—— *Altyidishe literatur fun di eltste tsaytn biz der haskole-tkufe*, vol. 6 of *Di geshikhte fun der literatur bay yidn*, 2nd ed. Vilna 1933; repr. New York 1943; Bernard Martin, ed. and trans., *A History of Jewish Literature, vol.* VII: *Old Yiddish Literature from its Origins to the Haskalah Period.* Cincinnati 1975.

Warnock, Robert G. "Wirkungsabsicht und Bearbeitungstechnik im altjiddishen 'Artushof.'" *Zeitschrift für deutsche Philologie* (Sonderheft *Jiddisch* 1981), pp. 98-109.

—— "Frühneuzeitliche Fassungen des altjiddischen 'Artushofs.'" In *Auseinandersetzung um jiddische Sprache und Literatur. Jüdische Komponenten in der deutschen Literatur – die Assimilationskontroverse*. Walter Röll and Hans-Peter Bayerdörfer, eds., Vol. 5 of *Kontroverse, alte und neue. Akten des VII. Internationalen Germanisten-Kongresses, Göttingen 1985*. Albrecht Schöne, ed., Tübingen: Niemeyer, 1986, 13-19.

Waxman, Max. "Judaeo-German Literature," 613-665 in *A History of Jewish Literature*, vol. II: *From the Twelfth Century to the Middle of the Eighteenth Century.* 2nd ed. New York 1943.

Weinberg, Werner. *Die Reste des Jüdischdeutschen.* Stuttgart 1969.

—— "Die Bezeichnung Jüdischdeutsch: Eine Neubewertung" *Zeitschrift für deutsche Philologie* 100 (Sonderheft *Jiddisch* 1981), 253-290.

Weinreich, Maks [Maks Waynraykh]. "Studien zur Geschichte und dialektischen Gliederung der jiddischen Sprache," part 1: "Geschichte und gegenwärtiger Stand der jiddischen Sprachforschung." 3 vols. Diss. Marburg 1923.

—— *Shtaplen: fir etyudn tsu der yidisher shprakh-visnshaft un literatur-geshikhte*. Warsaw 1923.

—— *Bilder fun der yidisher literatur-geshikhte*. Vilna 1928.

—— "Yidishe filologie." In *Algemeyne yidishe entsiklopedie*. Suppl. vol.: *Yidn B*. Paris 1940, 101-108.

—— "Yidish." In *Algemeyne yidishe entsiklopedie*. Suppl. vol.: *Yidn B*. Paris 1940, 23-90.

—— "Prehistory and Early History of Yiddish: Facts and Conceptual Framework," *The Field of Yiddish*, Uriel Weinreich, ed., Publications of the Linguistic Circle of New York 3 (New York 1954), 73-101.

—— "Ikerim in der geshikhte fun yidish," *Yidishe shprakh* 14 (1954), 97-110.

—— "History of the Yiddish Language: The Problems and Their Implications," *Proceedings of the American Philosophical Association* 103 (1959), 563-570.

—— "Old Yiddish Poetry in Linguistic and Literary Research, *Word* 16 (1960), 100-118.

—— "A yidisher sats fun far sibn hundert jor. Analis fun gor a vikhtikn shprakhikn gefins," *Yidishe shprakh* 23 (1963), 87-93 and 24 (1964), 61-62.

—— *Di geshikhte fun der yidisher shprakh.* 4 vols. New York 1981. Transl. of vols. 1 & 2 by Shlomo Noble and Joshua A. Fishman. *History of the Yiddish Language.* Chicago 1980.

Weinreich, Uriel [Waynraykh]. Preface to *The Field of Yiddish* 1. Publications of the Linguistic Circle of New York. Uriel Weinreich, ed., New York 1954, v-viii.

—— *College Yiddish*, 4th ed. New York 1965.

—— "Yiddish Language." In *Encyclopaedia Judaica* (New York 1971), XVI, 790-798.

Weinreich, Uriel and Beatrice. *Yiddish Language and Folklore: A Selective Bibliography for Research.* The Hague 1959.

Weissberg, Joséf. "The Vowel System of MS Cambridge T-S 10 K 22 Compared with Middle High German," *Journal of Jewish Studies* 14 (1963), 37-57.

—— "Das Konsonantensystem des 'Dukus Horant' und der übrigen Texte des Cambridger Manuskripts T.S. 10. K. 22, verglichen mit dem Mittelhochdeutschen," *Zeitschrift für Mundartforschung* 32 (1965), 1-40.

—— "Bemerkungen zu den Artikeln von J. W. Marchand," *Zeitschrift für deutsche Philologie* 85 (1966), 98-110.

—— "Zur Stellung der altjiddischen Literatur in der Germanistik," *Zeitschrift für deutsche Philologie* 91 (1972), 383-406.

Weißberg, Meïr. *Wölwel Zhazer, der fahrende Sänger des galizisch-jüdischen Humanismus.* Leipzig 1909.

Wexler, Paul. "Jewish Interlinguistics: Facts and Conceptual Framework," *Language* 57 (1981), 99-149.

—— "Reconceptualizing the Genesis of Yiddish in the Light of its Non-Native Components," *Language and Communication* 7 (1987, suppl.) pp. 135-142.

Wiener, Leo. *A History of Yiddish Literature in the Nineteenth Century.* New York 1899; 2nd ed., with a new introduction by Elias Schulman, 1973.

Wilhelm, Kurt. "Jüdisch-deutsche Spielmannslieder aus Ägypten. Ältestes Dokument in jüdisch-deutscher Sprache in Cambridge entdeckt," *Allgemeine Wochenzeitung der Juden in Deutschland*, 7 November 1958, 7.

Wolf, Siegmund. *Jiddisches Wörterbuch.* Mannheim 1962.

—— "Studien zum Vokalismus des älteren Jiddisch," *Phonetica* 8 (1962), 31-54,

—— ed., *Ritter Widuwilt.* Bochum 1974.

Yudkin, Leon Israel. *Jewish Writing and Identity in the Twentieth Century.* New York 1982.

Zunz, Leopold. *Die Gottesdientslichen Vorträge der Juden.* Berlin 1832; 2nd ed., Frankfurt 1892.

Author-Title Index

A

B

D

E

F

G

H

K

L

General Index

Scholar Index

P

R

S

T

W

Z